Slow
Northum
& Durham

including Newcastle, Hadrian's Wall and the Coast

Local, characterful guides to Britain's special places

Gemma Hall

Edition 1

Bradt Travel Guides Ltd, UK
The Globe Pequot Press Inc, USA

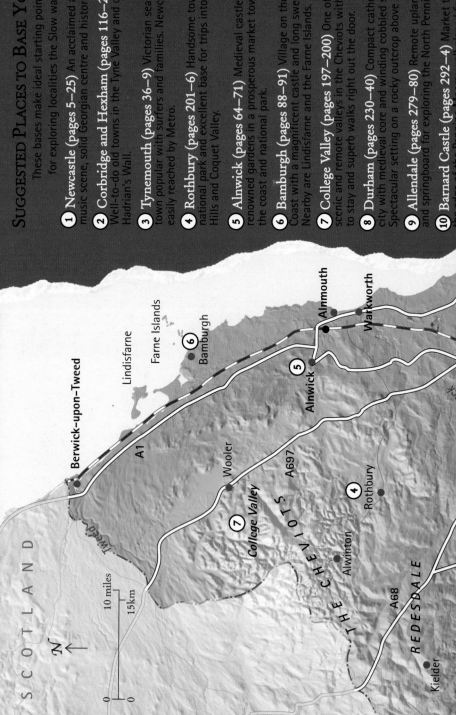

Suggested Places to Base Yourself

These bases make ideal starting points for exploring localities the Slow way.

1 Newcastle (pages 5–25) An acclaimed arts and music scene, solid Georgian centre and historic quayside.

2 Corbridge and Hexham (pages 116–26) Well-to-do old towns in the Tyne Valley and close to Hadrian's Wall.

3 Tynemouth (pages 36–9) Victorian seaside town popular with surfers and families. Newcastle is easily reached by Metro.

4 Rothbury (pages 201–6) Handsome town in the national park and excellent base for trips into the Cheviot Hills and Coquet Valley.

5 Alnwick (pages 64–71) Medieval castle and renowned gardens in a prosperous market town between the coast and national park.

6 Bamburgh (pages 88–91) Village on the Heritage Coast with a magnificent castle and long sweep of sand. Nearby are Lindisfarne and the Farne Islands.

7 College Valley (pages 197–200) One of the most scenic and remote valleys in the Cheviots with good places to stay and superb walks right out the door.

8 Durham (pages 230–40) Compact cathedral city with medieval core and winding cobbled streets. Spectacular setting on a rocky outcrop above a river.

9 Allendale (pages 279–80) Remote upland village and springboard for exploring the North Pennines AONB.

10 Barnard Castle (pages 292–4) Market town on

CHAPTER KEY

1
2
3
4
5
6
7

Tynemouth ③

Newcastle-upon-Tyne ①

Gateshead

Sunderland

Seaham

A1(M)

Hartlepool

Durham ⑧

Bishop Auckland

Darlington

A66(M)

Tyne

Corbridge

Hexham ②

A68

Stanhope

WEARDALE

Wear

A67

Barnard Castle ⑩

TEESDALE

Tees

North Tyne

A69

Allendale

⑨

HADRIAN'S WALL

Alston

South Tyne

A NORTHUMBERLAND & DURHAM GALLERY

There are no roads on the north side of Kielder Water, making motor-free transport the only way of reaching many of the lake's secluded banks and inlets.

The narrow-gauge steam locos from Alston can be a handy way of exploring the South Tyne Valley on linear walks and cycle rides (bikes travel for just 50p). (GH)

Hartlepool, Sunderland and South Shields may not be remote, but the 30-mile stretch of footpath that links them is wonderfully cut-off and tranquil for much of the way. (GH)

Cyclists will find many quiet lanes as well as dedicated cyclepaths and long-distance trails in the region. The popular Coast-to-Coast crosses the Pennine moors, river valleys and the vale of Durham. (GH)

The Pennine Cycleway (NCN Route 68) passes through valleys and over more remote areas of Northumberland National Park and the North Pennines *en route* from Berwick to the Peak District. (GH)

Getting around Slow style

Saddle up, put on your hiking boots and turn off those main roads in search of Northumberland's villages, green lanes and lonely hills.

St Cuthbert's Way long-distance path takes in some of the best hill and coastal scenery on its 62½-mile journey over the Cheviots from Melrose to Lindisfarne island. (GH)

Drop anchor in one of Northumberland's horseshoe bays or fishing village harbours. Alnmouth (pictured), Newton Haven, Craster, Lindisfarne and Berwick-upon-Tweed are recommended. (GH)

You can hire a boat in Durham and row along the wooded River Wear under the city's medieval bridges and take in the sight of the cathedral and castle above. (SF)

A clear highlight of a trip to the Northumberland coast is taking a boat from Seahouses to the celebrated Farne Island seabird colonies. (GH)

Terns migrate thousands of miles to the Northumberland coast to breed and raise chicks. You can see them on the Farne Islands and at Beadnell Bay and Coquet Island. (GH)

One of the most appealing fishing villages in the region, Craster draws walkers off the coastal path to its pub, art gallery and smokehouse set around an old harbour. (GH)

The Northumberland Coast

Sandy, crowd-free and dotted with medieval castles and historic fishing villages, the Northumberland Heritage Coast between Warkworth and Berwick is one of the most beautiful stretches of Britain's seaboard.

Much of Lindisfarne Castle, perched on an island south of Berwick, was built using stones from the nearby ruined priory. (GH)

Fishing along the North East coast is much diminished but at Seahouses you'll still see quite a few trawlers and the odd motor coble in the harbour. (GH)

SHOP
- CRASTER KIPPERS
- SMOKED SALMON
- SMOKED COD
- LOCALLY CAUGHT WHITE FISH
- CRAB/LOBSTER
- FRESH SALMON
- DAIRY PRODUCTS

Fishing nets and buckets, on sale at Whitley Bay (easily reached from Newcastle by Metro) are essential kit for a rockpooling expedition around St Mary's lighthouse. (GH)

You'll find excellent seafood restaurants, fish and chip shops and fishmongers at Craster, Seahouses, North Shields Fish Quay and Berwick. (GH)

Newton-by-the-Sea is one of the most family-friendly bays in Northumberland with a glorious expanse of sand, a nature reserve, rockpools and a good pub. (GH)

Another glorious summer's day on an empty beach in Northumberland. Sugar Sands is easy to reach on foot or by bicycle from Howick. (GH)

An increasing number of farms in and around Northumbrian villages offer B&B accommodation and food. This cheese farm near Birdoswald Roman Fort has a café and camping barn. (GH)

The model village of Blanchland is enclosed by trees, moors and the River Derwent and has changed very little over the last few hundred years. (GH)

The hamlet of Bowlees in Upper Teesdale delights passing cyclists and walkers with its white stone cottages and nearby waterfalls. (GH)

'A picture of rustic peace and beauty not easily surpassed in the county' is how one Victorian writer described the estate village of Cambo near Wallington Hall; those words ring true today. (GH)

A fine collection of church buildings in the hamlet of Chollerton not far from Hexham which includes the old hearse house (note the horse mount). (GH)

Many fishing villages had a row or square of 'sea houses' like at Newton-by-Sea (pictured) and North Sunderland (now better known simply as Seahouses). (GH)

Village life

Northumbria has many exceptionally intact 18th- and 19th-century villages, most of which are made of an apricot-coloured sandstone that glows in the evening light.

Medieval grave covers are built into the walls of many churches including at Ryal near Ponteland. Shears denoted a female and a sword was carved for a man. (GH)

Gentle farmland encloses the villages in the lowlands south of Hadrian's Wall detaching the likes of Matfen (seen here) from larger settlements and adding to their appeal. (GH)

Weardale's villages have many features that make them distinctly lead-mining settlements, such as Methodist chapels and reading rooms. Many historic details survive such as this cobbled square in St John's Chapel. (GH)

Striking churches are plentiful in the region, particularly those with defensive towers and Roman, Anglo-Saxon and Norman masonry. Kirkhaugh Church near Alston simply has a very unusual thin spire. (GH)

Sculptures with a difference lurk among the conifer trees and bracken at Chopwell Woods in the lower Derwent Valley. (GH)

Despite being on the outskirts of Gateshead, the National Trust's Gibside estate has miles of footpaths through beautiful old woodland. (GH)

In search of solitude

Northumbria excels at solitude and you will find miles of desolate moorland and beaches to explore as well as the darkest night skies in England.

Secluded plunge pools like this one in Harthope Valley are plentiful along the rivers and burns in the Cheviot Hills. (GH)

Hikes into the Cheviot valleys lead across hillsides and on almost traffic-free lanes such as in College Valley (pictured here). (GH)

Open roads and big valley views greet the touring cyclist in Upper Teesdale. (GH)

Snow falls thickly on the Pennine hills during hard winters attracting hikers to its frozen waterfalls, and snowsport enthusiasts to the ski-runs at Allenheads. (GH)

The rivers Tyne, Tweed and Coquet are some of the best salmon and trout fishing waterways in Britain. Thrum Mill on the outskirts of Rothbury is one of the most secluded wooded ravines. (GH)

Kielder reservoir is astonishingly tranquil thanks to its size, remote location on the border with Scotland and the surrounding 232 square miles of forest. (GH)

The rocky, heather-clad Simonside Hills between Redesdale and the coast are well-known to hikers but you can still walk for many miles without seeing anyone. (GH)

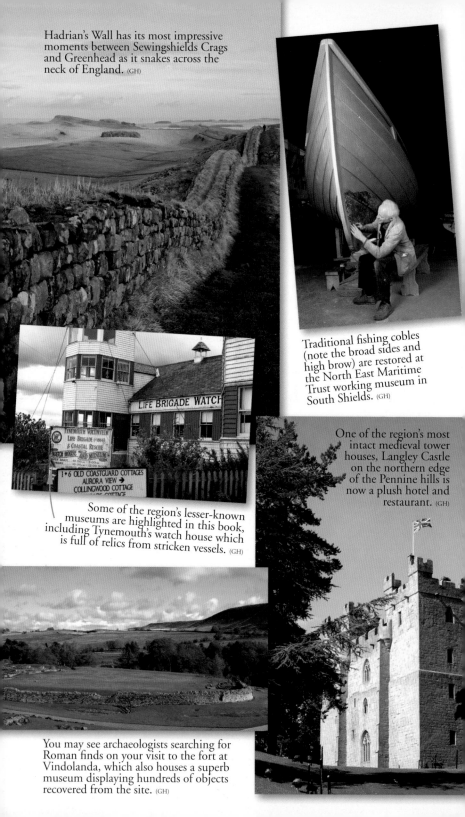

Hadrian's Wall has its most impressive moments between Sewingshields Crags and Greenhead as it snakes across the neck of England. (GH)

Traditional fishing cobles (note the broad sides and high brow) are restored at the North East Maritime Trust working museum in South Shields. (GH)

Some of the region's lesser-known museums are highlighted in this book, including Tynemouth's watch house which is full of relics from stricken vessels. (GH)

One of the region's most intact medieval tower houses, Langley Castle on the northern edge of the Pennine hills is now a plush hotel and restaurant. (GH)

You may see archaeologists searching for Roman finds on your visit to the fort at Vindolanda, which also houses a superb museum displaying hundreds of objects recovered from the site. (GH)

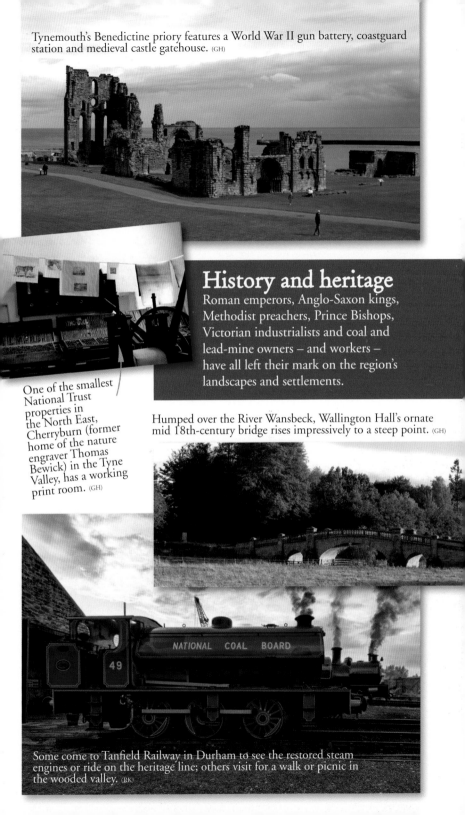

Tynemouth's Benedictine priory features a World War II gun battery, coastguard station and medieval castle gatehouse. (GH)

History and heritage

Roman emperors, Anglo-Saxon kings, Methodist preachers, Prince Bishops, Victorian industrialists and coal and lead-mine owners – and workers – have all left their mark on the region's landscapes and settlements.

One of the smallest National Trust properties in the North East, Cherryburn (former home of the nature engraver Thomas Bewick) in the Tyne Valley, has a working print room. (GH)

Humped over the River Wansbeck, Wallington Hall's ornate mid 18th-century bridge rises impressively to a steep point. (GH)

Some come to Tanfield Railway in Durham to see the restored steam engines or ride on the heritage line; others visit for a walk or picnic in the wooded valley. (BK)

A 20-minute walk north of Durham city centre and you could be wandering through some ten different gardens or gazing at Durham Cathedral over a cream tea here at Crook Hall. (GH)

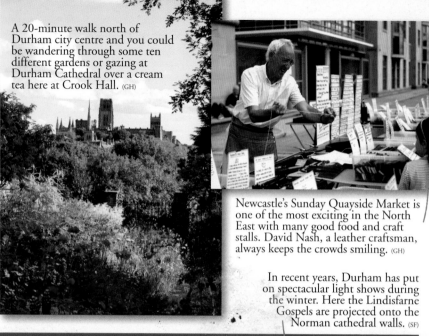

Newcastle's Sunday Quayside Market is one of the most exciting in the North East with many good food and craft stalls. David Nash, a leather craftsman, always keeps the crowds smiling. (GH)

In recent years, Durham has put on spectacular light shows during the winter. Here the Lindisfarne Gospels are projected onto the Norman cathedral walls. (SF)

Slow towns and cities

Even in big towns and cities, many visitors to the North East find the urban pace much less frantic than elsewhere in England. But it's not just the opportunity to slow down that appeals: there are plenty of unobvious historic corners, buildings and streets to entice as well.

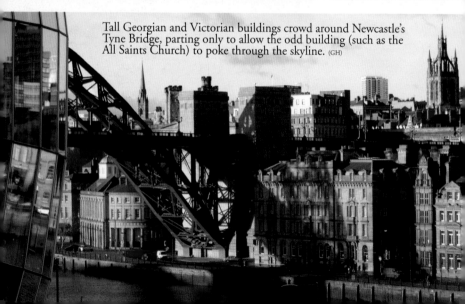

Tall Georgian and Victorian buildings crowd around Newcastle's Tyne Bridge, parting only to allow the odd building (such as the All Saints Church) to poke through the skyline. (GH)

Tynemouth Metro station's ornate metal work and original Victorian ticket office and waiting room provide an eye-catching backdrop to the weekend bric-a-brac, craft and antiques market. (GH)

It may be a busy workaday town, but Morpeth has many hidden delights such as Carlisle Park with its medieval architecture, woods and dreamy riverside. (GH)

Corbridge is one of the most attractive and unchanged sandstone towns in the Tyne Valley and is easily reached by train on the Tyne Valley Line. (GH)

Besides its very own *Harry Potter* trail, Alnwick imbues many other qualities with its eateries, old streets and farmers' market (last Friday of the month). (GH)

One of the most remote towns in England, Alston's historic streets, cafés and inns make it a popular stopping point for long-distance trail cyclists. (GH)

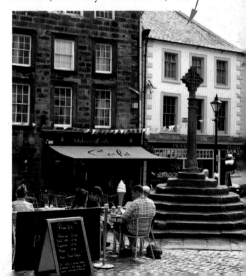

Many farms and smallholders sell fresh produce by the sides of roads like here near Hamsterley Forest. (GH)

Regional favourites such as the Northumberland Cheese Company, Cotherstone Cheese and Doddingtons are sold in this fantastic Morpeth shop. (GH)

Local food

Everywhere I visited during the research for this book, I found restaurants, pubs and B&Bs promoting local produce and regional dishes.

Memorably tasty seafood awaits at North Shields Fish Quay or one of the smokehouses at Craster or Seahouses. For fish and chips, a couple of favourites are Coleman's of South Shields and Gormans (*www. lovegormans.co.uk*) in Newcastle. (GH)

Berwick-upon-Tweed has a growing Slow Food movement with a farmers' market on the last Sunday of the month. (SM)

FABULOUS FRESH & FISH

FROM TODAY'S NORTH SHIELDS FISH QUAY...

The Great Northumberland Bread Company

www.greatnorthumberlandbread.co

Telephone: 01890 820562

Author

Gemma Hall (*www.gemmahall.co.uk*) is a freelance travel, nature and outdoors writer from the North East who began her career in journalism writing for *BBC Wildlife* magazine for which she's still a regular contributor. She also works for many other outdoor and heritage titles and, alongside writing and her professional photography work, she co-ordinates conservation projects in the UK and abroad. Her family live in Newcastle and Northumberland and she has extensively explored the coasts and hills of Northumberland and Durham on many sailing, cycling, birdwatching and camping trips. A keen walker, she's hiked many long-distance trails including Hadrian's Wall Way, St Cuthbert's Way and the Northumberland and Durham coast paths. Gemma has worked for the RSPB, National Trust and British Trust for Conservation Volunteers (BTCV) and is a Fellow of the Royal Geographical Society.

Author's story

My idea of contentment is camping in the Cheviots in October or walking along the coast when a fret is coming in off the North Sea, which sounds romantic but really it's because, as W H Auden wrote, 'I like it cold'. Perhaps this is explained by all the weekends spent as a young child knocking around in the dunes at Newton-by-the-Sea with my sister while dad was out sailing. Good things came of getting caught in poor weather and being left to our own devices – I discovered the Newton Pool bird hides for one, and I'm sure my interest in ornithology comes from the hours spent in there sheltering from the wind, looking at the wildfowl identification posters on the wall and peering out over the lagoons. Those wetlands and nearby rocks and grasslands are still some of my favourite birding sites though nothing beats Lindisfarne National Nature Reserve in November, Upper Teesdale in April and Allen Banks in May.

I discovered the Cheviot Hills later on in life and I'm still finding new routes to walk and cycle. I love it up there – all those bleak humps pressing into each other and happy burns and waterfalls. I have a favourite spot by an old thorn in College Valley. There are many more corners of the North East that I'm drawn to, including places discovered during the research for this book.

I'm also fascinated by the region's built environment: the shattered bastle houses of Redesdale, Newcastle's chares and bridges, the Roman forts, Northumberland's medieval castles and neo-classical manors and the lead-mining architecture in the North Pennines. The buildings that deeply affect me, though, are the uniform rows of red-brick terraces you see all over Durham, Newcastle and Gateshead. When the East Coast Main Line train nears Newcastle and before the Tyne Bridge comes into view, they are the first buildings that tell me I'm home.

Reprinted May 2014
First published June 2012
Bradt Travel Guides Ltd
IDC House, The Vale, Chalfont St Peter, Bucks SL9 9RZ, England
www.bradtguides.com
Published in the USA by The Globe Pequot Press Inc,
PO Box 480, Guilford, Connecticut 06437-0480

Text copyright © 2012 Bradt Travel Guides Ltd
Maps copyright © 2012 Bradt Travel Guides Ltd
Photographs copyright © 2012 Individual photographers (see below)
Illustrations copyright © 2012 Bradt Travel Guides Ltd (see below)
Series editor: Tim Locke
For Bradt: Anna Moores

ISBN: 978 1 84162 433 4

British Library Cataloguing in Publication Data
A catalogue record for this book is available from the British Library

Front cover artwork Neil Gower (*www.neilgower.com*)
Illustrations Francesca Simpson
Photographs
Stuart Forster/whyeyephotography.com (SF); Gemma Hall (GH);
Robert Knox (RK); Susan McNaughton/Berwick Food Festival (SM).
Photo of David Nash, Newcastle Quayside Sunday Market (*www.davidnashleather.
blogspot.com*), page 15 of colour section.
Maps Chris & Ingrid Lane (*www.artinfusion.co.uk*); colour map relief map base
by Nick Rowland FRGS

Typeset from the author's disc by Artinfusion Ltd
Production managed by Jellyfish Print Solutions; printed in India

Acknowledgements

This book would never have happened if I hadn't got chatting to Rachel Fielding from Bradt at a travel show. For her enthusiasm for a guide to Northumberland and Durham, I am very grateful. Particular thanks to Chris and Ingrid Lane for making sense of my maps, Chris Lane also for design and typesetting, Sara Chare for proofreading, Janet Mears and Ellen Hardy at Bradt, Francesca Simpson for creating such beautiful illustrations and Neil Gower for the enchanting front cover. Most of all, thanks to Tim Locke for editing my chapters and providing invaluable advice, guidance, snippets, enthusiasm, expertise and patience, and to the ever-upbeat and unflappable Anna Moores who did a fantastic job pulling this book together.

Many people provided suggestions of places to visit and insight on North East heritage, including Katrina Porteous, Geoff Heslop, Ian Tait and Edward Cassidy, experts at English Heritage, the National Trust, and rangers at Northumberland National Park, English Nature and the North Pennines AONB. Thank you very much.

I'm very fortunate to all those who put me up while away from home, including Dorothy Hall, Ros Heslop, Mary Hall, Ian Hall, and Richard and Elizabeth Greenhall. A huge thanks to dad for the cycling adventures and for help with fact-finding missions; Lucy Hall and Alexander Tilon; Don Salter for tales about Durham and reading early drafts; Louise Olverson, Rupa Patel, Lindsay Gray, Tommy Hodgson, Sue Hall, Frankie and Sarah Brownlee for their support and help; and Anna and Olivia Dickinson-Hall for brightening my day. Particular thanks to my husband, Owen Greenhall, for putting up with my absence from home, joining me on memorable hikes in the Cheviots and North Pennines, for his sound judgement and for willing me on. Most of all to mum for reading chapters, providing feedback and for her constant support and belief in me.

Local illustrator: Francesca Simpson is a self-taught artist and illustrator who lives and works in Lesbury, Northumberland. She is best known for her detailed acrylic paintings and pen drawings of Northumberland landscapes and animals.

CONTENTS

Going Slow in Northumberland and Durham

The Slow mindset
Hilary Bradt, Founder, Bradt Travel Guides

We shall not cease from exploration
And the end of all our exploring
Will be to arrive where we started
And know the place for the first time.
T S Eliot 'Little Gidding', *Four Quartets*

This series evolved, slowly, from a Bradt editorial meeting when we started to explore ideas for guides to our favourite country – Great Britain. We wanted to get away from the usual 'top sights' formula and encourage our authors to bring out the nuances and local differences that make up a sense of place – such things as food, building styles, nature, geology, or local people and what makes them tick. Our aim was to create a series that celebrates the present, focusing on sustainable tourism, rather than taking a nostalgic wallow in the past.

So without our realising it at the time, we had defined 'Slow Travel', or at least our concept of it. For the beauty of the Slow movement is that there is no fixed definition; we adapt the philosophy to fit our individual needs and aspirations. Thus Carl Honoré, author of *In Praise of Slow*, writes: 'The Slow Movement is a cultural revolution against the notion that faster is always better. It's not about doing everything at a snail's pace, it's about seeking to do everything at the right speed. Savouring the hours and minutes rather than just counting them. Doing everything as well as possible, instead of as fast as possible. It's about quality over quantity in everything from work to food to parenting.' And travel.

So take time to explore. Don't rush it, get to know an area – and the people who live there – and you'll be as delighted as the authors by what you find.

I've wanted to write this book for years. A comprehensive and independent guide to the North East that celebrates the hills, castles, beaches and villages as well as the urban centres seemed to be missing on the travel shelves of bookshops labelled 'North'. I hope this book has filled that gap and offered something a little different in its approach.

It's far-reaching in its scope: from Barnard Castle to Berwick-upon-Tweed and encompassing Tyneside and its hinterlands; the bays, islands and fortresses of Northumberland; Hadrian's Wall; the Cheviot Hills and Durham's cathedral city, dales and coastline. There's a strong leaning towards places with heritage appeal, adventures on foot and by bicycle, the lesser-known and the outdoors. That's not to say big-name attractions are not covered in detail. You'll find three pages devoted to Alnwick Castle and its gardens for example and Hadrian's Wall and forts dominate most of one chapter.

But what about that word 'Slow'? It's a deliberate nod to the Slow Food and Slow Tourism movements and you'll find this book embraces a similar ethos in its celebration of local distinctiveness, vernacular architecture, regional flavours and simple pleasures. It encourages visitors to seek out the unobvious, explore footpaths, railways trails, byways and B-roads – and linger awhile.

I spent a year researching and writing this guide, revisiting some of my favourite spots and picking through the hills and coastlines in search of the hidden and unsung corners of Northumbria. Friends, relatives and contacts provided tips and suggestions, but most of the curious and more unusual places peppered in these pages were gleaned by cycling the back roads, chatting to locals, driving along unclassified lanes, going for a wander and, most of all, having a nosey around.

Some places like those on my Wild Card list below (all covered in more detail in the following chapters) may be too obscure, unconventional or out of the way to tempt many visitors, but even if you don't seek them out, I hope you enjoy reading about them. Sometimes it's nice just to know places like this exist and to imagine as you read these words that a peregrine falcon is hunting for prey among the chimneys and pylons in Teesmouth, a Northumbrian pipist is playing a centuries old ballad in Morpeth Chantry, and the 7th-century sundial on Escomb's Saxon church is telling the time.

Northumberland and Durham

There are six areas in which Northumberland and Durham excel: castles, heather moors, industrial heritage, Roman architecture, sandy beaches and solitude. I can think of many more (prehistoric rock art, bridges, salmon rivers, railways, upland birds, waterfalls, Georgian architecture and fishing villages) but those are the six that really stand out.

Regarding solitude: a glance at a night sky map of England, shows the northeastern shank of the country is sparsely inhabited and supremely bleak in places. From the Cheviot Hills to the Pennine moors; through England's largest forest and across the empty beaches of Druridge Bay; over the rugged hills of Redesdale and the wild Whin Sill escarpment where the Roman emperor Hadrian built his wall – miles and miles of raw upland and coastal scenery beneath the most star-filled skies you will see anywhere.

Here you can hunker down in the dunes or walk all day through the heather and see only a handful of people; sit alone in one of the most wondrous Anglo-Saxon churches in Britain; pitch a tent undisturbed on the fells; experience a private viewing of a hen harrier skydancing; take the plunge butt-naked in a

Cheviot waterfall; and get up early and see Hadrian's Wall ribboned across the hills without another rambler in sight.

The poet, W H Auden, who dearly loved the North East's fells, isolation and climate, wrote in an article for *House and Garden* in 1947: 'the North of England was the Never-Never Land of my dreams . . . the wildly exciting frontier where the alien South ends and the North, my world, begins.' That sense of escape and wildness is undoubtedly Northumbria's greatest appeal.

Northern warmth and wit

Southerners are forever saying that those in the north – and particularly Geordies – are 'really friendly' and 'have a great sense of humour' (as well as a few less complimentary things). I've always been sceptical of such well-meaning words, partly because I suspect they've never been to the Bigg Market after Newcastle United have just lost to Sunderland, and partly because there is a tendency for those in the south to romanticise the north as a back-of-beyond region where uncouth pinched folk in hard towns make humour out of their meagre share of the cake.

Not so obvious Northumberland and Durham

Here's my Wild Card list of 20 unsung or lesser-known places and attractions, some of which are simply under-visited because they are out of the way or require a map and bit of detective work to find. They are all described (with directions) in this book. In no special order, they are:

1	Castle Eden Dene National Nature Reserve, Durham coast	10	Branxton's Cement Menagerie
2	Ross Sands, Northumberland coast	11	Old Bewick Church, Northumberland
3	19th-century railway architecture on the Newcastle–Carlisle line	12	Tees Transporter Bridge
		13	Dunston Staiths, Gateshead
		14	Preston Tower, Northumberland coast
4	Newcastle's Literary and Philosophical Society	15	Wednesday nights at the Cumberland Arms, Newcastle
5	North East Maritime Trust at South Shields	16	Great Wanney crags, Redesdale
6	Escomb Anglo-Saxon church near Darlington	17	Routin Linn Waterfall, Doddington
7	Newcastle's Civic Centre	18	Easington's coastal grasslands and pit shaft cage
8	North Pennine Methodist chapels	19	Darlington's railway museums
9	Hannah's Meadow, Upper Teesdale	20	The Bagpipe Museum at Morpeth

Certainly, Geordies like banter, but more so than a Cockney? And whenever I experience an act of kindness (the lady in a South Shields car park the other day who gave me 80p when I asked if she could change a tenner ('diven't be daft, pet,' she said with a wave of her hand when I protested) and the bus driver who got out of his cabin to give a passenger directions on the pavement), I remind myself this could happen anywhere in the country. I suppose the only difference is that it doesn't surprise me in the North East.

But, if there's one example of spontaneous humour that could only have occurred in the North East, it's the time a group of locals celebrating the Magpies reaching the FA Cup Final in 1998 made a Newcastle United football shirt large enough to fit the newly erected *Angel of the North*. They got up at dawn to hoist the giant top over the 65-foot sculpture using fishing lines, ropes and catapults, and in doing so they showed that, not only do Geordies worship football and have a fondness of ridiculing anything high brow, they also love a bit of mischief.

How this book is arranged

The **numbered points** on the map at the beginning of each chapter correspond with the numbered headings in the text. They are mostly larger settlements (not necessarily the most interesting places to visit) with attractions and smaller places nearby listed in the text under their own (unnumbered) headings.

On the **accommodation** front, I've been very choosy: this is not a review of all of the best places to stay in the region but a hand-picked selection of some of the special B&Bs, campsites, bunkhouses and small hotels I came across while researching this book. They were selected on the basis of how comfortable and clean they were with a preference for interesting or historic buildings, 'green' credentials and use of local produce. I've noted any that seemed particularly wheelchair friendly. No prices are stated (they change so frequently and often according to availability) so instead I've given an idea of how they compare to others in the area. As a guide, I took £70 for a double room to be about average.

An overview of **public transport** options are provided at the beginning of each chapter, but like the cuts in tourist information facilities, many bus routes are being discontinued so you should check timetables before setting off. Traveline (*www.traveline.org.uk*) is useful but it can be tricky to navigate. **Northumberland County Council's** information line and website (*01670 533998; www.northumberland.gov.uk*) really stood out (a real person

Impartiality

Reviews in this guide are totally independent. The accommodation providers, attractions, museums, restaurants and tour companies were selected on the quality of their services and no business paid to receive a mention in this guide.

with excellent local knowledge answers the phone). On their homepage, go to 'Experience Northumberland by Bus' by clicking on the letter 'E'. Here you'll find useful route maps and timetables. **Durham County Council** website (*0300 026 0000; www.durham.gov.uk*) also has a helpful bus map. For train services to all destinations in the UK including the smaller stops in the region, I find the **East Coast trains** website (*www.eastcoast.co.uk*) the most user-friendly.

Under **places**, I've listed contact information where it seemed useful and listed non-standard opening times. 'Open daily' means Monday to Sunday from around 09.00/10.00 to 16.00/17.00. Opening times change from year to year so it's always best to call and check. **Cafés**, **restaurants** and **pubs** are included that struck me for the quality of food and drink, location and surroundings. Sometimes, they appear as full listing and other times I've provided a round up, especially where no one eaterie stood out.

Many of my favourite **walks** (and the odd cycle ride and scenic drive) are mentioned in this book. I've tried to include enough of a route description so that anyone with an Ordnance Survey Explorer map (and map-reading skills) would be able to find their way. They are only meant to give an overview of the route and a taste of what to expect – in other words, just enough information to inspire and start you off in the right direction.

A number of **tour companies** operate walking, cycling and wildlife-watching holidays and trips in the North East. Two local outfits that stand out are:

Northern Experience Wildlife Tours ⓣ 01670 827465
ⓦ www.northernexperiencewildlifetours.co.uk. Specialise in birdwatching trips to Northumberland and Durham as well as pelagic boat tours in search of whales, dolphins, seals and seabirds. Martin Kitching and Sarah Barratt are excellent hosts and local birders with an intimate knowledge of the North East's wildlife and habitats.
Shepherd's Walks ⓣ 01830 540453 ⓦ www.shepherdswalks.co.uk. Established by Jon Monks, a former sheep farmer in Northumberland, and offering guided and self-guided rambles across the region including all the long-distance paths.

Feedback request

There are only so many special places and aspects of Northumberland life that you can focus on when limited by word counts and book length. We've done our best to include a good mix and to check facts but there are bound to be errors as well as inevitable omissions of really special places. If you send an email to info@bradtguides.com about changes to information in this book we will forward it to the author who may include it in a 'one-off update' on the Bradt website at www.bradtguides.com/guidebook-updates.html. You can also visit the website for updates to information in this guide.

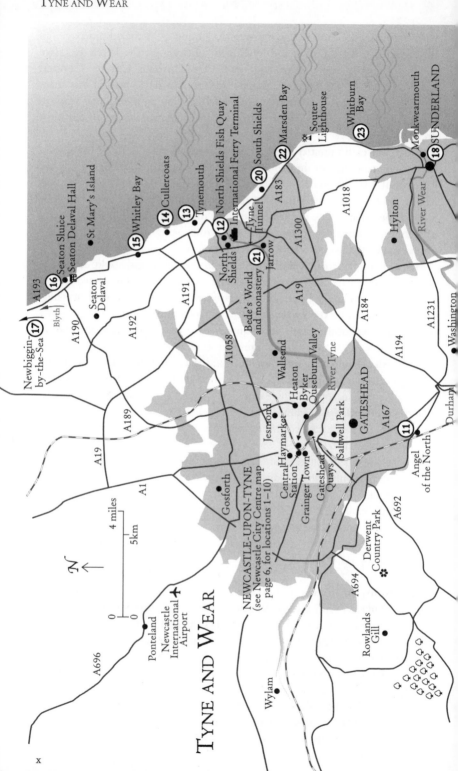

Tyne and Wear

SUNDERLAND 18
Monkwearmouth
River Wear
Whitburn Bay 23
Souter Lighthouse
Marsden Bay 22
South Shields 20
International Ferry Terminal
North Shields Fish Quay 12
Tynemouth 13
Cullercoats 14
Whitley Bay 15
St Mary's Island
Seaton Delaval Hall
Seaton Sluice 16
A193
Blyth
Newbiggin-by-the-Sea 17
Seaton Delaval
A190
A192
A191
A189
A19
A1
Gosforth
Ponteland
Newcastle International Airport
A696
Wylam
NEWCASTLE-UPON-TYNE
(see Newcastle City Centre map page 6, for locations 1–10)
A1058
Jesmond
Heaton
Byker
Ouseburn Valley
Central
Haymarket Station
Grainger Town
Gateshead Quays
Saltwell Park
Wallsend
Bede's World and monastery
North Shields
Jarrow 21
Tyne Tunnel
A183
A1300
A19
A184
River Tyne
GATESHEAD
A167
11
Angel of the North
Durham
A1018
Hylton
River Wear
Washington
A1231
A194
A692
A694
Derwent Country Park
Rowlands Gill

4 miles
5km
0

N

x

1. TYNE AND WEAR

Gone from the rivers Tyne and Wear are the dockyards, coal wagons, lead and glass works, ships, and all the ancillary businesses and buildings associated with being one of the largest industrial centres in the world in the 19th century. In their place are modern city flats, cafés, sculptures, arts centres, cycle paths, promenades and cultural venues.

Since the demise of heavy industry, the waterfronts of Newcastle and Gateshead have changed, not beyond recognition, but enough to surprise and delight a visitor who hasn't been here since the 1980s. The irony of the expression 'taking coals to Newcastle' used to describe a pointless activity, is that Tyneside actually imports coal these days, something our 19th- and 20th-century ancestors would find unbelievable.

Not everything has changed, however. In the centre of **Newcastle**, the elegant Georgian streets are as magnificent as ever, radiating from Grey's Monument in long rows of some of the finest neo-classical buildings in England. Grainger Town, as the area is known, was constructed during the boom years of the Industrial Revolution when Newcastle was a confident city out to impress.

In the same era, Victorian seaside resorts developed at places like **Tynemouth** and **Whitley Bay** providing a recreational space for Tynesiders to escape the city smoke and take in the fresh air. Then, as now, locals enjoy a walk along the promenade, a coffee on the seafront or a dip in the sea. **South Shields** and **Sunderland** also have good sandy beaches and 19th-century sea-facing terraces, but the landscape is more dramatic in places with breezy headlands and rocky coastal scenery.

People here talk much more about the 'cultural economy' defining the region and of a renaissance in the North. Certainly there is a buzz about the North East, renewed civic pride and a sense that, once again, this is somewhere to watch.

Getting around

Public transport in Tyne and Wear is excellent, thanks to the **Metro** system which connects Sunderland, Gateshead, Newcastle, the north and south Tyneside coasts, Central Station and Newcastle International Airport (25 minutes to Newcastle city centre). In Newcastle, the most useful stop for the city centre is Monument with Haymarket and Central Station close by.

There are no Metro stations on the waterfronts of Newcastle and Gateshead so you either have to walk (15 minutes down Newcastle's Grey Street for example) or take the yellow QuayLink electric buses.

QuayLink Q1 services Gateshead's quayside (for the Baltic, Sage and Millennium Bridge) from Newcastle Central Station to Gateshead's central

Tyne and Wear for young children – for free

Walk to the **Shoe Tree** in Heaton Park.

Spot the **Vampire Rabbit** behind Newcastle's St Nicholas' Cathedral.

Cross **Redheugh Bridge** on a windy day.

Go treasure hunting along the **River Tyne** at low tide from the promenade.

Fly a kite on the **Town Moor** or go sledging.

Watch planes coming into land at the end of **Newcastle airport's** runway (take the public footpath through fields at Low Luddick, Callerton Parkway).

Roll down the hill at **Tynemouth Priory**.

See **Fenwicks's Christmas Window**.

Cross the stepping stones in **Jesmond Dene**.

Find the walrus in **Mowbray Park**, Sunderland.

Visit the **Discovery Museum**.

Count the **Long Stairs** on the quayside.

Play among the chickens at the **Ouseburn Farm**.

Rockpooling at **St Mary's Island**.

Visit **Pets Corner** in Jesmond Dene.

Be king or queen of **Saltwell Towers, Saltwell Park**, Gateshead.

Look down at the kittiwakes from the top of the **Tyne Bridge**.

Find the Egyptian mummy in the **Great North Museum**.

Be the last one off the **Millennium Bridge** before it tilts.

Watch red kites from the **Derwent Walk Country Park** viaduct.

Feed the ducks in Newcastle's **Civic Centre**.

Go for a **swim** in the North Sea.

Take the lift down to **Marsden Grotto**.

Run to the end of **North Shields pier** to the lighthouse.

Build a sandcastle on **Tynemouth's Longsands**.

bus and Metro terminus. **Q2** goes to Newcastle's quayside from Newcastle city centre (Monument area).

A highly recommended (and cheap) **taxi** company in Newcastle is Blueline Taxis (*0191 262 6666*).

Walking and cycling

Newcastle city centre is compact and best explored on foot (there are few cycle paths and you can't ride in the main pedestrian shopping streets). Alongside the **river** and **seafront** are long promenades, perfect for strollers (and cyclists).

Heading upriver from **Newcastle to Wylam** (on Hadrian's Cycleway) the landscape becomes increasingly green and makes for a great afternoon's ride (*Chapter 3*, page 108).

You can also cycle from **Newcastle to Tynemouth** on an almost completely car-free route by following Hadrian's Cycleway and then National Cycle Network route 72 and route 1. The whole length is covered by the Coast to Coast route and is signed with 'C2C' markers. It gets a bit fiddly after Wallsend (where Hadrian's Cycleway ends).

Much of the **North Tyneside coast** (particularly north of Whitley Bay) is off-road. The **South Tyneside coast** can be cycled pretty much in its entirety from Sunderland to South Shields on traffic-free paths.

Cycle hire

The Cycle Hub Quayside, Newcastle NE6 1BU ① 0191 276 7250 ⓦ www.thecyclehub.org. Guided and self-guided long-distance trips, based on the coast-to-coast and Hadrian's Cycleway routes. Bike hire, repairs and café.

Scratchbikes These city hire bikes are dotted around the city. They operate by text message: you text a number and are given a code to release the lock; text again when you have finished using the bike (costs £1.50 per journey). Register your mobile phone number online to use the service (*www.scratchbikes.co.uk*).

Accommodation

Newcastle has a handful of very good small hotels (mostly boutique/minimalist style); if you want something a little more characterful, consider heading out of the centre and even to the Tyne Valley fringes and Durham (see *Chapter 3* and *Chapter 6*) where there's more in the way of rustic B&Bs and farmhouses.

At the **coast**, you'll find budget guesthouses along the seafronts of Roker, Whitley Bay and Tynemouth and on South Shields' Ocean Road. New contemporary **beach hut apartments** at Whitley Bay will offer novel accommodation when open but the launch had already been delayed for over a year at the time of going to press; see www.beachhutresorts.com. Also consider hiring an apartment such as South Cliff Apartments listed below.

Grey Street Hotel 2–12 Grey St, Newcastle NE1 6EE ① 0191 230 6777 ⓦ www.greystreethotel.com ⓔ enquiries@greystreethotel.com. Chic, paired back rooms with contemporary décor and black and white photographs of Newcastle. Considering the central location on Newcastle's most elegant street in a building with some old features delightfully exposed (mosaic flooring, marble staircase, wall tiles), prices for standard doubles are about average (but don't expect a huge room). Rooms overlooking Grey St are brighter but potentially noisier because you're on the edge of a busy drinking area.

Hotel du Vin Allan House, City Rd, Newcastle NE1 2BE ℗ 0191 229 2200 Ⓦ www.hotelduvin.com Ⓔ info.newcastle@hotelduvin.com. The sister hotel to Malmaison opposite the Millennium Bridge is similarly housed in a building with heritage appeal, in this case a former redbrick Victorian shipping company office. Plush, expensive rooms with Victorian features, contemporary furnishings and roll top baths as standard. Hotel du Vin is at the head of the Ouseburn Valley (not far from the quayside) where there's a good selection of alternative pubs, but you might want to stay put and sample the wines on offer here and enjoy a meal in the hotel restaurant (very good reputation; committed to sourcing local produce).

Jesmond Dene House Jesmond Dene Rd, Newcastle NE2 2EY ℗ 0191 212 3000 Ⓦ www.jesmonddenehouse.co.uk Ⓔ info@jesmonddenehouse.co.uk. One of Jesmond's finest 19th-century mansion houses is now an upmarket hotel and restaurant that's fairly reasonably priced considering the surroundings and standard of rooms. The house is set overlooking the tranquil wooded valley of Jesmond Dene (one of the most beautiful urban woodlands in the North East) and detached from the main residential area. Stylish, contemporary rooms furnished to a very high standard with decorative wallpapers and solid furniture. Arts and Crafts features throughout this historic building which has an impressive oak-panelled Great Hall.

Martineau House 57 Front St, Tynemouth NE30 4BX ℗ 0191 257 9038 Ⓦ www.martineau-house.co.uk Ⓔ martineauhouse@gmail.com. B&B right in the centre of Tynemouth and just a couple of minutes' walk from the Metro in one direction and the priory in the other. Cosy rooms with a cottage touch, original features (fireplaces, sash windows, etc) and sea views. Breakfasts made with local ingredients (Craster kippers for example) and home-made organic bread.

Sleeperz Hotel 15 Westgate Rd, Newcastle NE1 1SE ℗ 0191 261 6171 Ⓦ www.sleeperz.com/Newcastle. A very good economy hotel (clean, ultra minimalist and contemporary) next to Newcastle Central Station, with family rooms at hostel prices. Trains run past the back of the hotel which may be too noisy for some.

South Cliff Apartments 4 Southcliff, Whitley Bay NE26 2PB ℗ 0191 251 3121 Ⓦ www.southcliffapartments.co.uk Ⓔ southcliffapartments@theseaside. co.uk. Situated on a pedestrian terrace with direct views of the sea and close to Cullercoats and Tynemouth. Homely Victorian rooms (modern with some patterned wallpapers and the odd antique) and original features (fireplaces, high ceilings, etc), reasonably priced, spotlessly clean and friendly welcome.

Stables Lodge South Farm, Lamesley NE11 0ET ℗ 0191 492 1756 Ⓦ www. thestableslodge.co.uk Ⓔ info@luxurylettings.co.uk. Semi-rural setting in Gateshead and proximity to the A1 makes this a good choice for visiting Beamish and *The Angel of the North*. Newcastle is just a 10-minute drive away. Rooms are pretty sumptuous with rich fabrics, deep colours, solid wood furniture and floors and Molton Brown soaps. One room has a sauna. It's not cheap to stay in this room but there's a more average priced room available.

Staybridge Suites Buxton St, Newcastle NE1 6NL ① 0871 423 4876/0191 238 7000 Ⓦ www.staybridge.com. Staybridge Suites looks like a mid-range hotel with a reception and breakfast area and similar prices, but rooms have kitchens and a sofa and there are free laundry facilities, a gym and Wi-Fi. Contemporary décor throughout, comfy beds, modern, clean bathrooms. Location is on the edge of the city centre among student flats but it's only a 20-minute walk to Monument in one direction and the Ouseburn Valley in the other. Special rates at weekends, otherwise best for longer stays. Sofa beds/cots available for children under 12.

Townhouse Hotel 1 West Ave, Gosforth, Newcastle NE3 4ES ① 0191 285 6812 Ⓦ www.thetownhousehotel.co.uk Ⓔ bookings@thetownhousehotel.co.uk. Set on a residential road in an affluent suburb of Newcastle is this small, pricey Victorian terraced house hotel with plush, contemporary rooms (feature walls, luxury fabrics and furnishings, walk-in showers, etc). Gosforth High St, with its cafés and restaurants, is a minute's walk away. Easy access to Newcastle city centre by Metro.

Newcastle and Gateshead

Before the 1990s and *The Angel of the North*, Tyneside was famed for coal, steel, shipbuilding, fanatical football supporters, the Bigg Market drinking area and scantily dressed girls. Today, the heavy industries are gone; factories have been demolished or converted into art galleries, studios and loft-style apartments; and the Diamond Strip is the new Bigg Market (that alone tells you almost everything you need to know about the regional economy); but, Newcastle United football fans are still some of the most loyal of any club, and revellers have not taken to wearing coats in winter. The last two things will never change. Since the cessation of heavy industry, the region has been reinvented as an arts and cultural destination.

This is particularly true of Gateshead's South Shore Road on the riverfront, which was voted the hippest street in Britain in a Google poll on account of its contemporary architecture and arts venues. Irrespective of whether it really is the coolest quarter mile in Britain, Gateshead Quays is certainly vibrant and one of the highlights of a trip to the North East.

Any visitor who does not explore beyond the waterfront will miss out, however. Away from the contemporary buildings on the quayside, is the Tyneside of yesteryear: medieval alleys, 18th-century merchant houses, Victorian parks, Art Deco department stores, the evocative ruins of two monasteries, a Norman Castle Keep and the old town walls. In the centre are some of the most complete Georgian terraces in England, developed in the early 19th century by two men whose names are stamped about town: Grainger and Dobson. The architectural writer Nikolaus Pevsner said of Newcastle: 'Two things . . . distinguish Newcastle from Leeds or Bradford or Sheffield or any other industrial city of the North. One is the river, the other Richard Grainger and John Dobson.'

① Newcastle's city centre: Grainger Town

As for the curve of Grey Street, I shall never forget seeing it to perfection, traffic-less on a misty Sunday morning. Not even Regent Street, even old Regent Street London, can compare with that descending subtle curve.

Poet and architectural historian, John Betjeman speaking at the *Literary and Philosophical Society* in Newcastle, 1948

Grey's Monument marks the retail centre of Newcastle – and the heart of the city's celebrated Grainger Town where there are more Georgian buildings than anywhere outside the capital and Bath. The most distinguished 400 yards of beautifully dressed sandstone in Newcastle is found on **Grey Street** – a wide neo-classical boulevard that falls steeply away from Lord Grey's fluted column towards the River Tyne in the most graceful arc imaginable.

This 1820s and 1830s redevelopment of the medieval streets into the wide, stately thoroughfares you see today (including Clayton Street, Grainger Street, Neville Street, Nun Street and Hood Street) and the redirection of Newcastle's commercial centre from the quayside reflects the city's increasing confidence and aspirations during the industrial boom on Tyneside. **Grainger Town**, as it is known, is largely attributed to the grandiose vision of the property developer Richard Grainger and the architect John Dobson – said to be 'equal to Grainger in energy, superior in genius'. Dobson designed many of Northumberland's great country houses and churches as well as countless buildings in Newcastle.

One of the best views of Grainger Town is from the top of **Grey's Monument** (book tours through the tourist information centre in the Central Arcade). The Roman Doric column – which locals simply call 'Monument' – remembers British Prime Minister Earl Grey who lived in Northumberland (see page 77).

On Grey Street, the **Theatre Royal** (*0191 244 2500; www.theatreroyal. co.uk*) catches the attention with its towering Corinthian pillars. Newcastle's premier theatre (the regional home of the Royal Shakespeare Company)

Geordie-isms

aboot about

alreet alright, meaning 'okay'

aye yes. 'Why aye' means 'of course'

bairn child (from the Scandinavian 'barn')

belta really good

canny nice person

dee do

divn't don't

divvie stupid person

fatha father

gadgie man

gan/ganning go/going

haad hold, as in 'haad on!' ('wait!')

hacky dirty

hadaway get away (disbelieving)

ha-way! come on or hurry up

hinny term of endearment for a woman

hoose house

knar/knaa to know

mam mum/mother

man (often used at the end of sentences)

mi my eg: 'mi fatha', meaning 'my father'

na/naar no

neb/nebby nose or nosey

neet night

nowt nothing

pet term of endearment eg: 'are you alreet, pet?', meaning 'are you okay?'

radgie angry person

tab cigarette

toon town

Toon Army Newcastle United football supporters

us/uz/wuh me eg: 'give it to uz', meaning 'give it to me'

wor our, used before the name of a relative/friend (see the statue of footballer Jackie Milburn outside St James's Park, titled 'Wor Jackie')

yee you

yem home, from the Scandinavian 'hjem'

underwent major refurbishment three times: in 1901 following a huge fire, again in the late 1980s and in 2011 when the 1901 décor was brought back in all its red and gold splendour. Apart from Shakespeare, the theatre has an excellent reputation for contemporary dance performances, and this is the regional home of the Rambert Dance Company.

Also with an interior dating to the early 1900s, is the **Central Arcade** (50 yards downhill from Monument on the right hand side) – an exquisite Edwardian shopping centre decorated with mosaics and the finest Burmantoft's tiles from Leeds. The tiling is matched only by those in the old first-class waiting lounge at Central Station (now the Centurion Bar). The **tourist information centre** (*0191 277 8000; open daily*) is in the arcade. **Emerson Chambers** (now a Waterstones bookshop) faces Monument and is one of the more elaborate early 20th-century buildings in the city.

Grainger Market

Nelson St (near Monument), NE1 5QG; open Mon–Sat.

When opened in 1835, this covered market with its striking wrought-iron ribbed roof was one of the largest in the country occupying a site of approximately two acres. Much remains the same today with 187 stalls arranged along four alleys selling fresh produce (the fishmongers here are excellent – as is the cheese shop), cut-price clothing and homewares, though you'll also find secondhand books, music stalls, coffee shops and so on.

Wanderers with an eye for relics will find plenty here: old meat hooks on rollers, faded 1950s signs ('Hunter's High Class Provisions') and leaded glass windows. **Marks & Spencer's Penny Bazaar** has its original 1895 frontage painted maroon and gold and with decorative glass windows. The **Northern Optical Co. Ltd** is similarly unchanged and has the words 'Tortoiseshell spectacle frames' emblazoned in gold on its frontage. Like many shops in the Grainger Market, the optician's has been around since the market opened and in the same family for several generations. At lunchtimes, queues form outside the wonderfully preserved old **Weigh House** where for 30p (they've recently put the price up) you stand on the scales and a man on the other side of a counter hands you a print-out of your weight. Now an electronic scale is used but the original weigh machine stands in the corner.

Folk buskers

Young fiddle players, pipists and guitarists often perform traditional Northumbrian folk music in Newcastle city centre. The most reliable place to hear the music is at Monument, particularly inside the Central Arcade; an accomplished penny whistle player can sometimes be heard on Northumberland Street. Or you could just head to a folk session at the Cumberland Arms in Byker (page 33) or a concert at the Sage music centre in Gateshead.

1920s and 1930s buildings around Monument

A good number of Art Deco buildings survive in Newcastle's city centre, including the **Tyneside Cinema** and department stores such as nearby **Carliol House** down the same road, which features plain, long windows, a Portland stone façade, clean vertical lines and Egyptian-style Art Deco lion heads. The exterior of the old **Co-operative** on Newgate Street is similar with the addition of jazzy zigzag metalwork inside. The back entrance of **Fenwicks** on Blackett Street (opposite Monument) has a classic early modern cruise-liner shape to its 1937 frontage.

Shopping

Northumberland Street – a wide, pedestrian avenue running between Monument and Haymarket – is considered the Oxford Street of Newcastle where you'll find all usual high-street fashion shops as well as the city's most famous department store, **Fenwicks** (*0191 232 5100; www.fenwick.co.uk*). Its French Salon (and coffee shops) has been a firm favourite with well-heeled ladies since it opened in 1882 and the Fenwick's Christmas Window is as popular as ever. You'll find there's often a queue to walk the length of the shop front to see puppets acting out Christmas scenes. **Fenwicks's delicatessen** is huge and has excellent cheese and meat counters selling the very best produce from the North East.

During the 1960s redevelopment of Newcastle, Grainger's elegant **Eldon Square** near Monument was almost completely demolished and in its place was built a large, soulless indoor shopping centre of the same name. It's actually well concealed and does not impinge much on the rest of Grainger Town. Away from the chain shops in Eldon Square (*0191 261 1891; www.eldon-square.co.uk*) and Monument Mall, **High Bridge** is a bit of a scruffy street but has a good reputation for small independent shops and a long association with retro fashions and music.

Tyneside Cinema

10 Pilgrim St, NE1 6QG ℡ 0845 217 9909 Ⓦ www.tynesidecinema.co.uk; open daily until 23.00; bar and coffee lounges.

Newcastle's favourite arthouse cinema was extensively renovated in recent years to bring back the furnishings and fittings of the original 1930s building. Art Deco stained glass, lighting and ceiling roses were uncovered and brought back to their best and the grey lino in the foyers peeled back to reveal the original pink, green and cream mosaic flooring. Screenings in the revamped auditoriums include Hollywood films as well as world cinema, documentaries, cult classics and art house productions. Upstairs, the ever-popular Tyneside Coffee Rooms have been a favourite meeting place since the 1930s (see page 29).

When the Newcastle News Theatre, as it was originally known, opened in 1937, for sixpence, people could watch a 75-minute screening of world events played on a loop. The Tyneside, as locals call it, is the finest remaining of many such News Theatres that existed around the country in the 1930s.

Laing Art Gallery

New Bridge St, NE1 8AG ① 0191 232 7734 Ⓦ www.twmuseums.org.uk/laing; open Mon–Sat 10.00–17.00, Sun 14.00–17.00; free admission.

Newcastle's premier art gallery houses a good number of works by pre-Raphaelite and Impressionist painters, including *Isabella and the Pot of Basil* by William Holman Hunt.

Downstairs is the excellent **Northern Spirit** exhibition which showcases oils by the likes of Ralph Hedley, noted for his paintings depicting the lives of ordinary people in the North East (fishwives, miners, children, etc). Some of Thomas Bewick's woodblocks used in the creation of his celebrated *History of British Birds* are housed in a special display. Also here is a collection of oil paintings by artists working out of the fishing village of Cullercoats in the 19th century. *The Women* by John Charlton is one of the most stirring. The large, dark canvas tells the story of a famous ship rescue near Whitley Bay in 1861 (see page 39).

② Historic quayside: The Close, Sandgate and Side

There is something surprising in the sight of the Tyne, with its busy traffic, its fleet of keels and steam-tugs, coal-ships, and merchant vessels from the north of Europe . . . The banks are for the most part high and steep, rough and bare, or patched with ragged grass; pantiled cottages dot the slopes, or crowd the levels and hollows, and here and there dormer windows appear that look as if imported ready made from Holland.

Victorian view of the quayside from Walter White's *Northumberland, and the Border*, 1859

A wander along Newcastle's medieval roads and alleys reveals the city of past centuries when wealthy merchants lived by the Tyne and the riverside was a wall of masts and rigging.

Overshadowed by the towering legs of the High Level Bridge and screened by Customs House and the Guildhall are some of the oldest buildings on Tyneside, dating from the 16th to 18th centuries when the city was rapidly expanding and this was the commercial centre. The architecture of **Sandgate** and the **Close** evoke days when sailing ships and wherries lined the quayside, merchants occupied the now crooked timber and brick buildings set back from the river, and boatmen called keelmen transported coal along the Tyne to waiting ships.

One of the oldest buildings on the Close is the timber-framed **Cooperage** (pictured on page 11) beyond the Swing Bridge (where barrels were made), which dates to the mid 16th century; but the most striking of all the merchant houses and warehouses is **Bessie Surtees's House** (*0191 269 1200; www.english-heritage.org.uk; open Mon–Fri*), the wide Tudor-looking building on the corner of the Side. It has an equally impressive Jacobean interior with extensive wood panelling and ornate plasterwork and is named after a girl who eloped in 1772 with a man who would later become Lord Chancellor. She famously climbed out of a window (now marked with a blue pane above a panel describing the tale) and escaped Newcastle on horseback.

Around the corner on **the Side**, the **Side Gallery** (*0191 232 2000; www.amber-online.com; open Tue–Sat 11.00–17.00*) showcases a range of documentary photography and houses a small independent cinema with screenings on Tuesday evenings.

Continuing up the same medieval thoroughfare, you'll come to one of the oldest pubs in Newcastle: the **Crown Posada**, celebrated for its Victorian frontage and interior. Traditional partitions, wood-panelling, stained glass and a gramophone take you back in time.

Hidden quayside: back streets and alleys

Narrow passageways and streets called '**chares**' (possible Anglo-Saxon origins from 'cerre' meaning a bend or turning) connect the waterfront with the medieval markets near the cathedral and castle; they are full of surprises: the sudden appearance of the medieval town walls, an archway through the castle wall and a concealed Georgian church. There's even a staircase to nowhere that stops halfway down a bank between the Castle Keep and the Side. **Hanover Street** – a cobbled lane opposite the Copthorn Hotel – still has its smooth granite cart tracks.

Dog Leap Steps off the Side, **Long Stairs** next to the Cooperage and **Castle Steps** opposite the Swing Bridge, are still used by pedestrians. The latter passageway climbs steeply to the Castle Keep in 107 steps passing the crumbling masonry of the castle, a well and under an archway through the old castle wall. Once there were small shops selling old clothes and clogs here. Hundreds of years ago a sailor was reputedly murdered on Long Stairs and his body nailed on the wall by the side entrance to the Cooperage where there's an ancient wooden door. Last time I looked, a very large, old nail was protruding from the masonry to the left of the door, which made me wonder . . .

At the top of **Broad Chare** (next to the Law Courts) and just past a bonded warehouse that is now the well-regarded **Live Theatre** (*0191 232 1232; www.live.org.uk*), an archway leads to a medieval courtyard and one of the great historic buildings on the quayside: **Trinity House** (*0191 232 8226; visits by appointment*). It was originally a charitable guild formed by seafarers to support mariners in the city and was later given a charter by Henry VIII to levy a toll on ships entering the Tyne and maintain the light beacons at the mouth of the river (light dues). Highlights inside include a wooden chapel dating to 1505 and an 18th-century Banqueting Hall. On the hill above Broad Chare, reached by climbing **Dog Bank**, is the oval-shaped **All Saints Church** (see page 15).

Quayside Market
Every Sunday between the Tyne Bridge and Millennium Bridge; road closed and parking restricted (try Dean St or park in Baltic Sq on the Gateshead side of the Millennium Bridge).

Historical records of a market on the quayside go back to 1736. Today it's held on Sundays and is very busy with families. You can pick up local artworks, secondhand books, jewellery and handmade beauty products; there are also numerous food stalls selling such treats as Northumbrian cheese, artisan breads and chocolates.

You would never have seen foodie places like this a decade ago when the quayside market was a long row of stalls selling burgers, knick-knacks, household cleaning cloths and fake Newcastle United clothing (there's still a bit of that). The best thing about the market then was the traders who drew in the crowds with their cheerful banter – a rare sound today, though there is still a man who makes leather wallets, belts and pencil cases who always draws a laugh. The strap line to his business is: 'David Nash of London, Paris, New York, Tokyo, Rome and Blyth . . . But mainly Blyth.'

Bridges over the Tyne
Approaching Newcastle Central Station by train from the south is an arrival like no other city in England except perhaps for Berwick-upon-Tweed. An unbeatable vista opens of the river with the Swing, Tyne and Millennium bridges. In all, seven bridges link Newcastle with Gateshead. From east to west they are:

Gateshead Millennium Bridge is the newest (2001), flashiest and one of the greatest contemporary pieces of architecture on Tyneside. It was

Kittiwakes on the Tyne Bridge
To the seabirds that nest on the frame of the Tyne Bridge and on the ledges of its towers, this is as good a nesting spot as any coastal cliff. Kittiwakes took up residence here after Gateshead Council turfed them off the Baltic Flour Mill in the 1990s, and they are now a much-appreciated feature of the Tyne Bridge. Some market traders and councillors want to cover the bridge in netting to stop the birds nesting (because of the mess their droppings cause), but the powers that be have decided that the largest inland colony of kittiwakes in the world is an attraction and should not be moved – at least for now. Summers wouldn't be the same without their 'kittee-wake' calls resonating along the riverfront.

designed to complement the Tyne Bridge and it does something pretty special: it tilts, allowing boats to pass underneath. When the dual pedestrian and bicycle walkway rises (operated by two huge parabolic steel structures) counterbalancing the arch, the movement resembles a blinking eye.

Next upriver is the green **Tyne Bridge** which defines Newcastle more than any other building or structure. At the time of opening in 1928 it was the largest single-span bridge in Britain, and was designed by architects in Middlesbrough (the same company that built the Sydney Harbour Bridge that opened a few years later but was designed prior to the Tyne Bridge). When viewed from Newcastle's quayside (particularly the Side), its massive arms shoot across the skyline appearing to rest on the shoulders of the 19th-century houses by the river. You can walk across the Tyne Bridge that allows a closer inspection of its frame (and nesting kittiwakes below).

Joining the quayside promenades either side of the Tyne is the **Swing Bridge** – the eye-catching red and white wrought-iron bridge that pivots on a central point to allow ships to pass (a rare occurrence these days). It's driven by hydraulic engines and was engineered by the renowned Victorian industrialist, William Armstrong between 1868 and 1876.

Robert Stephenson's combined road and rail bridge, the **High Level Bridge**, marches across the Tyne at 120 feet above the water. Known as 'Lang Legs'

Ha'way the Lads

Geordies, if you haven't noticed, are obsessed with football. For fans not at the St James's Park stadium on a Saturday afternoon, there's no sound quite as joyous as the roar when Newcastle score. It's so loud in fact that as I write this from over two miles away, I can hear the cheers (two goals for Newcastle so far).

At no time are passions stirred more than when the players – known as the 'Magpies' on account of their black and white shirts – are playing Sunderland. Rivalry between the two teams goes back a long time and you'll quite often hear Geordies using the pejorative term 'Mackem' to describe not just Sunderland supporters, but anyone from Wearside. Its origins don't go back that far – perhaps only to the 1980s – and is thought to stem from the dockyards: Sunderland shipbuilders would make the boats and the Geordies would fit them out, hence 'mack'em and tack'em (make them and take them).

You can book tours of **St James's Park** by calling the number below. Incidentally, the stadium was re-named the 'Sports Direct Arena' in 2012 – a name as likely to stick as changing 'Tyne Bridge' to the 'Bupa Bridge' after the sponsors of the Great North Run. Otherwise, for a glimpse of fans in the arena (you can't see the pitch), take the lift to the roof of Eldon Square car park (the concrete spiral car park at the back of Marks & Spencer).

Strawberry Pl, NE1 4ST; 0844 372 1892; www.nufc.co.uk.

after it opened in 1849, its cream, wrought-iron frame is best appreciated from the pedestrian walkways which are encased by arches across its entire 450-yard length.

Next upriver is the Queen Elizabeth II **Metro Bridge** (brilliant blue crossing); King Edward VII **Rail Bridge** and the **Redheugh Bridge**, a lofty concrete crossing with a pedestrian footway that is as windswept as standing on the top of the highest hill.

③ Medieval Newcastle and China Town

In four things Newcastle excels; walls, gates, towers, and turrets.
William Gray, historian, 1649

Within bowshot of the Norman Castle Keep is Newcastle's medieval quarter characterised by winding streets and alleys that lead in one direction to the quayside and in the other to the markets around the cathedral. Cloth Market, Flesh Market, Groat Market and the Bigg Market (bigg was a type of barley) evoke a sense of what this area must have once looked (and smelled) like.

By the mid-14th century, Newcastle was enclosed by a stonking **town wall** that formed a protective two-mile loop around its perimeter with towers, gateways and turrets along its length. It was 25 feet high and seven feet thick and was said to 'far passith all the waulls of the cities of England and most of the cities of Europe'.

The **West Walls** near Stowell Street in **China Town** is the most substantial length of the barricade remaining with four towers and standing to full height. Elsewhere in the city, the odd bit of wall masonry crops up here and there: through a churchyard, tumbling down to the quayside, next to a busy roundabout.

Just within the protective boundary of the West Walls is the restored 13th-century **Blackfriars** cloisters (now workshops and a restaurant) on Monk Street. The cloisters' walkway is no longer covered but the building as a whole is worth seeking out and you can still see the outline of where the church once stood. Facing Westgate Road, the **Tyne Theatre** (*0191 243 1171; www. millvolvotynetheatre.co.uk; mainly family shows and comedy*) is one of the oldest working Victorian theatres in the world and houses its original stage machinery discovered hidden behind a screen in the 1970s. The sumptuous auditorium dates from 1867 and is largely unchanged, as is the Italianate frontage.

Castle Keep and Black Gate

Castle Garth and St Nicholas's St, NE1 1RQ ℗ 0191 232 7938
Ⓦ www.castlekeepnewcastle.org.uk; open Mon–Sat, and Sun afternoons.
Sixty-nine Dog Leap Steps connect Newcastle's quayside with the Castle Keep, one of the most intact Norman keeps in Britain. At the top of the stairs, a length of stone wall hidden under the archway of the railway bridge on your

Three remarkable churches

All Saints Church is one of Newcastle's great Georgian treasures. Access is from Pilgrim Street or Broad Chare but most impressively by climbing the King Street stairs (from the end of Queen Street) where you'll find the church at the top. A tremendously tall steeple and Grecian-styled portico hide its unusual oval body, a characteristic shared by just a handful of other churches in England. For such a remarkable building, it's surprising how few locals have even heard of All Saints, perhaps because it's tricky to find, drowned by modern buildings and only open to Sunday worshippers. Though lost from Newcastle's modern cityscape, when viewed from Gateshead it has quite an impact on the skyline, as its architects intended.

Compared to many of England's other cathedrals **St Nicholas's** (*St Nicholas's St; 0191 232 1939*) is neither stupendously impressive nor particularly elegant (with the exception of the steeple) mainly because it originated as a 15th-century parish church. However, it bears a number of beautiful – and curious – features including a small square of medieval coloured glass depicting the Virgin Mary breastfeeding Jesus. The steeple has eight turrets and finely carved stone pinnacles topped with vanes; its tower once contained a navigational lantern that helped guide mariners along the river.

St Andrew's Church near China Town (*Newgate St; 0191 222 0259; open Mon–Fri until 15.00*) is clearly very ancient and even contains a stretch of the old town wall running through the churchyard and stone slab roofing. Parts of the church were constructed in the 12th century, including the tall chancel arch and the lower section of the tower (the rest of the tower is mainly 13th century and was, incidentally, used as a gun platform during the Civil War). When open, the churchyard becomes a wonderful wooded sanctuary for the odd passer-by or office worker. Here lies Charles Avison ('England's Mozart') who lived in Newcastle and died in 1770, as well as 15 women executed in 1650 for witchcraft.

left is a relic of the wall that once enclosed the castle before the Victorians bulldozed their new railway bridge through the fortress. Because of the railway it's hard to gain a sense of the castle grounds and you'll see the keep is on one side of the bridge and the fortress's mid 13th-century entranceway and barbican on the other. **Black Gate**, as it is known, is a formidable beast of masonry with newer additions here and there and straddling a moat.

Newcastle gets its name from a 'new' timber castle built in 1080 by the son of William the Conqueror on the site of the old Roman fort, Pons Aelius. The wooden fortress was replaced a century later in stone under the orders of Henry II and it is this later Norman building (well, its keep at least) that still stands to this day. Situated so close to the Scottish border, the fortresses were necessary defences against invasions from the north.

By the late 16th century, the castle was 'old and ruinous' but it was strengthened in the years leading up to the Civil War of 1642. Not even Newcastle's mighty town walls could keep out the Scots who pounded the stone barricade with artillery fire and mines and finally stormed the city after a siege lasting three months. The castle and the Royalist mayor of Newcastle were taken a few days later and the Scottish army occupied Newcastle (as well as the whole of Northumberland and Durham) for three years. A reminder of the fateful year when the town fell is carved to the right of the fireplace in the King's Chamber; the names of the soldiers and the date '1644' are still visible.

Inside, a labyrinth of stone staircases leads into many chambers including the Great Hall and up to the roof where you gain a stupendous view of Newcastle's bridges and streets. Downstairs, cabinets contain many curious objects discovered during excavations including a bronze dodecahedron, an octagonal object the size of a child's fist with round projections on each corner. It looks like a torture instrument but is more likely to be a game. Only three have ever been recovered in the UK; there's another on display in the Great North Museum.

Amen Corner, the Vampire Rabbit and Milburn House

A narrow passage, **Amen Corner**, winds around the back of St Nicholas's Cathedral, revealing a few architectural curios including an elaborately decorated doorway, above which crouches an eccentric carving of a rabbit or hare. The **Vampire Rabbit**, as it is called, is painted black and has red claws and fangs. The celebrated nature engraver Thomas Bewick had his workshop on Amen Corner (note his bust on the wall).

Milburn House is a fascinating Edwardian building that deserves to be better known. Internally it was designed to resemble a cruise liner and each floor has a balcony overlooking a central light well and is even labelled as on a ship: A at the top and F on the ground floor. Some of the brass fingerplates on the office doors are engraved with ships and the whole building is decorated with ornate green and yellow tiles. It's fitting that Admiral Collingwood should have been born here and that the building was financed with shipping money. Access is from Amen Corner or Dean Street and though there is no general public access into the office block, no one seemed to mind me poking my head round the door.

④ Central Station and railway heritage

The entranceway to Newcastle's main station may be impressive, but the original plans were even grander and included an Italianate tower. Yet it is still a highly memorable station with its long curved platforms, elegant roofs supported by wrought-iron ribs and lattice-framed bridges arching over the railway lines. Beyond the ticket hall, the old first-class refreshment room now functions as a **brasserie and pub** (the Centurion) with an interior tiled throughout with sumptuous late 19th-century Burmantoft's tiles.

Newcastle's contribution to the Industrial Revolution – and particularly the legacy of the great railway engineers, George Stephenson and his son, Robert – is remembered in the buildings and monuments around Central Station. The **George Stephenson Monument**, 100 yards down from the station entrance, shows the 'father of the railways' standing above four figures representing the industries in which he made his name.

Behind Central Station is **Stephenson Locomotive Works** (*South St, just beyond the Royal Mail buildings; not usually open to the public; www. robertstephensontrust.com*), the workshops where the Stephensons' pioneering steam engines were built. A visitor in the mid 19th century described the buildings in their heyday when 1,500 men were constructing steam engines: 'The young man who showed me around, talked coolly [sic] of 50 locomotives being in hand for France . . . as a baker would talk of fifty loaves. I wanted to see The Rocket, and it was pointed out to me in a yard, standing neglected amidst a heap of rusty iron.' The engine is now rather better protected in the Science Museum in London.

Newcastle's contemporary reputation in the sciences is illuminated at the **Centre for Life** (*0191 243 8210; www.life.org.uk; open daily*), a science centre next door to Central Station. It features a large exhibition space with interactive machines, family events and a planetarium.

Literary & Philosophical Society

23 Westgate Rd (close to Central Station), NE1 1SE ⓣ 0191 232 0192 ⓦ www.litandphil.org.uk; open Mon–Thu until 19.00, Fri until 17.00 and Sat until 13.00; free admission.

Politics and religion were the only topics banned when this society was founded in 1793 as a 'conversation club'. Over the years, many distinguished engineers, historians and writers have lectured here including Oscar Wilde, Mary Kingsley and John Betjemen. The most famous lecture was given by Joseph Swan on 20 October 1880 during which he demonstrated the electric light. In doing so, this suitably grand building with a Greek Revival frontage just down from the Royal Station Hotel, became the first public building to be lit by electricity in the world.

The golden age of the 'Lit and Phil', as it is known, was at the peak of the Industrial Revolution when all the North East's big-name engineers and thinkers did a stint as president (the plaque at the top of the entrance staircase lists them all).

The tradition of public lectures continues today (see the society's website for upcoming talks), but most visitors come to use – and admire – the public library. The bookshelves extend almost to the dome glass skylights and are divided into a lower and upper tier by an elegant iron balcony. Oak chairs and tables, wooden coat stands and antique clocks evoke a bygone era. Even the toilet-door latches show period detailing and are opened and closed with the assistance of a brass cog. Note too the display cases which contain historic objects including one of George Stephenson's miners' lamps. In another is a copy of Thomas Bewick's *History of British Birds*.

Refreshments are served through a hatch and readers are permitted to return to their tables with a book and cup of tea or coffee.

Mining Institute

Neville Hall, Westgate Rd (close to Central Station), NE1 1SE ⓣ 0191 233 2459 Ⓦ www.mininginstitute.org.uk; open Mon–Fri 10.00–17.00. Free admission.

Next door to the Lit & Phil, this fascinating little known architectural gem has a Gothic Revival interior. It was founded at a time when coal was powering the railways (and the industrialisation of the modern world) and mines operated all over the North East. A deadly explosion at Seaham Colliery in 1852 prompted a group of mining men to establish an institute, the aim of which was to 'devise measures to avert or alleviate those dreadful calamities, which have so frequently produced such destruction to life and property . . . and to establish a Literary Institution . . . applicable to the theory, art, and practice of Mining.'

The **Neville Hall Library** has an outstanding interior with tiers of stained glass windows, a lofty central atrium and superb wood panelling and fittings, and contains journals, geological surveys and books on engineering, geology and mining.

Discovery Museum

Blandford Sq, NE1 4JA ⓣ 0191 232 6789 Ⓦ www.twmuseums.org.uk/discovery; open Mon–Sat, and Sun 14.00–17.00; free admission.

One of the most engaging and well-visited museums on Tyneside, devoted mainly to the region's industrial and maritime heritage, is conveniently found a short walk from Central Station. Dominating the interior is the 115-foot long *Turbinia* – the first ship to be powered by steam in the world. It's surrounded by an extensive collection of model ships as well as a couple of traditional full-sized wooden boats, a Science Maze and a water-based installation themed around activities on the River Tyne (waterproof aprons are provided for children). Temporary exhibitions bring to life different aspects of Tyneside's social history from fashion to football.

⑤ Haymarket and the Civic Centre

Haymarket Metro station at the top of Northumberland Street marks the end of the main shopping area. You have left the classical streets of Grainger Town and are now in a more modern space by the Civic Centre and Newcastle and Northumbria universities, albeit one with an imposing Victorian church and a scattering of old buildings. Apart from the university art galleries and the natural history museum are Newcastle's **city swimming pool** (*0191 277 1844*) on Northumberland Road where there's an old Turkish bath with marble fittings and wood panelled changing rooms, and **Northern Stage** (*0191 230 5151; www.northernstage.co.uk*), a well-known production theatre

1960s Newcastle

In Newcastle I wanted to see the creation of a 20th-century equivalent of Dobson's masterpiece . . . If this could be achieved, I felt, then our regional capital would become the outstanding provincial city in the country.
T Dan Smith *An Autobiography,* 1970

The Civic Centre was constructed as part of a major redevelopment of Newcastle in the 1960s to create the 'Brasilia of the North', a project much condemned for its destructiveness and disregard for historical buildings. It was in many ways as brutal and visionary in its scope as Grainger and Dobson's neoclassical redevelopment of the city in the early 19th century. T Dan Smith (a name that still evokes contempt from locals) was the then leader of Newcastle City Council and widely credited with the concrete brutalist architecture and dual carriageways. Not all the T Dan Smith era buildings in Newcastle are so derided, however, and though a number are now being demolished, some are cherished, including the Civic Centre. 'I know Smith was a bit of a rogue, but we are very grateful to him,' said a council worker in admiration of the building. And without the ring roads, the city centre would probably not be pedestrianised as it is today.

in the grounds of Newcastle University, showing modern plays, contemporary dance and exhibitions.

Civic Centre

Barras Bridge (Haymarket), NE1 8QH ☉ 0191 277 7222 ⓦ www.theciviccentre.co.uk; tours cost just a few pounds and must be booked in advance; watch Council Chamber meetings from the public gallery on the first Wednesday of every month.

The Scandinavian-influenced Civic Centre is much undervisited and underappreciated, except by architecture students. Externally, the most striking feature of the office building, designed in 1950 and opened in 1968 by King Olav V of Norway, is the square **tower** crowned with seahorses, but get in closer and you'll find **sculptures** including five steel swans (said to represent the Nordic countries) and an **auditorium** on stilts surrounded by a modern interpretation of a medieval moat.

The fantastically well-preserved interior will make Danish design aficionados weep. Unlike many buildings of its age, the Civic Centre was neither constructed in a hurry nor using inexpensive materials. George Kenyon, the architect, is said to have travelled all over Europe sourcing the finest marbles for the corridors,

Rapper sword dancing

Not the latest dance/music craze to hit the inner-city streets of Newcastle, but a traditional North East sword dance going back to at least the early 18th century. Performed almost exclusively by men, it shares similarities with Morris dancing, both in dress and movement, though it is somewhat more masculine, and not just because the dancers wield swords instead of handkerchiefs. Long, flexible swords are interlocked and crossed and various turns and the occasional flip are performed about a central point or in lines. The dance contains smooth transitions from one knitted sword position to another, and foot-taps and kicks not dissimilar to clog dancing.

Rapper competitions were popular in the 1800s in coal mining villages such as Winlaton, Swalwell, Westerhope and High Spen, but the tradition began to wane at the turn of the 20th century. It was momentarily saved by the intervention of English folk revivalist, Cecil Sharp, who recorded many of the near extinct rapper dances and encouraged teams to compete. Despite his efforts, almost every group died out during World War II. The High Spen Blue Diamonds is the only historic team that survives to this day.

In 1949, the tradition was again given a boost, this time by a professor from King's College, Durham. His team, the Newcastle Kingsmen, perform at festivals and public events. You can also see them practising at the Cumberland Arms (see page 33) in Byker on Wednesday evenings. The dancers are, of course, mostly university students, not coal miners, though they share the same fondness for performing in pubs. Surprisingly, rapper dancing has become popular beyond the Tyne and there are now teams elsewhere in England and overseas.

landings and staircases; woods for the ceilings, screens and banisters; and slates for the walls. The **chandeliers** in the entrance stairwell and banqueting hall, now priceless, are made of hand-cut Bavarian crystal with decorative features echoing the castles and seahorses on the city's coat of arms.

Upstairs in the **committee rooms**, walls are decorated in red silk and orange leather; the rosewood chairs, tables and sideboards are the work of Danish furniture maker, Arne Vodder. Light floods the rooms and corridors through floor-to-ceiling windows and there's a **spiral staircase** made from one piece of cast steel. The Council Chamber is superbly unchanged, still with its original 149 green leather chairs. The Lord Mayor's Silver Gallery is on the top floor.

Great North Museum and the Hatton Gallery

Barras Bridge, NE2 4PT ☎ 0191 222 6765 ⊛ www.twmuseums.org.uk/greatnorthmuseum; open Mon–Sat 10.00–17.00 and Sun from 13.00; free admission.
The building formally known as the Hancock Museum, in case you're asking a local for directions, houses the **Natural History Society's** collection of stuffed

animals, fossils and minerals as well as artefacts owned by the **Society of Antiquaries of Newcastle upon Tyne** (*www.newcastle-antiquaries.org.uk*), the second oldest antiquarian society in the world founded in 1813.

Children seem to enjoy having their photo taken in front of a shark with its jaw open, gawping at the Egyptian mummy and racing around the central atrium where the exotic creatures are displayed. The Roman and Hadrian's Wall galleries contain an impressive array of altar stones, and the World Cultures gallery exhibits well-presented ceremonial costumes including an impressive Samurai warrior display.

Always worth a look and with free entry, the **Hatton Gallery** (*0191 222 6059; www.twmuseums.org.uk/hatton; open Mon–Sat 10.00–17.00*) is part of the Great North Museum but is found tucked away in Newcastle University's old Quadrangle, opposite the Civic Centre. Exhibitions change regularly with contemporary solo artists and university students showcasing their work.

⑥ Ouseburn Valley and Byker

Stepney Bank/Lime St, Quayside East, NE1 2NP ℗ 0191 261 6596
Ⓦ www.ouseburntrust.org.uk.

Newcastle's east end, centred around Byker, has traditionally had a reputation as one of the poorest localities in the city. That image is changing somewhat with the arts-led regeneration of nearby Ouseburn Valley and the increasingly prosperous suburb of Heaton that borders Byker to the north. Byker Wall attracts architecture buffs and social historians (see page 24).

A concealed tributary of the River Tyne flows under the giant brick archways of Byker Bridge a mile east of Newcastle city centre, where there were once lead works, lime kilns, flour mills, iron foundries, glassworks and potteries at different times over the last 500 years; it remained a ramshackle sort of a place with modern factories, garages and scrap yards until the late 1990s.

One by one these have been converted into cultural venues, recording studios, and artist workshops, and the whole area named the Ouseburn Valley. Walking along the Ouse today you are more likely to hear the sound of a band practising than the clatter of machinery from the few remaining car workshops. The only other relics from the past still operating are a few pigeon crees on Lime Street.

Even the little **Ouseburn Farm** (*0191 232 3698; open daily*) by the river off Lime Street could not escape rebranding by the regeneration wizards (it used to be called Byker City Farm). The formerly rundown enclosures have been refurbished and it is now an even more inviting and engaging (though still delightfully higgledy-piggledy) farm where chickens and children roam freely among vegetable plots, and pigs snooze in pig heaps. Despite the cockerels competing with musicians from the recording studio, it's a tranquil spot. A café upstairs sells snacks and probably the cheapest cup of tea on Tyneside.

On sunny weekends, young and old lounge outside on the 'village' green between the Cluny pub and the city farm; horses from nearby Stepney

Bank Stables trot by and a steady stream of families wander in and out of the nearby Seven Stories Centre for Children's Books. Despite gentrification, the Ouseburn remains a laid-back, unpretentious place that is still agreeably scruffy round the edges. Regulars like it that way.

Industrial heritage

Evidence of the Ouseburn Valley's old industries and Roman roots are all around you. Between the farm and the Cluny is a ford said to have been in use when the Romans built Hadrian's Wall across this valley. The remains of a later slipway are still visible with two smooth granite tracks worn over the years by the wheels of many wagons transporting coal and grain from wherries (sailing barges). Today, the only boats are a couple of motor vessels but the river remains a grubby little waterway, albeit one frequented by grey wagtails and mallards and which smells of the sea when the wind is blowing from the east.

Also worth seeking out are the old flax mill (now occupied by Cluny and Seven Stories) and the brick furnace arches of a former glass works. The street names also evoke past industries: Lime Street, Foundry Lane and Maling Street (after the famous Sunderland pottery makers who had kilns here).

Unbeknown to casual visitors is a subterranean tunnel that runs right across Newcastle. The **Victorian Tunnel** (*0191 261 6596; www.ouseburntrust.org.uk; booking essential*) was opened in 1835 and designed for wagons to carry coal underground from a colliery near the Town Moor to the quayside, rather than through the streets. During World War II it served as an air-raid shelter. A 700-yard length of the narrow tunnel, which has an entrance on Lime Street, is open to the public booked on guided tours.

Seven Stories

30 Lime St, NE1 2PQ ① 0845 2710777 ⑩ www.sevenstories.org.uk; open Mon–Sun; half price admissions between 15.00–17.00 weekdays during term time; café.

Venture into the world of children's story books, their characters, authors and illustrators in this enchanting exhibition centre with changing displays and a permanent collection including an archive of Enid Blyton's work. Exhibits include original manuscripts and artefacts relating to the real-life characters who inspired stories. Upstairs, a story-teller in costume sitting on a huge comedy chair keeps children transfixed with lively readings. Elsewhere there are dressing up boxes with Gruffalo outfits and more, a café and a well-stocked bookshop.

Biscuit Factory

Stoddart St, NE2 1AN ① 0191 261 1103 ⑩ www.thebiscuitfactory.com; open Sun and Mon 11.00–17.00 and Tue–Sat 10.00–18.00.

When it opened in 2001, this large art gallery housed in a brick warehouse (and former Victorian biscuit factory) quickly became the premier contemporary art retailer in Newcastle. Claiming to be the UK's largest independent commercial art gallery it has a reputation for quality, range and affordability.

The gallery is arranged over two floors: crafts, jewellery and gifts occupy most of the ground floor, and larger paintings and sculptures are upstairs. You'll find works by local artists (there are always paintings depicting Northumbrian landscapes, for example) and international exhibits. You can often pick up an original painting or sculpture for under £100, though many paintings and sculptures are considerably more than that. The popular café on the top floor provides views of the city skyline and Byker Wall.

Millers Auction House
Algernon Rd, Byker NE6 2UN ① 0191 265 8080 ⓦ www.millersauctioneers.co.uk.
Millers has been operating for over a century (though not always out of Byker) and holds morning auctions on Tuesdays (china, collectables and glassware) and Wednesdays (antique and modern furniture). It's housed in the old Ringtons Tea warehouse and Maling Ware enthusiasts may recognise the building from the backstamp on Maling china tea caddies commissioned by the tea merchants. Even if you don't intend to buy anything, it's fun to squeeze into the often packed upstairs hall and watch proceedings.

⑦ Segedunum Roman Fort
Buddle St, Wallsend NE28 6HR ① 0191 236 9347 ⓦ www.twmuseums.org.uk/ segedunum; open daily from Apr–end Oct.
A tall viewing platform, which looks like an airport control tower looms over this industrial and archaeological site providing an amazing bird's eye view of the remains of the Roman fort and enhancing your appreciation of its scale. It provides an equally clear view of the Tyne above the famous Swan Hunter shipbuilding yards where you can still see the rectangular inlets where hulls including the *Mauretania* were constructed.

Segedunum (meaning 'strong fort') was built under the order of Emperor Hadrian and marks the end point of Hadrian's 73-mile wall across northern England (hence the town's name, 'Wallsend'). The site includes an indoor **museum** and a full-scale reconstruction of Europe's only fully working Roman **bath house**; part of the hot-room floor has been removed to show how the Romans engineered under-floor heating.

Other Roman buildings are marked out in lines of stones; they were only re-discovered when the terraces of Victorian housing running down to the shipyards were demolished.

⑧ Jesmond and around
During the mid 19th century, this leafy suburb a mile from the city centre gained a reputation as the city's most exclusive place to live, as many of Newcastle's industrialists and politicians settled here. Today, it shares the reputation with its two neighbours, **Gosforth** and to an extent, **Heaton**.

Modern city highlights

Newcastle is renowned for its neoclassical streets but also has some modern gems with many architectural and heritage credentials. The **Engineering Research Station** on Station Road, Killingworth, is one: built in the late 1960s, this clean block of painted concrete panels stands out for its funnel-shaped roof sculptures and geometric entrance archway.

The **Wills Building** on the Coast Road was a cigarette factory when completed in 1950 (to a pre-war Art Deco design). It's formed of a central clock tower and two red-brick wings, each with three tiers of windows. In keeping with the modernist tradition, the lines are clean and windows pared back and simple.

Newcastle Civic Centre near Haymarket Metro station has been preserved exceptionally well with its original 1960s furnishings. It's like stepping into a retro photoshoot for a plush interiors magazine (see page 19).

St Teresa's Church on Heaton Road is a much under-recognised building from 1972 and yet it's very striking: an octagon with steeply sloping gables giving the roof a zigzag appearance. A peculiarly short, thin copper spire rises from the centre. Inside, the church is light-filled and beautiful in its simplicity.

Jesmond Library on the corner of Sunbury Avenue and St George's Terrace is another circular building on one level, but one much more widely recognised for its design. Its low perimeter wall consists of a series of fins made of glass and red granite into which the bookcases are arranged creating a pleasing unity between the interior and exterior.

Much has been written about the design and social history of the **Byker Wall** and **Estate** inner-city housing project since its development in the 1970s and 1980s by Swedish-based architect Ralph Erskine. This complex scheme includes many different flats and housing types and requires time to explore (easily walked to from Byker Metro station). Byker Wall itself is a huge brown brick façade that contains domestic dwelling and was designed to act as a buffer between the noise of traffic on one side and the estate which it enclosed on the other (a motorway was proposed at the time of design). Its inner side, nothing like the exterior, features colourful balconies, timber detailing and large windows.

Jesmond is home to a burgeoning student population, hence all the pubs and cafés on the main thoroughfare, Osborne Road. It's very pleasant around here during the day and most of the bars have outdoor tables.

An afternoon wander around these prosperous Victorian streets might lead you to the **antiques 'village'** at the bottom of Fern Avenue. The likes of Shiners and the beautiful Antiquités Françaises specialise in vintage furniture and architectural items. **St George's Church** on Osborne Road, with its landmark Italianate tower and celebrated Art Nouveau mosaics, is really worth visiting. Not far from the church at the bottom of Reid Park Road is the 12th-century ruin of **St Mary's Chapel** by the entrance to Jesmond Dene.

Jesmond Dene

Access from Jesmond Dene Rd, Armstrong Bridge and Jesmond Park West (Heaton).

The former back garden of 19th-century industrialist Lord Armstrong is one of the most enchanting urban parks in the North East. The Dene, as it is known locally, is a mile-long wooded river gorge with all the hallmarks of a Victorian pleasure ground: a banqueting hall (now a picturesque ruin), rhododendrons, follies and a large number of mature yew and beech trees.

A short walk through the residential streets south of Osborne Road takes you to the top of a couple of steep paths that descend into the Dene. At the river, a wide paved track follows the Ouseburn which flows under ivy-covered bridges, past a ruined old mill, over waterfalls and between stepping stones to reach the River Tyne. Kingfishers often dart along the river and perch on overhanging branches, and you may see a dipper near Jesmond Vale's white wooden bridge. In Armstrong's time, there were also nightjars and even corncrakes, but that was before the meadows surrounding the Dene became the red-brick terraces of Jesmond. It's an inviting place to come for a walk or picnic or take children to the little **farm** (*open daily*) and coffee shop. The Dene is most magical first thing in the morning after a snowfall, when you can feel transported back to the late 19th century when Armstrong gave his woodland garden as a gift to the people of Newcastle upon Tyne.

Heaton Park, a continuation of Jesmond Dene, is reached by walking under Armstrong Bridge – the huge iron bridge spanning the gorge. On Ouseburn Road, go through a doorway on your left and up the bank. The **Shoe Tree** – a spontaneous creation by local kids and now listed by the council as a structure of Special Local Architectural or Historic Interest – is ahead. Note too, the old cattle run, old loos with slate walls dividing the urinals and windmill.

⑨ Town Moor, Exhibition Park and the Hoppings

Easily reached from the Royal Victoria Infirmary, Fenham and Jesmond.

Over double the size of London's Hyde Park, the open grasslands of Newcastle's Town Moor and Exhibition Park have been a centre for recreation and sporting competitions ever since the bowmen of Redesdale in Northumberland staged an archery competition here in 1792 – and probably before then too. Horse racing, boxing matches, cock-fighting – the Town Moor has hosted them all.

The first Temperance Festival was in 1882; it continues today but is better known as the **Hoppings**, a week-long event in June with all the usual fairground rides and stalls over a huge area.

For hundreds of years the herbage rights have been held by the City Freemen. Cows graze on the open pastures today alongside dog walkers, runners and winter tobogganists.

Exhibition Park with its bandstand, model boating lake, playground and bowling green blends into the Town Moor on the fringes of the city centre and is reached by following a footpath under a subway by Newcastle University Library (near Haymarket) or from Brandling Park in Jesmond.

Tyneside Flats

An overarching memory of central Gateshead is of the uniform red-brick terraces around Saltwell and Bensham. These early 1900s houses, known as Tyneside Flats, are unusual in consisting of two purpose-built flats one above the other, each with their own front and back doors.

A good number of these terraces, which are such a distinctive feature of Tyneside, were demolished in recent years (also in Newcastle's West End) as part of a widely criticised government scheme to rejuvenate post-industrial cities in the North by constructing new family homes. With the national economy stalling in the late noughties, demolitions stopped in favour of refurbishment and a good number of streets have been spruced up with new railings, front doors and gardens and look stunning. It's a great shame, though, about the displaced communities and ghostly neighbourhoods still with their street lighting and pavements but no houses.

⑩ Gateshead

Traditionally the smaller, less glamorous cousin of Newcastle on the south side of the River Tyne, Gateshead has attracted national attention in recent years for its daring contemporary architecture and arts venues – and made Newcastle sit up and take notice. Rejuvenating Gateshead's quayside began with the success of *The Angel of the North* on a hill outside of the town. Following Gormley's masterpiece, the forward-thinking council embarked on a major redevelopment of the riverfront which put Gateshead on the arts map of Britain, though Newcastle often gets the credit.

Gateshead lacks the Victorian architecture and stately streets of Newcastle but it does have a handful of buildings worth seeking out, including the Town Hall and Shipley Art Gallery and the National Trust's Gibside (see page 248). Saltwell Park is a superb 19th-century pleasure ground and easily visited with *The Angel of the North* if travelling by car.

The council has demolished many buildings in Gateshead in recent years, but the one that caused more outrage than any other was a big concrete 1960s car park dominating the skyline above the Music Centre. Known to film fans as the *Get Carter* **Car Park** after the epic 1970s film in which it featured, it was a fine monstrosity with a rooftop café that thousands tried to save and even more queued for hours to walk around before its D-day. Its legacy endures of course and the building is forever immortalised in the most famous gangster film ever made in Britain.

Gateshead Quays

South Shore Rd Ⓦ www.gateshead-quays.com; QuayLink bus Q1 from Gateshead Metro station or take Q2 (or walk) from Newcastle's Monument to the quayside and cross the Millennium Bridge on foot.

Gateshead's quayside is now a major culture and leisure attraction sharing similarities with cities like Bilbao in Spain that also underwent arts-led regeneration works in the 1990s. Our Guggenheim equivalent is **The Sage Gateshead Music Centre** (*0191 443 4661; www.thesagegateshead.org*) – an organic-shaped building wrapped in steel on a bank above the Tyne.

Sir Norman Foster's masterpiece has completely transformed the quaysides of both Gateshead and Newcastle.

Inside the Sage, it's airy, bright and voluminous and there's a well-placed café with views of the Tyne Bridge and Newcastle's waterfront.

If you come to a concert here you'll be able to appreciate the much-praised acoustics in the timber halls. Many big names and up and coming folk, indy and world music stars perform at the Sage; it's also the permanent home of Folkworks, the North East's traditional music organisation, as well as the Northern Sinfonia orchestra.

The **BALTIC Centre for Contemporary Art** (*0191 478 1810; www. balticmill.com; open daily; free admission*) faces the Music Centre and is reached from Newcastle by walking (or cycling) over the Millennium Bridge. A mid 20th-century flour mill, gutted, stripped and converted into an arts venue was hardly ground-breaking stuff for a post-industrial town in the mid-1990s when the Baltic renovation took place, but it was executed in Gateshead with much sensitivity to the original building. Over the years, there have been some superb exhibitions here, including the Turner Prize exhibits in 2011 and a couple of shows by the North's favourite contemporary artists, Anthony Gormley and Anish Kapoor. It's worth going in just for the views of the Tyne from the top floors.

Just over a mile upriver from the Sage, **Dunston Staiths** is another relic from Tyneside's industrial era. The late 19th-century pier-like structure, said to be the largest wooden construction in Europe, once enabled wagons loaded with Durham coal to transport their contents directly onto ships moored along its side.

At the peak of its use in the 1920s, 140,000 tons of coal destined for London and abroad were shipped from the Dunston Staiths every week; by the 1970s, just 3,000 tons departed the Tyne here. The staiths ceased operating in the 1980s but it remains largely intact, save for a middle section that was damaged by fire.

There is no public access but it is easily viewed from the promenade or railway bridge (when crossing the river by train, look upriver, away from the Tyne Bridge).

Saltwell Park

Saltwell Rd South, NE9 5AX ☉ 0191 433 7000; café and toilets at Saltwell Towers.

Named the 'People's Park' when opened in 1876, this Victorian pleasure park was intended as a tranquil outdoor space for Gateshead residents needing clean air. The park, just a short bus ride from Gateshead town centre, was recently restored and its bandstand, rose gardens, stable blocks, woodland gardens and Victorian mansion now look their very best. **Saltwell Towers** is an eccentric Gothic manor house dating to the mid 19th century that children tend to remember for its fairytale-like turret, which they can climb. A short walk over a wooded burn brings you to a large playing field, bowling green, model boat lake (a Victorian tradition still going strong) and larger lagoon with pedalos.

Shipley Art Gallery

Prince Consort Rd, NE8 4JB ☉ 0191 477 1495; open Mon–Sat 10.00–17.00 and Sun 14.00–17.00.

There's always an eclectic display of art at the Shipley – crafts, fine art, contemporary video installations and so on, but it's particularly known for its crafts shows and permanent collection of pottery and glass. Past exhibitions included portraiture from the 17th century to the present, chair design through the ages and a display of African bead work. At the back of the gallery hangs one of the most cherished North East paintings, *The Blaydon Races* – a lively depiction across a large canvas of the popular 19th-century event. The song of the same name is a well-loved Geordie anthem.

⑪ The Angel of the North

Signposted off the A1 south of Gateshead, also reached from the Durham Rd ☉ 0191 433 3000; parking on site; Angel Bus (Go North East services 21 & 22) from Eldon Square Bus Station in Newcastle or Gateshead Interchange.

Boasting a wingspan the breadth of a jumbo jet was something of a PR disaster when the then largest sculpture in Britain was unveiled in 1998. *The Angel of the North* was much criticised by locals who thought the 65-foot sculpture did indeed look like a plane and not the elegant, feminine form perhaps some had hoped for. Many residents hated the sculpture – really hated it – and wanted it taken down. Now if the council threatened to take away Antony Gormley's masterpiece, they would probably tie themselves to its enormous rusty red feet in protest.

The prominent hillock on which it stands was once a colliery and the mining history of the site – and the region – is very much reflected in the colour, steel fabric and form (undeniably masculine). It's said to be one of the most viewed pieces of public art in Britain being situated by the A1 and in sight of the London to Edinburgh railway line. It's definitely one of the highlights of a visit to the North. Other memorable sculptures around Gateshead include Sally Matthews's life-size metal goats below the blue Metro Bridge and *Cone* by Andy Goldsworthy (west of the High Level Bridge).

Newcastle pubs

Books have been written about Newcastle's drinking holes, but this is all you really need to know: **Jesmond/Osborne Road** has a reputation for attracting students and glitzy ladies from the town. The exception is the **Collingwood Arms** in Brandling Village (near Clayton Road) which is a quiet pub serving a few real ales (it's a bit like the Cumberland Arms in Byker but without the music and atmosphere). Pubs in the **Bigg Market** are always packed with hen and stag parties and sell £3 vodka trebles as standard; the **Quayside** is a mixture of all of the above with the odd smarter bar like the **Pitcher and Piano** and a step-back-in-time pub called the **Crown Posada** on Side where music is sometimes played on a gramophone. **Broad Chare** on the street of the same name is a gastro pub serving real ales. **The Ouseburn Valley** near Byker and Heaton is a melting pot of students, indy musicians, 'proper pub' devotees, artists and academic types (see page 32). That leaves somewhere called the **Diamond Strip**: the bars on Collingwood Street near Central Station now have an identity – and a brilliant name. It's like the Bigg Market after winning the lottery ('celebrities, footballers, young and loaded, champagne cocktails, VIP private booths' is how one venue describes the place). Among the more chic, (and expensive) bars is **Tokyo** on the Collingwood Road end of Westgate Road, and which has a roof garden.

Food and drink
GRAINGER TOWN

Café Royal 8 Nelson St, NE1 5AW ⓣ 0191 231 3000 ⓦ www.sjf.co.uk. Probably the best coffee on Tyneside. Café Royal does not skimp on quality with their drinks, breakfast or lunch dishes; all croissants and pastries are made in the on site bakery. Typical lunch menu includes fishcakes, posh burgers, soups (always excellent) and fancier dishes such as mushroom gnocchi with hazelnuts and spinach. For food this good, expect to pay above average prices.

Panis High Bridge ⓣ 0191 232 4366 ⓦ www.paniscafe.co.uk. Lively, youthful Italian bar and restaurant run by an Italian family of brothers and sisters. Consistently excellent seafood, meat, salad and pasta dishes, all very reasonably priced (Lasagne at lunchtime is just over £4). Ciabatta sandwiches are stuffed with fresh ingredients, as you find in Italy. Evening Italian classes.

Pumphrey's Grainger Market, Nelson St ⓦ www.pumphreys-coffee.co.uk. Newcastle-based Pumphrey's continues a tradition of selling coffee beans and loose tea that goes back to 1750. Numerous varieties are for sale at their Grainger Market stall where they also serve take-away coffee made by expert baristas.

Tyneside Coffee Rooms 10 Pilgrim St, NE1 6QG ⓣ 0845 217 9909 ⓦ www.tynesidecinema.co.uk. Unpretentious eaterie on the top floor of a restored Art Deco cinema where film buffs and ladies meeting for lunch mingle with students and elderly folk. This old favourite with Tynesiders has changed very little over the decades and serves delightfully unsophisticated dishes (sandwiches, fishcakes and even good old scrambled egg on toast).

NEWCASTLE AND GATESHEAD QUAYSIDES

Newcastle's waterfront is not short of bars and places to eat. You'll find a number of chain restaurants around Dean St and on the Quayside including the likes of Pizza Express and the Slug and Lettuce. The pubs on Sandgate and the Side are pretty rowdy, so you might want to walk to Broad Chare where three of Michelin-starred restaurateur Terry Laybourne's eateries are located, including **Broad Chare**, an upmarket freehouse serving food. Facing the Millennium Bridge, there's the **Pitcher & Piano** in a large glass building offering exceptional views of the river.

Gateshead has a couple of good places to eat including at the BALTIC arts centre (see below), the modern eatery at the **Sage Gateshead** and **Raval** (*0191 477 1700; www.ravaluk.com*), an upmarket Indian restaurant with a very good reputation at the end of the Tyne Bridge.

Café 21 Trinity Gardens, NE1 2HH (reached from Broad Chare on the quayside) ☉ 0191 222 0755 ⓦ www.cafetwentyone.co.uk. This is one of the premier places to eat in Newcastle: smart, unfussy and clearly upmarket, reflected in the superior service, furnishings and the quality and price of the food. Its distinctly more casual sister restaurant/bistro in Fenwicks department store on Northumberland St is a popular choice for high tea with all the trimmings.

Pan Haggerty 21 Queen St, NE1 3UG ☉ 0191 221 0904 ⓦ www.panhaggerty.com. Swish, boutique-style restaurant with a traditional British menu. Many locally sourced fish and meat ingredients, including pork from Durham, fish from the North Sea and, unusually, pigeon from Alnwick. 'Pan Haggerty', incidentally, is a traditional Northumbrian fried dish made with sliced potatoes and onions.

SIX BALTIC Centre for Contemporary Art, Gateshead Quays, South Shore Rd, NE8 3BA ☉ 0191 440 4948 ⓦ www.sixbaltic.com. Fabulous rooftop restaurant overlooking the River Tyne serving modern British dishes and cocktails. Somewhere you'd come for a treat as it's not cheap. Less pricey is the café on the ground floor.

Viva Café Live Theatre, 27 Broad Chare, NE1 3DQ ☉ 0191 232 1331 ⓦ www.caffevivo.co.uk. Owned by the same company as Café 21 but offering a more lively café-cum-bar atmosphere. Italian dishes (no pizzas).

Vujon, Queen St, NE1 3UG ☉ 0191 221 0601 ⓦ www.vujon.com. Upmarket Indian restaurant on the quayside which recently won the title of the British Curry Awards' 'best in the North East'.

MEDIEVAL NEWCASTLE AND CHINA TOWN

The restaurants here are concentrated on Stowell St and are easily reached from St James, Central Station or Monument Metro stations. A couple of Japanese restaurants on Westgate Rd (near China Town) worth trying are **Sagawa** (*0191 261 8323*) and **St. Sushi** (*0191 221 0222*) opposite the Tyne Theatre.

Blackfriars Restaurant Friars St, NE1 4XN ① 0191 261 5945 ⓦ www.blackfriars
restaurant.co.uk. Some of the best hearty traditional British dishes you will find
in Newcastle served in the 13th-century surroundings of a Dominican monastery.
North Sea fish, and lamb and beef from Northumberland. 'We grow herbs outside
the kitchen door, harvest walnuts from the trees in the courtyard, grow organic
vegetables on our allotment and collect wild garlic, nettles and blackberries from
Jesmond Dene and hedgerows out in the country.'

Little Saigon 6 Bigg Market, NE1 1UW ① 0191 233 0766 ⓦ www.littlesaigon.
uk.com. Excellent authentic Vietnamese restaurant that's becoming really well
known in Newcastle.

Nudo Noodle House 54–6 Low Friar St, NE1 5UE ① 0191 233 1133
ⓦ www.nudonoodles.co.uk. Contemporary restaurant serving Chinese and
Japanese dishes (sushi, rice dishes and a variety of stir fry and soup noodles).
Many locals rave about this place on account of the quality of the food and
low prices.

Tea Sutra 1st floor, 2 Leazes Park Rd (near Old Eldon Sq), NE1 4PF
① 07575010173 ⓦ www.teasutra.co.uk. The sort of café you might choose for a
private cup of tea ('I know a little place . . .' kind of a place). It's snug with floor
cushions (very Zen), world music playing and the smell of nourishing home-made
soup. Best of all is the tea. If you think different varieties should be served in
different types of pots, like the sound of a menu offering 100 teas and expect
your green tea served exactly at 80°C, then you'll love it here.

AROUND CENTRAL STATION

The station stands close to a clutch of pubs and cafés, including **The Telegraph**
(*0191 261 8991*) behind the station on Forth Street (laid back, indy music).
The Forth (*0191 232 6478*) on Pink Lane is lively and serves good pub grub and
speciality beers and ciders. The **Centurion Bar** (*0191 261 6611*) within Central
Station has a couple of real ales and serves very average coffees and lunches
but the real reason you should come here is for the interior which is every bit as
sumptuous as you'd hope of a Victorian first class waiting lounge.

Sachins Forth Banks, NE1 3SG ① 0191 261 9035 ⓦ www.sachins.co.uk. Ask a local
where the best Indian restaurant in Newcastle is and chances are they'll point
you in the direction of Sachins, which serves Punjabi dishes in contemporary
surroundings. It's not inexpensive.

Salsa Café 89–93 Westgate Rd, NE1 4AE ① 0191 221 1022 ⓦ www.salsacafe.
com. Wooden tables with tea-light candles, leather sofas and random old chairs
make this unpretentious bar serving tapas popular with those wanting a relaxed
evening.

Settle Down Café 61–2 Thornton St, NE1 4AW (round the corner from the Tyne
Theatre on Westgate Rd) ① 0191 222 0187 ⓦ www.thesettledown.com. Artsy
café with mismatched furniture popular with local artists who display their work;
wholesome, inexpensive light lunches (soup and sandwiches).

HAYMARKET

There's not much in the way of independent coffee shops and restaurants in the Haymarket area, but you could try **Flat Caps** on Ridley Place which is hidden away in the basement of a shop selling healing crystals and offering Tarot card readings. It's run by a young, award-winning barista who knows how to make a good flat white. Turkish and Greek coffees were on the menu when I last visited. The interior is nothing special but it's cosy and the sort of place where you could hide away on a cold winter's afternoon with a book.

OUSEBURN VALLEY AND HEATON

There are a couple of places to eat in the Ouseburn Valley and more choice on Heaton Rd, a mile's walk away (reached from Shields Rd in Byker).

Albaik 98 Byker Bank, NE6 1LA ① 0191 228 9000. Great bring-your-own Lebanese restaurant at the top of Byker Bank (that doesn't charge corkage). Moussaka, Lebanese breads and grilled meats come highly recommended.

Butterfly Cabinet 200 Heaton Rd, NE6 5HP ① 0191 265 9920 Ⓦ www.butterflycabinet.com. Note the queue coming out of the door. This laid-back café and bar with mismatched wooden furniture and a spacious interior is always packed with students and families at the weekend, many of whom come to enjoy the enormous all-day breakfasts. Fancy burgers are served for lunch.

David Kennedy's Food Social The Biscuit Factory, Stoddart St, NE2 1AN ① 0191 2605411 Ⓦ www.foodsocial.co.uk. Open plan restaurant in an art gallery with an excellent reputation. Mains are well priced considering one of the most acclaimed chefs in the North East is in charge. Expect Northumbrian lamb and steak and fish straight off the boats at North Shields. If you're after lunch or something lighter, choose from the 'tapas' menu, which has a British twist.

Heaton Perk 103–105 Heaton Park Rd ① 0191 276 2000. Vintage-style café with bookshelves crammed with secondhand books and board games. Paninis, scones coffees and cakes.

Sky Apple Café 182 Heaton Rd, NE6 5HP ① 0191 209 2571 Ⓦ www.skyapple. co.uk. Quirky, colourful little café/restaurant with just a handful of tables, specialising in vegetarian, vegan and gluten free breakfasts, lunches and dinners. Licensed but you can bring your own booze.

OUSEBURN VALLEY PUBS

It just so happens that four of the best 'proper' pubs on Tyneside are situated within a half-mile radius of the Ouseburn green. The décor is unconsciously vintage and a bit shabby and the music playing is likely to be Bob Dylan, The Pogues or folk. Live indy bands perform at the Cluny and the Tyne.

Cluny 36 Lime St, NE1 2PQ ① 0191 230 4474 Ⓦ www.thecluny.com. Has a young crowd and is especially known for attracting fairly big name bands and up and coming artists.

Cumberland Arms James Place St, NE6 1LD ℗ 0191 265 1725;
Ⓦ www.thecumberlandarms.co.uk. An old pub with an extensive range of local
drinks, very good food (especially Sunday lunches), wood furniture and floors,
open fires and a semi-resident ginger tom cat called Clarence. It's the kind of pub
where you can sit by the fire with a pint and play Scrabble. You'll often find folk
or ukulele musicians in the back bar. The Cumberland is best visited on a balmy
summer's evening when you can sit outside in the sun with a pint of cider, or on
cold nights in winter when the fires are roaring, the windows are steamed up and
the fiddle players are really going for it. The pub's only downside is that it is tricky
to find at the top of a steep bank overlooking the Ouse. From the Cluny, cross the
river, turn right onto Foundry Lane and then immediately left up a steep walkway.
From Newcastle city centre, take the yellow QuayLink bus Q2 to Cut Bank (bottom
of Byker Bank and walk uphill).

Free Trade Inn St Lawrence Rd (off Walker Rd), NE6 1A6 ℗ 0191 265 5764. A
likeable, scruffy little pub, a bit out of the way (reached by QuayLink bus Q1 from
Newcastle/the Quayside) but with an almost unbeatable view of the River Tyne
and its bridges. The jukebox is free, the regulars are a mix of students, artists
and university lecturers and the selection of ales is good. Don't expect sparkling
toilets or to get through a pint without Van Morrison playing three times. Like the
Cumberland and the Tyne, it has a beer garden that faces west and is soaked in
orange sunshine on summer evenings.

Tyne Bar Maling St, NE6 1LP ℗ 0191 265 2550 Ⓦ www.thetyne.com. A short
stroll along the river towards Newcastle quayside will lead you past this youthful
pub with a vibrant live music scene. It's tucked away under the archways of the
brick Glass House Bridge.

JESMOND AND GOSFORTH

Most of Jesmond's pubs are on **Osborne Road**. **Acorn Road** is the main shopping
street where there's a flurry of cafés but a few of the best eateries are on chi-chi
Brentwood Avenue next to West Jesmond Metro. **Gosforth** has some good places
to eat and drink including the **Brandling Villa** on Haddricks Mill Road which sells
Ouseburn Valley beers direct from the onsite brewery by its namesake river.

Adrianas 84–90 High St, Gosforth NE3 1HB ℗ 0191 284 6464 Ⓦ www.adrianos.
co.uk. Upmarket Italian with an elegant interior (olive trees in large pots, wooden
floors and chairs, and walls painted soft grey and white) serving very good, pricey
seafood, meat, pizza and pasta dishes. Lunch and early evening menu reasonably
priced.

Café 1901 Methodist Church, St George's Terrace, NE2 2DL ℗ 0796 251 2188.
There are three cafés in Jesmond that make an excellent coffee. This is the only
one where the service and ambience are also just about spot on. The mismatched
furniture, vintage artefacts and lofty church interior add to its appeal.

Café Arlos 36–8 Brentwood Ave, West Jesmond NE2 3DH ℗ 0191 281 4838.
Bright, contemporary café with artisan breads, gourmet sandwiches and quiches

and excellent coffee. Service used to be poor when it was called Stewart & Co but the new management might change that.

Café Zonzo Goldspink Lane, Sandyford NE2 1NQ ① 0191 230 4981. Superb Italian restaurant in the residential area of Sandyford (walking distance from Jesmond Rd). Inside the décor is light and contemporary; the dishes (regional Italian as well as a few pizza choices) are some of the best in Newcastle and very reasonably priced. Their early evening Peasant's Supper ('quality Italian basics, satisfying after a hard day in the field') is particularly good value.

Francesca's Pizzeria Manor House Rd, NE2 2NA ① 0191 281 6586. This restaurant has been around for years and locals are very fond of it. You can't book a table, but the wait is rarely long despite the queues out the door. Gone are the days when the fire surround was pinned with postcards from Italia picturing topless women but the food and atmosphere remain the same: good value, simple and authentically Italian.

Jesmond Dene House Jesmond Dene Rd, NE2 2EY ① 0191 212 3000 Ⓦ www.jesmonddenehouse.co.uk. Arts and Crafts mansion house turned restaurant and hotel. Upmarket lunches, posh breakfasts and afternoon cream teas (served from 15.00). Décor is contemporary but the surroundings are very traditional. Outside terrace overlooking Jesmond Dene's tree tops. Take a peek inside the oak panelled Great Hall before leaving.

Sambuca Jesmond Vale Lane, Heaton Park NE6 5JS ① 0191 276 0011 Ⓦ www.sambucas-restaurant.co.uk. When they say 'every hour is happy hour' they mean it. A margherita pizza will give you plenty of change from a fiver. While not the best pizza and pasta dishes around, they are pretty good; their bruschetta is very generous and piled high with tomatoes and olives – almost a lunch dish in itself. Restaurant interior is typical of an Italian pizzeria; the staff are mainly Italian and they know how to make a decent macchiato. Outside terrace under a Victorian pavilion shelter. Sister restaurants at Whitley Bay and North Shields.

North Tyneside Coast: North Shields Fish Quay to Seaton Sluice

Pleasure beaches at Tynemouth, Cullercoats and Whitley Bay became hugely popular during the 19th century when train travel made the seaside resorts accessible to ordinary people. Tyneside's coast is still easily reached by public transport with Metro stations at all the sandy beaches plus North Shields. The journey by Metro from Newcastle City Centre to Tynemouth for example takes just 20 minutes. You can also cycle to the coast very easily from Newcastle (see page 3).

North of Seaton Sluice, the settlements become of more interest for their maritime and industrial heritage but you'll also find a long sweep of sand with thick dunes and coloured beach huts south of Blyth, and one of the most celebrated National Trust houses in the North: Seaton Delaval Hall.

⑫ North Shields Fish Quay

Dance ti' thy daddy, sing ti' thy mammy,
Dance ti' thy daddy, my little man;
Thou shalt hev a fishy on a little dishy,
Thou shalt hev a haddock when the boat comes in.
Traditional North East folk song

When the boats come in at North Shields today, thou shalt usually hev a mackerel, crab or lobster. It's a lively scene when the fishermen are landing their catch: crates of fish being passed from the boats to the harbour wall, engines throbbing, seabirds swarming behind the trawlers as they travel up the Tyne, and the incessant cry of herring gulls announcing the start of another fishing day.

Even at quiet times, the Fish Quay is an appealing place to wander around with the old Victorian Customs House and Shipping Office buildings, open yards where rows of girls once stood over barrels filleting herring, fish shops, and eateries on the riverfront. It's all starting to feel quite gentrified around here and the Fish Quay is certainly somewhere to watch in coming years.

The area's fishing heritage goes back some 800 years since the monastery at Tynemouth developed fishermen's huts (shielings, hence North *Shields*) on the banks of the river. As the industry flourished, so did the town which is reached by climbing the stairs from the quay. High Lights and Low Lights are the two navigational white towers built in 1802 to warn mariners of the dangerous Black Middens Rocks, scene of numerous shipwrecks. Climb up the bank to High Lights for an expansive view of the Tyne.

The wooden dolly trail

The tradition of the North Shields wooden dollies goes back to 1814 when a ship's female figurehead was placed outside Customs House Quay on Liddell Street. She became a kind of good luck charm and seafarers would carve off chips from her torso to take on voyages. She lasted less than 50 years and has been replaced by successive dollies since; at one time appearing in the form of a fishwife with a creel (basket) on her back.

Dolly number five was also a fishwife and she stands in Northumberland Square. In the early 1990s, a new dolly (a buxom red beauty of the figurehead type) was placed back in the traditional spot outside Customs House Quay and the Prince of Wales pub. As if two wasn't enough, a third dolly – another fishwife – is now positioned outside the Wooden Doll pub on Hudson Street.

Food and drink

The Fish Quay is gaining a reputation for its seafood restaurants – not just fish and chip take-aways, and you'll find a string of excellent eateries along Union Quay including **Irvins Brasserie** (*0191 296 3238*) and David Kennedy's Food Social (see below). The excellent-value Italian, **Sambuca** (*0191 270 8891*) has three restaurants in North Shields (which says something of their popularity). There are a couple of fantastic **fishmongers**, including Taylors and Lindisfarne Seafoods that sells oysters from Northumberland.

> **David Kennedy's River Café** 51 Bell St ⓣ 0191 296 6168 Ⓦ www.davidkennedys rivercafe.com. Open Tuesday to Sunday. Everyone talks about this simple restaurant headed by one of Tyneside's top chefs. Seafood dishes include straightforward beer-battered smoked haddock and mussels but they also have more adventurous things on the menu like curry-battered haddock with lentils (it sounds wrong but was delicious). My lemon sorbet was clearly homemade. Their early bird three-course special for a fiver is extraordinary value.
>
> **Waterfront** Union Quay ⓣ 0191 296 1721. Visitors to the Fish Quay often have one thing on their mind: fish and chips. It's not hard to spot which is the locals' favourite take-away: it's the one with the queues coming out of the door. Waterfront has a reputation as one of the best places in the North East for fish and chips. Portions are very generous too.
>
> **Wm Wight Ltd** Union Quay. The old fashioned-looking food store on the riverfront has tempting tubs of boiled sweets on its shelves. They also sell coffees and huge bacon butties.

⑬ Tynemouth

The striking ruins of Tynemouth's 11th-century priory stand on a commanding rocky cape keeping watch over the North Sea and mouth of the River Tyne. The bustling town centre with all its cafés, bars, craft and antiques shops kneels behind and stretched along the seafront are the grand Victorian houses for which Tynemouth is celebrated. Tall and with decorative wrought-iron balconies, they line the Grand Parade forming an elegant arc at Percy Gardens. Unlike some Victorian seaside towns, there is no faded grandeur here or sense of abandonment, and neither is Tynemouth a retirement village – this is a buoyant resort with well-kept buildings, a youthful vibe, two top sandy beaches, a lively town centre and superb weekend flea market. Indoor activities include an **aquarium** and a **Toy Museum** above Longsands and **antiques emporiums** on Front Street.

Tynesiders have been coming here on day trips since the 19th century to enjoy the salty air and sea water; with easy access from Newcastle (20 minutes by car or Metro) you can see why it's still a favourite place to come at the weekend, even just to enjoy a coffee on the seafront. Until the 1990s, visitors could swim in the outdoor bathing pool above Longsands but it's now been drained of its sea water and filled in with rocks. It's sad to see this wonderful

1930s pool lose its gleaming white and blue paint (only just visible now) and abandoned at a time when there is such huge enthusiasm for outdoor swimming, but there it is, not lost to the sea, but not far off.

Tynemouth station and market

Tynemouth Metro station, Station Terrace NE30 4RE Ⓦ www.tynemouth-market.com; open every weekend 9.00–16.00.

Tynemouth's vibrant **flea market** is housed in the sumptuous Victorian train station (now the Metro station), which is surely one of the most ornamental stations of its era anywhere in England with a huge amount of decorative ironwork in the canopies and pillars. It's worth coming here even when the market is not on, just to see the 1882 station architecture.

The original covered timber bridge arches steeply over the railway from where you gain a near bird's-eye view of the market stalls selling bric-a-brac, restored vintage telephones, old records, books, jewellery, crafts, antiques and regional foods. On the third Saturday of the month, the station also hosts a farmers' market.

Tynemouth Priory

Pier Rd, NE30 4BZ ① 0191 257 1090; Ⓦ www.english-heritage.org.uk; open daily 1 Apr–30 Sep, mainly weekends for rest of year; English Heritage.

Built in 1090 on the site of an earlier Anglian monastery that had been destroyed by invading Danes, the current building survives remarkably well considering its position and age. Up close, the sandstone has been so heavily worn away that on some walls the stones have become bowls with only the mortar resisting erosion by the elements; the faces of headstones have formed strange patterns. But, stand back and the priory, though gaunt, is still impressive displaying soaring lancet window arches, a wealth of elaborate stone carvings and a 15th-century **chapel** with its rib vaulted ceiling and 33 roof bosses. Elsewhere are a ruined medieval **gatehouse** (Tynemouth Castle) and a **World War II battery**, complete with gun emplacements and store rooms containing the original mechanisms for transporting ammunition to the guns above.

Tynemouth Volunteer Life Brigade Watch House Museum

Spanish Battery (between Tynemouth and North Shields) NE30 4DD; easily walked from Tynemouth Priory ① 0191 257 2059 Ⓦ www.tvlb.org; open Tue–Sat 10.00–15.00 and Sun 10.00–12.00; free entry (but donations appreciated).

Thus it was that the lifeboat and rocket failed, and the spectators were left to idly and helplessly see their fellow-men drowning before their eyes, and in the sight of land . . . A few minutes after ten o'clock, the schooner, which had drifted a good way to the westward, was plainly seen going down, and the cries of those on board were heard as she sank.
Newcastle Guardian and Tyne Mercury, Saturday 26 November 1864

Surf School

When the sun's out and the waves are rolling into Tynemouth's sandy bay, surfers hit the beach at Longsands which has gained an excellent reputation among watersports enthusiasts over the years. The Tynemouth Surf Company, founded in 1995, and based on the promenade above the beach, offers lessons and hires equipment; you can't book sessions because it depends on the weather, so just turn up on the day. Wetsuits and boards are provided and lessons last a couple of hours; most of your time is spent in the water once you've learned some basic techniques on the sand.

Tynemouth Surf Company Tynemouth Longsands (opposite the boating lake) Grand Parade, NE30 4JH ① 0191 258 2496 Ⓦ www.tynemouthsurf.co.uk; surfing lessons Tue–Sun at 14.00 Mar–Oct.

Many ships have run aground and broken up on the Black Middens reef at the mouth of the River Tyne, but on 24 November 1864, disaster struck for two vessels: a boat carrying coal, and a steamship with 30 passengers on board. All through the night, lifeboats tried and failed to reach the stricken vessels and rocket lines, fired from land to the ships with a rescue sack (a breeches buoy) attached, weren't able to save passengers without causing further loss of life. In all, 32 people drowned.

One of the bystanders on the shore that night was John Morrison who saw the coastguards relying on spectators to help launch the rockets. He contacted some local dignitaries and tabled a meeting at the North Shields Town Hall, calling for a support unit of trained men to assist the coastguards. Less than three months after the shipping disaster, 50 volunteers attended the first practice drill of the newly formed Volunteer Life Brigade. Within the year, Cullercoats and South Shields had their own volunteer brigades.

A Watch House was built as a look out and had beds for shipwrecked survivors. When a ship was spotted in trouble, brigade members were called to duty by the firing of two shots. In 1887, a second timber building was constructed (the one standing today); both the Watch House and the Volunteer Life Brigade are still operational. When I visited one day in August, they had already assisted in 24 rescues that month. This is also a really special museum and one that deserves to be better known. Packed inside the striking blue, white and yellow wooden building is a hoard of artefacts amassed over the years: bells, clocks, old black and white photographs, a breeches buoy and several seafarers from shipwrecks. An old wooden lifeboat is installed at the back of the building.

Food and drink

Tynemouth's **Front Street** has many cafés, coffee shops and bars and a couple of upmarket places to dine (**Lui's Winebar** and **Allard's Lounge**, for example). For coffee (especially a mocha), try **Gareth James' chocolaterie** on the corner of Percy Park Road and don't leave without trying their Earl Grey truffle. The cosy tearoom at **No 61** (also a simple guesthouse) has a peaceful courtyard out the back where you can enjoy a good bowl of soup.

Crusoe's Longsands ① 0191 296 4152 ⓦ www.robinsoncrusoes.co.uk. Busy café on the beach serving light bites and with an outside terrace; where many locals come for a coffee when visiting Tynemouth. Excellent take-away chips.

⑭ Cullercoats

Very familiar indeed is the figure of the Cullercoats fishwife, as, clad in blue serge jacket, short petticoats with ample skirts, large apron and black straw bonnet she trudges along with a heavy creel of fish on her shoulders, calling, in shrill and not unmusical tones of voice 'Buy fee-s-ch.'
W W Tomlinson *Comprehensive Guide to Northumberland*, 1888

A mile north along the seafront from Tynemouth, this former fishing village faces the sea above a quiet sandy cove where Sunday strollers take in the salty air from the clifftop promenade and braver children – their legs and arms pink with the cold – jump off the little pier. This bay formed the backdrop to many paintings by the **Cullercoats Colony** of artists who captured the lives of local people here from around 1870 to 1920: men returning from sea in their wooden boats, women mending nets, collecting seaweed and carrying baskets of fish and scenes similar to those observed by the Victorian travel writer Tomlinson in the excerpt above.

A small number of these atmospheric paintings hang in the Laing Art Gallery in Newcastle including John Charlton's well-known 1910 masterpiece, *The Women*, which depicts the rescue of the Lovely Nellie ship that ran aground on New Years Day in 1861 near St Mary's Lighthouse. A storm prevented the Cullercoats lifeboat reaching the stricken vessel so it was pulled overland for two miles to where it could be launched. Everyone was saved except for the cabin boy. The focus in the painting is on the strong local women, shirts rolled up, heaving the boat in lashing rain alongside men and boys.

The old lifeboat station is still operational, but much has changed in the village: many buildings were razed in the latter half of the 20th century, and where Tomlinson counted some 40 fishing boats in his 1888 guide; today just one solitary green and white coble is seen in the bay.

Food and drink

Beaches and Cream 1 Victoria Crescent (opposite the promenade) ① 0191 251 4718. Period-style coffee house and fancy ice cream parlour with a contemporary twist.

⑮ Whitley Bay and St Mary's Island

The sharp bite of the saline waters at Whitley Bay is of the utmost value in all cases of debility,
and especially to the jaded business man.
Guidebook to Whitley Bay, 1909

Once the Blackpool of the North, Whitley Bay's popularity as a seaside resort began to wane in the latter half of the 20th century; today the words 'faded grandeur' come to mind but things are looking up for Whitley. The fine sea-facing Victorian buildings are being renovated and the landmark **Spanish City** pleasure hall – an eye-catching Edwardian building with a huge white dome and two towers will re-open in 2014 following a major revamp; the two dancing girls on either tower (one plays the cymbals, the other a tambourine) have also been cleaned and are now back to their copper-green best. When built in 1910 with a theatre and roof gardens it had the largest dome in the UK after St Paul's Cathedral in London.

From Spanish City to St Mary's Lighthouse, a wide grassy bank separates the **promenade** (pram- and wheelchair-accessible the whole way) from the road and town, making a stroll along the seafront very pleasant indeed. You can also walk on the **beach** of course – a gorgeous long expanse of beige sand that meets the black reefs of St Mary's Island at its northern end. Halfway along the promenade is the **Links Art Gallery** and café.

Children will love the **leisure pool** at Whitley Bay (*Waves, The Links NE26 1TQ; 0191 643 2600*), which has a wave machine and adventure slide.

St Mary's Island and Lighthouse

Whitley Bay NE26 4RS ⓣ 0191 200 8650 ⓦ www.friendsofstmarysisland.co.uk; open daily Apr–Sep, weekends and school holidays Oct–Mar (subject to tides).

St Mary's Lighthouse first shone her beam across the North Sea on 31 August 1898, following a tradition of beacons on the rocky isle that goes back to the 11th century. For the next 86 years the white tower helped keep mariners away from the dangerous rocks off the coast of Whitley Bay.

Though taken out of service in 1984, the lighthouse is open to visitors who have made the trip across the short causeway and are prepared to climb 137 steps up a dizzying spiral staircase to the top. I don't know which is more awesome: the view from the glass dome of the coast stretching from Blyth to the mouth of the Tyne, or looking 126 feet down through the hollow lighthouse.

At low tide, the reefs surrounding the lighthouse are a favourite hunting ground for children searching for sea creatures in **rockpools**.

This whole area is also of interest for its **bird life**, particularly because of its passage migrants in autumn, and in winter when large flocks of golden plover and lapwing roost on the nearby grasslands. In summer, look out for terns, fulmars and gannets.

Food and drink

Fish and chip shops, cafés and inexpensive Italian restaurants are fairly plentiful in the town, along the seafront and around Spanish City.

Links Art Gallery and café Whitley Bay promenade (Dukes Walk), NE26 1TP ⓣ 0191 447 5534. Situated right on the seafront, this café and gallery showcases local art and crafts and serves coffees in a building which retains a touch of Art Deco elegance about its frontage.

⑯ Seaton Sluice

The main reason you are likely to come here is to visit Seaton Delaval Hall (detailed below), a Baroque mansion which has far outlived the coal and glass industries on its doorstep. The settlement gets its name from the sluice gates in the harbour designed by one of the Delavals to keep the inlet clear of silt on each tide. This improved the export of salt, coal and glass – as did enlarging the harbour by blasting through the cliff. The colliery and the six 18th-century glassworks cones that used to frame the skyline are long gone. In 1862, 204 men and boys died at the nearby Hartley coal pit when the mine shaft caved in, imprisoning them underground.

Food and drink

Coastline Fish and Chips South Beach, Links Rd, Blyth NE24 3PL ⓣ 01670 797 428. Fish and chips and ice cream parlour just behind the beach.

Seaton Delaval Hall

The Avenue, NE26 4QR ⓣ 0191 237 9100 ⓦ www.nationaltrust.org.uk; open Thu–Tue 1 May–30 Sep and weekends Oct–end Apr; café; National Trust.

Since opening to the public in 2010, Seaton Delaval Hall has become one of the region's most visited historic properties, celebrated for its formal gardens and exterior by Sir John Vanbrugh (the most famous country house architect in England during the early 1700s), who died a few years before the mansion – one of his greatest – was completed in 1730.

A fire destroyed the interior in 1822 (the heat was so intense that the roof leading was said to have 'poured down like water') and the great hall remains gutted, but you gain a strong sense of how grand and lavish the entrance must have been before the disaster. Armless busts and statues line the walls and a wrought-iron balcony frames the first-floor landing. Either side of the portico and facing into the central courtyard are the stables (east wing) and the servants' quarters (west wing). To the rear of the great hall, two huge glass doors open out into the beautiful gardens: formal hedging, roses, herbaceous borders and a magnificent weeping ash planted at the time the manor was built.

The only furnished part of the house today is the west wing which was later used by the family. One of the highlights is a row of exquisitely embroidered

17th-century chairs. Portraits on a nearby wall include that of the only male heir of Sir John Delaval who died before his father. Apparently the young man was already a sickly creature when he was kicked in the genitals by a maid whom he had assaulted. He never recovered from his injuries. The boy is buried in the church at Doddington in north Northumberland which was painted black for 25 years after his death.

Walking to Seaton Delaval Hall from the coast

By taking the riverside path from below the Melton Constable pub, you can walk to Seaton Delaval Hall in 2½ miles from the coast at Seaton Sluice. You'll need Ordnance Survey Explorer map 316. The scenery is quite dreamy with lots of trees crowding the water meadows; the second half is across fields with Seaton Delaval's obelisk coming into view through a parting in the trees.

Near the hall is the Norman **Church of Our Lady** on the edge of the National Trust estate (*open May–Sep on Fri, bank holidays and Sun afternoons*). It dates to 1102 and was for 700 years the private chapel of the Delaval family.

Return to Seaton Sluice by bus X4 (bus stop right outside the hall) or walk the short distance (under a mile) to Seaton Sluice along the main road (quick enough and on pavement).

⑰ Newbiggin-by-the-Sea and around

From Seaton Sluice, a thick belt of dunes criss-crossed by sandy trails and a paved path leads to **Blyth**. Though its town centre is rundown, Blyth's **South Beach** – a popular bay with dog walkers and families – is pleasant enough. A colourful array of beach huts faces the sea and a World War I and II **battery**, stand prominently in the dunes. The pale pink and grey observation towers and gun emplacements are a striking feature of the seascape here and, though you can't enter the buildings, children seem to enjoy running around them.

North of Blyth is **Cambois Bay** (another desolate expanse of sand) and **Newbiggin-by-the-Sea**. A wicked northeasterly was blasting the promenade when I last visited. I met a woman and her dog both walking sideways to the wind. It wouldn't be unfair to describe this former seaside resort as a rather pinched-looking place, but that shouldn't stop those with an interest in maritime heritage from paying a visit. Below the 14th-century **St Bartholomew Church** is the wonderful **Maritime Centre** (*01670 811951; www.newbigginmaritimecentre.org.uk; closed Mon in winter; modern, sea-facing café*), which tells the story of the local community and the fishing and coal-mining heritage along this coast. The main attractions are the *Girl Anne* coble and the *Mary Joicey* traditional lifeboat.

The Pitmen Painters

Here I found an outlet for other things than earning my living. There is a feeling of being my own boss for a change and with it comes a sense of freedom.
Harry Wilson, founder member of the Ashington Group, quoted at the *Woodhorn Museum*

The story of how a group of coal miners from Ashington became painters is an unlikely one, hence its appeal (and success as a theatre production that made it to Broadway and the West End of London in recent years). In 1934, a group of miners hired a lecturer from Durham University to teach them about art appreciation. Instead they learned to paint and were encouraged to capture their surroundings on canvas. They did this for 50 years to much acclaim while continuing to work in the colliery.

Their unsentimental paintings depict men working underground, domestic life, the close communities in which they lived and their leisure activities (growing leeks, dog-racing, bowling, pigeon-keeping and so on). A superb collection of their paintings is on permanent display in the Woodhorn Museum near Ashington (see below).

A short way along the promenade, between a fleet of tractors and a fine collection of fishing cobles, is the **RNLI lifeboat station**, the oldest working station in the UK, established in 1851. On Sundays you can see the modern lifeboat and artefacts collected over the last 160-odd years. Every recorded incident in the lifeboat station's history is detailed on the blackboards lining the walls. Before the first tractor pulled the lifeboat to the sea in 1949, an army of women volunteers assisted the crew. The services of the legendary women lifeboat launchers of Newbiggin were utilised quite recently when the old *Mary Joicey* lifeboat was brought to the Maritime Centre, and elderly ladies, children, mums and UGG boot-wearing teenagers came out to pull the boat to its final resting place.

Woodhorn Museum
Ashington NE63 9YF ① 01670 528080 Ⓦ www.experiencewoodhorn.com; open daily during school holidays and Wed–Sun at other times; free to enter but a small charge for parking cars; café.

A few miles inland is the best surviving example of a late 19th-century northern colliery complete with winding houses, yards and pit-pony stables. It has an excellent contemporary visitor centre. Without the miners, horses, smoke and clatter of machinery and wagons, it's hard to get a true sense of what it was like here before the colliery closed in the 1980s but the approachable stewards, some of whom are former miners, bring that side of the colliery to life.

Life and work in and around the colliery is highlighted in the indoor exhibition, which takes you forward in time from the height of coal mining through to the strikes and closures in the late 20th century. The museum also provides insight into the domestic life of miners and their pastimes. Nowhere is this more vividly represented than in the **Ashington Group gallery** with its collection of artworks by the Pitmen Painters (see box, page 43). Outside the gallery is a display of old miners' banners (rousing socialist slogans and images of a better future).

Close to the museum, the **QEII Country Park** is a large lake with picnic tables and a lakeside trail; a narrow-gauge railway line runs for a few hundred yards from Woodhorn Museum at weekends. Many years ago this tranquil lagoon, which is now inhabited by many swans and ducks, was the largest spoil heap in Europe.

Sunderland, Ryhope and Washington

Sunderland and its outlying towns tend to get overlooked by visitors to the North East, yet a number of places around the River Wear are really worth seeking out, such as the Ryhope Pumping Station, Washington Old Hall, the National Glass Centre and the Anglo-Saxon church of St Peter's.

⑱ Sunderland

Sunderland is a lively city straddling the River Wear with an acclaimed glass museum and theatre and some eye-catching buildings. The **city centre** and historic **Sunniside** area are on the south side of the river around Sunderland Metro station and Fawcett Street (the main shopping street). The **tourist information centre** is in the library on Fawcett Street (*0191 553 2000*).

With the exception of Sunniside's Georgian brick terraces, the city lacks the architectural uniformity and grandeur of Newcastle, but Sunderland does have some notable buildings. Look out for the Gothic red-brick **Cordor House**, the classical façade of the **Hutchinson's Building** and eccentric red and cream **Elephant Tea Rooms** (Italian Gothic meets Disneyland in 1877, but described by its architect as 'Hindoo Gothic' [sic] in a style apparently inspired by the East to reflect the exotic teas sold inside; note the elephants between the windows).

Sunderland Empire (*High St West; 0844 871 3022; www.sunderlandempire. org.uk*) boasts a terrifically opulent Edwardian interior and is the largest theatre in the North East with a tradition of attracting big name stars such as The Beatles, Laurel and Hardy and Charlie Chaplin. Today the Empire draws audiences from all over the North for its opera, ballet and touring West End productions from London.

In coming years, a new landmark bridge will span the Wear (expected to open in 2015) to add to existing crossings, the most prominent of which are

Sunderland Cottages

Built between 1840 and 1930, striking single-storey dwellings known as Sunderland Cottages were designed for industrial labourers, particularly shipyard workers, and are a distinctive feature of the city. Kitchener Street, Nora Street and Hawarden Crescent on the edge of Barnes Park have good examples.

the bow-arched road and rail bridges that mirror each other in form. The **Wearmouth Road Bridge** shares an uncanny similarity to Newcastle's Tyne Bridge. It was built in 1929 to replace an earlier bridge originally designed in cast iron by Thomas Paine in 1796 and reconstructed by Robert Stephenson in the 19th century. It features on many of Sunderland's lustreware jugs.

At the height of the industrial boom in the mid 19th century, Sunderland was a major centre for glass, pottery and rope making and was the biggest shipbuilding port in the world with 65 shipyards. You encounter industrial relics and buildings about the city including an impressive 18th-century **ropery** at Deptford. Elsewhere, Sunderland's industries are remembered and celebrated in a number of its museums.

Arranged over several floors in the **Sunderland Museum and Winter Gardens** (*Burdon Rd; 0191 553 2323; open daily Mon–Sat and Sun 14.00–17.00; free admission*) are exhibition spaces dedicated to Sunderland's industrial heritage, an art gallery showcasing 19th-century and contemporary works (including paintings by L S Lowry), natural history section and a large collection of **Sunderland lustreware** pottery with the distinctive pink colouring that makes these ceramics valuable collectable items. Many people come here for the tropical Winter Gardens, which houses a fish pond and exotic plants and trees. The museum overlooks **Mowbray Park** – a beautiful Victorian pleasure ground with gardens, a lake and bandstand.

National Glass Centre

Liberty Way, SR6 0GL ☏ 0191 515 5555 ⓦ www.nationalglasscentre.com; open daily; free entry.

Sunderland's glass museum on the north side of the Wear showcases contemporary glass art and tells the story of the first stained glass artists in Anglo-Saxon times and how Wearmouth became a major bottle, tableware and window manufacturer in the 19th century. Live **glass-blowing demonstrations** are held twice daily and the museum puts on temporary glass art **exhibitions** every year. On the ground floor and with views of the riverside is a good shop selling jewellery and glassware by leading glass artists, and a bright café. You can stroll along a pleasant riverside promenade here.

St Peter's Anglo-Saxon Church

Monkwearmouth SR6 0DY (close to the National Glass Centre) ☏ 0191 567 3726

Ⓦ www.wearmouth-jarrow.org.uk; open daily 10.30–14.30; café.

Stained glass production in Britain goes back to the 7th century when Frenchmen were brought to Sunderland to work on the windows of St Peter's Church at the new monastic centre of Wearmouth-Jarrow. Amazingly, parts of the Anglo-Saxon church and fragments of its coloured glass have survived into the 21st century. Incidentally, it's fitting that the contemporary National Glass Centre with glass artists' workshops should face St Peter's at the mouth of the Wear, continuing a tradition of glass-making more than 1,300 years old.

As soon as you enter the church grounds, it's very obvious which is the oldest remaining part of the church. The slim tower with small windows and a porch date to AD674 when the church was founded by the nobleman Benedict Biscop on land provided by the King of Northumbria. Inside the vaulted porch are stone balusters with carvings of animals.

Monkwearmouth Station Museum

North Bridge St, SR5 1AP ① 0191 567 7075 Ⓦ www.twmuseums.org.uk/ monkwearmouth; open Mon–Sat and Sun 14.00–17.00; free admission.

Before the railway bridge was built across the River Wear, this was the last stop on a line that ran to Gateshead and Newcastle. The original station building of 1848, now a small museum, has an imposing neoclassical portico grand enough to be the entranceway to a national museum or art gallery. It certainly wouldn't look out of place in Newcastle's Grainger Town; not surprisingly it is the work of North East architect John Dobson. Its interior includes the original 1866 booking office and station furniture (benches, fireplaces and ticket booths), railway memorabilia, dressing up boxes and changing art exhibitions.

Ryhope Pumping Station

Ryhope Engines Museum, Waterworks Rd, Ryhope SR2 0ND ① 0191 521 0235 Ⓦ www.ryhopeengines.org.uk; open a few weekends of the year and Easter week.

You could describe this relic from the 19th century – the only working example of its kind in existence – simply as an engine house with machinery used to pump clean water for drinking from underground to supply the city, but it is so much more than that. When you walk through the door, you are immediately faced with the sight of two formidably large and powerful pumping beams moving up and down (like something from a Texas oil field), spinning flywheels and clattering rods. Keep a close eye on little ones as there are a lot of moving cogs, rods, cranks and wheels here (all behind barriers, but all the same . . .). A viewing hole in the floor allows you to peer 250 feet down to the water twinkling beneath the limestone.

Outside, the reservoir is now grassed over but you can still see its outline, and two cooling ponds (now inhabited by ducks). Other buildings house steam engines, a blacksmiths, and a museum and café in the old superintendent's residence. Original artefacts and furnishings and a film tell the story of Thomas Hawksley, the Nottingham engineer responsible for the Ryhope Pumping

Station who was involved in 150 water supply projects across England. Even when it's closed, the buildings in their parkland setting are worth seeing from the outside.

Food and drink

D'Acqua Basement 26–8 John St, SR1 1JG ☏ 0191 565 1988 ⓦ www.dacqua. co.uk; open Wed–Mon. Contemporary upmarket restaurant hidden downstairs in one of Sunderland's historic city centre streets (very close to the Winter Gardens). Mediterranean dishes with a British twist and grills. Fresh seafood from local fish quays.

Paprika 46 Frederick St, SR1 1NF ☏ 0191 564 0606 ⓦ www.paprikacafe.co.uk. Small restaurant in the basement of one of Sunniside's Georgian houses offering gourmet sandwiches and wraps for lunch and substantial evening meals (traditional steak, lamb and fish dishes) that come recommended by locals.

An hour at Mr Surtees's Famous Pigeon Cree

A humble 1950s weatherboard pigeon house, Mr Surtees's Famous Pigeon Cree is the only building of its type in England to be Grade II listed. Not bad for a single storey pigeon loft. It's a quirky addition to the tourist trail, painted brilliant blue, red and white with decorative timber edging and a series of windows behind which Mr Surtees's racing pigeons are heard cooing.

Maurice was not around when I visited the ramshackle Ryhope Allotments which look out to sea on the outskirts of Sunderland, but another allotment holder showed me around. George Yarnell said the allotments have been here for 50 years and that there used to be tens of pigeon crees, but now there are only seven. He opened the doors of his lofts and his birds flew out in a flurry of feathers, circled the allotments a few times and then swooped back into their shelter.

On my way out, with my arms full of onions and beetroot kindly given to me by George, I met Alexander, a cheerful chap wearing a cap who remembers when horses and carts used to go up and down the lane and the allotment holders weren't facing eviction. 'They want us off,' he said referring to the landowner who wants to develop the site. Bailiffs were expected on New Year's Day 2008 but the allotment holders put up a fight and even had their case heard in Parliament. In the end, having a listed building on site seems to have saved the day – for the time being. 'We love it here,' said Alexander. 'It's a place to get away to and we're not a bother to anyone; we just sit in our rocking chairs with the fire on, looking out to sea and telling lies to each other.'

Ryhope Allotments, Back Ryhope St, Ryhope SR2 0JP

⑲ Washington

Washington's historic village is the most attractive part of this otherwise modern town made up of 14 districts. Though not of immediate appeal to tourists, Washington does have a number of places worth visiting, including the excellent **Wildfowl and Wetlands Trust** centre (*0191 416 5454*) with its flamingos and many indigenous birds (numbers swell with migrants in winter); the landmark **Penshaw Monument**, a folly and replica of the Temple of Hephaestus in Athens; and the National Trust's **Washington Old Hall**.

Industrial heritage enthusiasts might enjoy the **F-Pit Museum** (*Albany Way, NE37 1BJ; 0191 553 2323*), one of nine coal mines owned by the same company, each identified by a letter of the alphabet. When the colliery closed in the late 1960s, the engine house and winding wheels (headgear) were given to the people of Washington as a monument. Today the museum highlights coal mining in the area on the site of a pit sunk in 1777, and is only open on a few weekends of the year, but from outside you can see the huge headgear that lowered pitmen underground 1,000 feet in 28 seconds and brought coal back up.

Coal mined at Washington's collieries was taken by train along the Bowes Railway to the Tyne where it was loaded onto ships. The **Bowes Railway Museum** (*Springwell Village, near The Angel of the North, NE9 7QJ; 0191 416 1847; www.bowesrailway.co.uk*) is the only standard gauge rope-hauled railway still operational in the world. This railway mechanism was one of the earliest methods of coal transportation and involved horses pulling wagons on flat terrain and uphill. On the return, a man controlled the speed of the wagons using brakes. The outdoor museum is on a site with a couple of working forges and a station platform (in use) and has a number of engines.

Washington Old Hall

Washington Village NE38 7LE ① 0191 416 6879 ⑩ www.nationaltrust.org.uk/Washington-old-hall; open 1 Apr–31 Oct, Sun–Wed; café; National Trust.

The crowning glory of Washington's old village is this stone mansion and its tranquil gardens, the home of the first US president's ancestors, the de Wessyngtons. The oldest parts date to the 12th century, but it was mostly rebuilt in the 17th century and contains impressive rooms with wood panelled walls and dark Jacobean furniture. Upstairs and on the staircase walls is a huge amount of memorabilia including US flags, stamps and portraits of George Washington that have been donated over the years. Staff and volunteers really go to town celebrating America's heritage, particularly at Thanksgiving and Halloween when there are special events. The tea room is staffed by extremely friendly and chatty volunteers. Beyond the formal Jacobean gardens are a croquet lawn (with mallets available for visitors) and a meadow with beehives.

More stars and stripes

Next stop on the American heritage tour should be the medieval **Hylton Castle** on the outskirts of Sunderland in North Hylton. The embattled ruin, originally only the gatehouse of a larger building, is incredibly stern. A few stone figures guard its turrets. American visitors will be interested in the 'stars and stripes' coat of arms of the Washington family displayed above the doorway, the design of which is said to have influenced the American flag.

Food and drink

Blacksmith's Table The Green, NE38 7AB ⓣ 0191 415 1788
Ⓦ www.blacksmithstable.com. Close to Washington Old Hall in the historic part of town is this cosy upmarket restaurant in a 400-year-old smithy. Traditional British meat dishes and Sunday lunches with some locally-inspired choices including Washington Wellington (venison with haggis, mushrooms and redcurrant sauce). A good choice for a romantic meal, but it's not cheap.

South Shields, Jarrow and the South Tyneside Coast

Between the rivers Tyne and Wear is a rugged stretch of **coastline** characterised by heavily indented cliffs, rock stacks, flower meadows, piers, a couple of sandy beaches and a lighthouse. It's built up in places but you can escape the Coast Road and streets between Whitburn and Marsden by walking along the headland. In fact, you can **cycle** (or **walk**) the whole way between Sunderland and South Shields along off-road trails (largely on promenades and clifftop paths).

It's said that more ships have run aground between Sunderland and South Shields than on any other six-mile stretch of coastline in Britain; twenty ships hit rocks in one year alone in 1869. The need for better resources to rescue mariners from stricken vessels led to the creation of the world's first purpose-built lifeboat in **South Shields** – a large town with maritime and Roman heritage attractions.

Next door to South Shields on the south bank of the River Tyne is **Jarrow**, famous for miners' solidarity, Barbour jackets, an Anglo-Saxon church and as the birthplace of England's first historian, the Venerable Bede.

⑳ South Shields

Enclosed by river and sea, South Shields is a busy town with a couple of good sandy bays, two piers, a pleasure park, a boating lake, a Roman fort – and a large number of curry houses. In the late 19th century, thousands of Yemeni sailors found work at South Shields's port, many of whom settled in the town permanently.

The **tourist information centre** (*Amphitheatre, Sea Rd; 0191 455 7411; open daily*) is on the beachfront not far from all the kitsch ice cream stalls and fairground rides.

The **High Street** is a pleasant enough long pedestrian street with a busy outdoor market at its head. It's just behind where the Shields Ferry docks and the **Customs House** (*Mill Dam; 0191 454 1234; open daily and late on performance days*) – a grand Victorian building facing the river which now houses a theatre, cinema and contemporary art gallery with regularly changing exhibitions.

Set back from the waterfront are a scattering of heritage sites and museums including the **Tyne Lifeboat**, one of the oldest lifeboats still in existence in Britain (see page 54), and the **Arbeia Roman Fort & Museum** (*Baring St; 0191 456 1369; open daily 1 Apr–1 Sep*) which was once a military supply base for garrisons based on Hadrian's Wall. Reconstructed buildings, including the mighty West Gate, stand on the foundations of some of the actual Roman structures discovered during archaeological research. The contrasts between the civilised commander's quarters and the cramped rooms of the ordinary soldiers' barracks really brings the place to life. **South Shields Museum & Art Gallery** (*Ocean Rd; 0191 456 8740; open daily Mon–Sat; free admission*) highlights the history of the area from the Bronze Age, with a special focus on the social history of South Shields in the 20th century. Changing exhibitions of paintings focus on coal mining, maritime and other aspects of South Shields' heritage.

A little way out of the centre, near Chichester Metro station, is **Westhoe Village** – a single avenue of period houses (mostly Georgian) that rates as one of Tyneside's best-looking residential streets.

Coble boat builders of South Shields

The traditional wooden fishing boat peculiar to the North East (pictured on the front cover of this book) was for a long time a very familiar sight all the way along the Northumbrian and Yorkshire coasts. Painted bright colours and with broad sides and a characteristic flat bottom (easy for hauling up the North

Tyne Pedestrian and Cyclist Tunnels

This architectural relic (*www.tynepedestrianandcyclisttunnels.co.uk*) from the mid 20th century is worth seeking out if you're in the South Shields/Jarrow area. Work began on the tunnels (one for walkers, the other for bikes) in 1939 but it didn't open until after World War II. It was the first purpose-built bicycle tunnel in the UK, running for 900 feet under the river and connecting Jarrow with Howdon.

Inside, the tunnels are clad with tiles, but most eye-catching are the original escalators which are the longest wooden-step escalators in Europe. The tunnels are being refurbished at the time of writing with the loss, sadly, of two of the escalators which are being replaced with lifts, and the installation of 'feature lighting' on the remaining escalators. Perhaps it will look better than it sounds.

East's sandy beaches) and high bow, cobles have operated out of fishing villages and ports for many hundreds of years. Some say the design originates from Viking boats.

You still see a scattering of cobles in places such as Newbiggin-by-the-Sea, Craster, Boulmer and North Shields, but most were abandoned or scrapped during the collapse of the North Sea fishing industry in the 20th century. There are probably only around 40 left, a very small number of which are the original sailing type. The most famous coble belonged to Grace Darling and is now housed in her namesake museum in Bamburgh (see page 88).

At one time there were many boat yards on the River Tyne where cobles were built and repaired; today there are just a couple on Wapping Street (a ten-minute walk north from South Shields Metro along Mile End Road).

Few people know of the **North East Maritime Trust** (*Wapping St, NE33 1LQ; 07969 908123; usually open Tue, Wed and Sat, but call to check*), a fascinating working museum run by friendly local volunteers. 'David is a retired engineer, Alan worked in the shipyards, Charlie used to drive a wagon and Davie was a boiler maker,' the Trust's founder, Peter Weightman, explains. All sorts of old boats are lovingly restored here in the time-honoured way, including salmon fishing boats, lifeboats and cobles of course. When I last visited, men were hammering away under the hulls of cobles, planning wood, varnishing timber and sharing a joke over a cup of tea. Moored in the river in front of the workshop are cobles still used by fishermen and a rare sailing coble. Information panels inside explain the heritage of the boats and the fishing industries on the Tyne.

Next door is the workshop of master boat-builder, **Fred Crowell** (*0191 536 2336*), who also specialises in restoring traditional fishing boats and welcomes visitors. 'I left school at 15 and one week later I got a job building boats; I've been here ever since', he says. His workshop is quite a sight with ropes, planks of wood, tools and chains hanging from the rafters and walls. More surprising is the collection of rubber ducks Fred has fished out of the Tyne over the years.

Food and drink

The curry houses on South Shields's **Ocean Road** are legendary, hence the local name 'Curry Row'. A few worth trying are the **Spice Garden** (*0191 455 9867*), **Monsoon** (*0191 4556103*) and **Jai Ho** (see below). Also consider **Lasun** a little further away (see below).

Coleman's Fish and Chips 176–186 Ocean Rd, NE33 2JQ ⏱ 0191 456 1202 🌐 www.colmansfishandchips.com. Four generations of the same family have perfected the batter on the now legendary Coleman's fish and chip dinner which has won a string of awards over the years. Many people will tell you this is the best fish and chip restaurant in the North East. There's a good choice of fish on

Barbour

If you walk down South Shields's High Street you may notice a number of locals wearing Barbour jackets, the traditional country brand that originated in the town in 1894 and is currently enjoying a revival. The company has its headquarters in South Shields where their classic waxed jackets are still manufactured by hand. Large groups of tourists arrive regularly from Spain and Italy to empty the contents of the factory shop in Jarrow (adjacent to Bede Metro station). You can pick up some bargains here (discontinued lines and seconds) as well as the latest range of clothing.

Barbour Retail and Factory Outlet Monksway, Bede Estate, Jarrow NE23 3HL; 0191 428 4707; www.barbour.com; open daily.

offer (not just cod and haddock) and an appealing eat-in restaurant.
Jai Ho 118 Ocean Rd, NE33 2JF ⓉEl 0191 455 5133 Ⓦ www.jaihosouthshields.co.uk. Expect a wide choice of classic and modern Indian dishes in this well-regarded Ocean Rd restaurant, recognised by the British Curry Awards as one of the best newcomers in the North East. This is not your average curry house and the surroundings are daring and contemporary (ice-white walls and flash of electric blue). Reasonably priced menu.
Lasun 50 Dean Rd, NE33 4DZ Ⓣ 0191 454 5111 Ⓦ www.lasun.co.uk. All the classic dishes you'd expect from a Balti house with a few twists, and unusual ingredients including crab and monkfish.

㉑ Bede's World and monastery

Church Bank, Jarrow NE32 3DY Ⓣ 0191 489 2106 Ⓦ www.bedesworld.co.uk; open daily year round.

Dedicated to the 'father of English History', this ambitious museum adjoins the monastery and church of St Paul's where Bede, the scholar and priest, lived from the age of seven. Bede's life and his written works are only part of the focus of the museum; displays also explore the world of Benedict Biscop and Ceolfrith – two key figures in the development of the twin monastery of Wearmouth-Jarrow and the cultural flowering of Northumbria during the 7th century.

Part of the museum is outdoors, on a large site where there's a **farm** with reconstructed thatched Anglo-Saxon dwellings, ancient breeds of live farm animals, and herbal gardens with typical plants grown for medicinal use in those days.

Also making up the monastic estate is **Jarrow Hall**, Georgian manor house set in gardens. There's not a huge amount to see inside, but it does have a small exhibition space and a pleasant café.

A visit to **St Paul's Church** and **monastery** next door to the museum completes the story of Bede and the monastic community at Jarrow. Take your time to get your bearings at St Paul's which is composed of several buildings constructed – and reconstructed – at different times over the last 1,300 years. Its nave is Victorian and the chancel, once a separate church entirely, Anglo-Saxon; a tower stands between the two parts. A dedication stone over the tower arch is inscribed with the date: 23 April AD685 making this the oldest surviving dedication stone in England. The ruined walls of a medieval monastery are clearly visible outside, but look at the ground and you'll see stone slabs from the original monastery around the time of Bede.

Inside, a host of 7th-century finds includes stones carved with plants and animals and elaborate designs that were novel and exotic when they were produced. In the middle window on the south chancel wall is the original aqua, yellow, green and brown stained glass from the 7th century – some of the earliest coloured glass in Britain. Astonishingly, it was recovered by excavators in the 1960s and restored to its original position. 'It was like picking up jewels',

The twin monastery of Wearmouth-Jarrow

Though 10 miles apart, St Paul's on the Tyne and St Peter's on the Wear were part of the same monastic community founded in the 7th century by an important figure in Anglo-Saxon Northumbria, Benedict Biscop. St Peter's in Wearmouth was built first on land provided by the Northumbrian king, Ecgfrith, in AD674; St Paul's in Jarrow came later. Benedict Biscop travelled to Rome several times collecting books and religious artefacts for his monastery. He was very much inspired by the arts and ecclesiastical traditions in Italy and returned to the River Wear with his collection of pictures and books – as well as with French stonemasons and glaziers, and the choirmaster from St Peter's, Rome.

This sparked a period of investment in the arts, crafts and learning which is often referred to as the **Golden Age of Northumbria**. It was during this period that we see the creation of fine stone carvings, illuminated books such as the Lindisfarne Gospels and the Codex Amiatinus (a version of the Bible), and stained glass windows – the latter being something that was completely new to Britain when Benedict Biscop introduced the craft to his church.

The Venerable Bede was very much apart of this cultural centre having been brought up at the monastery under the care of Benedict Biscop and later under Benedict's successor, Ceolfrid. 'I have spent all my life in this monastery, applying myself entirely to the study of the scriptures,' he wrote in his seminal work, *Ecclesiastical History of the English People* – the first history book of Britain. 'It has always been my delight to learn or to teach or to write.'

recalls the lead archaeologist, Rosemary Cramp, speaking on an audio guide produced by English Heritage.

㉒ Marsden Bay

The flat grasslands behind Marsden's clifftop footpath haven't always been here: before the local colliery closed in 1968, a complete village stood on the site with a church, post office, school and nine streets of 19th-century miners' houses. The whole lot was demolished in the years after the mine closed. Dog walkers and those on the coastal path enjoy the open, car-free area today. Botanists will find the magnesium limestone cliffs of interest in the summer when orchids, rock rose, cowslips, bird's-foot trefoil and field scabious blossom.

Below the cliffs are lime kilns and the **Marsden Grotto** – originally a cave that was enlarged by a North Pennine miner (brilliantly named 'Jack the Blaster') in the late 18th century and made into a home and later an inn. It was a favourite haunt of smugglers and now functions as a restaurant and bar; it gets busy with locals at the weekends (see food and drink listing below).

Marsden Rock is a huge craggy block of limestone that had a picturesque archway until it collapsed in 1996. It's an important landmark and a known nesting site for **seabirds**. Scan the ledges for fulmar, cormorants and kittiwakes.

In fact, this whole stretch of coastline is excellent for **birdwatching** throughout the year. Following strong easterly winds in autumn, unusual

Lifeboats

A reward of two guineas will be given to any person, producing a plan of a boat, capable of containing 24 persons, and calculated to go through a very shoal heavy broken sea. The intention of it being to preserve the lives of seamen, from ships coming ashore, in hard gales of wind.
Advert in *The Newcastle Courant* 2 May, 1789

The challenge to design a lifeboat was set in the wake of a terrible shipwreck in 1789 during which eight men on board the Newcastle vessel, *Adventure*, lost their lives. Only two people responded to the above advert and neither design was fully adopted (which caused future controversy over who could lay claim to being the inventor of the lifeboat: Willie Wouldhave or Henry Greathead?); nonetheless, work began the same year on construction of the *Original*, which was launched in February 1790 – the first purpose-built lifeboat in the world.

The *Original* was superseded by many lifeboats, including the *Tyne* – a beautifully preserved blue-and-white vessel now installed under an ornate wrought-iron and timber canopy on the edge of South Marine Park on Pier Parade in South Shields. Built in 1833, the wooden boat operated out of the town, saving over 1,000 lives.

migrants often get blown onto land. They show up in curious places: burial grounds, gardens and allotments. **Marsden Quarry** (half a mile west of Souter Lighthouse) is a hotspot – also for orchids in the summer.

Souter Lighthouse

Coast Rd, Whitburn SR6 7NH ℗ 0191 529 0909 ℗ www.nationaltrust.org.uk; usually open daily Mar–Nov and school holidays, 11.00–17.00; closed Fri outside summer holidays; café; National Trust.

Standing on a grassy headland (and increasingly closer to the cliff edge) on the southern edge of Marsden Bay is an arresting red and white lighthouse and a beautifully preserved lighthouse keeper's cottage. Built in 1871, Souter made history by becoming the first lighthouse in the world to be powered by electricity. It closed in the late 20th century and is now open to visitors who wish to climb to the top of the lighthouse, visit the cottages and see the engine room. The foghorn sounds most Sundays but brace yourself – it's apparently the loudest in the UK.

Food and drink

Marsden Grotto Coast Rd, South Shields NE34 7BS (near Souter Lighthouse) ℗ 0191 455 6060 ℗ www.marsden-grotto.co.uk. Modern restaurant and bar (with a smuggling history – see above) built into Marsden's cliffs. You arrive in the grotto by way of a lift from the clifftop – an experience in itself. Average pub food, light lunches and seafood dishes (sandwiches, fish and chips, mussels, etc) served in the rock cave. There's a seating area outside looking over the beautiful bay and famous rock stack.

㉓ Whitburn Bay, windmills and walruses

The long expanse of sand at **Whitburn Bay** was once enjoyed by *Alice in Wonderland* author, Lewis Carroll (real name Charles Dodgson), who had ties to the area. His poem 'The Walrus and the Carpenter' is said to have been inspired by visits here, hence the bronze statue of a walrus at the Victorian Mowbray Park in Sunderland (erected in his memory). Whitburn is known for its beach and three windmills – two of which have sails (like something out of a Constable painting, plonked in Sunderland).

Fulwell Windmill (*near Seaburn Metro station; 0191 516 9790; www. fulwell-windmill.com; occasionally open to the public*) was built for Joseph Swan (of lightbulbs fame) in 1808 and has its original mechanisms. **Whitburn Windmill** is on the Coast Road (A183), just north of Whitburn centre, the little Catholic Church and Poplar Drive. It dates to 1790 and was restored in the 1990s with new sails.

Rockpooling

Shattered limestone rock stacks, cliff walls, rock-strewn bays and sandy beaches characterise the coastline (much of which is managed by the National Trust) between Sunderland and South Shields – an area well-known for its birdlife and rockpools. Popular spots for exploring at low tide are the shores and coves between Whitburn and Lizard Point, each fairly easily accessed from prominent car parks. Besides limpets, barnacles, hermit crabs and winkles, you may find brittle stars, butterfish, crabs and sea scorpions and sea anemones lurking beneath the bladder wrack and sea lettuces. Pick up fishing nets and buckets in Whitburn village (try the newsagents on Percy Terrace). National Trust rangers at Souter Lighthouse run occasional rockpooling events during the summer.

Birdwatching along the Durham and South Tyneside coasts

This is seriously good birdwatching country. From Hartlepool to South Shields, birders can pretty much choose any cove, shore or ravine and come away after a morning with an impressive species list.

In summer, nesting **seabirds** (cormorants, kittiwakes and fulmars) on Marsden Bay's carboniferous rock stacks are an impressive sight (see page 54) and you may also spot passing razorbills and guillemots as well as those great ocean-wanderers, the terns. For woodland birds, take a walk through the enchanting coastal gorges of Hawthorn and Castle Eden Dene (see page 261).

The pace and diversity of birds completely changes come the end of the summer when most of the breeding seabirds head out to open waters and **migrants** are on the move: that's when things get really exciting. It's the unpredictability of passage birds, chance of rarities and size of flocks that draws birders from all over the UK to the North East coast at this time of the year, no matter how poor the weather may be. In fact, the worse the better in some ways: ideally, a strong easterly wind, an overcast sky and a bit of drizzle is what you're looking for. Under such conditions weary migrants are blown onshore and turn up in the most curious of places: allotments, gardens, churchyards, cemeteries, urban parks, trees in residential streets – basically anywhere there's a bit of cover. Whitburn and Hartlepool Headland are well known to birders. Large falls of thrushes and smaller passerines like goldcrests are likely with the odd wryneck and rare warbler, wagtail and flycatcher thrown in.

Poking around the likes of Mere Knolls Cemetery and Marsden Quarry is not for everyone so you might want to head to Souter Point, Lizard Point (around Souter Lighthouse) or Whitburn Coastal Park in the hope of spotting divers, grebes, red-breasted mergansers and eider ducks at sea. Lucky visitors may also see **passage ducks, geese and skuas** such as goldeneye, common scoter and pink-footed geese.

Food and drink

Latimer's Shell Hill, Bents Rd, SR6 7NT ⓣ 0191 529 2200 ⓦ www.latimers.com.
Fantastic fishmonger on the seafront at Whitburn, renowned locally and winner
of quite a few national awards over the years. Seafood comes straight in off the
boats at Whitby, Sunderland and North Shields. At the time of writing Latimer's
was about to re-open its new seafood café/restaurant which will have outdoor
seating with a sea view. In the past, the only thing they didn't serve was chips and
that is likely to be the case when it re-opens; besides, anyone who wants fish and
chips goes to Coleman's of South Shields.

Throughout autumn and winter, **wading birds** gather in large numbers on the
rocky shores and coastal grasslands (Whitburn is always good). They are the
easiest birds to see in many ways because of their predictability and preferred
roosting sites which are mostly within sight from coastal footpaths and beaches.
Apart from the shoreline, where you may see oystercatchers, dunlins, redshank,
turnstones and purple sandpipers, also check out the fields around the **Whitburn
bird observatory** where golden plover and lapwings huddle in dense flocks. Keys
for the hide, which is accessed from the car park at Whitburn Coastal Park, can
be purchased from Souter Lighthouse for £12.

Lines of gulls along South Shields's pier are always worth scanning for the odd
Glaucous, Mediterranean and Iceland gulls as well as the usual suspects. The
added advantage here is the proximity of one of the best fish and chip shops in
the region on Ocean Road (Coleman's – see page 51).

TOP BIRDWATCHING SITES BETWEEN SOUTH SHIELDS AND HARTLEPOOL

1   South Shields' pier
2   The Leas grasslands
3   Marsden Bay and Rock (see page 54)
4   Marsden Quarry
5   Lizard Point
6   Whitburn Coastal Park
7   Souter Point
8   Whitburn Bay rocks
9   Hawthorn Dene
10 Blackhall Colliery
11 Castle Eden Dene National Nature Reserve, Peterlee (see page 261)
12 Hartlepool Headland (see page 262)
13 Teesmouth National Nature Reserve/Saltholme RSPB Reserve

River Tweed

A1

A689

B6354

A1

B6353

St Cuthbert's Way

B6525

St Cuthbert's Cave

B6349

B6348

A697

B6346

N

0   4 miles
0   5km

NORTHUMBERLAND COAST

(19) BERWICK-UPON-TWEED
Tweedmouth
Spittal

Lindisfarne (Holy Island)
(18)
Lindisfarne NNR

Ross Sands

(14) Farne Islands

(16) Budle Bay
(15) Bamburgh

(17) Belford

B1340 (13) Seahouses

Northumberland Coast Path

(12) Beadnell
Beadnell Bay

A1

(11) Preston Tower

(10) Low Newton-by-the-Sea

Embleton Bay
(9) Embleton
Dunstanburgh Castle
B1339
(8) Craster

Rennington

(7) Howick Hall

(6) Sugar Sands
Boulmer

Northumberland Coast Path

A1

(5) Alnmouth

Denwick
ALNWICK (2)
A1068

B6341

B1338

(4) Warkworth
Amble

A1

(3) Coquet Island

Hauxley Nature Reserve

B6345

River Coquet

East Chevington Nature Reserve

(1) Druridge Bay

2. NORTHUMBERLAND COAST

'There's nothing like the Northumberland coast, is there?' said a cheerful angler passing me without stopping as I walked towards Dunstanburgh Castle one sunny morning in August. Anyone who makes a trip along the dune-backed shores between the outskirts of Tyneside and Berwick-upon-Tweed will know what he means. Where else in England can you walk along a pristine sandy beach on a summer's day and only meet a handful of people? The Northumberland coast is like this for much of its 70 miles.

Besides beaches, you'll find old fishing villages, offshore islands and a number of medieval castles. Nowhere are these landscape features more conspicuous than between Warkworth and Berwick-upon-Tweed (the Northumberland Coast Area of Outstanding Natural Beauty, also known as the Heritage Coast). Here you'll find most of the best bathing **beaches**, the **Farne Islands** nature reserve, **Lindisfarne Priory,** excellent guest houses and holiday cottages and all the **castles**.

But, don't overlook the south Northumberland coast. Some of the longest and most silky stretches of beach are found around **Druridge Bay**. Birdwatchers, walkers, those with an interest in industrial heritage, surfers, and anyone looking for some of the best fish and chips in Northumberland should come here. Tyneside's coastal strip between Tynemouth and Newbiggin-by-the-Sea is covered in *Chapter 1*.

Getting around

If you're using public transport to access the north Northumberland coast, you'll have to be well organised as **buses** are infrequent and the train stations are set back at least a few miles from the shore. A couple of useful buses are the **501** (Newcastle to Berwick via Alnwick, Alnmouth, Craster, Embleton, Seahouses, Bamburgh and a few other places) and the **505** (Newcastle to Berwick via places on the A1 including Alnwick). For Lindisfarne, take the **477** from Beal which connects with the 505. See www.arrivabus.co.uk.

A combination of **bicycle** and **train** (stations at Berwick, Alnmouth and Chathill) is a better way to get around if you don't have a car.

NCN Route 1 runs the length of the county, staying close to the coastline for much of the way. However, one of the most beautiful stretches of the Northumberland coast, between Embleton and Lindisfarne, is currently not accessible on two wheels, forcing a detour inland.

Taxis on the coast include: A2B (*Berwick & Lindisfarne 07732 520 385*); Croft Cabs (*Belford 01668 213639/07803 496 278*); Hunters Taxis (*Seahouses 01665 720400*); Knights Taxis (*near Alnmouth 01665 714555/07760 751 667*); and the Yellow Taxi (*Alnwick 01665 541250*).

Walking

Linear walks along Northumberland's beaches are unbeatable and are well marked thanks to the 64-mile **Northumberland Coast Path** from Cresswell to Berwick-upon-Tweed. The long-distance path is easily walkable in six days with few challenges (except perhaps for the hike over the Kyloe Hills).

Inland the countryside is flat and really not in the same league, so mostly you're confined to the coast itself. If you want to vary a linear route along the coast, you're best off along the beach on the outward journey and walking on the headland or dune paths (or vice versa) on the return. You can do this on walks for much of the way between Dunstanburgh Castle and Beadnell, for example. Also, see the Craster to Howick circular route described on page 79.

Popular half-day routes are Warkworth to Alnmouth; Craster to Howick; Newton-by-the-Sea to Craster or Beadnell; Seahouses to Bamburgh; and the Lindisfarne round-island walk. Druridge Bay is the ultimate beach for a windswept walk.

Horseriding

Horseriders trotting through the surf on the beaches at Bamburgh, Lindisfarne and Newton-by-the-Sea are always an enviable sight. If you want to join them (experienced riders only) try **Slate Hall Riding Centre** (*01665 720320; www. slatehallridingcentre.com*) at Seahouses who offer trips on the bays at Bamburgh, Beadnell and Embleton. **Kimmerston Riding Centre** (*01668 216283; www. kimmerston.com*) in Wooler go to Lindisfarne regularly in summer.

Accommodation

Holiday cottages

Midrange and luxurious holiday cottages are plentiful on the coast. Some of the more unusual cottages you'll find include a dovecote (see below), the Victorian bathing house near Howick (see page 76), and Newton-by-the-Sea's coastguard cottage and rocket house (used during shore-based rescues by local Volunteer Life Brigades in the days before modern rescue boats).

Reputable holiday cottage companies in the area include **Grace Darling Holidays** (*01665 721332; www.gracedarlingholidays.com*) and **Coastal Retreats Northumberland** (*0191 285 1272; www.coastalretreats.co.uk*). Both offer a consistently high standard of accommodation often in stone buildings that have had interesting former lives. **Lindisfarne Bay Cottages** and **Outchester and Ross Farm Cottages** are described below.

The Ducket Outchester and Ross Farm Cottages, near Waren Mill ①01668 213336 ⑩ www.rosscottages.co.uk. The couple behind Lindisfarne Oysters own a number of cottages west of Budle Bay and at Ross Sands. This 18th-century dovecote is by far the quirkiest. The farmland setting is not spectacular, but the coastal view from the top of the 65-foot high tower really is something special. It's not spacious inside, obviously, but the round rooms are cosy and perfect for love birds. It's expensive to stay in the Ducket but the other cottages nearby are very reasonably priced.

Lindisfarne Bay Cottages West of Fenwick on the shores of Lindisfarne National Nature Reserve (NNR) ☏ 07565 891795 ⓦ www.lindisfarnebaycottages.co.uk. I could have spent most of the morning sitting in front of the floor-to-ceiling window of the Byre gazing out over the stunning Lindisfarne NNR to the castle and watching huge flocks of wading birds feeding and taking to the air. Waking up to the sound of the wind in the trees, curlews and geese flying overhead was a wonderfully soothing start to the day. Birdwatchers or those looking for a tranquil escape will love it here. The three cottages, which stand together on the shores of the nature reserve, were originally part of an 18th-century millhouse. They are all exceptionally well-appointed and pretty luxurious (feather duvets, heavy curtains, original artworks, the odd antique and a kitchen better equipped than most homes). It's not cheap to stay here but the accommodation is superb.

Camping, wigwams and bunkhouses

Campers will be disappointed on the coast, though less so if you're a member of the Camping and Caravanning Club. Considering how many beautiful bays are cut into Northumberland's shores, you'd think that somewhere there would be a secluded independent campsite with a divine view of the sea, but there's not and camping in the sensitive dunes is strictly forbidden.

Beadnell Bay Camping and Caravanning Club Site Beadnell NE67 5BX ☏ 01665 720586 ⓦ www.campingandcaravanningclub.co.uk. One of the closest sites to a beach. Shame about the road preventing a hop, skip and jump into the sea. Open to non-members for an additional fee. You could also try **Annstead Farm** (*01665 720387; www.annstead.co.uk*) further north on the same road. Camping and Caravanning Club members only but they also have a bunkhouse.

Joiners Shop Bunkhouse Chathill NE67 5ES ☏ 01665 589245 ⓦ www.bunk housenorthumberland.co.uk ⓔ bunkhouse.wal@btinternet.com. Old stone building close to Preston Tower (4 miles from the sea); shabby (in a good way) and great for groups with a big dining table, wood fire and curtained off bunkbeds.

Pot-a-Doodle Do Wigwam Village Scremerston, south of Berwick ☏ 01289 307107 ⓦ www.northumbrianwigwams.com ⓔ enquiries@ northumbrianwigwams.com. Wigwams a-plenty at this family-friendly site (set back from the coast) with extras like pottery painting and play areas. You can also sleep in a Finnish hut or a yurt.

Springhill Farm West of Seahouses NE68 7UR ☏ 01665 721820 ⓦ www. springhill-farm.co.uk ⓔ enquiries@springhill-farm.co.uk. Wigwams, modern bunkhouse and spaces for tents and caravans.

Tewart Arms Cottage Camping & Caravan Site Near Chathill NE67 5JP
① 01665 589286. Rustic campsite (read: basic, quiet and small) for tents and
caravans, 4 miles west of Seahouses.

Guesthouses

Courtyard Gardens 10 Prudhoe St, Alnwick NE66 1UW ① 01665 603393
Ⓦ www.courtyardgarden-alnwick.com Ⓔ info@courtyardgarden-alnwick.com.
The owners (who are antiques magpies) have spared no expense transforming
this Georgian townhouse into an upmarket period-styled B&B. The two rooms
at the top of a lofty stairwell (surprisingly not that much more expensive than
an average guesthouse) are furnished with heavy, opulent fabrics and both
have stripped floors and the odd decorative antique. Charming black-and-white
photographs from the early 20th century hang on the walls. Best for a romantic
treat. If you're heading inland to the Cheviots, the owners have a cottage you can
rent in Alwinton which has their stylish touch.

Greycroft Croft Pl, Alnwick NE66 1XU ① 01665 602127 Ⓦ www.greycroft.co.uk
Ⓔ info@greycroft.co.uk. Exceptionally clean, above average-priced B&B set in a
private street close to the centre of Alnwick. Contemporary rooms with no clutter.
Enjoy Craster kippers for breakfast in a light-filled dining room overlooking the
secluded garden. Family room available (no children under ten).

Harbour Lights Whin Hill, Craster NE66 3TP ① 01665 576062 Ⓦ www.
harbourlights-craster.co.uk Ⓔ info@harbourlights-craster.co.uk. There are
few average-priced B&Bs on the Northumberland coast that are as chic (and
ecologically minded) as Harbour Lights. Rooms are decorated with soft greys,
blues and neutrals and local artworks. Great location with view over the harbour.
Kippers for breakfast from the smokehouse.

Northumbrian House 7 Ravensdowne, Berwick-upon-Tweed TD15 1HX
① 01289 309503 Ⓦ www.7ravensdowne.co.uk. Diana and Ian are gradually
restoring this elegant period townhouse back to its Georgian roots. Expect high
ceilings, stripped wooden floors and an antique touch. Bathrooms are modern,
new and spotless. Prices a little above average. The attention to detail impressed
me (leaf tea in bedrooms, for example). Ian is hugely enthusiastic about local
produce (as well as being a Slow Food devotee) and what he doesn't grow in the
walled garden, he sources from local farms. His full English breakfast is possibly
the best I've ever eaten. Also try the porridge with whisky and the gorgeous
homemade marmalade. Ian's background is in geology and he leads guided tours
along the Northumberland coast.

Old Vicarage Guesthouse 24 Church Rd, Tweedmouth, Berwick-upon-Tweed
TD15 2AN ① 01289 306909 Ⓦ www.oldvicarageberwick.co.uk Ⓔ stay@
oldvicarageberwick.co.uk. When I visited this slightly above average-priced B&B
one cold November's evening, I was welcomed into the elegant drawing room
which was furnished with many turn of the century antiques and warmed by
a roaring fire. Antiques are scattered throughout the house which is full of
character. Rooms (some better than others) are spacious with high ceilings and

original fireplaces. The owner, Ruth, is very active in Berwick's Slow Food culture and you can be sure that not only do her breakfasts and four course dinners come with glowing recommendations, pretty much everything on your plate is locally produced.

Roxbro House 5 Castle Terrace, Warkworth NE65 0UP ℗ 01665 711416 ⓦ www. roxbrohouse.co.uk ℮ info@roxbrohouse.co.uk. Period wallpaper, bold colours, antique furniture and a touch of decadence make this above average-priced B&B an excellent choice for couples wanting somewhere that feels a little bit special. Prime location opposite Warkworth Castle (direct view from some rooms).

St Cuthbert's House 192 Main St, Seahouses NE68 7UB ℗ 01665 720456 ⓦ www.stcuthbertshouse.com ℮ stay@stcuthbertshouse.com. Gorgeous B&B in a converted chapel just outside of Seahouses village. Neutrally decorated rooms have a luxurious feel and are exceptionally clean and comfortable. Prices are a little above average but the standard of accommodation is far higher than most (St Cuthbert's House was awarded best North East B&B of the year for a reason). The owners go that extra mile to ensure everything on your plate is sourced locally, including the fish from the smokehouse down the road and honey from their hives. I also liked the fact the honesty bar is stocked with bottled local ales.

① Druridge Bay

Northumberland's most desolate beach is a sweeping expanse of sand that extends for six wind-whipped miles from Cresswell to just south of Amble. The shore is sheltered somewhat by high dunes, but it's hard to completely escape the bracing winds. Perhaps this explains in part why Druridge Bay is not the most popular bucket-and-spade beach. You'll easily find a spot to yourself where the nearest family is several hundred yards away. Walkers and kite-boarders will love it here.

Behind the dunes is a broken chain of (sheltered) lagoons fringed by reedbeds and farmland that attract large numbers of wildfowl in winter. They are linked by the Northumberland Coast Path which takes a varied route along the beach, tracks and grassy dunes.

The wetland **nature reserves** which were reclaimed from old coal mines attract rare migrants, as well as over-wintering species including pink-footed geese, bitterns, short-eared owls and whooper swans. In recent years marsh harriers have returned to Northumberland after a 130-year absence and successfully raised chicks at East Chevington Nature Reserve, and in 2011, avocets nested at Cresswell Ponds Nature Reserve (the most northerly record in the UK).

Within the **Druridge Bay Country Park** (access from Red Row) is the family-friendly **Ladyburn Lake** where you'll find a visitor centre, large picnic area and watersports on offer including canoeing and windsurfing (call the **visitor centre** on 01670 760968 for information).

East Chevington Nature Reserve

Nestled behind Druridge Bay's high dunes is a wetland reserve managed by the Northumberland Wildlife Trust and one of the best places to watch birds on the Northumberland coast. The reedbeds, woodlands, rough grasslands and dunes are usually reached from Hadston via Druridge Bay Country Park though there is also a lane from Red Row. You can walk around the whole reserve on soft ground but there's one long stretch along the above mentioned paved lane. You'll see a good variety of birds, particularly in autumn and winter when large flocks of waders and geese descend on the grasslands and pools. Splinter paths lead to the beach, and bird hides (I've spotted reed buntings and reed warblers here in summer and I once saw a bittern clamber out of the reedbeds in a rare burst of extroversion; they are not uncommon in winter when the UK's population expands with European bitterns).

Hauxley Nature Reserve

At the northern end of Druridge Bay is this Northumberland Wildlife Trust reserve which is reached by walking along the dunes (great coastal views) or by track from High Hauxley. Viewing hides are good, but don't overlook the scrubby areas and meadows (flowering plants, butterflies and dragonflies in summer; and finches and tits throughout the year). The reserve has a thriving population of tree sparrows (like a sparrow but with dark patches on either cheek) which feed on bird tables close to the visitor centre.

Amble Links

Extensive dunes and another long sandy beach lead you from Low Hauxley to the fringes of this busy work-a-day fishing town. The bays nearer Amble are not as pristine but you'll find what some say is the best **fish and chips** in Northumberland if you continue to the north end of the town. Harbour Fish Bar (*01665 710442*) is the place to go (tucked out of sight on the corner of Leazes Street and Broomhill Street).

② Alnwick town and castle

'Alnwick is ever under the spell of the dreamy past', a late 19th-century visitor to the town observed. Today, you might also say it is under the spell of *Harry Potter*, whose fans flock to the town's famous medieval castle, better known to some as Hogwarts. For others, even without its castle and celebrated gardens, Alnwick (pronounced 'Annick') is one of the most vibrant and historically interesting market towns in the North East.

Alnwick

At its centre, three venerable streets wrap around a piazza which boasts an outdoor café culture, market and summer folk music festival. To the north are the castle, gardens, museum and church. The most memorable approach to the town centre is from the south under the **Bondgate Tower** – a mighty stone gateway which has served as a main entry point into the once walled town since its construction in 1450.

Before you reach the arch, you'll pass **Barter Books** (see page 66) on **Bondgate Without**. Opposite is a moving **war memorial** designed by Ralph Hedley in 1921. The three bronze figures of a soldier, sailor and airman warrant close inspection. Close by is the **Percy Tenantry Column**, a fluted pillar surmounted with a lion and guarded at its base by four other feline beasts. It was erected in 1816 by the tenants of the 2nd Duke of Northumberland after he reduced rents during tough economic times. The lion is the emblem of the Percy family of Alnwick Castle and is seen in many places about town, notably on Lion Bridge.

Art buffs should head up Prudhoe Street to the **Bakehouse Gallery** (*01665 602277; www.thebakehousegallery.com*). Many of the region's best local painters have their work displayed here, alongside ceramics, handmade jewellery and various other craftwork.

Bondgate Without becomes **Bondgate Within** (that is, within the town walls) after you pass under the medieval arch. Here, a wide thoroughfare of Georgian and Victorian buildings leads to the **Market Place** where you'll find the **tourist information centre** (*01665 511333*), the imposing Georgian Town Hall and a couple of good eateries. One building on Bondgate Within to look out for is the **White Swan** (*01665 602109; www.classiclodges.co.uk*). In the 1930s, the then owner of the hotel bought all the fittings and artworks from the decommissioned *Olympic* cruise liner (the *Titanic's* sister ship) and reconstructed them to make an opulent dining room. You don't need to stay at the hotel to enjoy an evening meal in the sumptuous oak-panelled restaurant which transports you back to the era of trans-Atlantic cruises, Edwardian style.

Fenkle Street is a long run of old merchants' houses with a chocolaterie on the corner (an old photo inside shows that there was once a chocolate shop here in 1923) that curves gently to meet **Narrowgate**. It's fairly swish in this area with a scattering of tea rooms, interiors shops, an antiques emporium, art gallery, deli and 'boutique' wine shop. Don't miss the dusty bottles in the window of **Ye Olde Cross** pub at the junction with Pottergate. They are said to be cursed and have not been touched in 200 years.

St Michael's Church and Alnwick Castle stand either end of Bailiffgate, Alnwick's most elegant street of sandstone houses. The former Catholic church is now the **Bailiffgate Museum** (*01665 605847; www.bailiffgatemuseum.*

Alnwick International Music Festival

A market town in Northumberland is an unlikely venue for an international gathering of musicians, but Alnwick is a vibrant place. It's a folk dance and music festival really, with performers from eastern Europe, France, the USA and Northumberland. Expect swirling dresses, traditional costume, sword dancers, fiddle players, concertinas and ukuleles out in force. The popular event is usually held early in August and always in the Market Square. See www. alnwickmusicfestival.com.

co.uk) which gives a comprehensive introduction to the history of Alnwick district – its buildings, industries and people.

St Michael's Church

Opposite end of Bailiffgate from the castle. Open most afternoons May–Sep.

'Don't tell me the Victorians were good engineers', said the church warden pointing to a bowed wall which began to tilt in the years following a 19th-century reconfiguration of the medieval edifice. Despite this, St Michael's certainly gives the appearance of strength and steadfastness with its short, castellated tower supported by wide buttresses. The unusual turret on the southeastern corner of the church served as a lookout point during the centuries of Border fighting.

Inside, the faces on some stained glass windows have faded because an inferior black pigment was used in their creation. Those corner-cutting Victorians have caused no end of strife for the current warden. The two stone effigies are of interest. The female figure is thought to be Lady Isabella de Vesci, wife of William de Vesci, the last Baron of Alnwick (before the illustrious Percy family). Take a closer look at the knight's garment: the eight buttons look unremarkable but back in the 14th century they were quite novel, having only come to Europe in the previous century.

Barter Books

Alnwick Station (Bondgate Without) NE66 2NP ☏ 01665 604888
Ⓦ www.barterbooks.co.uk. Open daily (until 19.00 in summer); café.

An hour or two in this acclaimed secondhand bookshop on the southern edge of Alnwick will not be forgotten. Housed in the old train station, Barter Books oozes old-world charm and character with its rickety bookshelves, waiting room café, crackling open fires and child's train track suspended from the ceiling. The incessant sound of the toy train is a much loved feature of the building.

Painted under the domed ceiling is a huge **mural** of 33 life-size well-known writers including Charlotte Brontë, Salman Rushdie, James Joyce and Alan Bennett. It took two years to paint and has sparked many a debate among visitors as to which figures from the world of literature are worthy of a place on the wall.

On the books front, there's something for every enthusiast here. Children, rare book lovers and railway fans are particularly well catered for. You'll find antique books upwards of £10,000 and those costing just a few pounds.

Barter Books is also home of one of the original 'Keep Calm and Carry On' World War II posters, which was found among a stash of books bought at auction. The crinkled poster is displayed in a frame. It's not for sale of course, but the owners are doing a roaring trade in facsimile copies of the posters as well as mugs and the other Keep Calm paraphernalia that has become so ubiquitous.

House of Hardy

Willowburn (south Alnwick, off the A1) NE66 2PF ℗ 01665 602771
Ⓦ www.hardyfishing.com.

Even those not particularly interested in fishing may find this small museum and large showroom appealing. Anglers will be in heaven. For those not in the know, Hardy is a well-regarded Alnwick company making fishing rods and reels. Old black and white photographs of the company's craftsmen at work over a hundred years ago and exhibits displaying the evolution of the famous Hardy rods and reels (the 'Rolls Royce of fishing reels' the helpful chap behind the counter proudly described them) are displayed next to the shop. The Hardy traditional bamboo rods cost thousands but are still sold to those with a fondness for the craftsmanship of yesteryear; American visitors and people like Prince Charles, for example.

Hulne Park

Ratten Row, Alnwick; generally open all year from 11.00 until sunset; no dogs or bicycles permitted; free access.

Not far from St Michael's Church is the imposing gateway to Hulne Park – a huge area of woods and open parkland enclosed by walls and owned by the Duke of Northumberland. Several miles of footpaths wind through the trees, over stone bridges, past dells and across open grasslands. If Alnwick wasn't already stuffed with so many old buildings, perhaps more would be said of the

Aln Valley Railway

From the late 1800s until the 1960s, a branch line operated from Alnwick to the coast at Alnmouth. Plans have been afoot for well over a decade to restore the heritage line and build a new station to replace the original which now houses Barter Books. Steam and diesel locomotives will eventually operate out of a new station called Lionheart (a nice nod to the Percy family at Alnwick Castle). See www.alnvalleyrailway.co.uk.

romantic ruins of Hulne Priory founded by Carmelite friars in 1265. Also in the park is one of the most outlandish Gothic follies in England, Brizlee Tower, and the imposing 14th-century gatehouse of Alnwick Abbey, a striking turreted tower that stands alone in open parkland by the River Aln. Once you're past the working sawmill, you'll find the parkland a wonderfully tranquil place to visit for an extended walk or morning jog.

Alnwick Castle

Where Bailiffgate meets Narrowgate NE66 1NQ ① 01665 510777
Ⓦ www.alnwickcastle.com. Open 1 Apr–31 Oct; café and restaurant (see food and drink listing for Alnwick) free guided tours by knowledgeable stewards are highly recommended.

Alnwick Castle is often referred to as the 'Windsor Castle of the North' in tourism literature on account of its size and imposing buildings. Like Windsor, it's home to royalty, well, Geordie royalty at least. The Duke and Duchess of Northumberland are historically one of the most powerful aristocratic families in England; they own huge amounts of land and property, including this almighty fortress.

Alnwick has been the Percy family's principal seat for 700 years ever since Henry de Percy bought the castle from the Bishop of Durham in 1309. Stonework from the earlier Norman building is seen in the archway into the keep, but the castle was extensively rebuilt in the 14th century and again in the latter half of the 18th century.

The present buildings are largely medieval and the castle roughly retains its original layout with a circular keep about a courtyard and an inner and outer bailey. Miniature stone warriors guard the parapets. From a distance, they look life-size and were intended to give the impression of a well-armed castle. Indeed, Alnwick was very much built with military use in mind, and its strength has been tested several times by the Scots. The formidable barbican is said to be one of the best examples of its kind in the country.

Inside the keep hangs a Canaletto depicting the ruinous castle as it was in 1750 before the Georgian restoration under the 1st Duke of Northumberland. He directed the transformation of the castle into a stately home, and the countryside beyond the castle's north walls into a landscaped parkland.

The current 12th Duke and Duchess of Northumberland have certainly left their mark. The Duchess is responsible for the much publicised 42-million pound redevelopment of the gardens and establishing Alnwick Castle and The Alnwick Garden as the North East's leading paid-for attractions and two of the top ten attractions in Britain. Former head of Disneyland Paris was employed as chief executive of the castle and is said to be behind attractions like Knight's Quest. There's no denying the castle has a theme-park edge.

Ever since the filming of *Harry Potter* at Alnwick in 2000, the fortress has become known to many young visitors as Hogwarts School of Witchcraft and Wizardry. The managers of Alnwick Castle are only too happy to indulge them and you'll find broomstick-riding lessons (as entertaining for spectators) among the array of wizard- and medieval-themed activities.

Alnwick Castle is clearly a huge hit with families, but there's also much to interest those with a love of porcelain, fine art (the castle houses a distinguished collection of Renaissance art including six paintings by Canaletto and three Titians) and, of course, gardens (see The Alnwick Garden, page 70).

A taste of the Duke of Northumberland's riches are revealed in the **State Rooms**. The dining room, library and drawing room are sumptuously furnished with highly decorative ceilings, fireplaces and wallpapers, etc. When the dining room underwent restoration in 2005–06, it took five men five weeks just to polish the ceiling. Paintings by Canaletto, Velasquez and Turner hang on the walls and an extensive collection of Meissen porcelain is displayed in the China Gallery.

Two of the most treasured items in the castle are the ornately carved and painted Italian **Cucci cabinets**, made out of ebony for Louis XIV's Palace at Versailles in the late 17th century. They are thought to be two of the most valuable pieces of furniture in the world.

The **Inner Bailey** is spectacular – for its size, tremendous walls and the 18th-century view from the ramparts. Below, an expansive, tree-studded **parkland** falls away from the walls and rolls to the River Aln and beyond. It is one of the most beautiful designed landscapes in Northumberland and, not altogether surprisingly, the work of local landscape architect, Lancelot 'Capability' Brown. The parkland can be enjoyed along a public footpath north of the river which requires the visitor first to cross the showy **Lion Bridge** built in 1773. The view looking across the river and up to the castle is highly memorable.

Harry 'Hotspur'

I'll empty all these veins, And shed my dear blood drop by drop in the dust.
William Shakespeare *Henry IV, Part One*

Of all the Percy men through the centuries, the most legendary is Harry 'Hotspur', a fearless and impulsive knight who fought in several conflicts at sea and on land during the 1300s including the midnight Battle of Otterburn in 1388. Hotspur went on to lead the rebellion against Henry IV in the Battle of Shrewsbury in 1403 and like all infamous knights he died in combat when an arrow pierced his skull (I'm not sure how historically accurate this detail is, but it has certainly helped to perpetuate the Hotspur legend). Shakespeare immortalised Hotspur in *Henry IV, Part One*.

Today, Hotspur is remembered in many place and building names in the North East and in the London football club, Tottenham Hotspur, so called because the Percy family owned land where the club originated.

The Alnwick Garden

Denwick Lane, NE66 1YU ① 01665 511350 ⓦ www.alnwickgarden.com. Open daily; café and Treehouse restaurant (see opposite).

The newly restored gardens at Alnwick are unashamedly bold and contemporary and designed to thrill. Jane Percy, the 12th Duchess of Northumberland steered the development of the overgrown gardens in 1997 into the pleasure grounds experienced today, but not without criticism.

The centrepiece is the **Grand Cascade**, a huge modern waterfall lined with fountains that plunges over many tiers into a pool. The cascades must have been designed with families in mind, because the layout makes it possible for parents to sit in the outdoor café and keep an eye on their children driving toy dumper trunks under the spray of water. They looked like they were having great fun and some had stripped down to swimming costumes.

Around the Grand Cascade are a number of distinctive gardens which, with the exception of the more traditional enclosures like the **Rose**

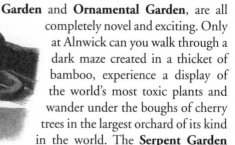

Garden and **Ornamental Garden**, are all completely novel and exciting. Only at Alnwick can you walk through a dark maze created in a thicket of bamboo, experience a display of the world's most toxic plants and wander under the boughs of cherry trees in the largest orchard of its kind in the world. The **Serpent Garden** uses water to creative effect in a sequence of mesmerising contemporary installations and is not to be missed. Ditto the Treehouse restaurant which is quite magical (see opposite).

A steward told me the quietest time to visit the gardens is on Fridays. I visited late one Friday afternoon in August and can honestly say I was one of very few people in the gardens.

Food and drink

Bari Tea 28 Narrowgate, NE66 1JG ① 01665 510508 ⓦ www.baritea.co.uk. Fantastic, recently opened café celebrating distinctively Northumbrian fare including pan haggerty (a potato and cheese dish) and singing hinnie (traditional fruit scone). Posh tea (loose-leaf and not cheap). 'Bari' ('baa-ree'), incidentally, is a Northumbrian word meaning 'delicious'.

Carlo's Fish and Chips 7–9 Market St, NE66 1SS ① 01665 602787 ⓦ www.carlosfishandchips.co.uk. Posh fish and chips (take away or eat in restaurant) at reasonable prices.

Fleece Inn 49 Bondgate Without, NE66 1PR ① 01665 603036. Live folk music in a real ale pub on the third Wednesday of every month.

Grannie's Tearoom 18 Narrowgate, NE66 1JG ① 01665 602394. The smell of fresh bread and tea wafts up the stairs of this tiny café hunkered down on the ground floor of a 400-year-old building. It looks straight out of the pages of a nursery book with copper kettles hanging from the ceiling, a drying rack with knickerbockers and a range among its furnishings. Homemade cakes, scones, pies and soups.

Prima Deli Market Pl, NE66 1HS ⓣ 01665 605610. Excellent value (and quality) delicatessen and café in sunny spot opposite the market cross. Italian cured meat and cheese platters, salads and paninis.

Treehouse Alnwick Castle, Denwick Lane, NE66 1YU ⓣ 01665 511852 ⓦ www.alnwickgarden.com. You'll need to book at least two weeks in advance to secure an evening table in this enchanting restaurant built in a tree canopy within the grounds of Alnwick Gardens (no ticket required for evening dinners). Dishes prepared using local seafood and organic Northumberland meats are not cheap, but the surroundings are unique and a few times a month folk musicians fill the treehouse with regional tunes.

Turnbull's of Alnwick 33–35 Market St, NE66 1SS ⓣ 01665 602186 ⓦ www.turnbulls-of-alnwick.co.uk. For a bite to eat while you wander through Alnwick, try this well-known butchers opposite the market square and dribbling 18th-century pant. Turnbull's has been here for over 100 years and sell inexpensive sandwiches (cold or with hot meats) and pies to take out. Their steak and ale pie made with Farne Isle ale costs little more than £1. BBQ packs recommended for holiday-makers. Turnbull's was behind the opening of **Louis Bistro & Steakhouse** in the Market Place (*01665 606947; www. louis-steakhouse.co.uk*). Steaks sourced from north Northumberland farms via Turnbull's butchery.

The Northumberland Heritage Coast

Northumberland's beaches don't get creamier or softer than those between Boulmer and Lindisfarne within the area designated as the Area of Outstanding Natural Beauty (AONB). The likes of Sugar Sands, Embleton Bay and Beadnell Bay are extremely popular with families and walkers and often top polls of Britain's best beaches. Despite this reputation, they are surprisingly crowd-free, even in high summer. The coast from Warkworth to Berwick (the scope of this section) is not short of old villages, visitor attractions, castles (four within 20 miles) and good quality accommodation.

③ Coquet Island

Near Amble ⓣ 0300 777 2676 ⓦ www.rspb.org.uk; RSPB.

From mid-April, thousands of seabirds descend on this grassy 16-acre lighthouse isle a mile off the coast of Amble and begin squabbling over the best nest site. To see the 30,000 puffins, eider ducks and tens of terns, kittiwakes and fulmars on the RSPB-managed reserve, take a boat tour from

Amble (spring and summer only). Landing is not permitted because of the sensitivity of the site, but you'll get excellent views of the birds, and spy-hopping grey seals.

Coquet Island is home to the only colony of Britain's rarest breeding seabird, the roseate tern, which nests on this tiny isle and almost nowhere else in Britain. Each pair is provided with a ground nest box that the birds 'decorate' with shells, shingle and objects washed up on the shore. The island's manager, Paul Morrison (aka 'Captain Coquet'), told me that one year he found a nest adorned with daffodils and another with fragments of paint. 'I've also seen a Gothic "hut" decked out with rabbit bones', he said. Some birds are so particular that they return to the same nest box every year. Warming seas and availability of sand eels (the main food of puffins and terns) threaten the survival of the seabirds here and elsewhere along the coast.

The lighthouse was built in 1841 on top of a Benedictine monastery (the stone base of which is still visible). You will also see recently restored stone cottages (built in 1840 in the ruins of a 15th-century monastic chapel).

〜〜〜

Getting there
Omega Charters (*07872 639521*) and **Puffin Cruises** (*01665 711975*) boat trips operate out of Amble Quayside between Easter and the end of September, and last around an hour. Call in advance to check sailing times and book tours (just a few pounds). The seabirds depart the island in July and August but it's still possible to see seals, eiders, oystercatchers and so on for the rest of the summer.

④ Warkworth
Warkworth Castle rears over the rooftops of a long row of sandstone houses that step down to the River Coquet, linking the parish church at the bottom with the castle at the top. The Coquet forms a hairpin loop around the settlement, protecting it on three sides (the castle guards the fourth base to the south) before opening to the sea a mile or so beyond the 14th-century bridge. Warkworth's medieval layout is one of the most intact and celebrated in the whole of England.

At the foot of the village, the Coquet flows around **St Lawrence Church** making coastal Warkworth feel much more like a riverside settlement. Despite its protective loop, the river was not enough of a barrier to keep the Scots out in 1174 when they raided Warkworth and massacred the men, women and children sheltering in the church. A church has stood here since Saxon times, but the present building dates to 1130 with medieval and Victorian modifications. Inside, its Norman origins are immediately apparent in the chancel with its, now slightly crooked, arch and impressive stone vaulted ceiling. The only medieval stained glass to survive is in the top of the east window.

Opposite the church is the **market cross** where, on the 9th of October 1715,

Warkworth became the first public place in England to proclaim James III as King during the fated Jacobite Rebellion. The night before, the legendary Earl of Derwentwater (page 120) and 40 rebels dined at the nearby **Masons Arms**. The event is recorded on a beam inside the pub and described on a plaque outside. Today the pub is also known for its **Sea Shanty Nights** on the first Thursday of every month. Singers and musicians with concertinas and mandolins perform traditional songs and the chef serves up seafood pies, lobster and fish from the North Sea.

On the **main street** leading away from the church and market cross, you'll find several pubs and shops, a contemporary art gallery selling pottery, sculptures and paintings of local landscapes, and a few cafés.

The **river** is crowded with trees and is a pleasant place to go for a short walk, feed the ducks, picnic or row a boat (hire station is close to the hermitage landing). Half a mile or so upriver from the church is the crossing point for the medieval **hermitage** – a 15th-century rock-cut chapel concealed by trees on the north side of the river (*01665 711423; www.english-heritage.org.uk; Apr–Sep*). To get there, you must take the rowing boat operated by English Heritage (small charge).

From Warkworth, a glorious long stretch of sand shoots north to Alnmouth and Boulmer. To reach the **beach**, take the paved track heading east from the north side of the medieval bridge.

Warkworth Castle

Castle Terrace, NE65 0UJ ⓣ 01665 711423 ⓦ www.english-heritage.org.uk. Open daily from Easter, and weekends from end Oct; English Heritage.

Warkworth is a fortress to be reckoned with. Though much ruined internally, its 14th-century keep still maintains a heavy presence at the head of the village. The perimeter walls and restored gatehouse date from around 1200 and have resisted the ravages of time better than many of the medieval buildings inside.

Percy is a name you will have heard on your travels along the coast, especially if you've already visited Alnwick Castle, currently the Duke of Northumberland's main seat. Several centuries ago, Warkworth was the Percy family's principal residence, hence the lion motif stamped about the place. Nowhere else is the beast more strikingly carved than above the doorway to the Lion Tower at Warkworth. Its bushy mane and snarl immediately catches the eye on entering the bailey. The castle ('worm-eaten hold of ragged stone') and legendary Percy knight, Harry Hotspur, were immortalised in Shakespeare's *Henry IV, Part One*.

The impressive **keep** is formed of four polygonal wings arranged around a central square. Its roof, battlements and turrets are long gone, exposing the building's ribcage to the sea air, but you still get a good sense of the layout of rooms and can imagine the Duke of Northumberland's medieval banquets in the Great Hall. From his private chamber, he could look over the village and, as today, see all the way to Coquet Island and beyond.

Food and drink

Masons Arms 3 Dial Pl, NE65 0UR ☎ 01665 711398
Ⓦ www.masonsarmswarkworth.co.uk. Poached mackerel, crab cakes, grilled
lobster and monkfish are typically served at the Sea Shanty Nights on the first
Thursday of every month. Fish dishes are also served at other times (I enjoyed
their mussels with cider, cream and parsley sauce). Wednesday is steak night. A
decent serve-yourself carvery is on Sundays.
Topsey Turveys 1 Dial Pl, NE65 0UG ☎ 01665 711338 Ⓦ www.topseyturvey.co.uk.
Cosy and a decent choice for average-priced jacket potatoes, sandwiches, soups,
etc. Evening meals are a little pricey.

⑤ Alnmouth

From a distance, this old fishing village with its colourful row of houses
surmounted by a church spire appears marooned offshore because of the River
Aln which separates the settlement from the mainland to the south and west.

The usual approach for those travelling by road is across a multi-arched
Victorian bridge that skims the river. If travelling on foot over dunes and beach
from Warkworth, you get tantalisingly close to Alnmouth only to find that
you can't cross the estuary (dangerous except at extreme low tide) and have
to backtrack and take the more roundabout trail. Before you do, take in the
view: from **Church Hill** (the grassy knoll with a cross), you'll see small fishing
boats bobbing in the estuary, waders feeding on the riverbed and the red-tiled
roofs of Alnmouth's cottages crowded above creamy sands. It is one of the most
distinctive and picturesque panoramas on the Northumberland coast. As its
name suggests, a church once stood on this hillock, but it was destroyed during
a storm in 1806 that was so violent, it changed the course of the river, cutting
off Church Hill from the village. Fragments of an Anglo-Saxon cross were
found on this spot, indicating the presence of an even earlier church.

Alnmouth's main road, **Northumberland Street** opens generously to
sand dunes at its southern end. Along its length are shops, a church and a
number of pubs and cafés. Some of the Victorian houses on terraces leading
off Northumberland Street are surprisingly tall and austere, contrasting with
the quaint cottages seen elsewhere. The sharp-eyed visitor will notice that a few
buildings have irregular shaped windows (the row leading away from the post
office on the main street, for example). They were built as granaries during the
18th century when Alnmouth was a busy port and exported large amounts of
corn.

At the sand dune end of the main street in the side of a stone house is a
small window displaying an old **barometer** that was given to the Alnmouth
coastguards in 1860 by the Duke of Northumberland. It is a pleasing object,
as is the small window and description of its history.

Drop down onto the creamy-coloured sands at the very end of the road
and enjoy the very special walk along one of Northumberland's most perfect-
looking bays.

Food and drink

Bistro 23, 23 Northumberland St, NE66 2RJ ① 01665 830393. This is the place
to eat in Alnmouth, or indeed if travelling anywhere along this stretch of the
coast. It's a fairly simple eatery with limited menu and opening hours (*café open
daily except Tue; evening meals served on Wed and Sat; only Sat in winter*)
but the owners prepare dishes from scratch using locally sourced ingredients
such as Cheviot lamb, crab from the North Sea and cheeses from Blagdon.
Northumberland beef is always on the menu.

Red Lion 22 Northumberland St, NE66 2RJ ① 01665 830584
Ⓦ www.redlionalnmouth.com. Alnmouth is not short of pubs, but the Red Lion
is one of the best. It is a typical old inn with a low-beamed ceiling and open fire.
It's deliberately rustic inside but not at all pretentious and there's an outside
drinking area overlooking the estuary. The restaurant serves traditional meat
and fish dishes made largely with local ingredients, as well as sandwiches. B&B
accommodation upstairs is above average in price and quality.

⑥ Sugar Sands and around

Whin Sill outcrops and limestone between the fishing villages of Boulmer
and Craster come together to create a very striking and unusual shoreline.
Near Craster, horizontal sheets of rock heave in great shelves onto the
beach. Hidden along this rocky coastline are three sandy bays popular with
families, sea kayakers and anglers. The middle beach is Sugar Sands – one of
Northumberland's finest secluded coves.

The bays are reached in quick succession from the coast path (a rough track
for most of the way from Boulmer to Howick and suitable for cyclists). If
driving or cycling to Sugar Sands, you're best off taking the paved lane east from
Longhoughton where there's a rough parking area at the end of Howdiemont
Sands.

Boulmer

This straggling old fishing village with a rocky shore and RAF base was once
legendary for its smugglers. 'As many as twenty or thirty of them, mounted on

The Great Whin Sill

Three hundred million years ago, hot, molten rock from the Earth's core surged
through to the surface and solidified, forming hard basaltic outcrops rising
sporadically – and dramatically – throughout Northumbria. These ridges have
caught the eye of emperors, Saxon settlers, dukes – and seabirds. It is what
Hadrian's Wall teeters along, Bamburgh Castle rises from and what makes the
Farne Islands such a special sanctuary for wildlife. On the coast near Craster the
combination of hard Whin Sill outcrops and softer limestone has created many
contorted, serpent-like formations on the shoreline.

horseback, would come to Boulmer for gin, and carry it to the centre of the county and the wilds of Coquetdale, not without many hair-breath escapes and lively encounters with the excisemen', says Tomlinson in his *Comprehensive Guide to Northumberland*. The centre of the illicit activities was the Fishing Boat Inn. Tomlinson says casks of liquor are sometimes still dug up on the coast – but he was writing in 1888, so there's little chance of contraband finds today.

Rumbling Kern

Such an evocative name for a beach (just north of Sugar Sands) piled with rocks and with plenty of holes and channels for the sea to roar through. At low tide, this is a great bay for rockpooling and beachcombing. At the north end of the cove, there's a tempting swimming hole cut into the rock.

The Victorian house on the headland (now a very popular holiday cottage, see www.northumbria-byways.com) is the **Bathing House**, built by former Prime Minister, the 2nd Lord Grey of nearby Howick Hall for his 15 children to stay in while enjoying a dip in the sea and pools below.

⑦ Howick Hall Gardens

Howick NE66 3LB ① 01665 577285 Ⓦ www.howickhallgardens.org. Open early Feb–mid Nov, winter Wed–Sun 10.30–16.00, British Summer Time, daily 12.00–18.00; other times Wed–Sun 10.30–16.00; tea room (open to visitors to gardens only).

Howick shipwreck

Just south of Rumbling Kern there's an old ship's boiler that belonged to a French steam trawler that hit rocks nearby in March 1913 on its way to Icelandic fishing grounds. According to a newspaper report at the time, the lifeboat from Boulmer and many local people came to the aid of the fishermen. They rescued 25 men but five sailors (one just 16 years old) drowned. A few of the deceased had tied themselves to the rigging and mast to avoid being washed away in the storm and had to be cut down. The newspaper described the scene as so harrowing that the coastguard ordered all local children away from the shore. The Frenchmen are buried in the church on the Howick Hall estate and the event summarised on the memorial stone.

Earl Grey tea

This delicate tea was especially blended with bergamot to offset the taste of the lime-rich water from the spring on the Howick estate. Earl Grey tea became popular among London's political elite when Lady Grey served the brew at social events. Twinings were brought in to market the blend but, sadly for the ancestors of the Grey family, the trademark was not registered and no royalties have therefore ever been received.

Leaf Earl Grey tea is served in the beautiful old ballroom on the Howick Hall estate where floor-to-ceiling windows look over the gardens. Their cream tea is one of the very best in Northumberland (fruit scones are particularly excellent). To eat here, you must purchase a ticket for the gardens.

'The gardens at Howick are deliberately aimed at garden lovers', say the Howick family. The season starts with a dazzling display of snowdrops followed by daffodils then flowering rhododendrons, camellias and magnolia trees. In high summer, the **Bog Garden** is a visual treat: a water garden with a lake surrounded by bushy lupins, roses, delphiniums and poppies spilling over into grassy paths. Some 11,000 trees and shrubs were planted in the arboretum by the current Lord Howick who is an ardent collector of exotics. Many specimens were grown from seeds gathered on expeditions to China and elsewhere.

The **Woodland Garden** is one of the highlights, especially for its eye-catching stone bridge, spring-flowering shrubs and the way it merges naturally into the woods beyond the road. Here, a path called the **Long Walk** follows the bubbling Howick Burn for 1½ miles to Sugar Sands. You are permitted to walk its length (see page 78 for access information). The 2nd Earl Grey, of whom more later, had an unusual way of preventing his 15 children from developing a fear of the dark. On the first full moon in the July following their tenth birthday, they had to walk to the sea on this trail at midnight and return with a stem of grass of Parnassus, a white flower that grew (and indeed grows to this day, albeit in an inaccessible location) on rocks at the coast. In recent years, the tradition was revived by the estate on midnight guided walks in July (check website for future events).

The house (not currently open to the public, although access is being planned) was built in 1782 and rebuilt following a fire in 1926. It has been the home of the Grey family (and later inherited by the Howicks) since 1319. The most illustrious figure was **Charles, 2nd Earl Grey**, who served as Prime Minister from 1830 to 1834. He is best known for the Great Reform Bill of 1832 which influenced the development of our modern democracy. He loved the family home at Howick and stayed in Northumberland as much as he could, to the frustration of colleagues in London. Described in an estate leaflet as 'one of Britain's greatest Prime Ministers, and one of the century's greatest truants', he is buried in the estate's church.

⑧ Craster

The smell of burning firewood wafts through the streets of stone cottages gathered around a snug harbour in the fishing village of Craster. There's no mistaking where the famous **smokehouse** is situated: it's the stone building with white plumes pouring out of wooden vents in the roof. Herring has been smoked here by L Robson & Sons (*01665 576223; www.kipper.co.uk*) for over a hundred years.

Today, herrings are split using machines and hung on hooks above smouldering oak sawdust and whitewood shavings for up to 16 hours, but once local 'herring girls' did the unenviable task by hand. You can buy kippers over the counter or have them for lunch in the adjoining restaurant or the Jolly Fisherman.

Craster has become somewhat gentrified in recent years, hence the contemporary café, gastro pub and art gallery. **Mick Oxley** (*01665 571082; www.mickoxley.com*) is a well-regarded local artist whose paintings capture the Northumberland coast in all weathers and lights. His gallery is just up the road from the Jolly Fisherman. West of Craster harbour is the main visitor car park with a **tourist information centre** (*01665 576007; open daily; Apr–Oct, weekends only Nov–Mar*).

Coastal walks from Craster

Two fantastic coastal routes start/end here. The first is a linear trail from Newton via Dunstanburgh Castle outlined on page 82; the second is a six-mile circular walk to Sugar Sands via Howick Hall, described briefly here.

A glance at an Ordnance Survey map reveals no obvious way of walking a circular coastal route from Craster to Sugar Sands without taking the long (and unappealing) inland route via Longhoughton. You'll wish there was a public right of way along the meandering Howick Burn that connects the historic gardens at Howick with Sugar Sands. As it happens, you are permitted to walk its length, under certain conditions, enforced by a gate at the Howick Hall end. When the gardens are closed from November to January, the gate is always open and you can walk in either direction. When the gardens are open,

---

Rennington Scarecrow Festival

Rennington (a village between Alnwick and Craster) goes a little bit bonkers during the August Bank Holiday weekend. Scarecrows are out in force in almost every garden. Elvis, Harry Potter, R2-D2, Snow White and Pippa Middleton have all made appearances in recent years. 'It's a great fun event for all, celebrating eccentric English village life at its daftest,' say the organisers. Besides scarecrows, expect a hog roast, refreshments, stalls selling cake, plants and books, and a coconut shy as well as 'Splat the Rat' and 'Nail the Bale'. Whatever they might be, they sound like they might be fun.

the gate permits one-way travel (from the estate to the coast) for those who have paid to see the gardens.

A shorter circular route can be made from Craster to Howick Hall Gardens which excludes Sugar Sands (and the above mentioned gate), but does take in a good section of beautiful coastline. At Rumbling Kern, strike off inland on a lane towards Howick.

You'll need Ordnance Survey Explorer map 332 for this walk (and make sense of the gate business) from **Craster to Sugar Sands via Howick Hall Gardens**. For the reason stated above, you must walk anti-clockwise from February to November (ie: north up the coast on the return). Set foot from Whin Hill (behind the Craster smokehouse) and take the path that goes round the back of houses and skirts gorse-clad Howick Scar. Go under craggy Hips Heugh and approach Howick Hall along a quiet track from the north. After visiting Howick Hall Gardens, walk southeast out of the estate through woodland. When you meet a road, you'll see the one-way gate on the other side. Enjoy the Long Walk following Howick Burn on its winding course to the sea.

For Sugar Sands, cross the modern footbridge and walk south for a short while along the coast path. Before you do, those with an interest in ancient history might like to climb an **Iron Age earthwork**, accessed via a gate on the left just north of the footbridge. Good views of the coast all the way to Seahouses are had from the top of the earthwork (not particularly impressive in itself).

After Sugar Sands, return to Craster on the coast path, passing the Bath House at Rumbling Kern and the **Cullernose Point** bird cliffs where you'll see nesting fulmars and kittiwakes. An outstanding view of Dunstanburgh Castle enriches the return route for much of the way.

Food and drink

Picknickers are well catered for in Craster. Try opposite the harbour where there's a well-placed bench, or south of the village on the rocky shore beyond the playground. The smooth boulders here make good seats and you'll have a view of Dunstanburgh Castle.

Jolly Fisherman Haven Hill, NE66 3TR ① 01665 576461. Once a routine pub in a prime, seafront location and now an upmarket place to eat with an even more expansive view of Dunstanburgh Castle. The owners have built an outside terrace and brought in the decorators (and a very reputable chef). You'll still find old favourites like the crab soup, crab sandwiches and Craster kipper pâté (now served on an olive board with toasted soda bread).

Shoreline Café Corner of Church St and Haven Hill ① 01665 571251. Contemporary café with outdoor seating serving reasonably priced coffees, sandwiches and cakes. Good refuelling station for walkers on the coast path. Open daily.

Dunstanburgh Castle

Craster ① 01665 576231 Ⓦ www.english-heritage.org.uk. No road access (1½ mile-walk from Craster); open weekends in winter and daily from Apr–end Oct; toilets inside the castle; free entry for National Trust members; English Heritage.

Viewed from the north, Dunstanburgh is a shattered ruin clinging to the edge of a cliff formed of Whin Sill rock. Through sun haze or sea fret, the medieval edifice rarely looks anything but rough and moody: its crumbling turrets and curtain walls almost always seen in silhouette form. But from the south, Dunstanburgh bears its formidable chest, appearing more brutish – and terrifically romantic. The sight of the huge drum gate towers greeting the sun, and the sea pounding nearby rocks, cannot be beaten. It doesn't matter that most of the fortress has succumbed to the wind and sea and is now under the ownership of fulmars and kittiwakes.

But for all its might, the 14th-century stronghold of Thomas Earl of Lancaster, the richest man in England after the king, was more a show of power than an important military base. Dunstanburgh never came under attack by the Scots (though plenty of local inhabitants and their livestock were driven by Scottish raiders to within its protective walls); but it was besieged during the War of the Roses in 1462. On one of two attacks, the garrison, which had taken to eating their horses, only really surrendered to the Yorkists out of starvation. After the execution of Lancaster for treason, the castle was inherited by John of Gaunt, son of Edward III, who built a gateway bearing his name in the west curtain wall (still visible today). By the mid-1500s, Dunstanburgh was a ruin – in any case, after the Union of England and Scotland in 1603 it had become militarily redundant.

For a castle of which little remains, Dunstanburgh still holds its own in the line of Northumberland's great coastal fortresses. But, unlike Alnwick, Bamburgh or Lindisfarne, it has not been patched up or altered much over the centuries by its owners. You'll find, firstly, that most of what you see today dates

to its original construction in 1313, and secondly that there's not much to see behind its walls, besides a view of the coast from Liburn Tower and a number of medieval garderobes.

The legend of Sir Guy the Seeker – and his ghost which is said to haunt Dunstanburgh – is immortalised in a ballard that begins:

Sir Knight! Sir Knight! If your heart be right,
And your nerves be firm and true,
Sir Knight! Sir Knight! A beauty bright
In durance waits for you.

Searching for shelter one stormy night, the knight met with a wizard who ushered him through Dunstanburgh Castle to the bedside of a beautiful maiden lying asleep under a spell. She was guarded by two skeletons: one holding a sword and the other a horn. The fate of the maiden rested on the knight choosing the sword or the horn. He wrongly opted for the latter and spent the rest of his life being taunted by the wizard's words:

Now shame on the coward who sounded a horn
When he might have unsheathed a sword.

⑨ Embleton

Set back from the sea between Craster and Newton-by-the-Sea, Embleton draws in visitors because of its good range of holiday accommodation such as Embleton Mill Cottages (*www.embletonmillcottages.co.uk*) and its pleasing cluster of pubs and houses set around a triangular village green. Parts of the Holy Trinity Church, including the nave arcades, date from the 13th century, and the lower parts of the tower to even earlier.

Food and drink

If you're looking for a pub, the **Greys Inn** at the top end of the green is your best bet.

Eleanor's Byre Spitalford NE66 3DW ☏ 01665 571371. As you head south out of Embleton, you'll come to this unexpected café and pretty gift shop. Excellent coffee and a tranquil, sunny courtyard.

⑩ Low Newton-by-the-Sea

Newton hasn't always been so gentrified. Despite second home owners from Newcastle swallowing up the place and the reinvention of the much-loved shabby pub into more of an upmarket restaurant, the hamlet's square of whitewashed stone cottages about a green is still very appealing.

In 1859, the travel writer Walter White in *Northumberland, and the Border* observed boys coming and going from herring boats and the cottages in the square where 'women fling their household slops and fish offal' and 'are content to live within sight thereof.' White was not impressed. 'Newton is not pretty or pleasing', he wrote. He never would have guessed that 150 years later, well-off families would be hob-knobbing on the green, eating lobster in the pub, attending folk music concerts in the tiny corrugated iron church (tucked away by the side of the road as you enter Newton and, incidentally, bought in kit form over a hundred years ago), and paying extortionate prices to buy the holiday shacks in the dunes.

Fear not, Newton is hardly the Padstow of the north and even on hot days in summer, kite-boarders can still find an empty stretch of beach, and children can be lord of their own dune. Back in the 1980s, Newton was one of the first

Birdlife around Embleton Bay and Newton Haven

From the shoreline in summer, look out for gannets plunging into the sea in open water and terns cruising overhead (all five British breeding species could show up). Fulmars and kittiwakes nest on the cliffs under **Dunstanburgh Castle** and at **Cullernose Point** (south of Craster).

Behind the dunes and north of the boat park at **Newton Haven** is a large freshwater lake overlooked by a couple of bird hides (one is wheelchair-accessible). All the usual suspects are found here (coots, swans, geese and gulls). The surrounding damp fields are often more exciting, especially in winter when flocks of wading birds and migrating geese gather to feed. Don't overlook the scrubland as you walk to the bird hides; migrant passerines rest here in autumn on their journey south.

If you are walking north on the headland path from Newton to Beadnell, you may find yourself accompanied by the silver chain song of skylarks. In winter, the wave-washed rocks at **Newton Point** are reliable for eider ducks, lapwings, turnstones, red-breasted mergansers and even goosanders. Flocks of linnet, twite and goldfinch regularly pass overhead from September. The fields around **Newton Links** brim with golden plover, curlew and lapwing and you sometimes see ruff and bar-tailed godwit.

places to promote the then new sport of windsurfing (the windsurfing school has since closed but locals still refer to the large house next to the telephone box as the Windsurfing Centre).

The return **walk** to Dunstanburgh Castle and Craster is one of the most popular on the coast. It's around five miles and has all the ingredients of a perfect coastal trail: sandy beaches, a castle and a great pub at either end. It's straightforward to navigate: head south along the beach until Embleton Bay comes to an abrupt end by a mass of boulders. Climb onto the headland, skirting the golf course on your right and a World War II pillbox (one of many dotted around the Northumberland coast), and make your way under the castle walls to the south entrance. Note that a rivulet that runs across Embleton Bay can sometimes be crossed at low tide without taking off your boots; otherwise, go inland along the edge of the golf course and over a couple of little bridges.

If it really does get too crowded for you at Newton, wander north over the headland to **Football Hole** and hunker down in the dunes.

Food and drink

Joiners Arms High Newton-by-the-Sea NE66 3EA ☏ 01665 576112. There's a gastro pub feel to this revamped inn at the bottom of the hill as you approach Low Newton. Since it re-opened in 2011, it's always been busy and has gained a good reputation for its food. My cod and chips were spot on.

Ship Inn Low Newton-by-the-Sea NE66 3EL ⓣ 01665 576262
ⓦ www.shipinnnewton.co.uk. You may see a local fisherman walking up Newton
Haven beach with a few lobsters for the restaurant. It almost goes without saying
that if you want lobster for dinner, you'll need to put your order through in
advance. Apart from the supremely fresh seafood, most meats and dairy products
are also sourced in Northumberland and the beer comes from the onsite brewery.
Unsurprisingly, the Ship is always overflowing with cheerful families and walkers.
What's not to like? Fighting for a table.

⑪ Preston Tower

Preston (near Cathill) ⓣ 01665 589227 ⓦ www.prestontower.co.uk; open daily until
dusk or 18.00, whichever is earlier.

A well-preserved medieval tower dating to 1392 stands in landscaped parkland
just a couple of miles southwest of Beadnell. Very few fortified towers quite
as special as this are open to the public and provide such a vivid sense of the
border clashes that were so frequent in Northumbria until the 17th century.
Rooms are furnished with items typical of the period, including animal skins,
wood stools and a spinning wheel. I like the way you are free to visit on any
day and enjoy the tower at leisure; just remember to switch off the light when
you leave.

Though Preston Tower looks like a complete building, it is in fact one half
of a four turreted 'castle', part of which was pulled down when the threat of
violence from marauding clans waned. At one time the entrance would have
been on the first floor (accessed by way of ladders which were then lifted off
the ground). Livestock were housed on the ground floor. The slit windows and
seven-foot thick walls would have been very difficult to penetrate.

From the turrets, you can see all the way to the sea (the coastguard cottage at
Newton-by-the-Sea is just visible). A clear highlight is the 1864 **clock** which,
the information panel tells you, has a similar mechanism to Big Ben. On the
hour, cogs start spinning and a metal arm is depressed, triggering another lever
that pulls a cord that moves the hammer which strikes the deafening half-ton
bell at the top of the tower – to the great excitement of children and adults
alike. The dilemma you'll have is whether to watch the whirring mechanism

Dune flowers

In late summer, bloody crane's-bill puts on a deep pink-purple display among the
marram grass, sea campion and the odd burnet rose. The grasslands behind the
Beadnell Bay dunes are covered in pyramidal orchids in localised areas (visible
from the coast path from June to August). Lindisfarne's dunes are particularly
well known for their orchids. At Newton, the herb-rich meadow below the old
coastguard cottage, flowers with kidney vetch, clovers, knapweed and buttercup,
drawing in many bees and butterflies.

or experience the powerful, bone-vibrating gong of the bell. Fortunately, you can see both if you are quick enough up the stairs (be careful – there's no hand rail at the top). Note that there's a pause between the when mechanism kicks into gear and when it really gets going. I stood for what felt like a few minutes with my hands clasped over my ears waiting for the bell to strike.

Three short **trails** lead around the estate, providing a view of the mansion house, built in 1802, and the mature ornamental trees including redwoods and a beautiful copper beech.

⑫ Beadnell

Beadnell has two pleasant enough historic areas (the harbour and village) connected by a number of sprawling roads with modern houses. This one-time fishing village is now mainly a holiday area which boasts one of the most unspoilt sandy beaches in the North East. The **village centre** is set back from the seafront at the northern end of the village.

Those who make the approach on foot from the south across Beadnell Bay will find the knot of curious buildings above the tiny **harbour** rather appealing. They include 18th-century lime kilns, a turreted stone guesthouse and a 13th-century chapel, now completely ruined. If you continue north along Harbour Road with the sea to your right, you'll come across a couple of ramshackle 19th-century fishermen's huts (there used to be more but some were demolished in 2011). Unfortunately they are not protected and are in a poor state of repair. Below them is **Beadnell Haven**, once used by fishermen (see box opposite).

Beadnell Bay

A pristine sandy beach padded with dunes and lapped by sapphire-blue water is not easily found anywhere in England, but to come across one as crowd-free as Beadnell is rare indeed. Families, walkers and birdwatchers will love it here.

Halfway along is Long Nanny – an inlet by a hut which is well-known for its colony of around 700–900 pairs of **arctic terns** that nest in the dune grasses. It's probably the largest colony on mainland Britain. The hut is manned by National Trust wardens round the clock and it is the best place to watch the birds at close range without disturbing them. Sometimes they land on the fence right in front of you. A handful of little terns (Britain's second rarest breeding seabird after the roseate tern) also nest here.

⑬ Seahouses

Seahouses is a bustling fishing town, now busier with tourists popping into gift shops for buckets and spades than with fishermen, but its harbour is still very much a working port. Ten fishing vessels were docked when I last visited and, as always, the lobster pots were stacked on the harbour wall. A couple of fishermen with caps and waterproofs stood around chatting: a timeless scene.

One of the greatest pleasures at Seahouses is to sit on the terrace of benches

Fishing heritage

Katrina Porteous, local historian and editor of The Bonny Fisher Lad

Most of north Northumberland's coastal villages have been strongly shaped by fishing. Traditionally this was carried out from 'cobles', small open wooden boats launched from the beach. The fishing year was divided into the winter season, when long lines were used to catch cod and haddock, and summer, when herring were caught using drift nets. All the family was involved: women sold fish inland and, with their children, gathered mussels and limpets to bait the 1,400 hooks of each line.

Herring became a major industry from the early 19th century, and villages such as Seahouses prospered. In summer the men fished at night, and women worked in teams, gutting and packing herring into barrels for export, or smoking them as 'kippers'. Although herring are no longer caught locally, Craster and Seahouses still have active smokehouses. In **Seahouses** the remains of several 19th-century herring yards can be seen, now converted into cottages. Walk along South Street looking for blocked-off 'bowly-holes' in the walls, where cartloads of herring were shovelled into troughs for gutting. Nearby, the gateway of Chapel Row is marked by grooves made by generations of fisherwomen sharpening their limpet-picking tools on their way to the rocks.

On **Lindisfarne**, at the Castle and the Ouse, old upturned herring drifters are used as sheds, and on Harbour Road at **Beadnell** two tarry fishermen's huts, now disused, mark the Haven where cobles were launched. Near them, beside the footpath to the sea, stand the remains of a row of 18th-century 'bark-pots'. These square structures consisted of a hearth, chimney and large metal tank, and were used to boil nets, ropes and sails in a tannin-rich liquid to preserve them. This seashore is full of hidden clues to its past, such as mussel-beds, lobster ponds and rectangular troughs called 'bratt holes', only visible at low tide, where fish were stored for live export in sailing sloops to London.

Today, fishing on this coast has greatly diminished. Where it still exists, it is mostly confined to catching crabs and lobsters. But look out for cobles still working traditional summer salmon nets in Boulmer Haven.

facing the harbour eating some of the best fish and chips you will find anywhere in the UK.

Seahouses grew as a holiday resort in the 1920s. Then, as now, the Farne Islands are the reason many people came here and today you'll find a number of boat tour companies by the RNLI building on the harbour. Opposite the kiosks are Seahouses's well-preserved **lime kilns**, dating to 1841. As at Beadnell and Lindisfarne they were ideally situated for the easy transportation of lime by boat.

A short **walk** south from the harbour along a row of cottages lined with starlings and jackdaws provides a good view of Bamburgh Castle and the Farne Islands. Depending on whether the tide is high or low, there are between 15 and 28 islands in the chain. On **South Street** you'll see evidence of the 19th- and 20th-century fishing industry, including a very old smokehouse known as the Fisherman's Kitchen (see below). Continuing south on the headland, the wind picks up as you press on to Beadnell Bay.

Food and drink

Neptune's or Pinnacles for fish and chips? That's the dilemma that faces every visitor to Seahouses. I usually opt for a take-away from **Pinnacles** on Main Street (*01665 720708*) and plonk myself on one of the benches overlooking the harbour, but **Neptune's** (*01665 721310*) on the other side of the road has a pleasant dining area where you might want to shelter if the fog is rolling in off the sea. Really, you can't go wrong anywhere in Seahouses: the fish comes straight off the boats a few hundred yards away and most restaurants have had decades of perfecting the batter.

The Fisherman's Kitchen 2 South St, NE68 7RB ① 01665 721052 ⓦ www.swallowfish.co.uk. Herring have been smoked here since 1843. It's worth visiting the smokehouse even just to see the old photos on the wall above an old iron range, and herring baskets and anchors hanging from the ceiling. You can buy everything you need for a fish BBQ: locally caught mackerel, scallops, king prawns, whole crab and lobster.

Olde Ship Inn Main St, NE68 7RD ① 01665 720200. This is a great seafarers' pub with bags of character (and nautical artefacts), overlooking the harbour. Expect real ales, an open fire, a beer garden and convivial chatter.

⑭ Farne Islands

① 01665 720651 ⓦ www.nationaltrust.org.uk; toilets on Inner Farne; no refreshments; National Trust. Boat trips depart hourly Apr–Oct 10.00–15.00 (weather depending) and can be booked from the kiosks at Seahouses harbour. Note most seabirds will have left the islands before the end of summer. Eider ducks, cormorants, shags and seals are seen year round, and winter migrants from early autumn. Allow for a round trip (including the Inner Farne stop off) of 3 hours. Boat prices do not include admission onto the island, which must be paid to the National Trust on landing. Birdwatchers and photographers may want to combine a trip to Inner Farne with Staple Island.

'A boat may be secured for fifteen shillings. In addition to this charge, the boatmen expect to be provided with refreshments, solid and liquid.' Visitors to the Farne Islands no longer need to supply the skippers of the Seahouses tour boats with food and drink, as they did in the late 19th century when the above advice was penned in a guidebook. But, little else has changed here since Victorian tourists came to experience the famous bird islands.

Everyone who has visited these rocky isles scattered a couple of miles northeast of Seahouses will remember ducking and flinching from the dive-bombing arctic terns. A wave of the hands usually keeps the birds, which are ever so protective of their chicks running at your feet, from striking, but you might want to wear a hat just in case.

From the moment you step ashore, you'll see puffins crash-landing with beaks stuffed full of sand eels, terns wheeling in the sky or spearing fish from the sea, cormorants sitting proud on their castles of dried seaweed, and guillemots standing on rock stacks painted white with guano. There is no other wildlife experience quite like this anywhere else in Northumberland.

But only for a few months of the year. Come mid-August, the birds depart for open waters, abandoning their empty nests to the wind and sea.

The islands are divided into two main groups by Staple Sound. Inner Farne, the closest island to the mainland, is of most interest to visitors and is also the disembarking point for boat tours. Boardwalks guide visitors on a half-mile long circular walk around the island. Tens of thousands of puffins nest here in burrows they dig themselves (not old rabbit burrows as is sometimes thought), while razorbill, kittiwakes and guillemots lay their eggs on the columnar sea-facing rocks (part of the Great Whin Sill that peaks in several places along the Northumberland coast). Sea campion covers much of the ground that isn't bare rock.

Inner Farne was inhabited by hermits and monks for 900 years; the most well-known was Cuthbert, who lived twice on the island, before and after he became Bishop of Lindisfarne. The second time, in AD687, he returned to his much-loved sanctuary to die. The only other person to have lived on the island for as long as Cuthbert is the lively National Trust Head Ranger, David Steel.

Cuddy's Duck

Several hundred eider ducks nest on the Farne Islands. Most of them inhabit Inner Farne, where they have received sanctuary for over 1,300 years ever since St Cuthbert lived here in the 7th century. The saint afforded the ducks special protection and is sometimes referred to as the first bird conservationist. His love of eiders is the reason why Cuthbert is sometimes depicted with the bird at his feet and the origins of the local name: Cuddy's Duck.

Nothing remains of Cuthbert's simple shelter and prayer room, but you will see a few old stone buildings, including a chapel built around 1300. The 17th-century wood stalls inside came from Durham Cathedral.

Two lighthouses still operate on the Farne Islands, both dating to the early 1800s. The red and white beacon on Longstone is the famous 'Grace Darling lighthouse' from where the lighthouse keeper and his daughter rowed through a storm on 7th September 1838 to the aid of the survivors of a shipwreck (see box opposite). In the years after the rescue, Victorian tourists would visit the famous family at the lighthouse and delight in hearing of the extraordinary event first hand. Today, you'll need to visit the Grace Darling Museum in Bamburgh.

⑮ Bamburgh

The wind can really kick up on the wide, long bay connecting Seahouses and Bamburgh and you can find yourself walking through streamers of sand being blown lengthways down the beach like wisps of smoke. The bracing walk is rewarded with the sight of Bamburgh Castle rising majestically from the dunes – all rock, turrets and battlements. It is undoubtedly one of Britain's most romantic castles and this is one of the most unspoilt and dramatic coastal panoramas with the Farne Islands visible to the south and Lindisfarne Castle silhouetted on its rocky perch to the north. The view is most expansive from the castle's Battery Terrace.

In the **village**, the castle maintains its heavy presence despite keeping close watch over the North Sea. My 19th-century travel guide describes Bamburgh as 'clean and cheerful' and a 'model village'. Nothing has changed in that respect. The village centre is almost entirely made of stone and centred about a wooded green. Two roads fork either side of the trees; the southern one (Front Street), being the most touristy on account of its pleasing run of 18th-century stone cottages, red telephone box and pillarbox, eateries, pubs and B&Bs.

Keep heading up hill and you'll reach **Bamburgh Gallery** on Lucker Road (*01668 214420; Apr–Oct open daily, Nov–Mar Thu–Sun*), the sister studio to the Chatton Gallery near Wooler. Most works are by the celebrated landscape painter, Robert Turnbull and wildlife artist, Zana Juppeniatz.

Bamburgh does get a little crowded in summer, but if you're feeling hemmed in, just wander down to the generous beach or cycle along **The Wynding** (a quiet paved lane north out of the village that hugs the seafront and provides a superb view of the coastline all the way to a light beacon and golf course). Walkers can continue ahead to Budle Point and drop down onto the sandy shore. A beach towel comes in handy here.

Facing the sea to the northwest of the village on Radcliffe Road, is the modern RNLI station and enchanting **Grace Darling Museum** (*01668 214910; www. rnli.org.uk/gracedarling*) that perpetuates the memory of the Victorian heroine who helped saved shipwrecked passengers off the Farne Islands. The collection of memorabilia in the small museum is elegantly presented. You'll find out about events on that fateful night, the life of the lighthouse keeper and his family and Grace's rise to fame in the years following the rescue – an intriguing tale in itself.

The main exhibit is the famous Darling rowing boat, a shapely old coble and object of great beauty. Around the boat are paintings depicting the rescue, including Carmichael's romantic scene of Grace and her father rowing through violent waters away from the lighthouse. Also on display are letters and clothes such as Grace's black cloak.

Next door but one is **3 Radcliffe Road**, where Grace was born (a plaque above the doorway gives the date: 24 November 1815) and, in the churchyard opposite, is where she is buried, facing the sea, as is fitting.

Grace Darling

I had little thought of anything but to exert myself to the utmost, my spirit was worked up by the sight of such a dreadful affair that I can imagine I still see the sea flying over the vessel.

From a letter by Grace Darling in her namesake museum at Bamburgh

In the early hours of 7th September 1838, the paddle steamer SS *Forfarshire* hit the corner of Big Harcar off the Farne Islands. Knowing that the lifeboat from Seahouses would not be able to reach the stricken vessel in such poor conditions, William Darling, the lighthouse keeper on Longstone Island, launched his wooden rowing boat and, with the help of his daughter, Grace, they rowed for a mile to reach the nine shipwrecked survivors. If you take a boat trip to the Farne Islands, you will know how choppy the waters around the islands can get so you can imagine how rowing through a storm in a wooden rowing boat would have been difficult and dangerous. The Darling's boat could only carry five passengers so a second trip was made until all survivors were brought to the lighthouse.

Following the rescue, the story was widely printed in the papers and it seems the Victorian readership couldn't get enough of the romantic tale of the lighthouse keeper's daughter, who became famous in her lifetime. She sat for endless portraits and received many gifts including £50 from Queen Victoria. Four years later, she died of tuberculosis aged 26. Her story endures, though the events and Grace's character have been much romanticised. Wordsworth penned the following verse, an extract of which appears on a memorial on the Farne Islands:

Pious and pure, modest and yet so brave,
Though young so wise, though meek so resolute —
Might carry to the clouds and to the stars,
Yea, to celestial Choirs, Grace Darling's name!

Her **grave** is reached by following the trampled grassy trail to a large Gothic memorial (rebuilt in 1993 to the same design as the older sandstone structure that had become worn by the weather).

Inside **St Aidan's Church**, Grace Darling is represented in a series of stained glass windows in a small chapel to the left of the altar. She stands in one looking like a goddess with, strangely, blond curly hair and is only identifiable by the oar on her arm. The words 'charity', 'fortitude' and 'hope' appear beneath the three main figures.

The church dates for the most part from the end of the 12th century and is notable for many reasons, including its long chancel (the size of some parish churches) and many arcades. It stands on the site of a much earlier church founded by St Aidan in 635. The only relic from that time is thought to be the wooden girder in the baptistery. According to legend, it was the same beam that the saint died leaning against and is said to have survived two fires.

Bamburgh Castle

Bamburgh NE69 7DF ① 01668 214515 ⑩ www.bamburghcastle.com; open daily from mid Feb–end Oct and weekends at other times; good café in the Clock Tower.

Many writers and architectural historians have declared Bamburgh the most wondrous of all England's coastal castles. You may well agree when you see the mighty edifice strikingly situated on a fist of dolerite rock thrust 150 feet from sea level through sand dunes. Bamburgh is certainly the stuff of fairy tales.

Its enviable situation proved a valuable vantage point for settlers from ancient times and almost certainly the Romans. From the Anglo-Saxon period to the present day, Vikings, kings, earls and dukes have seized, pounded and abandoned the castle in various states of ruin. Some of the Anglo-Saxon objects

Whales, porpoises and seals

I've seen the odd **minke whale** and **porpoise** while boating offshore from Newton, but it's just luck whether you happen to see one from the headland. A local cetacean enthusiast told me he once saw a dozen white-beaked dolphins off the coast of Bamburgh. He described the sight as 'like a Miami marine park'. Northern Wildlife Tours (*01670 827465; www.northernexperiencewildlifetours. co.uk*) run special pelagic boat trips from Seahouses and North Shields near Newcastle to look for cetaceans and seabirds. More reliable are the **grey seals** that bask on the outermost Emblestone rocks at Newton-by-the-Sea. You will always see them on a boat trip to the Farne Islands or Coquet Island and on sand banks near Lindisfarne. Occasionally in autumn white pups lie on the beach (I've even come across them on the causeway to Lindisfarne). Some well-meaning people shoo them back into the sea not realising that they are resting and should be left alone.

retrieved from the fortress are on display inside the castle's Archaeology Room, including part of a stone throne.

After the Viking raids, the Normans rebuilt the castle in stone. The keep you see today dates to the reign of Henry II. Bamburgh stood strong for several hundred years and survived invasions from north of the border until 1464 when its walls were razed by the Earl of Warwick during the Battle of the Roses. Connoisseurs of trivia will take pleasure in knowing that Bamburgh was the first castle in England to surrender to gunfire.

The fortress was extensively rebuilt in the 18th century and contains later additions, such as the stables, added by the Victorian industrialist Lord Armstrong, whose family has owned the castle ever since. Much of the interior dates to this period, including the **King's Hall** (the former banqueting hall), a magnificent wood-panelled room of ballroom proportions with a false hammer-beam roof and stained glass. A newspaper report from 1932 describes the annual Bamburgh Castle Ball as 'a beautiful fashion parade at which quite the most swagger gowns imaginable were worn'. As a rule of thumb, the pinkish outer walls are medieval, and those with a grey hue are Victorian.

In addition to the King's Hall, don't miss the **views** from the **Court Room** and the intriguing **bottle-shaped doorway** at the bottom of the stairs. This allowed knights on horseback to swiftly enter the building without having to dismount (how's that for style?). The **Billiard Room** and adjoining **Faire Chamber** evoke the era of high society social events where aristocratic men played pool in one room and ladies gossiped in the sumptuous surroundings of the chamber next door. You can almost hear the ladies chatting, and smell the tobacco smoke wafting through from the Billiard Room.

Food and drink

You'll find a couple of **tea rooms** on Front Street. For **picnic food**, try the tumbledown **greengrocer** opposite the church. Out the back there are crates and carts stuffed with plants for sale and an old man of an apple tree standing among fallen fruit. Also try **Carters** ('Butcher Baker Sausage Roll Maker') on Front Street. A board in the window reads: 'Home to the original prize winning Bamburgh Banger. Available by the ton'. **The Pantry**, also on Front Street, has a good deli. Grace Darling died here in 1842. For a drink, try the **Victoria Hotel** further up Front Street (also good B&B accommodation).

Mizen Head Lucker Rd, NE69 7BS ① 01668 214256 ⑩ www.mizen-head.co.uk. 'You can't get fresher', the manager says of the hotel's seafood dishes which are prepared using produce straight from the North Sea, including oysters from Lindisfarne, Craster kippers and salmon. The restaurant is incorporated into the hotel which was being refurbished at the time of writing to give it more of a boutique finish. When I visited, the rooms were quite plush and hardly looked in need of redecorating.

⑯ Budle Bay

By road from Bamburgh to Belford or on the coastal footpath, you gain far-reaching views of the swirling sand and mudflats sheltered in this deep, wide bay. Non-birdwatchers travelling with birders in autumn and winter beware: from here to Lindisfarne and beyond is serious binocular and field guide country. One of the best places to see some of the thousands of ducks, geese and waders that descend on the flats is from the roadside path and pull-in areas along the coast road east of Waren Mill. As the tide comes in, the birds are pushed closer to land.

The large corn mill which gives **Waren Mill** its name has been converted into domestic dwellings (and rental accommodation) and stands overlooking the head of the bay. South of the settlement is a wooded dene, to the east of which are the **Spindlestones Heughs** crags, and to the west, a tall dovecote, now a holiday cottage (see page 60). There are a couple of caravan parks and campsites in the area, none of which hold huge appeal, except for their proximity to the coast.

Ross Sands

The beach at Ross is a gloriously deserted sandy spit that extends for three breezy miles from Budle Bay almost to Lindisfarne. Access is via a mile-long footpath (no bicycles allowed) through Ross Farm and across the dunes, which puts off the few travellers who venture to this remote place. Your reward is an unbeatable panorama: all sky, sea and white sands with Lindisfarne Castle at one end and Bamburgh Castle and the Farne Islands at the other. One Saturday afternoon in winter, I walked for over two hours without seeing another person.

Those binoculars will come in handy again, both to check out the seals lazing on sand humps opposite Lindisfarne Castle and to scan the sea for divers, grebes and scoters in winter, and terns in summer. Also in winter, check the dunes for snow bunting, twite and any other migrants taking refuge. At the northern end of the spit on **Guile Point** (out of bounds from May to July because of nesting birds) you'll see two triangular navigation towers.

Lindisfarne Oysters

Oysters have been harvested for hundreds of years on the mudflats of Lindisfarne. Past owners of the oyster beds include the monks on Lindisfarne in the 14th century and a Victorian landowner. The industry died out but was resurrected in 1989 by a local farmer who spotted oyster shells on the sand. Current owners, Christopher Sutherland and his wife, Helen, inherited the business in 2003. You can buy their oysters at the Lindisfarne Oysters smokehouse in Seahouses, online, or direct from Ross Farm (between Budle Bay and Lindisfarne) if ordered in advance (*01668 213870; www.lindisfarneoysters.co.uk*).

They help keep mariners on the right course through the dangerous waters which have claimed many boats, including the remains of two shipwrecks you see by walking the length of the beach. From the main access point onto the sands (roughly the midway point of the spit) the towers look deceptively close but they take over an hour to reach.

Many years ago, a boat used to transfer pedestrians to Lindisfarne. The sand flats at low tide are, like at Budle Bay, perilous, and should not be crossed on foot. Another word of caution: make a mental picture of where the footpath enters the beach (currently marked with a large bough forced deep in the sand), as it is difficult to find on your return.

⑰ Belford

Since the A1 was diverted away from this market town between the coast and the Cheviot Hills, it's become very quiet in Belford … The High Street is a long row of grey stone houses curving away from the top of the village.

Someone very interested in local history in Belford has put together a number of informative guides to the buildings and old ways of life. You'll find them in the excellent **Belford Craft Gallery** (*01668 213888; www.belfordcraftgallery. com; open Tue–Sat and Sun afternoons*) on Market Place. I was impressed by the large collection of crafts, paintings and local history books and pamphlets on display and definitely recommend stopping here. It's good to see specialist shops like **Border Stoves and Cookers** on the High Street. Now you know where to come next time you need a new log basket or hearth brush.

St Cuthbert's Cave

Northwest of Belford, St Cuthbert's Way long-distance path from the Cheviot Hills to Lindisfarne passes a small wood near Holburn Grange (four miles west of Budle Bay) where there's a cave made of boulders. Monks carrying Cuthbert's body are said to have rested here when they fled from Viking invaders on Lindisfarne at the end of the 9th century. A grassy track leads steeply uphill from a car park at Holburn Grange. If you continue on the St Cuthbert's Way over the hills, you gain a spectacular panorama of Lindisfarne and Bamburgh.

⑱ Lindisfarne (Holy Island)

Lindisfarne Castle seemingly rises out of the sea off the coast of north Northumberland, but from the causeway that connects the island to the mainland at low tide, it sinks out of view and the island as a whole appears as a long grey-green streak across a glistening expanse of sea and sandflats.

When the tide retreats, it exposes the causeway and a seabed that stretches for what appears to be several miles, though it is impossible to tell where it meets the sea when the tide is out. Even when it's overcast, the reflected light is sharp and the sky perfectly mirrored in the flat, silvery expanse. Seals rest on exposed sandbanks here.

The wildlife of Lindisfarne

Ducks, wading birds and geese begin arriving from late summer and early autumn on the grazing marshes, dunes and tidal mudflats surrounding Lindisfarne island where they spend the winter. Most of the time they are busy prodding the mud for food or avoiding death by peregrine. On the occasions that a raptor does swoop by (sparrowhawk and hen harrier are also possible) a pandemonium of birds takes to the sky.

There are so many vantage points, but some trusted favourites are the mainland shores of the **Fenham Flats** where shelduck, redshank, wigeon, bar-tailed godwit and curlew congregate in good numbers. This is a favourite feeding area for Brent geese. You can walk along the shore here though the ground is very muddy. Thrushes gorge on berries in the thorn hedges by the shore (this being many migrants' first fuelling station since departing Scandinavia).

Lindisfarne causeway (from the bridge) is good for close up views of waders and ducks on your way to the island, as are the damp **fields** on the left as you walk to the castle (masses of teal, wigeon, lapwing and golden plover here). If walking across the island's **dunes** in November and December you have a very good chance of seeing the day-flying short-eared owl. The last time I visited, I saw at least three individuals here.

The reserve is also known for its grey seals and flowering plants. Dunes on the northwest side of Lindisfarne island blossom with orchids in summer. Look out for the purple northern marsh and early marsh orchids as well as the Lindisfarne helleborine and marsh helleborines, which are well distributed.

For ducks and waders, the mudflats are a giant bird table with enough marine creatures on offer to support tens of thousands of birds. Their numbers swell from early autumn until spring when over-wintering migrant birds from the continent join in the banquet.

Lindisfarne is best known as a place of **Christian pilgrimage**. For over 1,000 years, worshippers have arrived on the island by foot over the mudflats – a tradition that continues today by following a line of posts that steer walkers around dangerous quicksands.

A monastic community led by St Aidan was established on Lindisfarne under the instruction of Oswald, King of Northumbria, in AD635. St Cuthbert came to the island 50 years later when he left the Farne Islands to become Bishop of Lindisfarne. On Cuthbert's death in 687, his body remained perfectly preserved – an apparent miracle that inspired thousands of pilgrims to travel to the island, and the creation of the celebrated Lindisfarne Gospels.

Danish raids forced the monks of Lindisfarne to flee the island, carrying Cuthbert's coffin and the gospels. Over a hundred years later they finally came to rest in Durham where a shrine was constructed that was later rebuilt (the same magnificent Norman cathedral you see today). The Viking invaders are depicted on a 9th-century stone carving, now housed in the **Lindisfarne Priory Museum**, which shows a line of rudimentary figures waving swords and axes.

Most visitors arrive by car and some take the infrequent 477 bus from Berwick (*www.perrymansbuses.co.uk*) to the **village centre** where there's a lively local community, post office, a few eateries, pubs, holiday cottages and a couple of places offering B&B accommodation. Opposite the village green is **St Aidan's Winery** (*01289 389230; www.lindisfarne-mead.co.uk*), distillers of the famous Lindisfarne Mead. The **Lindisfarne Centre** (*01289 389004; www. holy-island.info/lhc*) on Marygate serves as a **tourist information centre** and has an excellent bookshop and three exhibition spaces, one of which is devoted to the story of the Lindisfarne Gospels and includes a facsimile of the AD698 illuminated manuscript.

The ruins of the early 12th-century **Lindisfarne Priory** (*01289 389200; www.english-heritage.org.uk*) and 13th-century parish church face each other on the southwestern tip of the island, just a few steps away from the village green. Nearly 900 years of wind and rain as well as damage during the Reformation have badly worn the stones of the arcades and arches of the priory, which was founded by Benedictine monks from Durham Cathedral. Enough structures and geometric patterns remain to appreciate the layout of the building and recognise its architecture as Norman – and even to notice similarities with the nave at Durham. At dusk, the naturally blushed sandstones deepen in colour to that of a red night sky. The view from the churchyard looking over the gravestones with the priory to the left and the castle and boats in the bay to the right, is exceptionally picturesque.

The oldest parts of **St Mary's Church** date from the time of St Aidan in the 7th century, but most of it is 13th century. Notice the different style of

Lindisfarne Gospels

It is remarkable that this exquisite illuminated manuscript survived 600 years of battles, invasions and unrest in this once lawless region. The gospels are considered one of the most treasured religious and artistic works in the UK and for that reason are stored for safe-keeping at the British Museum in London. Durham Cathedral, Chester-le-Street and Lindisfarne all have facsimiles of the book; the latter is displayed in the Lindisfarne Centre on Marygate. The highly decorative pages were painted using animal and vegetable dyes in one unified style by Eadfrith who was Bishop of Lindisfarne in the late 7th and early 8th centuries.

the facing arcades: the arches on the south side are pointed and date from the 13th century while those on the north aisle are Romanesque. There's an eye-catching stained glass window above the north altar of fishermen, and 20th-century glass in the west wall depicting St Aidan and St Cuthbert. The wood sculpture of monks carrying Cuthbert's coffin is identical to the bronze version in Durham city. They mark the start and end points of the monks' journey.

A circular walk of Lindisfarne

It only takes a couple of hours to complete the six-mile round-island trail. It's a beautiful walk with almost constant views of the castle, sea and dunes, and culminates in the priory and castle. You hardly need a map for this walk; just a sense of the shape of the island and the location of the village and castle in relation to the dunes and causeway.

A few yards south of the first ticketed car park you come to on reaching the island, there's a footpath by a kissing gate that crosses into farmland and over dunes. On veering right through the dunes, you soon reach a quiet sandy bay on the north side of the island. Cross the beach and climb up to a white triangle day marker that serves as a warning to passing boats.

Turn southwards and follow the field edge with the sea to your left and castle ahead. The Farne Islands, Bamburgh Castle and the Cheviots are all within view. A lough with a **bird hide** is reached by a footpath off to the right. Continue straight ahead for the castle.

The path curves towards **lime kilns** on a raised embankment (an old waggonway that was used during the late 19th century for the transport of lime). According to the National Trust who care for the kilns, they are some of the best examples of Victorian lime kilns anywhere in England. Kilns are also located at Castle Point on the northwest of the island, though they are not so well preserved. Also note the remains of two timber jetties – or staiths – near to the gate at the bottom of the castle path. Lime was loaded onto moored ships from wagons which ran along the structures.

The three upturned boat hulls (now storage sheds) are a cherished feature of the Lindisfarne landscape. Two were destroyed by fire in 2005 but have been replaced. The path to the left leads to the castle. To the right of the castle in farmland is a pretty little **garden** designed by Gertrude Jekyll in 1911 and protected on four sides by a drystone wall. Roses, sweet peas, fuchsias and delphiniums bring colour and scent to the isolated enclosure in summer. The story of the garden's creation and restoration to the original layout is told in an informative leaflet you can pick up near the shed.

From the castle, continue downhill towards the village centre, passing the harbour on your left. A pleasant approach to the priory and village green is made by walking around the harbour and up and over the grassy heugh. Skirt the priory and turn right onto Church Lane from where you'll find the entrance to the ecclesiastical buildings.

Lindisfarne Castle

① 01289 389244 ⑩ www.nationaltrust.org.uk; check website or call for opening times (dependent on the tides), generally open daily (except Mon, Mar–Oct) and only on selected weekends in winter; National Trust flag flies when castle is open; National Trust.

Lindisfarne Castle crowns a conical-shaped mound of Whin Sill rock on the south of the island. The Tudor fortress appears to naturally emerge from the dolerite, rather than being built upon it, which is all rather pleasing from a visitor's point of view. The castle dates from 1542 and was fortified in Elizabeth I's reign but the strength of the impenetrable-looking walls has never been fully tested. Two Jacobites held the castle for a couple of days during the uprising of 1715, having taken the garrison by surprise, but they were quickly removed from the castle and imprisoned.

For many visitors, the most intriguing period in the building's history was the evolution of the castle into an Edwardian house by architect Edwin Lutyens under the instruction of Edward Hudson, editor of *Country Life* magazine. Domestic rooms were created in every chamber and connected by way of passages.

The interior has much rustic appeal and is simply furnished, including with items designed by Lutyens. Uncluttered rooms allow appreciation of details like the arcades, spiral staircases, vaulted ceilings and patterned flooring made with bricks arranged in herringbone formation (a Lutyens trademark). 'I want to amuse myself with the place', said Edward Hudson. He certainly did that – not just in transforming the castle, but by holding summer parties.

Lindisfarne causeway

It's frustrating to reach the causeway to find you've missed the safe crossing time by minutes, but don't be tempted to blast across. I can say from experience that the safe crossing times listed on the information board at either side of the crossing are very accurate, having myself made a foolish dash for it many years ago in a car and almost conked out. I was not ten minutes over the safe crossing limit, but the sea was already rushing across the paved track frighteningly quickly. There is a refuge on stilts for those who don't make it. The RNLI will take care of you, but your car will be washed away. A record 24 cars were abandoned in 2011. Plan ahead by checking the timetable online at www.northumberlandlife.org/holy-island.

Walkers following the **pilgrims' way** across the tidal mudflats should be very cautious. It takes around an hour to walk the three miles from the mainland to the island (following the line of posts so as to avoid dangerous quicksands). This should only be attempted if you can reach the other side by the mid-point of the safe crossing period. There is a refuge accessed by ladders halfway across.

Food and drink

A couple of cafés and two very average pubs serve food. **Pilgrims Coffee House** on Marygate is home to the best latte on the island. For evening meals (*May–Oct*), try the **Bean Goose Restaurant** (*01289 389083*) which serves up local lobster, crab, fish and beef from the Borders.

Barn at Beal Beal Farm, TD15 2PB ① 01289 540044 ⑩ www.barnatbeal.com; open daily until 16.00/17.00 winter/summer and in the evenings at weekends. On the approach to Lindisfarne Causeway, travellers pass this large eatery housed in a modernised 19th-century cart shed which stands on a hill gazing at the island. Monks at Lindisfarne Priory are said to have kept their beehives here. The busy café/restaurant serves excellent reasonably priced hot and cold lunches made with local meats, cheeses and fish. Next door is a bird of prey centre.

⑲ Berwick-upon-Tweed

The salmon-fishers rowing in their boats from Spittal Snook, looked strange and spectral through the mist; and if Tweed had anything to say concerning his birthplace in the western hills, and his travel along the Border land, it was stifled by the gloom, and I heard it not.
Walter White *Northumberland and the Border*, 1859

Salmon are still caught on the Tweed in the time-honoured way using traditional wooden boats and nets, but on a sunny day, the river is nothing like as brooding as the description above. The same is true of the town itself, which is really a very cheerful-looking place with its red-tiled Georgian houses gathered along the river's edge and large colony of swans. The approach from the south is made all the more memorable by an old stone bridge that skims across the water in 15 low leaps leading you into the centre of Berwick in the most pleasing of ways.

Berwick has an uneasy identity because of its position on the wrong side of the river. Scottish or English? A lot of folk to the north and south are never quite sure because the northern banks of the Tweed are in Scotland, except at Berwick. At least that's the case today. But, this is a town that has yo-yoed from one side of the border to the other some 13 times. It doesn't help that Berwick's football team plays in the Scottish division and the town has various other allegiances to north of the border. It's understandable therefore why many locals don't affiliate themselves to either country, preferring the description: 'Berwicker'. Their accent is equally non-committal: neither Northumbrian nor Scottish Borders (I think more Scottish, but a Highlander may beg to differ).

Border disputes in the Middle Ages eventually led to the complete fortification of the town under Elizabeth 1. These distinctive 16th-century century **ramparts** remain largely intact and are said to make Berwick an outstanding example of a fortified town.

A wander around Berwick

From a visitor's point of view, the ramparts encircling the town make a great walk offering views through Berwick's streets. This is the best way to get to know England's northernmost town. Without deviation, the circuit takes an hour or so, but most likely you'll want to hop off and on and see places of interest as you go. Information panels explain the form of the curtain wall, moat and impressive artillery bastions.

Starting at the eastern ramparts, your first calling point should be **Berwick Barracks** – the oldest post-Roman army barracks in Britain – dating to 1719. The quadrangle on the Parade houses a museum which traces the military history of the King's Own Scottish Borderers regiment, formed in 1689 to defend Edinburgh against the Jacobites. This isn't just a military heritage centre, however: in the clock building, you'll find the **Berwick Museum & Art Gallery** (*01289 304493; www.englishheritage.org.uk; open 1 Apr–30 Sep*) with its recreated garrison town and fine art gallery. The Burrell Collection (an offshoot of the magnificent Burrell Collection in Glasgow) includes paintings from the 16th century to the early 20th century from Britain, France and the Netherlands. There's a Degas pastel here, but just as intriguing are works by local artist, James Wallace, who painted scenes of everyday life in the 1900s, including salmon fishermen on the Tweed. Also in the barracks is the **Gymnasium Gallery** (*01289 304535; open Apr–Dec; access from the ramparts; free entry*) which specialises in contemporary artworks.

Nearby, don't miss the **Holy Trinity Church** on Wallace Green. The mid 17th-century building is one of very few churches constructed in Cromwellian England and is strikingly different to any other church you will see in the North East, particularly because it has no tower or spire. The interior is a mix of Gothic and classical styles.

When you reach **Scot's Gate**, one of the main entrance archways into the town, you are pretty much in the centre of Berwick. If you continue south on the ramparts towards the river, you'll reach **Meg's Mount** (the westernmost bastion on the ramparts and one of Berwick's finest vantage points). **Marygate** is the long street running under Scot's Gate. It's basically the town's high street with all the usual chain shops as well as the **tourist information office** (*01289 301780*) and the mid 18th-century **town hall** – easily the most prominent historic building on the street (tours daily in summer at 14.00).

The Lowry Trail

Berwick's many cobbled lanes and irregular shaped buildings caught the eye of L S Lowry who painted some of his most memorable street scenes here from the mid-1930s until his death in 1976. The **Lowry Trail** (pick up a leaflet in the tourist information office on Marygate) allows you to compare his paintings (shown on panels at each stopping point) with reality.

Sloping downhill from Marygate to the river is **West Street** – a narrow, cobbled lane worthy of a few photographs. **Bridge Street** is the long road set behind the river and Quay Walls and is recommended for a drink or lunch (see page 101). Look out for **Dewar's Lane** halfway along. It's a tight little cobbled alley with a bulging 200-year-old **granary** (now an excellent, modern YHA and art gallery). Access to the granary is from **Quay Walls**, itself worth a stroll for its handsome row of Georgian houses.

Along the riverside: Berwick's bridges

East Coast Main Line trains from Edinburgh to London chug across Robert Stephenson's 1850 **Royal Border Bridge** offering a spectacular view of the Tweed. The clear problem here is that you only very briefly see its 28 towering arches, but the bridge's magnificence is sensed in the way it makes you feel at 126 dizzying feet above the river. It's such a Victorian pleasure.

The other way to get up close to all those long, colourful stone legs is to stroll downhill on a leafy path that connects the station with the river. Cowering underneath the Border Bridge arches is the ruin of **Berwick Castle**, founded in the 12th century. Those ruthless Victorians bulldozed the fortress to make way for the bridge and station.

Continuing downriver on the **promenade**, you'll pass a boathouse and then **New Bridge** (opened 1928). Peering through its undersides is one of the great pleasures to be had in Berwick. Perhaps I'm overstating the experience but it's certainly very sculptural and won't go unappreciated by photographers.

In comparison to Stephenson's gazelle, **Old Bridge**, last in the trio of Berwick's bridges, is rather squat and stumpy, but such adjectives don't convey quite how graceful and romantic this 17th-century bridge of 15 arches appears as it crosses the Tweed

Spittal and Tweedmouth

Facing Berwick on the south side of the river is Tweedmouth – a largely residential area but with many 19th-century buildings near the river which serve as reminders of the area's once thriving grain, herring and salmon fishing industries. Here, **Brewery Lane** has an intact run of 19th-century brewery buildings; it's rare to find all the elements of a Victorian brewery (drying sheds,

Food heritage

Berwick has a very active **Slow Food** movement (*www.berwickslowfood.co.uk*) and an annual **Food Festival** in September. The organisers have produced two excellent **trail guides** (available from the tourist information centre on Marygate) which explore the streets of Berwick and Tweedmouth highlighting the town's once flourishing fishing and grain industries. Following the Fishy Trail you'll pass herring yards, ice-houses, fishing shiels and a whaling house. The Barleycorn Trail explores breweries, maltings, the old corn exchange and Dewar's Lane granary.

malt kilns and the 'brewery tap' – the nearest pub to the brewery) as well-preserved as this.

On Tower Hill and with an expansive view of the Tweed, is **Tower House Pottery** (*01289 307314; www.towerhousepottery.com*). When I visited, the owners were immersed in their craft, painting vases, plates and cups with their trademark floral designs and local scenes. The outlook from the workshop windows provides plenty of inspiration.

Keep going along Dock Road to reach **Sandstell Road** with its old herring sheds and salmon fishermen's shiel. **Spittal beach** and its Victorian promenade (painted many times by L S Lowry) is recommended for a blustery walk.

Food and drink

Fish and chip shops in Berwick are numerous. I tried **Cannon's** on Castlegate (*01289 331480*) which was recommended by several locals. It did not disappoint. **Prior Chippy** on Grove Gardens, Tweedmouth (*01289 308936*) also has an excellent reputation.

Barrels Ale House 59 Bridge St, TD15 1LZ ① 01289 308013. Characterful pub full of local chatter just off the Old Bridge. Inside, old skis and a big fish hang from the wall and ceiling along with a load of other random objects. Punters sit on barrels and in an old barber's (dentist's?) chair enjoying a (cheap) pint of real ale.

Café Curio 52 Bridge St, TD15 1AQ ① 01289 302666. The windows of this charming little café were steamed up when I visited which made it feel even more cosy and inviting. Inside, early 20th-century French music was playing and the smell of coffee and hearty food filled the room. The antique chairs, tables, pictures (and cutlery!) are for sale. The owners are keen supporters of Berwick's Slow Food movement and serve excellent lunches and dinners.

Queen's Head 6 Sandgate, TD15 1EP ① 01289 307852 Ⓦ www.queensheadberwick.co.uk. It's not cheap (most mains upwards of £15), but the food is made with a lot of care by reputable chefs and many of the ingredients are sourced locally. French and traditional British dishes (steak, venison, salmon, etc).

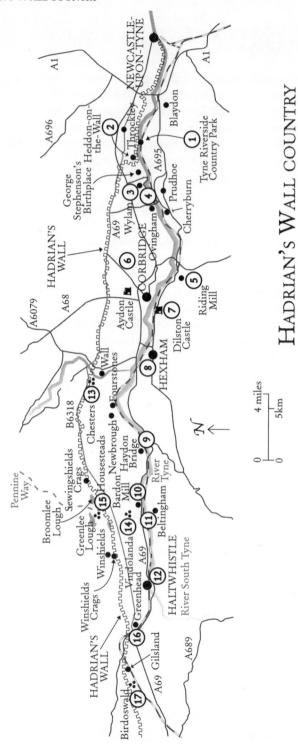

HADRIAN'S WALL COUNTRY

3. Hadrian's Wall Country

From Newcastle to Carlisle, road, river and railway ribbon across the neck of England through a wide, fertile valley. A mile north, spanning 73 miles from west to east, is the region's most famous attraction: **Hadrian's Wall** – a World Heritage Site and, according to English Heritage, 'the most important monument built by the Romans in Britain'. The best-preserved stretch, between Chesters and Brampton, rides the tops of the highest hills where undulating grasslands roll far into Cumbria and down through the Tyne Valley. This is superb walking country indeed.

The countryside between the river and Wall is all fields and woodland as far as you can see with a scattering of farms and settlements hunkered down by the water's edge. From Haltwhistle, the South Tyne hurries eastwards past ruined castles, manor houses and historic market towns on its way to meet the North Tyne near **Hexham**. Here, the two rivers become one, forming the River Tyne for the final run through Newcastle and on to the coast. The countryside is not remote and neither is it what you might call dramatic, but there is much beauty in this broad-sided valley that is filled with light owing to the relative flatness of the land.

Border clan clashes and invasions by the Vikings and Scots in centuries past have left their mark, and you'll see a number of defensive buildings (bastles and pele towers) in every town and village in this region. They are unique to the Border Country and are explained in more detail in *Chapter 4*.

Mining and industrial production over the last few hundred years greatly changed the character and fortunes of settlements in the Tyne Valley and Pennines. These industries expanded with the aid of the railways in the 19th century and towns and villages grew as a result. Many have retained characterful uniform terraces of sandstone and brick, village greens and stone bridges. If they were situated in the south of England, they would be crowded with Sunday day-trippers, but not here; the remoteness of Northumberland does have its advantages.

Getting around

By train or bus or a combination of the two, you can pretty much reach every town and visitor attraction along Hadrian's Wall and the Tyne Valley. Motorists, cyclists and walkers are also extremely well looked after.

The dead straight Military Road (B6318) runs parallel to Hadrian's Wall and offers views of the wall and surrounding upland landscape, but cars fly along this road and cyclists should be very cautious. The old Roman road, the Stanegate (see page 125), is a mile or so south of the Military Road and is a recommended alternative for cyclists – and motorists who like to tootle along.

Bus

The **Hadrian's Wall Country Bus** (*01434 322002; www.hadrians-wall.org*), route No. AD122, stops at every jumping-off point for the Roman ruins between Hexham and Carlisle, including Chesters, Housesteads, Once Brewed, Vindolanda and Birdoswold. It operates seven times a day between Easter and the end of October. Multi-day Rover passes allow unlimited travel.

Buy single trip and one-day **tickets** from the driver and multi-day **passes** online or at tourist information centres at Newcastle, Hexham, Once Brewed, Haltwhistle and Carlisle. There are concessionary tickets; disabled badge holders travel for free (buses have low floor easy access). Unusually, they can take bikes: there's no charge, but it's a first come-first served service and only two bikes are permitted per bus. When no buses run (outside summer), take the train to Bardon Mill and walk across country to Vindolanda Roman Fort by following Chainley Burn, or take a **taxi** from Hexham train station (*Hadrian's Wall Taxis 01434 606565*).

Train

The best way to get a sense of the lie of the land and enjoy the big, bright views in the Tyne Valley is to take the frequent **Newcastle–Carlisle** train on what is sometimes referred to as the Tyne Valley Line (and occasionally the slightly misleading Hadrian's Wall Country Line). Railway and river intertwine the whole way and the train stops at most riverside towns and villages. It is very convenient and the surrounding green and yellow fields dotted with sheep, cows, woods and farmsteads are just lovely. On the down side, it's no Bullet train and it rattles along like a tin can.

For those visiting the **Roman sites**, the Hadrian's Wall Country Bus (see above) connects with Corbridge, Hexham, Haltwhistle and Brampton train stations. Ask for a combined rail–bus ticket ('Hadrian's Wall Country Bus add-on-fare') or consider a Northern Rail Day Ranger ticket, which allows unlimited travel.

Bikes travel free on Northern Trains (two per service). No need to book.

The Tyne Valley Line

The Newcastle–Carlisle railway, dating from the 1830s, was one of the earliest railways ever built. The stations have retained much of their original Victorian

Whistlestop pubs

You are never far from a 'proper' pub after a day's sightseeing in the Tyne Valley. A good number are conveniently located close to train stations, as detailed in an inspired leaflet produced by CAMRA (Campaign for Real Ale). Pick up a copy of *Whistle Stops* in pubs and tourist information centres or download it at www. cannybevvy.co.uk.

character and North Eastern Railway Company architecture. Waiting rooms with tall chimneys, big station clocks, signal towers, old water tanks and decorative iron footbridges painted cream and red add to the historic appeal of the villages and towns the stations serve. At Haltwhistle station all the elements above come together, making it one of the most interesting on the line. Hexham, too, will catch your eye, not just for its station architecture but also for its hanging baskets.

Cycling

Cyclists are in for a treat in Hadrian's Wall country. The landscape is varied enough to offer something to suit most grades of cyclists: strenuous rides up and down hills and through forests, flat riverside paths, and pub trails on country lanes. What's more, you can make use of the excellent train and bus network and take on long linear routes. **Haltwhistle** and **Hexham** make good bases for cycle rides north to Hadrian's Wall and south into the North Pennines.

An introduction to the countryside around Hadrian's Wall is described in brief on page 132. The 15-mile route follows the lofty **Pennine Cycleway** (NCN Route 68) into Northumberland National Park. This long-distance trail also extends south from Haltwhistle making for a very ample day's jaunt into the North Pennines along a disused railway line to Alston (described on page 270).

The Brampton-based company, **Pedalpushers Cycle Hire** (*016977 42387*) offer bike transfer along Hadrian's Wall. Bicycle repair shops are also found in Corbridge, Prudhoe Industrial Estate Hexham and Newcastle. The Hub on Newcastle's quayside also arranges tours and bike hire (see page 3).

Walking

Ramblers will find no shortage of excellent walks in and around the Tyne Valley and Hadrian's Wall. Rough upland grasslands, wide valleys and wooded gorges await, plus stone ruins, Roman forts and villages with pubs where real ales, good food and a roaring fire welcome walkers after a day on the hills. A couple of recommended routes are outlined in the following pages. You'll find all the classic trails described in various walking guidebooks on sale at the Once Brewed Visitor Centre (see page 130) and in the well-stocked shops at the major Roman fort sites.

Shepherds Walks (*01830 540453; www.shepherdswalks.co.uk*) is a reputable local travel company that offers self-guided and led trips along Hadrian's Wall (see page ix). Also try **Hadrian's Wall Ltd** (*01434 344650; www.hadrianswall.ltd.uk*). If you are walking independently and want someone to take your bags, **The Walkers' Baggage Transfer Co.** (*0871 4238803; www.walkersbags.co.uk*) will deliver your luggage for a few pounds per bag. **Hadrian's Haul** (*07967 564823; www.hadrianshaul.com*) offer a similar service.

Accommodation

I found many of the best B&Bs were outside of the larger towns, and for some reason, Gilsland on the Cumbrian border had a disproportionate number of good ones. Try **Willowford Farm** (*016977 47962; www.willowford.co.uk*) – beamed rooms, and evening meals made with lamb from the farm; **Tantallon House** (*01697 747111; www.tantallonhouse.co.uk*) – spacious rooms with Victorian fireplaces and furnishings; and **Brookside Villa** (*0845 8731992; www.brooksidevillabandb.co.uk*) – Victorian detached house with contemporary rooms and stripped wood floors.

There are not many places to camp near Hadrian's Wall; try **Hadrian's Wall Campsite** near Haltwhistle (*01434 320495; www.hadrianswallcampsite.co.uk*).

Angel Inn Main St, Corbridge NE45 5LA ℗01434 632119
ⓦ www.theangelofcorbridge.com ⓔ info@theangelofcorbridge.com. Leather armchairs and open fires make this plush old coaching inn the kind of place you hope to fall into after a day's sightseeing. The restaurant is pretty good but, like the rooms, it is not cheap. Rooms are divided between the inn and the Radcliffe on the other side of the road. The latter is recommended (quieter than the inn). Ask for a room with a view of the river and bridge.
Ashcroft Guesthouse Lanty's Lonnen, Haltwhistle NE49 0DA ℗01434 320213
ⓦ www.ashcroftguesthouse.co.uk ⓔ info@ashcroftguesthouse.co.uk. Rooms are spacious and have an antique touch without being fussy. Some have balconies; one sleeps four and has a kitchen; and all are immaculate. Views of the terraced gardens and hills from the dining room. Oil paintings and a grandfather clock stay true to the building's Victorian heritage. Average prices.
Carraw B&B Carraw Farm, Humshaugh NE46 4DB ℗01434 689857
ⓦ www.carraw.co.uk ⓔ relax@carraw.co.uk. Top B&B, 3 miles west of Chesters Roman Fort with impressive green credentials. The stone mansion has a complex history, having been a coaching inn, fortified manor house and reputedly the summer retreat for monks from Hexham priory. The four south-facing rooms (two are family rooms) are immaculate, bright and contemporary with pine furniture and stripped floors. Dinners must be booked in advance. Laundry and drying facilities and secure cycle storage.
Causeway House holiday cottage The Stanegate, Vindolanda, near Bardon Mill ℗01628 825925 ⓦ www.landmarktrust.org.uk ⓔ bookings@landmarktrust.org.uk. This late 18th-century cottage stands on the entrance drive to Vindolanda Roman Fort and is said to be the only heather-thatched house in Northumberland. It sleeps four and is not too expensive. The rooms are decorated with antique rugs and furniture and the building has much character with its stone flag flooring, exposed timber beams and early 20th-century cast-iron kitchen range which can be used by guests as a (gas) fire. A note in the visitor book reads: 'Arrived at this lovely house, pitch black, hadn't a clue what we'd be waking up to. Daylight ... greeted by a short-eared owl sitting on the fence post.'

Chapelburn House Gilsland, Brampton CA8 2LY ①016977 46595
ⓦ www.chapelburn.com Ⓔ stay@chapelburn.com. Chapelburn House combines
the best of what you want to be modern (showers, curtains, lighting, bedding)
with antique detailing and furniture, to stylish effect. You won't find any
fussiness or clutter in either of the two guest rooms, but neither is the décor
bland or boutique either. For the standard of accommodation, it is not expensive.
The owners, who are very eco-minded, will accompany children who want to see
the pigs or collect eggs for breakfast. Produce is sourced mostly within a 20-mile
radius. Sausages and bacon are made using the family's pigs and the bacon is
smoked in the grounds of the house. The jams and marmalade are homemade.
Also expect trout from Brampton, Bowness-on-Solway salt marsh lamb, cheese
from Birdoswold and Chapel Burn's own eggs and honey.

Fairshaw Rigg B&B Lowgate, near Hexham NE46 2NW ①01434 602630
ⓦ www.fairshawrigg.co.uk Ⓔ info@fairshawrigg.co.uk. Unlike other B&Bs in the
Northumberland countryside, at Fairshaw Rigg you are more likely to see alpacas
grazing outside your window than sheep. The setting is pleasant enough, with easy
green farmland all around and historic Hexham a short distance away (3 miles).
The owners sell gorgeous hats and scarves made with the soft wool from their
herd. Three clean and bright average-priced rooms in the barn conversion are
fitted with Ikea-style white and pine furniture. Ever slept under an alpaca duvet?
Now's your chance. They're light and warm, and you may never want to go back
to an ordinary duvet.

Grindon Cartshed Self Catering and B&B North Rd, near Haydon Bridge
NE47 6NQ ①01434 684273 ⓦ www.grindon-cartshed.co.uk Ⓔ dave@grindon-
cartshed.co.uk. The converted barn on a hill surrounded by 600 acres of farmland
and a woodland inhabited by native red squirrels is thoroughly Northumbrian.
Enjoy the view (and the sight of rare-breed sheep) from the floor-to-ceiling glass
windows in the dining room. Tuition on wool weaving is provided for a fee. The
inexpensive rooms, though on the small side, are simply decorated with pine
furniture. One is wheelchair accessible. From October to Easter, Grindon Cartshed
operates self-catering accommodation only (sleeps six).

Once Brewed YHA Military Rd, near Bardon Mill NE47 7AN ①0845 3719753
ⓦ www.yha.org.uk Ⓔ oncebrewed@yha.org.uk. It's not plush but you can hardly
find a more convenient or modestly priced place to stay for visiting Hadrian's
Wall. Set back from the Military Road half a mile from the Wall and with an
excellent tourist information centre next door, a pub down the road (Twice
Brewed) and close proximity to Vindolanda and Housesteads, you'll be set for your
trip into Roman Northumberland. Family rooms are available in addition to dorms.
Good bike storage, laundry facilities and a restaurant.

Ovington House Ovington, near Prudhoe NE42 6DH ①01661 832442
ⓦ www.ovingtonhouse.co.uk Ⓔ stay@ovingtonhouse.co.uk. Inexpensive B&B
with big Georgian windows, period fireplaces and a mix of antique and shabby
chic-style furnishings. Self-catering cottage also available. Free range hens greet
guests on arrival in the pretty garden which includes an orchard, stables and

patio seating area. Locally sourced breakfast ingredients, including meat from the local farmer and eggs from the henhouse.

Peartree Cottage Sandhoe, Hexham NE46 4LU ①01434 608072/07891 893 530 Ⓦ www.peartree-cottage.com Ⓔ mail@peartree-cottage.com. Stone cottage with three bright, average-priced rooms tastefully painted in soft greys and duck-egg blue. Wood-burning stove in cosy lounge. Tranquil setting, reached along a wooded lane just outside of Corbridge. Large garden and wildflower meadow.

Newcastle to Ovingham

As you travel upriver from Newcastle, the landscape becomes increasingly rural from Newburn onwards. Some of the greenest and most tranquil stretches of the River Tyne are found here and are easily reached by following the riverside path out of Newcastle city centre, described below, or by taking the train to Wylam or Prudhoe.

Little effort is needed to lure passing tourists to Wylam and Ovingham with their affluent Victorian terraces, riverside settings and old pubs. However, there are a few other places nearby that should not be overlooked, including Bywell, noted for its castle (not open to the public) and two very old churches, and Heddon-on-the-Wall. On reaching this pleasant village overlooking the Tyne Valley, don't be surprised if locals greet you in the street. Welcome to Northumberland.

Newcastle to Wylam by bicycle

This easy, ten-mile off-road cycle path takes you west along the Tyne Valley under Newcastle's famous bridges and into tranquil countryside. It follows the well-signed Hadrian's Cycleway (NCN Route 72). The footpath for walkers (Hadrian's Wall Path) follows the same route, except between Scotswood and Newburn Bridge (the section you may wish to cover by bus 22 from Newcastle Central station because it follows a busy road).

From Newcastle's historic quayside, follow the riverside promenade west from the **Tyne Bridge** passing under the High Level, Metro, Rail and Redheugh bridges in that order. The countryside doesn't get going until your back is to Newburn, but the urban fringes should not be overlooked as you hurry towards the leafy banks of the Tyne further west. Birdwatchers and those with an interest in industrial architecture will find several reasons to pause on the outskirts of Newcastle.

At the Newcastle Business Park (not as ugly as it sounds) you'll get a good view of the **Dunston Coal Staiths** (see page 27) jutting out from the riverbank and into the Tyne. In winter, shelduck, teal, lapwing and the odd curlew dabble in the exposed mud at low tide.

The mile-long stretch to the ancient woodland of **Denton Dene** is a big, busy concrete affair (albeit one on a footpath and cycle path), but once you enter the Dene's woody confines, the Scotswood Road and its juggernauts seem far away. If you've heard the famous North East song *The Blaydon Races*, you'll recall the often recited line: 'There were lots of lads and lasses there, all with smiling faces, ganning along the Scotswood Road, to see the Blaydon Races.'

Just after Blaydon Bridge, the cycle path turns to the river and follows it closely to Newburn. Continue straight ahead if you want to see the 120-foot high **Lemington Glass Works cone** – the only one of four late 18th-century brick cones still standing here and one of the last remaining in England.

The historic **Tyne Rowing Club** is just beyond the Newburn Bridge. After a very pleasant half mile through the **Tyne Riverside Country Park** (see below), the path swings north where you will meet with the old **Wylam Waggonway** (see page 112). Even if you don't go into **George Stephenson's Birthplace** (see page 112), the little café annexed to his birthplace house is a welcome stopping point.

From Wylam, NCN Route 72 continues to Ovingham on the south side of the river via a manmade chalk grassland.

① Tyne Riverside Country Park

Information Centre, Grange Rd, Newburn NE15 8ND ☎0191 264 8501.

You'd never guess a coal mine once stood on this 200-acre meadow and wetland parkland near Newburn. Unless, that is, you look carefully for clues in the landscape (the remains of four beehive coke ovens can still be seen at Blayney

Rowing on the Tyne

In the 19th century, rowing was as popular a spectator sport on Tyneside as football is today. Crowds would gather on Newcastle's crossings and along the banks of the Tyne to watch races between the High Level and Scotswood bridges. As with football, rowing had its heroes: Harry Clasper, Robert Chambers and James Renforth were the Jackie Milburn, Paul Gascoigne and Alan Shearer of their day. To give you an idea of their fame, when Clasper died in 1870, more than 100,000 people are said to have turned out on the banks of the Tyne for his funeral procession.

At the height of the sport's popularity in the mid-to late-1800s, there were dozens of rowing clubs along the Tyne. Today there are four. The oldest, established in 1852, is the **Tyne Rowing Club** at Water Row near Newburn Bridge. In recent years, however, rowing is once again growing in popularity. In May 1997, the inaugural **University Boat Race** between Durham and Newcastle took place on the Tyne, and in 2007 the **Tyne United Rowing Club** was resurrected on the banks of the river, 50 years after it closed.

Row, for example). Today, the site, which extends to the south side of the Tyne at Prudhoe, is popular with dog walkers, families and those cycling and walking Hadrian's Wall. From Newburn, two trails keep tight to the riverbank (one exclusively for walkers). The Tyne flows lazily here, tugging the branches of overhanging shrubs and trees. If visiting at dusk in winter, you'll walk under the noisy flight-path of hundreds of jackdaws and rooks that roost in nearby trees. **The Spetchells** (see page 116) near Prudhoe is a unique manmade chalk grassland habitat with an interesting assemblage of plants and butterflies.

Food and drink

The Keelman's Lodge and **Big Lamp Brewery** Grange Rd, Newburn NE15 8NL ⓣ0191 267 1689 ⓦ www.keelmanslodge.co.uk. The large playground next to an outdoor seating area shouts 'family-friendly pub'. If travelling from Newcastle, the Keelman will probably be the first country pub you come to. It's not really in the countryside as such but the leafy riverbank setting gives that impression. The building dates to the mid 19th-century and was formally a water pumping station. Decent pub food, but the best thing, aside from the historic buildings and setting, is the beer, which is brewed on site.

② Heddon-on-the-Wall

As you approach Heddon from the east, look out for the long stretch of Hadrian's Wall crossing a field on the left of the Hexham Road. The friendly village centre is reached by turning off left where the wall ends. If you come for lunch at the **Swan Inn** on Towne Gate (see below), make sure you visit **St Andrew's Church** opposite, parts of which date to the Saxon period. A wide Norman arch spans the sanctuary and a large fragment of a Celtic cross rests to the left of the altar.

Food and drink

Dingle Dell Deli and Tearoom 3 Taberna Close, NE15 0BW ⓣ01661 854325 ⓦ www.dingledelldeli.co.uk. This little foodstore and café is close to the Hadrian's Wall Path and sells freshly made baps for a few pounds.
Swan Inn The Towne Gate, NE15 0DR ⓣ08442 435395 ⓦ www.greatbritish carvery.co.uk. Popular, family-friendly pub and carvery in the centre of Heddon. The dining room interior is contemporary and uncluttered with wooden floors and furniture and has a gastro pub feel. Sit in the beer garden and take in the expansive view of the Tyne Valley.

Wylam Brewery

South Houghton Farm, Heddon-on-the-Wall NE15 0EZ ⓣ01661 853377 ⓦ www.wylambrewery.co.uk.
Go to any decent pub in Northumberland serving real ales and chances are you

will come across a favourite like the Rocket or Red Kite from the celebrated Wylam Brewery (now based in Heddon-on-the-Wall). You can sample their beers at the Black Bull pub on Wylam's Main Street or by going on a brewery tour lasting an hour or so. Tours cost £8 and run on Fridays and Saturdays at selected times (depending on demand).

③ Wylam

For a small place, Wylam has produced a surprising number of the great railway pioneers of the 18th and 19th centuries. **George Stephenson** and **Timothy Hackworth** were both born here and **William Hedley**, who was raised in nearby Newburn, worked at the Wylam Colliery and tested his famous steam engine prototypes on the Wylam Waggonway. The town itself makes a very pleasant stopping point on your travels along the Tyne. Grand stone houses and brick terraces either side of the river reflect the affluence that came with being a railway town in the 19th century. Stephenson Terrace, which connects with the Wylam Waggonway on the north side of the river, is particularly attractive with its river outlook and weeping willows.

Two **bridges** span the Tyne at Wylam. The most striking is the 1876 railway bridge (now only open to cyclists and pedestrians) at Hagg Bank. The single span structure is reminiscent of Newcastle's Tyne Bridge which was built half a century later. The bridge further east directly connects the two sides of Wylam town and retains its 1899 Toll House.

Wylam's **centre** is on the north side of the river and reached by following the Main Road away from the bridge and memorial green. It's pleasant enough with a few bistros, shops, a post office and a couple of pubs (note the old stone horse mount outside the Black Bull) but unless you need some food, there's not a great deal to warrant the uphill walk.

On the south side of the Tyne is Wylam Station which conveniently stands next to **The Boathouse** (*01661 853431; www.theboathousewylam.co.uk*) a good traditional pub with 15 real ales and ciders on tap.

If you continue south on Station Road, you will eventually come to **Sled Hill** – a winding lane that passes the lovely Bradley Nursery and Walled Garden.

Bradley Gardens

Sled Lane, NE41 8JH ⓣ01661 852176; open Tue–Sun (café only open until 15.00 in winter).

At the time of writing, this Victorian walled garden, nursery and tearoom was up for sale. I hope the new owners keep it open to the public as it is one of the most enchanting gardens in the region, with its walkways draped in climbers and its early 20th-century glasshouse (now the café). On sunny days you can sit outside looking at the green hills rising beyond the old brick walls. Next to the tea room is a gift shop and small antiques emporium. The entrance is tucked away down a quiet lane south of Wylam train station and next to a lake with many water birds.

Wylam Waggonway

Today it is a recreational path surrounded by trees that runs for a few miles between Wylam and Blayney Row but at the turn of the 19th century, this waggonway (that then extended to Lemington) played an important role in the development of modern railway travel.

Wagons were used to transport coal from Wylam Colliery to ships docked at Lemington staiths on the River Tyne, some five miles away. Originally they were pulled on wooden rails by horses, until the owner of the colliery, Christopher Blackett, set his mind to making the transfer of coal more efficient.

In 1808 he replaced the wooden rails with cast iron ones and enlisted the engineering skills of his colliery manager, William Hedley, to develop an engine to replace his horses. Hedley experimented with different designs until the Puffing Billy was unveiled in 1814. The stout locomotive (now housed in the Science Museum in London) was created with the assistance of two local engineers, Timothy Hackworth and Jonathan Forster, and is the oldest surviving steam engine in the world. The train carried coal along the Wylam Waggonway for 50 years, but its greatest contribution to the Industrial Revolution was in demonstrating that smooth iron wheels could run on flat iron tracks without derailing. This was an important step in the evolution of the modern train, enabling the locomotives of the future to travel at high speeds.

Wylam Railway Museum Wylam Library, Falcon Terrace, NE41 8EE ①01661 852174. Open Tue and Thu 14.00–17.00 and 17.30–19.30, Sat 09.00–12.00. This small museum housed in the public library traces Wylam's railway heritage and the legacy of the great Victorian engineers associated with the town.

George Stephenson's Birthplace

Wylam Waggonway NE41 8BP (about ½ mile east of Wylam village)
①01661 853457 ⓦ www.nationaltrust.org.uk. Open Easter–end Oct, Thu–Sun; café selling drinks and snacks; National Trust.

Halfway along the old waggonway to Wylam is a small limewashed stone cottage built for mining families around 1760. It was here, in 1781, that the great railway engineer George Stephenson was born. In his early days, he would have watched horses outside pulling wagons laden with coal from Wylam Colliery.

Stephenson lived with six other family members in one room of the four-bedroom building. It has been furnished in the style of an 18th-century dwelling and houses George Stephenson's Jacobean rocking chair. The floor would have been bare earth back then. With just one room open to the public, there is little to see inside, but the National Trust stewards really go to town bringing the legacy of George Stephenson and the golden era of railway development to life.

Food and drink

Even if you don't go inside the house, the little **café** next to the cottage makes a welcome resting point on a summer's day, especially if walking or cycling the Wylam Waggonway. The pretty garden café (small selection of cakes, teas and cold drinks) has enough seats for about eight bums. The homemade chocolate and beetroot cake is deliciously moist.

④ Ovingham

By any Northumbrian standard, the lively riverside village of Ovingham (Oving-jum) is one of the most appealing to visitors in the region. The area around St Mary's Church is particularly quaint with its red phone box, cottage gardens and streamside pub (the Bridge End Inn).

Those who arrive by train, or by bike along the traffic-free route from Newcastle via Wylam, will enter the village over the **Ovingham Bridge** from Prudhoe. The single-lane rickety road crossing, dating to 1883, doesn't strike one as particularly sturdy, especially when cars cross and the whole structure shudders. The adjoining pedestrian bridge (added in 1974) is worth walking over for the river views (and bone-rattling sensation when cars pass on the road bridge).

The Tyne is extremely lush and overgrown here. Mature trees and bushes crowd the riverbank where fly-fishermen whip the water with their lines and kayaks take it in turn to whoosh down the rapids. All the pushing and shoving of trees towards the bright river's edge has inevitably resulted in toppled trunks, but some have taken root on banks of green debris and many islets now appear in the Tyne serving as stepping stones for giants.

St Mary's Church is built on the site of an early Saxon building of which the tower is the only relic. It is thought part of the west side of the tower was built using Roman stones and the structure may have been designed with habitation in mind during the post-Roman centuries when invasions were feared. As you walk to the main doorway, you'll see the grave of the celebrated 18th-century nature artist, Thomas Bewick, who lived at Cherryburn over the river and went to school in Ovingham.

The last time I visited Ovingham, I was drawn from the busy streets into St Mary's churchyard by the sound of children singing along to a piano. Despite the commuter traffic outside and the mini-scooters stacked in the church porch (the same entranceway that Thomas Bewick used as a canvas for his chalk drawings when he had run out of notebook pages) there was something quite old-fashioned about the scene. It struck me that Ovingham has a sense of tradition and community, but at the same time is a vibrant modern village.

Whittle Burn is crossed by way of an old packhorse bridge. It is very pleasing, both in form (two narrow stone arches) and location. From here you

Ovingham Goose Fair

The tradition of selling birds and other livestock at the village's annual Goose Fair seems to have died out some time in the early 20th century but was revived in the late 1960s; the fair is now held on the third Saturday in June. Visitors are entertained with Morris and rapper dancers and traditional Northumbrian folk music, with a procession beginning from the old Goose Fair Cross. Cakes, plants, ice creams and crafts can be purchased from stallholders, while children can have their face painted and participate in the fancy dress competition. It's all good, traditional country fun.

can trace the waterway upriver along a quiet footpath. Nineteenth-century records of Whittle Burn note the occurrence of fairies. If a quiet woodland with a shallow, stony stream and overhanging trees is the kind of place that attracts fairies, then this should indeed be a favourite haunt.

Cherryburn

Station Bank, Mickley, Stocksfield NE43 7DD ☏01661 843276 ⓦ www.nationaltrust. org.uk. Closed Wed and 31 Oct–1 Mar; small café; National Trust.

The eventful day arrived at last … I can only say my heart was like to break; and, as we passed away, I inwardly bade farewell to the whinny wilds, to Mickley bank, to the Stob-cross hill, to the water banks, the woods, and to particular trees, and even to the large hollow old elm, which had lain perhaps for centuries past, on the haugh near the ford we were about to pass, and which had sheltered the salmon fishers, while at work there, from many a bitter blast.

A Memoir of Thomas Bewick Written By Himself, 1862

The year was 1767 and 14-year-old Thomas Bewick was leaving his birthplace on the banks of the River Tyne to begin an apprenticeship at an engraving workshop in Newcastle. His fondness for the family home at Cherryburn and the woods and rivers surrounding the farmhouse stayed with Bewick for the whole of his life. Though he is most famed for his woodcut blocks of birds and his celebrated 1797 *A History of British Birds*, on every other page of the book there is a vignette depicting rural scenes typical of the Tyne landscape in the 18th century: boys sail toy boats on the river in one picture while in another a farmer cuts his meadow with a scythe. There is humour too, like the man holding onto a cow's tail while crossing a river with a drunkard on his back. Bewick's engravings evoke nostalgia for the rural way of life and draw us into his childhood along the Tyne Valley where fishermen stand knee high in water, men play the fiddle and it is almost always summertime.

The National Trust looks after Bewick's much-loved Cherryburn with great care and makes much of the stone cottage, cobbled courtyard and farm outbuildings huddled near the Tyne. It's a very appealing museum with a fascinating print room, displays of Bewick's works, and live folk sessions in the garden (first Sunday of the month from May to October).

From Cherryburn, you can **walk** through countryside and along the river to Ovingham on the north side of the Tyne where Bewick went to school. A leaflet detailing the route is available from the National Trust. Woodland and river birds are plentiful on this walk but to see Bewick's namesake swan (a rare winter migrant) you'll have to venture further north into Northumberland.

Fifiefofum Fine Art

Westside Farm, Newton, near Corbridge NE43 7TW ℗01661 843778 ⓦ www. fifiefofum.com. Open Mar–Dec, Wed–Sat (times may vary; also open by appointment). Sue Moffitt used to help her brother on his dairy farm but found she was more interested in painting the cows in the fields than milking them. Over the last decade she has become well-known for her distinctive portraits of animals and so she established a contemporary art gallery (apparently the largest in Northumberland) ten years ago above the Tyne Valley. Affordable paintings and glass and ceramic works by a number of artists are displayed in a converted farm building at the family home, which also includes a dreamy five-acre lake populated by swans.

Food and drink

Bridge End Inn West Rd, Ovingham NE42 6BN ℗01661 832219. Friendly local pub serving a real ale from Wylam Brewery. On weekend evenings in summer there's always a convivial atmosphere in the patio area outside. No food.
Duke of Wellington Newton, nr Corbridge NE43 7UL ℗01661 844446 ⓦ www.thedukeofwellingtoninn.co.uk. Advertised as traditional British food but really it's more like an upmarket restaurant with a range of continental dishes alongside standard favourites like steak and chips. The wood furnishings, original

The salmon run

In November and December, salmon turn upriver and embark on an arduous journey to their breeding grounds, leaping over rapids and boulders as they swim. The Tyne, being the number one salmon river in England and Wales, is a good place to witness the spectacle (try the Wylam Bridge).

In the early 1800s, the Tyne was, as it is today, a very good salmon river. On one day in June 1833, between 400 and 500 salmon were fished from the Tyne and taken to market in Newcastle. But, back in the 1950s there were virtually no salmon left, owing to pollution. Cleaner water and hatcheries have reversed the salmon's fortunes quite dramatically. Record numbers were recorded in the Tyne in 2011.

artworks and stone floors and walls give the Duke of Wellington a gastro pub feel. Good selection of beers, views of the Tyne Valley, a wood-burning stove and plush B&B accommodation upstairs. Sunday lunches should be booked in advance.

Vallum Farm Eastwallhouses, Military Rd, NE18 0LL Ⓣ01434 672652 Ⓦ www.vallumfarm.co.uk. Open daily. Dishes (and ice creams) prepared using local ingredients from the family dairy farm and vegetable gardens. Meats locally sourced. Playground and ice cream parlour will keep children very happy.

Prudhoe

From the valley basin, **Prudhoe Castle** (*01661 833459; www.english-heritage. org.uk; open 1 Apr–30 Sep Thu–Mon*) can be seen poking through the trees at the top of a steep bank. The 12th-century ruin is easily the most striking historic attraction in Prudhoe, not that it has much competition in this modern settlement and former coal mining town, known today for the manufacture of paper towels and its ferret rescue centre.

The castle, said to be the only fortress in the North never to be taken by the Scots, is more spectacular close up than from a distance. Its ten-foot thick curtain wall, elevated position and moat no doubt provided good protection. Originally the stronghold of the Umfravilles, it was eventually inherited by the powerful Percy family at Alnwick Castle.

Also of interest in Prudhoe (again, no stiff competition) is the **Spetchells** – a grassy embankment that runs parallel to the river between Hagg Bank and Prudhoe. Dubbed 'The White Cliffs of Tynedale', it was created by waste chalk from an ICI chemical factory which became colonised by shrubs, trees and lime-loving plants. Walkers and cyclists will find an assemblage of plants more usually found in the downlands of southern England, including wild marjoram, St John's wort, bird's foot trefoil and kidney vetch. Also look out for the dingy skipper, a brown butterfly with beige speckles.

Corbridge to Haltwhistle

Following the South Tyne upriver from Ovingham to the western edge of Northumberland, the traveller dips in and out of a string of market towns and hamlets with plentiful historic buildings and attractions.

Almost anywhere along this stretch of the wide, low-sided valley of the South Tyne, you will find far-reaching views of farmland and glimpses of church towers and manor houses peeping through the trees.

⑤ Riding Mill

When you arrive by train from Newcastle, Riding Mill feels like the first stop in the Northumberland countryside. There are no attractions to speak of except for a couple of defensive **bastle houses** in **Broomhaugh**, the 17th-century **Wellington Inn** (good pub for Sunday lunch) and the **old mill house** opposite, but the leafy setting, stone cottages and closeness to the River Tyne make this village a pleasant stopping point. The construction of the Newcastle–Carlisle line made it possible for Tyneside businessmen and their families to live in the countryside hence the tall townhouses you see today that were built with Victorian commuters in mind.

The **riverside** is easily reached from the station. From the platform on the north side of the line, take the paved footpath that continues for a few hundred yards to Broomhaugh. Turn left at the Methodist church and continue to the end of the street where a dirt path near an old bastle house leads to the river.

A very pleasant, albeit muddy, **walk** follows the southern bank of the Tyne to Corbridge. A longer walk continues to Devil's Water (a wooded gorge) and Hexham; return by train from either town.

Food and drink

Wheelbirks Ice Cream Parlour Stocksfield NE43 7HY ☏01661 842613
Ⓦ www.wheelbirks.co.uk. Open Tue–Sun. Café serving lunches, cakes and farm-produced ice cream in a converted Victorian stable. Exceptionally family-friendly with an indoor 'pre-school play area' and outdoor playground.

⑥ Corbridge

On entering the town from the east, the wide main thoroughfare with its large double-fronted houses, makes quite a first impression. In the centre, art galleries sit next to a posh delicatessen on Hill Street; ladies chat outside smart dress shops on Middle Street; and several vintage-inspired cafés, a florist, bookshop and 1950s-style sweet shop circle the Market Cross. A number of shop fronts have original 18th- and 19th-century wood detailing and a few are among more than 60 listed buildings in Corbridge.

Prosperity has not always been associated with Corbridge, however. In the 14th century, the town was attacked and ransacked by the Scots on several occasions. The Black Death later wiped out much of the remaining population. For several hundred years, Corbridge remained a small, insignificant settlement, until 1835 when the Newcastle to Carlisle railway opened. Wealthy businessmen moved here from Newcastle, gentrifying Corbridge into the smart town it is today. Most of the streets date to this period though the layout is medieval.

There were several earlier booms in the town's history that ought to be mentioned, notably in the 13th century, when Corbridge was said to be (regionally) second only to Newcastle in wealth, and during Roman times.

The church, opposite the Market Cross, is a good starting place for a walkabout. Before you enter the church, note the **vicar's pele tower** in the churchyard. The defensive structure, where vicars of centuries past would have taken refuge during attacks on the town, is thought to date to around 1400. English Heritage ranks it as the best example of its kind in Northumberland.

Tucked out of sight to the right of the pele tower (outside the church boundary) is the **old market cross** – a simple stone structure mounted, according to the plaque on the wall, on a Roman altar. It stood in the Market Cross for 600 years before being replaced with the newer cross in the early 1800s.

St Andrew's Church is one of the most interesting ecclesiastical buildings in Northumberland. The walls you see today date mainly to the 13th century, though there is evidence of Norman construction as you enter the south porch, and the tower is Anglo-Saxon. Perhaps most striking of all is the 16-foot high Roman arch which forms the entrance to the baptistery. Like many buildings in Corbridge, we can hazard a good guess as to where this stone treasure was sourced. Equally as impressive and standing over double the height is an Early English archway dating to the 13th century. There are other features of interest (such as the large number of medieval gravestones) which, had they been in another church not so rich in stone workmanship, would be worthy of greater attention here.

As you depart the church grounds, turn right to see the exterior of the Saxon tower and the intriguing 700-year-old **King's Oven** built into the church wall. A plaque between the two wooden doors explains that it was 'the communal oven for the baking of the village's bread and meat'.

Hill Street is home to a couple of small contemporary art galleries, the **tourist information centre** and good market town shops including a butchers and a posh deli, the **Corbridge Larder** (*01434 632948; www.corbridgelarder. co.uk*). Like many buildings in settlements around Roman forts, the **Golden Lion** pub on the corner with Princes Street contains recycled Roman materials. The stones were sourced from nearby Dilston Hall (demolished in the late 18th century) but originally came from nearby Coria. A wander up Princes Street reveals more stone work that looks suspiciously Roman. But then, after a while of wandering these streets, you can convince yourself that any frontage is constructed with Roman stone.

Heading south towards the river, Princes Street meets the busy junction with the plush **Angel Inn** – a 17th-century pub and B&B and once the stopping place for mail coaches. In the 1800s, locals used to gather at **The Coigns** seating area opposite to hear the weekly newspaper from Newcastle being read aloud by the landlord of the Angel Inn. Today it's a meeting place for ramblers.

The Tyne flows fast over rapids as it passes Corbridge and it is not difficult to imagine the destructive power of the waterway after prolonged rain. In 1771 the flooded river was strong enough to wash away every crossing along the Tyne, except for the magnificent seven-arched **bridge** you see today at Corbridge which has spanned the river since 1674. You can access the northern bank of the Tyne by walking down the path at the side of the bridge.

The **riverside trail** is tranquil and especially beautiful late in the afternoon when the sun turns the sandstone bridge a deep golden hue. Late one October afternoon, I walked this path and met some young boys fishing in the river. The bridge in the background and the ducks that had gathered under a willow added to the timelessness of the setting. If it weren't for the BMX bikes on the ground, it could have been a rural scene from any autumn day in the last few hundred years.

Food and drink

Corbridge has very good selection of cafés around St Andrew's Church including **Tea & Tipple** on the Market Place with its slightly industrial 1940s–60s style furniture. Over the road on the corner, **Watling Coffee House** has a bright, vintage interior. Also try the **Café House** on Middle Street – good cakes and bright cottage-chic décor (lots of bunting and white furniture).

Angel Inn Corbridge (see accommodation; page 106).
Black Bull Middle St, Corbridge NE45 5AT ①01434 632261 ⓦ www.blackbull-corbridge.co.uk. Low beamed ceilings, stone walls, old wood chairs and tables, a coal fire, real ales and excellent value food make this 18th-century pub a favourite with locals and ramblers. Meat lovers are spoilt with a large selection of beef and lamb dishes to choose from; fish is also on offer.
Brockbushes A69 roundabout east of Corbridge NE43 7UB ①01434 633100 ⓦ www.brocksbushes.co.uk. Open daily. A pick-your-own strawberry and raspberry farm with a café and well-stocked farm shop.

Coria

Corchester Lane, NE45 5NT ①01434 632349 ⓦ www.english-heritage.org.uk. Open daily 1 Apr–31 Oct and weekends at other times; English Heritage.

Before Hadrian's Wall was constructed, the Roman garrison town of Coria (sometimes known as Corstopitum, but we now know from the Vindolanda tablets that the Romans called it Coria) on the western edge of Corbridge, built circa AD85, was an important settlement at the junction of two major Roman roads: Dere Street and the Stanegate (old English meaning 'stone road'). It also held a strategic position at a crossing of the river and later acted as a supply town for the Wall.

Visitors can wander around the stone foundations of market buildings and peer underneath the large flagstones covering the granary floor. Also of note is the base of what was once an impressive fountain which was fed by an aqueduct. One of the most treasured finds at Coria is a freestanding stone carving of a lion with a bushy mane poised on top of a captured deer (or is it a goat? The English Heritage jury is still out on that one). **The Corbridge Lion** is on display in the on-site museum.

Aydon Castle

Aydon, near Corbridge NE45 5PJ Ⓣ01434 632450 ⓌWww.english-heritage.org.uk.
Open 1 Apr–30 Sep, Thu–Mon; English Heritage.

Not a true castle as such, but more a fortified manor house, albeit one of the most intact and formidable of its period. The stone buildings stand on an elevated fist of farmland overlooking a wooded ravine and are well preserved owing to the fact they were continuously occupied for the best part of 700 years until the late 1960s.

Aydon Castle was originally unfortified when it was built by a Suffolk merchant in the late 13th-century, but that was before warring between Scotland and England threatened settlements across Northumberland. In 1312 the Scots burned nearby Hexham and Corbridge, prompting the construction of a high stone wall around three sides of the manor. The south side was already protected by the steep bank of a ravine.

You can wander through the courtyards and bare chambers, stables, hall and kitchen. The orchard makes a nice place to take a rug and some sandwiches. Alternatively, take your packed lunch down to the wooded ravine below and enjoy a walk along Cor Burn – a shallow river that rushes over stones and fallen branches on its way to meet the Tyne.

⑦ Dilston Castle

Dilston, near Corbridge NE45 5DW ⓉO1661 844157 ⓌWww.friendsofhistoricdilston. org; check website for opening times.

The ruins of a mid 15th-century castle stand high above the wooded slopes of Devil's Water, surrounded by parkland and a 17th-century chapel and gatehouse. The surroundings couldn't be a more fitting setting for the romantic and tragic tale of the legendary 3rd Earl of Derwentwater, James Radcliffe.

Dilston was the ancestral home of the powerful Radcliffes for 200 years, but its links to the family and the last, much loved, Earl of Derwentwater were extinguished in the years following the Jacobite Rebellion of 1715.

The Earl was well-liked by peasants and nobility, and was said to be a generous man known for his charity and hospitality, but his life was cut short for his leading role in the Rising against George I. He was just 26 and newly married. The Jacobite army had been initially successful in many towns in Northumberland, but when they proceeded south through Lancashire, they were defeated at Preston. For his part, the Earl of Derwentwater was imprisoned in the Tower of London and later executed. Tomlinson in his 1888 *Comprehensive Guide to Northumberland* reports:

> On the night of his fatal 24th of February 1716 an exceptionally brilliant display of the aurora borealis took place in the north, staining the waters of the Devil's Water with its crimson glow …

Thereafter, the Northern Lights were, says Tomlinson, known locally as

'Lord Derwentwater's Lights'. The Earl apparently haunts the grounds around Dilston Castle and his wife is said to appear on top of the tower, forever watching for her husband.

The wooded slopes rising from **Devil's Water** (name derived from the 12th-century settlement, Dyvelston) are as scenic today as when Tomlinson wrote this account:

> *Under the shade of pine, beech, rowan and birch trees the visitor saunters along the winding pathway, by banks covered with the trailing flowers ... Crossing a narrow plank, he proceeds to the right, along a rustic pathway, through a tangled copse, perfumed by the honey-suckle and wild rose, until he reaches the haughs already seen from the heights above. Here he seems to stand in the arena of a vast amphitheatre, with tiers on tiers of foliage sloping upwards from the river's edge ...*

Many of the plants, trees and foliage observed in 1833, colour Dilston's woods and meadows to this day.

Gardeners and those interested in the medicinal use of plants should visit nearby **Dilston Physic Garden** (*Dilston Mill House, NE45 5QZ; 07879 533875; www.dilstonphysicgarden.com; open mid Apr–mid Oct, Wed and Sat 11.00–16.00*). An abundance of medicinal plants (over 600 species) grow in the two-acre site which was created by a neuroscientist at Newcastle University researching the healing properties of plants. Visitors can wander round the winding paths and enjoy the profusion of scents and colour. Day courses include tuition on meditation, yoga, foraging for edible plants and medicinal herbs (see website for details).

⑧ Hexham

The Tyne Valley's most significant market town is engulfed by so many trees that it appears much smaller than its true size when approached by train or from the riverside. The historic centre stands on a plateau above the Tyne and is reached by heading uphill in the direction of the abbey tower (one of the few buildings to break the green canopy). You'll pass an excellent **tourist information centre** (in the car park in front of the station) on your way. On reaching the marketplace – a bustling square with a higgledy mix of Victorian, Georgian and medieval buildings – it is clear why Hexham was once voted England's favourite market town by *Country Life* magazine. The criteria were charm, accessibility and sense of community, all of which are apparent to the visitor.

Hexham's buildings have been burned and pillaged many times over 1,300 years since it began life as a monastery on a terrace above the Tyne. In the Middle Ages, farming and lead mining were the principle industries, but Hexham later became a centre of leather production and was famed for its gloves known as Hexham Tans. According to A B Wright in his 1823 *History of Hexham* some 280,000 pairs of gloves were produced annually. If you walk down Gilesgate, a narrow alley on the left leads into a large courtyard with a few old buildings and a shallow stream running over a channel of cobbles. Where now you see a car park, until the 1920s, there were large tanning pits where animal skins were soaked. Wright also notes the town had two woollen manufacturers, two rope makers (one can still be seen on Argyle Street), 16 master hatters and a 'very considerable brewery'. I suppose it would have to be of some size in order to have supplied some of Hexham's 32 inns and pubs. A number of those historic taverns are still extant and serving ale today.

A wander round the streets radiating from the **marketplace** reveals the shops and industries of bygone times. The stone-pillared shelter prominently standing in the marketplace is known as **The Shambles** – a medieval meat market. Goods are still sold here but you are more likely to find potted plants and clothes.

One of the most fascinating streets in Hexham, **St Mary's Chare** is tucked away down a passageway next to Paxton's fish and chip shop, which stands on the site of an old chapel from which the street gets its name. You can see the outline of one of the chapel's windows to the side of the entrance arch. The cobbled lane has many Victorian shop fronts and a couple of pubs.

Running parallel to St Mary's Chare is **Fore Street**, a busier pedestrian street with an equal number of old shop fronts. The **Old Pharmacy** is a curious building: its black and red frontage with decorative grapevines was designed by a Belgian refugee in 1916 and looks totally incongruous – and far too special to be a Poundstretcher. When you get to the end of the street, look up at the top of the **Old Bank** and smile back at the grinning ram.

Snaking downhill from the marketplace is **Market Street** – a road with plenty to tempt shoppers with its art gallery, posh interiors shops and huge antiques emporium. Bargain hunters will be in their element in **Ashbourne House Antiques** (*01434 607294*), which is stuffed with china, bric-a-brac, copper pots, furniture and architectural salvage. You could find anything here from a cast-iron Victorian radiator to a hookah pipe.

Hexham Old Gaol

Hallgate, NE46 1XD ☏01434 652349
Ⓦ www.northumberland.gov.uk. Open Apr–Sep, Tue–Sat and Oct–Mar, Tue and Sat only.

'No, people weren't sent here to be punished', the steward at the oldest purpose-built prison in England (completed 1333) says, correcting my false assumption. 'This was a holding cell until suspected criminals were tried. If found guilty, *then* they were punished.'

It's hard to see how being kept in a windowless stone cellar living on scraps of charity food for sometimes over a year (trials of prisoners were only held every quarter so you can imagine the backlog of cases) cannot be seen as a punishment. Perhaps that is why records show that three quarters of prisoners in the Middle Ages were found not guilty when they were shackled and walked the few hundred yards to the Moot Hall where they were brought before a judge. For the remaining 25% who were found guilty, stocks, the ducking stool, branding and the whipping post were some of the punishments they could expect – if they weren't hung. Executions were performed behind the Moot Hall in the Market Place but were rare because the Archbishop of York ruled Hexhamshire and the church was not in favour of the death penalty. The Archbishop was, however, in favour of collecting fines and 'board and lodging' from inmates. The gaol was in use until the 1820s.

The stone tower, made with hugely thick walls, has four levels open to visitors. Each floor has an exhibition room dedicated to a different aspect of local history: the Border Reivers, rural life and the history of the gaol itself. The dungeon is reached by way of a glass lift that doesn't open but pauses long enough for visitors to gawp at the impenetrable walls and imagine being imprisoned in the cold, dark surroundings.

Hexham Abbey

Market Sq, NE46 3NB ☏01434 602031 ⓦ www.hexhamabbey.org.uk.

Founded in AD674 by Wilfrid, Bishop of York, the abbey was originally built as a monastery but very quickly became a church. It was said by a follower of Wilfrid's (Eddius Stephanus) to be of greater beauty than anything 'this side of the Alps'. Today, the only surviving part of Wilfrid's wondrous building is the **crypt**, reached by descending a stone staircase in the nave. The warren of tight passages and chambers was constructed using masonry from nearby Coria, in which you can see Roman carvings and lettering.

Danish raids in the 9th century damaged the original Saxon building, which was restored as a priory some two hundred years later (the remains of the priory cloisters lie in the abbey's southwest grounds). Most of what you see today dates to the 12th and 13th centuries.

You may find the view of the abbey from the street underwhelming, but wait until you step inside. What appears from the outside to be a rather stout, manly building with a short tower, is elegant and lofty indoors. The best vantage point is from the broad stone staircase in the south transept. The **Night Stair** used to lead to the canons' dormitory and today provides visitors with a superlative view of the crossing and choir. The soaring lancet windows in the north transept and the three tiers of arched windows opposite drive the walls skywards, creating a sense of space and height. At the bottom of the Night Stair is a Roman tombstone with a startling engraving of a **standard-bearer** on horseback trampling over a cowering, primitive-looking Briton.

Many more treasures are found in the aisles and around the altar, including an **Anglo-Saxon chalice** and a **frith stool** (a bishop's throne) that may have been built for Wilfrid in the 7th century. A number of rare medieval **wood panel paintings** are nearby.

In the chancel, you'll find the **Dance of Death** painted across four panels; Death is depicted in each as a frightening skeleton hovering next to a cardinal, king, emperor and pope. Above the altar in the **Leschman Chantry chapel** is an unusual wood painting depicting Christ emerging from a coffin. Kneeling at the head of the coffin is Prior Leschman whose stone effigy (carved with a hooded robe pulled over his eyes) is also in the chapel. Also note the curious stone-carved figures on the side of the chapel, depicting a jester, a harpist and a bagpipe player.

Abbey Grounds and the Sele

Every corner of this pleasure ground commands a good view of the abbey and the church. It is now the mall of the fashionables, the privileged playground of the lower classes, and the place of exercise and amusement for all.

This observation of Hexham's historic parkland was made in 1823 and largely rings true today.

Twenty acres of green space surrounds the abbey on all but one of its sides, divided into three distinct areas: the Abbey Grounds with its 20th-century bandstand; a large open area of grassland called the Sele; and the gardens and bowling green in front of the Georgian mansion, **Hexham House**. Visitors won't struggle to find a tranquil corner to put down a picnic rug. To the side of the bowling green is a wooded area with a lively burn that trickles through a 13th-century archway and under the boughs of oak and fir trees.

A pleasant stroll follows the burn uphill past the bandstand on your left and the Sele to your right. At the top, a secluded narrow passage on your left, called Seal Terrace, leads past a row of diminutive early 19th-century cottages. At the Fox pub, turn left onto Hencotes and return to the abbey by continuing downhill to Beaumont Street. The **Queen's Hall Arts Centre** (*01434 652477; www.queenshall.co.uk*) puts on regular dance, music and theatre performances.

〜〜〜

Food and drink

For great coffee, and hot chocolates so thick with cream and marshmallows they look like cakes, head straight to the **Creamy Coffee Pot** on St Mary's Chare. **Mrs Miggins' Coffee House** on St Mary's Wynd is also popular. For something more substantial than paninis and scones, **Paxton's Fish and Chips** in the Market Place have perfected the traditional British take-away over the last 60 years. It may be a chain pub (Wetherspoons) and the bar area can get rowdy, but walk down the steps at the back of **The Forum** on the Market Place and into the café area. The mint green and gold paintwork and high ceilings will take you back to the days when this was an Art Deco cinema. Coffees and inexpensive pub grub (burgers, etc).

Bouchon Bistrot 4–6 Gilesgate, NE46 3NJ ☎01434 609 943 ⓦ www.

The Stanegate

In the years before the building of Hadrian's Wall, the Romans built a military road linking several settlements between Corbridge and Carlisle. The line of the Stanegate (a medieval name meaning 'Stone Road') is a mile and a half south of Hadrian's Wall but is not to be confused with the much busier B6318 Military Road that runs tight to the wall.

The eight-mile stretch of the Stanegate from **Fourstones to Vindolanda** makes a very pleasant route to Hadrian's Wall from the Hexham area and offers views of upland meadows and pastures the whole way.

Between **Fourstones** and **Newbrough** the road is flanked by a scattering of stone cottages, a curious bright green clapboard chapel dating to the late 19th century, two pubs and a picturesque stone church. **The Red Lion** (*01434 674226; www.redlionnewbrough.co.uk*) at Newbrough has been recently refurbished and is a recommended place to refuel (also a good B&B). The lane to the side of the pub heads north to **Carr Edge woodland** – the site of the **Lookwide Campsite**, the first official Scout camp led by Lord Baden-Powell in 1908 (a year after the famous Brownsea Island experimental camp). To locate it, follow the road for a mile and a half, then turn off right along a footpath signed to Carr Edge; a memorial cairn in the woods marks the spot.

Climbing out of Newbrough on the Stanegate, the road flattens and the views of farmland become even more expansive. Lines of dry-stone walls follow the sloping contours of the land towards Hadrian's Wall, sheep and cows graze in fields and, in spring, the sky is filled with the song of curlew and skylark. This is very good cycling country.

Grindon Lough is one of four natural lakes in the Hadrian's Wall area and is sometimes visited by migrant whooper swans and pink-footed geese in winter.

The last three-quarters of a mile stretch of the Stanegate to **Vindolanda** is lost under grassland and re-emerges at the Roman site where it formed what was essentially a Roman high street.

bouchonbistrot.co.uk. Posh French restaurant in Hexham's old town centre, awarded the accolade of 'best local French Restaurant in the UK' on Gordon Ramsey's TV programme, *The F Word*.

Danielle's Bistrot 12 Eastgate, NE46 1BH *01434 601122. Bare candle-lit tables in no-fuss Italian restaurant serving traditional Mediterranean (and some British) dishes like roast duck, salmon, and ravioli (no pizzas).

Dipton Mill Inn Dipton Mill Rd, Hexham NE46 1YA *01434 606577 W www.diptonmill.co.uk. Pub in a tranquil setting on the outskirts of Hexham serving ale direct from the landlord's Hexhamshire Brewery (*www.hexhamshire.co.uk*). Sandwiches and traditional pub lunches are served in the 17th-century old mill, but on a summer's day you'll probably want to be outside in the beer garden by the stream.

Rat Inn Anick NE46 4LN ☏01434 602814 ⓦ www.theratinn.com. Exceptional pub food made with the very best Northumbrian meats. The old drovers' inn sits high above the Tyne and dates to 1750. Beer garden for sunny days and blazing fire inside when it's frosty outside. Ales from local microbreweries. Booking essential for Sunday lunch.

⑨ Haydon Bridge

'Haydon', as the locals call it, has become considerably quieter in recent years since a bypass diverted the main Newcastle–Carlisle trunk road away from the centre. The cessation of juggernaut convoys thundering through the streets has greatly improved the town's appeal both for residents and visitors. Two bridges connect the town, which straddles the river, including the graceful, six-arched pedestrian bridge built in 1776. From here you gain a good view of Haydon's distinctive old stone houses rising directly from the river, and the hills beyond.

The long, uniform streets of stone make the north side the most popular with visitors. The street backing onto the Tyne is **Ratcliffe Road**. Number 1A was bought in 1962 by Monica Jones, the long-term girlfriend of Philip Larkin. According to the poet's biographer, Andrew Motion, some of the couple's happiest times were spent in Haydon Bridge and surrounding countryside: 'They lazed, drank, read, pottered around the village and amused themselves with private games. The place always cheered them both up.'

A sulphurous spring once popular in Victorian times is reached on a short walk east from the Anchor pub (south side of the bridge) on a tranquil riverside path. The **Spa Well** has suffered a few landslides over the years but is currently open.

Food and drink

General Havelock 9 Ratcliffe Rd, NE47 6ER ☏01434 684376. The interior is not posh, but that does not reflect the food, which is very good indeed. The chef and his wife make everything you eat on site, even down to the breads, pastries and ice cream, hence the limited menu. The setting couldn't be more appealing with a garden overlooking the river.

⑩ Bardon Mill

By road or railway between Haydon Bridge and Haltwhistle, you will pass Bardon Mill, a small settlement with a village store, post office, pub and green set either side of a burn.

Next door to the **Bowes Hotel** bar (*01434 344237*) is **Errington Reay & Co. pottery** (*01434 344245; www.erringtonreay.co.uk*), which stands on the site of a 17th-century woollen mill. You can't miss it: it's the open yard with garden pots lining the road and two tall brick chimneys. The company started producing ceramic chimneypots and piping in 1878. Look at the roofs of houses in the village and you will see that some are an unusual design, looking a little bit like an upside down plant pot placed on top of a stump. Known locally as the 'Marriage Save Pot' it was developed at the pottery and remained in production until very recently. It was a successful solution to the problem of smoke billowing back down chimneys into homes, which was a frequent nuisance in this exposed village.

The manager, Karl Jacques, is enthusiastic about the pottery's heritage and may let you see where the pots are made if you ask (tours can be booked for groups of six or more). Once there were a number of potteries in the Tyne Valley but, says Karl, they closed when the manufacture of cheap, plastic water pipes took off. Errington Reay survived by clever adaptation of their machinery to make garden plant pots. Five hundred pots are produced here every week, all hand-finished by a couple of men sitting at potter's wheels, and traditionally made using a salt-glaze (one of very few potteries in Britain still producing pots in this way). There's a large selection of seconds for sale.

Ghost-hunters should speak to Karl about the resident phantom, Harvey, allegedly an aggrieved ex-employee from centuries past who set fire to the old mill. He was caught and sent to prison, where he later died. 'There's a lot of spooky goings-on up there', says Karl pointing to the top floor of the pottery. 'You sometimes hear someone banging and running across the floorboards. I just yell "shut up Harvey!" and he stops.'

⑪ Beltingham

Roughly a mile southeast of Bardon Mill on the south side of the river is Beltingham – a hamlet of half-a-dozen houses about a church and green whose existence is not recognised by Google Maps. But, what it lacks in size, it makes up for in superlatives: Beltingham is home to the oldest yew tree and the only Perpendicular-style church in Northumberland. It also has the smallest village green in England (you could just about pitch a four-man tent on its circle of grass) and is the most picturesque hamlet in the county. At least I think so. In truth, I can only objectively verify one of the above claims (the oblong church) but the yew tree at the north end of the churchyard (the one whose torso is being pulled in by metal belts) is truly ancient. The church guide refers to estimates of it being 2,000 years old, though it is more likely to be closer to 900 years old.

As for the 'most scenic hamlet in Northumberland' award, except for possibly Cambo in Wallington, I can't think of any other hamlet with such an agreeable arrangement of houses, church and green, and where the stone buildings have been quite so faithfully preserved according to their original design. The farmland setting and nearby wooded ravine add to the appeal of this little idyll by a burn.

Of course, there is little to do here, few places to see and nowhere to eat or drink (unless two well-to-do ladies invite you in for coffee with the vicar) but you can stay in the plush **Beltingham House** (*01434 609521;*

www.beltinghamhouse.co.uk), a Georgian mansion which was visited more than once by the late Queen Mother who popped in to see her relatives, the Bowes-Lyons. It is now a holiday cottage that sleeps 14.

A wooden lych gate marks the entrance to 16th-century **St Cuthbert's Church**. Some believe an earlier timber structure stood here and was visited by monks carrying St Cuthbert's body in the 10th century, hence the church's name.

There are two very pleasant **walks** from Beltingham. Heading west across farmland you come to **Willimoteswyke Castle** – an impressive, albeit derelict, 16th-century fortified manor house with seven-foot thick walls and an intact pele tower; going east you descend into the most beautiful wooded gorge in the whole of Northumberland, **Allen Banks** (see page 276). I did say this was a hamlet of superlatives.

⑫ Haltwhistle

'Welcome to Haltwhistle – Centre of Britain'. Most visitors would never have guessed the geographical centre of Britain is so far north. As it happens, it's not. Well, at least if you believe the inhabitants of Dunsop Bridge in Lancashire or Allendale in the North Pennines who also claim the title. It depends on how the centre is calculated, of course.

What is true is that this market town was, for 300 years, the centre of many clashes between the Scots and the English and warring Border clans. The constant threat of violence explains the large number of defensive **bastle houses** (see page 154) along the High Street. In fact, Haltwhistle claims (quite accurately) to have more of these defensive buildings in and around its town than anywhere else in the North East. A good number are found clustered around the marketplace. Look for two-storey dwellings with irregular windows and prominent stones at pavement level such as at the Centre of Britain building and the fish and chip shop. If it weren't for the blue plaques, you might struggle to distinguish them from ordinary domestic dwellings as they have been modified over the years. The Bastle Trail leaflet available in the **tourist information office** on Westgate provides more clues.

Haltwhistle's centre is, in essence, one long, main thoroughfare with a park at the western end and the marketplace in the centre. Before pressing on into the town, take a moment to admire the **railway station**, which is one of the most unchanged on the Newcastle–Carlisle line. Haltwhistle retains its original waiting room, ticket office and cast-iron footbridge, as well as the old water tank (a relic from the days of steam, set back from the line and supported by a square stone building with arched windows all around). Note the engineer's plates dated 1861 with their decorative seahorses. The signal box is an elegant building made of weatherboards that curve outwards from a narrow rectangular brick base.

Haltwhistle has boasted a lively mix of shops since the town became an important industrial hub in the 18th and 19th centuries. A directory of commercial businesses in 1834 lists, among other shops: two blacksmiths, eight pubs, one stonemason, two saddlers, one straw-hat maker, one slater and three clog makers. Today you will still see some of the original inns as well as various food and clothes shops, newsagents, cafés and gift shops. But there is one specialist shop open today that you wouldn't have come across in the 19th century, despite its antique appearance: the **Newcastle Bookshop** opposite the marketplace is a working bindery where the restoration, printing and sewing of book covers is done by hand. The interior is stuffed with old books and plan chests containing trays of woodblock letters.

Nearby is the **Centre of Britain Hotel and Restaurant** (see below), an old coaching inn noted for its 15th-century pele tower. Inside, a narrow stone staircase climbs curiously to a window, and an underground tunnel (revealed under a glass panel in the floor) is said to connect with the vicarage.

Tucked behind the marketplace is the early 13th-century **Holy Cross Church**. As you enter the building, you'll see what is clearly a very old stone stoup supported on a column. Its age is disputed though some believe it could be Roman. As you walk down the nave, three lancet windows simply decorated with stained glass by William Morris & Co. rise elegantly above the altar. On passing the pulpit, note the memorial stone standing on the floor. The Latin inscription is translated in the church guidebook and reads:

To God the greatest and the best
After a short, difficult, useless life
Here rests in the Lord
Robert Tweddle
Of Monkhazelton Durham
Dies 1735. Aged 23

Continuing eastwards along Main Street, the shops peter out and domestic dwellings made of sandstone sit side by side with agreeable uniformity. Soon the noises of the town are replaced by the cheerful chatter of sparrows in garden bushes and jackdaws clucking on rooftops.

Mill Lane on the left leads to **Haltwhistle Burn**. A footpath hugs the waterway for 1½ miles upriver passing a number of relics from the days when Haltwhistle became a prosperous industrial town in the 18th and 19th centuries, including a brickworks. If you continue northwards, you will soon reach the Military Road and Hadrian's Wall.

Food and drink

There's not a great choice of restaurants in Haltwhistle. The **Centre of Britain** (*01434 322422; www.centre-of-britain.org.uk*) is the most upmarket. The **Black Bull** on Market Square (*01434 320463*) serves standard pub food and an excellent selection of real ales. There are several cafés on Main Street.

Hadrian's Wall and Roman forts

North of the River South Tyne, the hills begin their gallop towards Scotland but are momentarily stopped dead in their tracks by a surge of rock between Sewingshields and Greenhead. To the north of this east–west ridge, the land falls away quite dramatically. This natural wall was made even more impassable by the construction of a ten-foot high stone barricade along its uppermost edge by the Romans. Two thousand years later, this central section of Roman wall is still a mighty structure and awe-inspiring feature of the rugged Northumberland landscape.

When built on the orders of Emperor Hadrian in AD122, the **Wall** extended for 73 miles from coast to coast with a 25-mile extension south through Cumbria. The structure took three legions consisting of 5,000 men as little as, perhaps, a decade to build. But, they didn't just build a mighty wall with a deep channel on its north side: 16 **forts** were constructed, as well as the **Vallum** – a 20-foot ditch with a mound either side running the whole length of the south side of the Wall. According to English Heritage, this immense earthwork likely functioned as 'the Roman equivalent of barbed wire'. Now, if it weren't for the colossal and visually more striking wall, perhaps more would be made of the Vallum in history books. It really is a remarkable feat in its own right.

Although the Wall had a defensive role, it mainly functioned as a barrier marking the northwest edge of the Roman Empire (Hadrian being more concerned with containing his kingdom than expanding it). It was, say English Heritage, a kind of Berlin Wall, and controlled the north–south flow of human traffic for some 250 years until the collapse of the Roman Empire in the 5th century.

To this end, a number of guarded posts were built along its length, one every Roman mile. Between these **milecastles** were two observation towers – or **turrets**. Some, like milecastle 37 west of Housesteads with its arched gate, are impressive to this day. Little kindles the imagination more than on a wet, misty morning when the Wall rises and falls through the fog and the walker is forced to seek shelter on the inside wall of a milecastle. One can only imagine what Roman soldiers thought about being stationed up on this remote ridge.

Despite the 'recycling' of wall stones in the towns, villages and farmhouses in the Tyne Valley in the centuries that followed the retreat of the Romans, it is still considered the most important Roman monument in Britain. The **best-preserved section** lies between Chesters and Brampton where the greatest Roman forts are also situated. Chesters, Vindolanda, Housesteads and Birdoswold all have their highlights and some have superb on-site museums housing Roman treasures unearthed over the last few centuries. The excellent **National Park Visitor Centre** (*Military Road, NE47 7AN; 01434 344396*) is at Once Brewed YHA (not far from Vindolanda).

The preservation of the forts and Wall in this central section has been greatly assisted by the rough, inaccessible countryside. Of course, this is also what makes Hadrian's Wall exceptionally good **walking and cycling** country and an increasing number of visitors come here to take on the 84-mile **Hadrian's Wall Path** or 160-mile **Hadrian's Cycleway**.

Walking the Hadrian's Wall Path

The 84-mile long-distance trail from Bowness-on-Solway on the Cumbrian coast to Wallsend in Newcastle is now fully accessible to walkers along its entire length and is well signposted. What many visitors would call 'the best bit' is the well-preserved section of Wall in the central area, roughly between Chollerford and Brampton. That said, just because the Wall breaks up and often vanishes altogether either side of these settlements isn't to say the walking is not scenic. The Solway Estuary is birdwatching heaven and the tumbling farmland through the Tyne Valley is quite dreamy in parts. Even Wallsend has a certain appeal: it is as manmade as Sewingshields Crags is wild, but there is something very raw and powerful about the industrial scenery with its cranes and old shipbuilding yards at Swan Hunters.

But, back to 'the best bit'. Between Sewingshields and Greenhead, the hills rise for 12 spectacular, thigh-busting miles, holding the Wall to the sky and out of the reach of builders of past centuries.

To really appreciate the beauty of this landscape, hope for bad weather. Okay, not lashing rain, but a misty morning when the clouds cover the roads and all signs of modern life, and the Wall rollercoasters across the landscape peeking up through bowls of fog wherever the Whin Sill crags rise high enough. It's evocative moments like this that will stay with the walker.

Winter walkers will experience solitude that those walking the path during the rest of the year will miss out on. However, bear in mind that this upland countryside is famously damp underfoot and some accommodation providers, attractions and information centres close from October to spring. Also, it gets dark before 16.00.

At any time of year the **weather** can be foul in the uplands of Northumberland and, just like soldiers 2,000 years ago, you may find yourself huddled under the wall sheltering from the wind. Chillproof clothing is recommended throughout the year.

Direction of travel is a tricky one. Most people walk east to west, usually because Newcastle is better connected than the Cumbrian coast, but on balance I think it is best travelled in the other direction. You'll most likely have the wind and rain to your back and the view of the Whin Sill escarpment is most spectacular when viewed from the west. Lastly, you can't start a walk at a place called Walls*end*! Go with the Romans on this one and walk eastwards.

It goes without saying that especially on the remote stretches, make sure you set out with good **supplies** as there are few places on the Wall to pick up water and food. You'll find plenty of villages to refuel at nearby, but you may have to walk perhaps a couple of miles off the Wall in remote parts.

Even though the route is well signposted, you should take Ordnance Survey **maps** (the orange Explorer ones) 314, 315, OL43 and 316. You'll be grateful when a weather front rolls in.

Cycling in the heart of Hadrian's Wall country

Some of the very best wall, hill and river valley scenery is experienced on a 15-mile circular trail from Bardon Mill. You'll need OS Explorer OL43. Cycle north past Once Brewed and cross Hadrian's Wall by Steel Rigg. Descend into the endless hill-farming country bordering Redesdale and continue as far as Edges Green. For the return, head west via Whiteside. An outstanding view of the Roman wall snaking across the backbone of the Whin Sill escarpment comes into sight as you pedal south to the **Milecastle Inn** (*01434 321 372; www.milecastle-inn.co.uk*) on the Military Road. Continue due south up Shield Hill and then free-wheel into Haltwhistle. The final leg east dips in and out of some pretty settlements including Melkridge with its old stone cottages and green, and offers glorious views of pastures and farms in the South Tyne Valley.

⑬ Chesters Roman Fort

Chollerford NE46 4EU ① 01434 681379 Ⓦ www.english-heritage.org.uk; open daily in summer; weekends only in winter; English Heritage.

If Housesteads is 'the fort with the loos' and Vindolanda the one with the high street and writing tablets, then Chesters is all about the bath house. At least that's what it has become known for. Of course, Chesters also boasts a **museum** which has been open to visitors since 1896 and is filled with an astonishing collection of Roman treasures amassed by John Clayton between 1840 and 1890. It is thanks to him that so many Roman artefacts and buildings in Northumberland survive at all.

Clayton bought a number of forts and stretches of Wall to stop them being plundered for stone, and put the most precious objects in his 'Antiquity House' in the garden. Even if he had only saved a handful of the Roman stone plinths, altar stones, reliefs of gods, memorial stones, metal tools and jewellery on display in the museum created after his death, you would be impressed, but there are hundreds of Roman finds here.

The **fort** stands on a hill above the River North Tyne, near Chollerford, in parkland laid out by the Clayton family in the early 19th century. In the centre is the colonnaded courtyard of the headquarters building, still with its paved flooring and well (notice the phallic good luck symbol carved into the paving). Next door is the commanding officer's house, complete with its private bath house (by the tree). To the left are the remains of three barrack blocks.

A large **bath house** lies outside of the fort wall by the wooded riverside and represents the best example of its type in Britain, as well as being one of the most intact Roman structures on the whole of Hadrian's Wall. You gain an idea of how soldiers would have moved from the changing room (the large room with a row of arched 'cubby holes' which may have been used for hanging clothes or could even, an expert at English Heritage told me, have held statues of the seven days of the week) into progressively warmer chambers. Treatment rooms include a sauna and a steam room and hot and cold baths. Like all Roman bath houses, it was a place to wash (using oil, not soap) and socialise. Here soldiers had their skin cleansed, played board games and chatted. At Segedunum Roman Fort in Wallsend, a replica bath house has been created based on the ruins at Chesters.

By now you will have appreciated the **view** of the North Tyne, which forms rapids as it rushes on its way to join the South Tyne at Hexham. Note the stones on the other side of the river – these are the remains of the abutment of two Roman bridges. You can take a closer look by crossing the bridge at Chollerford and taking the path immediately off to the right.

Food and drink
George Hotel (*01434 681611; www.coastandcountryhotels.com*) on the west side of Chollerford Bridge is open for lunches and dinners to non-residents. The restaurant overlooks pretty gardens and is one of the few places serving food close to Chesters Roman Fort. Better still is the **Barrasford Arms** (*01434 681237; www.barrasfordarms.co.uk*) a few miles north of Chollerford (see page 176). For light bites, **Lucullus Larder** (open only in summer) within the grounds of Chesters Roman Fort is recommended (teas, coffees and generously filled sandwiches).

⑭ Vindolanda

Near Bardon Mill, NE47 7JN
Ⓣ 01434 344277 Ⓦ www.vindolanda. com. Open daily; café.
A mile upstream from Bardon Mill where the land is green and bumpy all around is this Roman military station and museum housing some of the most important Roman finds ever recovered. The Roman military fort and village were built in AD85, several decades before the construction of Hadrian's Wall a mile north. Over the following centuries the site was rebuilt several times and continued as a settlement with shops and domestic dwellings after the retreat of the Roman Empire.

Inside the **fort** walls, which would have once been at least 16 feet high, are the remains of a granary, the commanding officer's quarters and the headquarters building. Equally as fascinating are the food and textile shops, domestic dwellings, tavern and workshops that face each other along a main street outside the western fort gate.

Drains line either side of the road and are covered with stone slabs at intervals marking the entrances to individual buildings. One even has the name of the 5th- or 6th-century owner crudely engraved into the stone: 'RIACVS' is clearly visible on the left as you enter the fort and could be a post-Roman name. With a little imagination you can imagine the smells, bustle and noise along what was essentially a high street.

After exploring the fort and the convincing replica stone tower (climb to the top to gain a bird's-eye view of the site and wider countryside), take the path that leads downhill to a wooded ravine and a 19th-century house (and the Trust's excellent museum). A stream runs through the gardens where there is outdoor seating for the café.

Taking the footpath from the back entrance of the museum, you can **walk** to Bardon Mill along the river. A shorter stroll to the stables at Low Fogrigg and back takes under an hour. The path passes many mature oaks and horses in a paddock as you rise away from the bubbling Chainley Burn. On returning to the museum, continue uphill to the Roman road (the Stanegate) where you will see a stone pillar, the only **Roman milestone** in its original location.

The Roman writing tablets

I want you to know that I am in very good health, as I hope you are in turn, you neglectful man, who have sent me not even one letter …

Are we to return with the standard … to the crossroads all together or just half of us … My fellow-soldiers have no beer. Please order some to be sent …

Thanks to the damp, anaerobic soil at Vindolanda, a large number of leather, textile and wooden items that would otherwise have quickly rotted away survived here for almost 2,000 years until first discovered by archaeologists in 1973.

What excited the team most were the hundreds of small writing tablets about the size of a postcard. At first archaeologists thought they were wood shavings until they noticed a script scrawled across the fragments of birch, alder and oak. Among the tablets are the quartermasters' book-keeping records listing supplies for the garrison, the correspondence of commanding officers, and messages of a more personal nature: letters to family members and notes accompanying parcels. Perhaps the most treasured card is the famous birthday party invitation from Claudia Severa to Sulpicia Lepidina; it is the earliest record of female correspondence and Latin handwriting in western Europe.

It was probably only a matter of time before archaeologists at Vindolanda came across a message that would disclose a derogatory term Romans used to refer to native Brits. Tablet 164 revealed the slang word *Brittunculi*, meaning 'wretched Britons'.

The most treasured artefacts at the **Vindolanda museum** are the **Roman writing tablets** (see box opposite) discovered on site beneath a protective layer of clay in 1973. They are the earliest collection of written material in Britain and provide a glimpse of life in Roman Britain. Most of the 1,400 tablets recovered thus far are stored in the British Museum in London but nine are on display at Vindolanda. A short film tells the fascinating story of their discovery which includes the enthusiastic recollections of the eminent archaeologist, Robin Birley, who led the excavations.

The rest of the museum is devoted to the remarkable array of other objects excavated at Vindolanda, including many ceramic vessels, tools, animal bones and weapons as well as intriguing domestic items such as a brush made from pig hair, basketware, a lady's wig, jewellery, leather shoes and a child's textile sock. One of the most exciting finds of recent years is a fragment of a bronze blade-like instrument which has holes punched along its length and the word 'SEPTEMBER'. It is thought to be a Roman calendar or a water clock and is the only example ever found in Britain.

Excavations are ongoing at Vindolanda and adults over the age of 16 can join the team on an **archaeological dig** for one week or longer. Applications open in early November each year for the following season.

⑮ Housesteads

Off the Military Rd, near Haydon Bridge, NE47 6NN ☏01434 344363 ⓦ www.english-heritage.org.uk. Usually open daily but check times in case of scheduled conservation work; café and museum; English Heritage.

The most complete Roman fort in Britain and the most visited of the four main forts in Northumberland owing in part to its dramatic position. Housesteads was built in the years following the construction of Hadrian's Wall and sits snug to the stone barricade, teetering on the edge of the Roman Empire.

The fort is typical in its arrangement of buildings with its centrally located headquarters building, granaries, hospital and commanding officer's residence. The latter consists of rooms arranged around a courtyard and has an excellent example of Roman under-floor heating technology. The floor, now mostly removed, was raised on rows of pillars under which hot air circulated.

The well-preserved **latrine** in the southeast corner of the fort often interests visitors most. The room is oblong with a raised central area with a gutter running around its perimeter. Two wooden benches with holes for around 30 bums once bridged the gap between the central stone plinth you see today and the outer walls. It is thought soldiers cleaned themselves using a kind of natural sponge made of moss attached to the end of a stick. The functions of the trough and bowl are not known for certain though plenty of people have made guesses.

The four **gates** around the curtain wall are of interest, particularly the west gate, still with its door pivot holes, and the east gate with its stone flooring deeply worn by the wheels of carts. These grooves show the wheels were just shy of five feet apart – the same dimension adopted in the centuries thereafter. It is also, not coincidentally, the same width as standard railway gauges in Britain (4 feet 8½ inches). Before the invention of steam engines, horses pulled carts on wooden tracks so it is thought the same standardised axle length was applied when they were replaced by metal rails and 'iron horses'. It's nice to think that the great Victorian railway engineers based at Wylam some 20 miles away from Housesteads developed the railway line based, by default, on the measurements of Roman carts.

A classic Hadrian's Wall **walk** is the seven-mile circular route from **Steel Rigg to Housesteads**, which is described in nearly every walking guidebook to the region. The outward journey from the Steel Rigg car park is along a grassy trail north of the Wall that runs parallel to the Whin Sill crags; the return follows the wall. It takes in the most breathtaking scenery in Hadrian's Wall country and gives you two perspectives of the wall: from the Whin Sill looking down across farmland and loughs into 'barbarian' country, and looking up at the crags and mighty Wall.

⑯ Greenhead and Gilsland

On your way out of Northumberland and into Cumbria while pottering around the Wall, you come to two very pleasant villages in quick succession. **Greenhead** is reached first. The riverside setting, stone terraces, church and village hall make it a welcome stop for ramblers, cyclists and motorists. If you are looking for somewhere to eat your sandwiches, I recommend the picnic area (Millennium Green) by Tipalt Burn (opposite the church).

On a hillside half a mile north of Greenhead is the ruin of **Thirlwall Castle** – a 14th-century fortress reached by following the riverside footpath out of the village (turn up Station Road by the phone box and turn right at the gate signed for the castle). The castle is soon upon you – all bitten and crumbling now – but clearly once a mighty edifice. It was built to defend the wealthy inhabitants from raiding Scots and was abandoned in the 1700s. The walls are nine-feet thick in places and were built using masonry from nearby Hadrian's Wall. The same stones have been robbed and recycled a second time and are seen in nearby houses.

Gilsland sits in a secluded dip in the hills next to the River Irthing. This quiet village of stone about a green is reached from Greenhead by following a road high up over hilly farmland or by foot along Hadrian's Wall Path. The village was popular in Victorian times with visitors who came by train to enjoy the sulphur-rich waters just north of the village.

Gilsland Spa (*016977 47203; www.gilslandspa.co.uk*) is an 18th-century mansion and exclusive hotel above the River Irthing where it is said that Sir Walter Scott met his future bride when he visited in 1797. The wooded grounds of the hotel are particularly scenic and are accessible along a public footpath. A few hundred yards north of the footbridge is a large boulder and two small rounded ones by the river: the Popping Stone (presumably the largest one) is said to be where Scott 'popped' the question to his lover, though the tale is without evidence.

Opposite Gilsland green, on Hall Terrace, is a 17th-century cottage – and former hostelry – known as Mumps Hall which is now the **House of Meg Tee Rooms** (*016977 47777; www.houseofmeg.co.uk*). It is famed for the legend of a notorious landlady nicknamed Meg of Mumps Hall who was said to have murdered and robbed many passing travellers in the 18th century. She was immortalised in Sir Walter Scott's *Guy Mannering* as the character, Tib Mumps.

A good stretch of **Hadrian's Wall** can be found by continuing uphill from the House of Meg tea rooms, passing the Methodist Church on your right.

South of the railway line, **Milecastle 48** is one of the most intact of all on the Wall. It is also known as the Poltress Burn Milecastle after the river it watches over.

The landscape around Gilsland and Walltown is varied and offers good day **walks**. You'll experience some of the best Roman wall scenery: open farmland, wooded rivers, ruins and one of the tallest sections of Hadrian's Wall, while avoiding the crowds. The crumbling 14th-century Thirlwall Castle marks the centre point of two great circular walks: east to Walltown along Hadrian's Wall and return via the vallum; and west to Gilsland village following the vallum and return via Gilsland Spa, the River Irthing and farmland.

Roman Army Museum

Carvoran, Greenhead CA8 7JB ⓣ01697 747485 ⓦ www.vindolanda.com/Roman-Army-Museum; open daily; buy a 'joint site ticket' which includes entry to Vindolanda and a saving of 20%; café.

Vindolanda's sister museum delves into the world of the fierce and unstoppable Roman army in all its spear-thrusting, shield-bearing magnificence. Different aspects of the Roman military are detailed across three galleries and include the daily lives of legionnaires and auxiliaries. You'll learn about the life of Hadrian and the wider context of the army in relation to the Roman Empire and see life-size models of soldiers.

Everyone raves about the museum's 3D film, *Edge of Empire*. Re-enactments of ambushes and clashes with native Britons and the life of soldiers on Hadrian's Wall are brought to life in a Hollywood blockbuster-style format. Step outside into the 21st century where children can make their own Roman re-enactments in the shadow of one of the tallest sections of Hadrian's Wall (Walltown Crags) and the fort at Carvoran (now largely an outline).

⑰ Birdoswald Roman Fort

Gilsland CA8 7DD ⓣ01697 747602 ⓦ www.english-heritage.org.uk. Open daily from 1 Apr–31 Oct, weekends only rest of year; café and small museum; English Heritage.

Compared to Housesteads and Vindolanda, the fort at Birdoswald is more ruinous and with fewer buildings, but its curtain wall, granaries and gates are worthy of note – and, wow, what a view. Situated at the top of a steep, wooded escarpment, the fort and the centuries-old farmhouse look across several miles of undulating fields and Roman wall. The two granaries date to the early 3rd century but were demolished and rebuilt in the following century. The wooden posts you see show where a later timber hall once stood.

The 30 miles of Hadrian's Wall to the west of Birdoswald was originally a turf construction but was later replaced with stone. You can see this older turf wall by exiting the fort through the south gate and following the footpath heading west. Plunging **views** of the River Irthing snaking through woodland in the valley below await. A pleasant 45-minute walk, which returns via a lane outside the estate, is described in a leaflet in the information centre.

Ten memorable bridges in Northumberland

Chesters Roman Bridge *River North Tyne, Chollerford (B6318)*
It's not the mid 18th-century multi-arched road crossing at Chollerford that's of interest here (though it is a handsome sandstone bridge and one of the oldest on the Tyne and its tributaries) but the ruined Roman bridge below. The only surviving parts of this relic that used to connect with Hadrian's Wall and the Roman fort at Chesters are its piers and an abutment.

Cragside's Iron Bridge *Rothbury*
Lord Armstrong built several metal bridges in the North East, including the Swing Bridge and Armstrong Bridge in Newcastle. At Cragside (see page 204), a slender 1870s footbridge with elegant ironwork reaches across the Debdon Burn at some height offering a superb view of the industrialist's mansion through the trees. Nearby is an old stone packhorse bridge.

Featherstone Bridge *3 miles south of Haltwhistle*
This curious lopsided bridge arching over the wooded River South Tyne on an unclassified road not far from Rowfoot is really worth seeking out. It dates to 1775 and is set within a dreamy riverscape lined with mature trees.

Warkworth Old Bridge *Northumberland Coast*
Clearly a venerable structure, Warkworth's 14th-century bridge over the River Coquet features cutwaters between its two arches and a fortified tower (once used as a toll house). It's a cobbled pedestrian bridge these days but you get good views as you enter the village from the newer road bridge (the B1068/ continuation of Bridge Street).

Kielder viaduct *Kielder Forest*
Northumberland and Durham have an impressive number of viaducts owing to the extensive railway network that once ribboned across the whole of region. Lambley viaduct over the River South Tyne and the Royal Border Bridge at Berwick are particularly eye-catching (detailed elsewhere in this book) as is this unusual castellated viaduct over the North Tyne near Bakethin Reservoir. The 1862 crossing is well used by cyclists and walkers today but was originally built to carry the now defunct Border Counties Railway on its journey from the

Food and drink

Scypen Café and Birdoswald Cheese Slack House Farm, Gilsland (near Birdoswald Roman Fort) ☏01697 747351 ⓦ www.slackhousefarm.co.uk. Variable opening times in summer and winter; camping barn. High on a hill in a tumbledown working farm is this cosy organic café serving snacks and lunches. Tori Bird is passionate about healthy, home-produced food and makes unusual scones (I recommend the apple variety). Cheese and yoghurt are made on site to a 1688 recipe. Milk is taken straight from the herd of brown and white Ayrshire cows in nearby fields and immediately worked for up to five hours. The cheese is then left to mature for up to six months.

Tyne Valley to Scotland. It was engineered with seven 'skew arches' that were individually shaped so the viaduct aligned with the river.

Bellasis Bridge *1 mile north of Horton Grange on Green Lane, Ponteland*
It comes as quite a treat to chance upon this medieval stone crossing humped over the River Blyth. You're most likely to find it if travelling on the back roads to the cheese farm. I once met a couple of cyclists here who told me the grouting was made with sand from near Tynemouth Priory, hence the fragments of shells between its stone blocks. Not the most enthralling discovery, but a curious one. Look over the left-hand side of the bridge as you approach the crossing from the south and you'll see shell fragments between the stones.

Lion Bridge *The Peth, Alnwick (B6346)*
Castellated parapets and faux arrow slits mirror the masonry of Alnwick Castle rearing above the River Aln to the south, adding to the appeal of this much photographed bridge dating to 1773. An arresting statue of a lion (emblem of the Percy family of Alnwick Castle) guards the crossing and entrance to the town.

Lowford Bridge *Morpeth (B6343)*
A mile or so west of Morpeth on the road to Mitford, you come to a sharp bend in the road where Lowford Bridge carries the B6343 over the Wansbeck. Though not magnificent or as appreciated as some other sandstone bridges in the area, the early 19th-cenutry crossing is memorable for its huge square blocks of honey-coloured stone and wooded surroundings.

Haltwhistle Station footbridge *Haltwhistle, Tyne Valley*
If you take a trip on the Newcastle to Carlisle Railway, you'll pass a chain of Victorian stations still with many original features including their cream-and-maroon iron footbridges. This one is particularly fetching because of the old signal box, water tank and waiting room completing the 19th-century scene.

Weetwood Bridge Chatton *(B6348)*
Curving high over the River Till on the road from Chatton to Wooler is a wondrous medieval bridge constructed with rose-coloured sandstone – originally in the 16th century but modified later. Its height above the water, colour, splayed parapets, conical finals to its piers and view of the Cheviots are not easily forgotten.

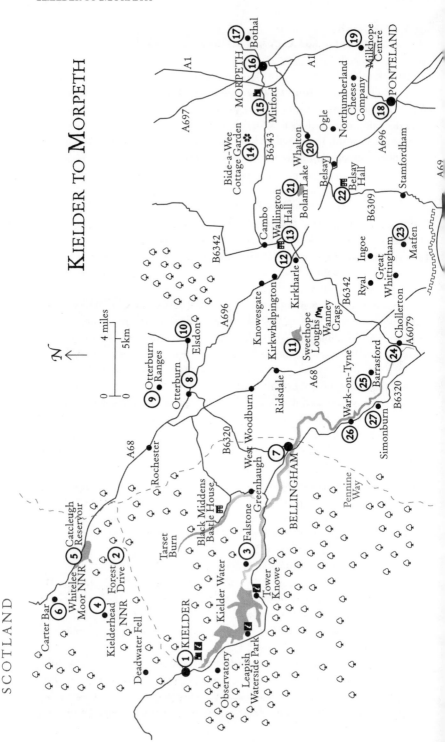

KIELDER TO MORPETH

SCOTLAND

4 miles
5km

N

Carter Bar ⑥
Whitelee Moor NNR ⑤
Catcleugh Reservoir
Kielderhead NNR ④
Forest Drive ②
Deadwater Fell
KIELDER ①
Observatory
Leapish Waterside Park
Kielder Water
Tower Knowe
Falstone ③
Tarset Burn
Black Middens Bastle House
Greenhaugh
Rochester
A68
B6320
West Woodburn
BELLINGHAM ⑦
Pennine Way
Otterburn ⑧
Otterburn Ranges ⑨
A696
Elsdon ⑩
Ridsdale
A68
Simonburn ②⑦
Wark-on-Tyne ②⑥
Barrasford ②⑤
Sweethope Loughs ⑪
Wanney Crags
B6342
Chollerton ②④
A6079
Knowesgate
Kirkwhelpington
Kirkharle ⑫
Wallington Hall ⑬
Cambo
B6342
Ryal
Ingoe
Great Whittingham
Matfen ②③
Bolam Lake
⑫① Hall ②①
B6343
Bide-a-Wee Cottage Garden ⑭
Whalton
Belsay ②⓪
Belsay Hall ②②
B6309
Ogle
Stamfordham
Northumberland Cheese Company
A696
A69
Mitford
⑮
MORPETH ⑯
Bothal ⑰
A1
A697
A1
Milkhope Centre ⑲
PONTELAND ⑱

140

4. KIELDER TO MORPETH

Five hundred years of cross-border warfare and clan fighting made this stretch of upland countryside a very dangerous place to live. Those lawless years ended after James I came to the English throne in 1603, but parts of **Redesdale** (from Kielder to Otterburn and as far north as Carter Bar on the Scottish border) still have a wild edge. Dark forests, lonely fells, rough farmland and Cheviot moors dominate the landscape, enticing ramblers and cyclists who savour solitude.

Kielder, England's largest forest, is a vast uninhabited expanse of conifer trees on the western edge of Northumberland. Its remote location, hilly terrain and large reservoir make the area popular with mountain bikers, watersport enthusiasts, walkers and wildlife watchers. The countryside becomes increasingly inhospitable as the trees peter out giving way to exposed heather-covered slopes and the Cheviot Hills.

Travelling east out of Redesdale, it's a completely different picture. The hills collapse into the lowland farmland around **Ponteland** and **Morpeth** and you'll find yourself dipping in and out of well-to-do villages, tootling along green lanes and glimpsing country houses between the trees and hedgerows. Northumberland's gentle corner is well known to Tynesiders, but less so to visitors from further afield (not altogether surprising with Hadrian's Wall and the national park nearby). Here you'll find two of the region's finest manor houses (Wallington and Belsay) and a number of picturesque villages and gardens to visit. Cyclists will enjoy the quiet country lanes connecting all these places.

Getting around

Saddle up and hit the road. **Cycling** around the countryside covered by this chapter is a joy: plenty of quiet back roads, high passes with far-reaching views and an excellent network of bike-friendly trails around the whole of the Kielder area.

Otherwise, you'll probably need a car unless you want to tightly plan your holiday around the infrequent **buses**. If travelling from Newcastle to Kielder by bus, you'd better make it a Sunday in summer (more options from Hexham). Morpeth town is easy to reach from Newcastle with **trains** running hourly (fewer services on Sundays) and buses every 15 minutes.

There are three **buses** to note: the **880** from **Hexham to Kielder** via Bellingham (*all year on Tue, Fri and Sat*); **714** from **Newcastle to Kielder** via Ponteland, Belsay and Otterburn (*Sun and bank holidays in summer*); **508** from **Newcastle to Rothbury** stopping at Ponteland, Belsay and Wallington (*Wed, Fri, Sun and bank holidays in summer*).

Northumberland County Council has an excellent **information line** (see page viii).

Accommodation

B&Bs and self-catering

Battlesteads Hotel & Restaurant Wark NE48 3LS ℗ 01434 230209 ⓦ www.battlesteads.com Ⓔ info@battlesteads.com. This old farmhouse on the outskirts of Wark and just a few miles from Hadrian's Wall beat the likes of the Savoy in London to become crowned Green Hotel of the Year. It's not quite the Savoy in terms of the standard of rooms, but what really makes this inexpensive hotel (with some wheelchair-friendly rooms) stand out, apart from having a carbon-neutral heating system and a genuine environmentally friendly ethos, is its restaurant (see page 176).

Boat Farm Bellingham NE48 2AR ℗ 01434 220989 ⓦ www.boatfarm.co.uk Ⓔ info@boatfarm.co.uk. B&B accommodation in a farmhouse by the wooded River North Tyne. Homely, average-priced rooms, some with river views. Two small self-catering stone cottages located side by side next door (modern interior with exposed beams and wood-burning stoves). Bellingham is reached on foot by following a riverside track.

Falstone Barns Falstone, near Kielder NE48 1AA ℗ 01434 240251 ⓦ www.falstonebarns.com Ⓔ info@falstonebarns.com. Four sumptuous stone apartments individually styled (eg: French Bourgeois, Romantic Medieval) with opulent fabrics, luxury bathrooms and wood-burning stoves. It's not cheap to stay here but this is somewhere you might come for a couple of nights as a romantic treat. That said, children are very welcome and there are family orientated activities on offer including bush crafts, pony trekking, willow weaving and wildlife-watching. Activities (run by Wild North Discovery) also available to non-residents.

The Hytte Bingfield (5 miles north of Corbridge) NE46 4HR ℗ 01434 672321 ⓦ www.thehytte.com Ⓔ srgregory@thehytte.com. This Norwegian-inspired timber cabin just off the A68 has a turf roof, sauna and hot tub and gets booked up far in advance. It's an unusual self-catering lodge (sleeps eight) with over an acre of wildflower meadows and lawn. The Hytte was rated 'exceptional' for accessibility by the National Accessible Scheme and is very welcoming to wheelchair users. The price works out reasonably for large groups.

Kielder Water Lodges Leaplish ℗ 01434 251000 ⓦ www.nwl.co.uk/kielder Ⓔ kielder.holidays@nwl.co.uk. Family-focused with a small indoor swimming pool, mini-golf and restaurant/bar on site. Lodges furnished to a high standard but they are not cheap. Some have wheelchair access. The **Calvert Trust** near the Bull Crag Peninsula (*01434 250232; www.calvert-trust.org.uk; enquiries@ calvert-kielder.com*) run a small number of lodges overlooking a burn. They are not luxurious but are comfortable and have been designed with those less mobile in mind.

Old Church Cottages Chollerton NE46 4TF ℗ 01434 681930 ⓦ www.chollerton-oldchurch.co.uk Ⓔ enquiries@chollerton-oldchurch.co.uk. Characterful, low- to average-priced cottages in converted church buildings (two cottages in the church and one in the stable), set in pretty gardens. Exposed beams, rustic décor and wood-burning stoves. Somewhat out of the way on a hillside with expansive farmland views but within easy reach of Hadrian's Wall, Hexham and Redesdale's countryside.

Pheasant Inn Stannersburn, Kielder NE48 1DD ℗ 01434 240382 ⓦ www.thepheasantinn.com Ⓔ stay@thepheasantinn.com. Very clean and comfortable rooms with modern bathrooms; set away from the restaurant and bars around a garden courtyard. Slightly above average prices. Exposed stone walls add to the appeal of this 400-year-old farmhouse, but what will win you over most of all is the standard of food in the restaurant (see page 148).

Shieldhall Wallington NE61 4AQ ℗ 01830 540387 ⓦ www.shieldhallguesthouse.co.uk Ⓔ stay@shieldhallguesthouse.co.uk. You can see the National Trust's Wallington Hall from the gardens of this 18th-century farm. The surrounding countryside is like stepping into a parkland laid out by Capability Brown, which is fitting because the great landscape gardener's family used to live here. Within Shieldhall's ten acres, there's a lovely woodland walk. Rooms have their own entrances and are reached from a central courtyard; the décor is 'country farmhouse' with the odd antique and old print and solid wood furniture (some pieces hand-crafted by the owner and his son who have a cabinet-making business at Kirkharle). Four-poster oak bed in one room. Homemade dinners on request.

Southlands Farm Cottages Gunnerton, south of Wark NE48 4EA ℗ 01434 681464 ⓦ www.southlandsfarmcottages.co.uk Ⓔ enquiries@ southlandsfarmcottages.co.uk. Three stone cottages (side by side so good for large family groups) in a hamlet surrounded by hills and farmland. Each cottage furnished to a high standard (modern décor and fittings with a touch of the old; very cosy with wood-burning stoves) hence the above average price. The ecologically minded owners have rare-breed cattle, pigs and free-range hens. Help yourself to veg (with permission) from the organic kitchen garden. A welcome basket of fresh produce is provided on your first day.

Camping, wigwams and bunkhouses
Boe Rigg Campsite & Bunkhouse Charlton, east of Bellingham NE48 1PE ℗ 01434 240970 ⓦ www.theboerigg.com Ⓔ info@theboerigg.com. Recently opened large timber-framed bunkhouse (more of a very comfortable hostel really)

and bistro in pretty farmland setting. Tranquil campsite in field opposite. Even if you're not staying here, it's a good place to grab a bite to eat if passing.

Demesne Farm Bellingham NE48 2BS ① 01434 220258 ⓦ www.demesne farmcampsite.co.uk ⓔ stay@demesnefarmcampsite.co.uk. Located in the centre of Bellingham and close to the start of the Hareshaw Linn walk (see page 154). Bunkhouse in a sensitively converted old barn; camping in a field with free-range hens around.

Kielder Campsite ① 01434 250291 ⓦ www.kieldercampsite.co.uk. Set by the river and close to the castle and Kielder village, this community initiative has a small shop, a few timber-framed huts for hire, and space for 40 tents. Caravans also welcome. You could also try the **Caravan Park** at Leaplish Waterside Park (*01434 251000*). Backpackers and those wanting somewhere more remote should enquire about the Forestry Commission **bothies** and **wild pitches** (see page 147). There's also a **youth hostel** in Kielder village run by the YHA.

Wild Northumbrian Thorneyburn, Tarset (east of Kielder) NE48 1NA ① 01434 240902 ⓦ www.wildnorthumbrian.co.uk ⓔ info@wildnorthumbrian.co.uk. Luxury tipis and yurts in beautiful upland setting by a burn and not far from Kielder water and forest. Bushcraft, bat detecting, pottery making and many more workshops on offer.

Kielder's forests and lakes

Solitude is not difficult to find in England's largest forest which covers 230 square miles of upland terrain. As you drive into Kielder along the lakeside road, the tall Sitka spruce trees gather around you, and for a while the landscape takes on the appearance of the great Highland forests. The scenery is made all the more Scottish in character by vast areas of open moorland and the presence of ospreys and red squirrels. Ospreys only recently returned here as a breeding species after an absence of 200 years and they are now one of the star attractions during the summer months.

Kielder is no untouched wilderness, however, this being a plantation forest surrounding the largest reservoir in northern Europe and supplying 25% of England's domestic timber. It may be a young landscape, created in the aftermath of World War I to replenish timber supplies, but it is still astonishingly scenic. The Campaign to Protect Rural England described Kielder as the most tranquil place in the country with the darkest night skies. If you'd like to be

Before you set off

Kielder is a remote place with no petrol stations, mobile phone signal or large food shops. Opening times of visitor centres are variable and limited in winter. Phone ahead to check. Also see www.visitkielder.com.

Forest Art

One of the most exciting initiatives at Kielder in recent decades was the commissioning of 20 sculptures sited around Kielder Water. Each is unique (and some have won architectural awards) and they are all inspired in some way by the landscape and experiences in this vast forest. A giant timber head, stone maze, huge rotating metal seats and a 'forest' of twinkling silver disks should give you an idea of what to expect. Some double as shelters for mountain bikers and walkers caught out in bad weather. The locations of all the works are listed on the Visit Kielder website (*www.visitkielder.com*) and at the three information centres around Kielder Water.

Wave Chamber is a conical stone hut and camera obscura a mile west of the Hawkhope car park on the north side of Kielder Water. Inside it's pitch black at first, but when your eyes adjust, you'll see a real-time image of the reservoir projected on the floor. The building echoes the sound of the waves on the shore outside, adding to the experience. It's best visited in the afternoon and/or on a sunny day.

Skyspace is reached on the track to the observatory and would not be out of place in a retreat centre. It's another round chamber (wheelchair accessible) with a hole in the roof which draws your eye to the clouds (or stars) above. It's incredibly relaxing. Outside, a rock ledge provides a far-reaching view of the forests, moors and lakes.

convinced of this, I recommend a dusk walk to the observatory. Halfway up is a large boulder by the Skyspace sculpture where you can sit looking out over the trees and reservoir. The chorus of songthrushes on spring and early summer evenings is quite something. As the light fades and only the silhouette of the hills and treetops can be seen against the indigo sky, the first planets appear. Stay here long enough and you will see more stars than you have seen anywhere else in England.

① Around Kielder Water and Kielder village

Kielder's activity centres, information points, lodge accommodation and camp/caravan sites are dotted along the southern shores of the reservoir. The main hubs are Kielder Castle and village where you'll find bike hire stations as well as the start points of many walks and cycle rides, and Leaplish Waterside Park.

Tourist information

There are three **tourist information centres** on the south side of Kielder Water. Variable opening times; call to check.

Tower Knowe Visitor Centre (*0845 1550236*) is reached first if coming from the east. It is a large lakeside visitor centre, with a café and picnic benches.

Leaplish Waterside Park (*01434 251000*) is halfway along the lake. Many visitors to Kielder stay here (caravan park and lodges) and make use of the

Osprey Ferry

Kielder Water's motor cruiser operates a 'hop on, hop off' service four times a day (roughly 10.00 to 16.00) from 1 April to end of October. It's useful if you're doing a linear walk or cycle ride on the Lakeside Way (the ferry takes a limited number of bicycles, pushchairs and wheelchairs). It stops at Belvedere, Leaplish and Tower Knowe (buy your ticket at either of the latter two places). Call 01434 251000 or see www.visitkielder.com to check times. If you're lucky, you may see an osprey.

watersport activities on offer. You'll also find a pub serving evening dinners, a **bird of prey centre** (*01434 250400; demonstrations at 13.30 and 15.00 daily in summer; 14.00 in winter*), a small indoor swimming pool and a shop selling outdoor clothes. Information point only.

Kielder Castle Visitor Centre (*01434 250209*) at the western end of the reservoir is a popular starting point for trips into the forest. There's a café and information centre here and the bike hire stations, village and campsite are all nearby. The **salmon hatchery** (*01434 250269*) has also has a visitor centre.

Outdoor activities at Kielder

The Forestry Commission maintains a superb network of trails for cyclists, walkers, horseriders and wheelchair users. One of the most accessible (and beautiful) is the **Lakeside Way** multi-user trail – a paved track of 26 miles that circumnavigates the reservoir. It lends itself well to marathons for obvious reasons. See www.kieldermarathon.com or call 01434 689040. If you don't want to walk (eight to ten hours) or cycle (three to four hours) the whole way around, you can return using the Osprey Ferry (see above).

Kielder is well known for its off-road **cycling** and **mountain bike trails**. They range from family-friendly green routes such as the loop of the Bull Crag peninsula, to red routes like the Deadwater Trail (and its black route extension) that climbs to the summit of Deadwater at 1,900 feet. At the top you can see the Pentland Hills just south of Edinburgh and the Lake District. **Bike hire** at Purple Mountain (*near Kielder Castle; 01434 250532; www.purplemountain. co.uk*) and the Bike Place (*Kielder village; 01434 250457; www.thebikeplace. co.uk*).

For **watersports**, contact the Calvert Trust (*01434 250232; www.calvert-trust.org.uk*) based between Tower Knowe and Leaplish. They also have a climbing wall, a King Swing (a horrifically thrilling trapeze) and various other adventure activities. The charity works closely with disabled children but anyone can hire their canoes, have a go on the climbing wall, etc. If staying in the lodges or caravan park at Leaplish, you have access to land- and water-based activities. Merlin Brae Water Ski club near Tower Knowe (*01434 250037; merlinbraewaterski.co.uk*) offers waterskiing and wakeboarding.

Fishing permits and basic equipment for novices are available to hire at the Leaplish.

Hillwalkers have plenty of choice, which you'd expect as Kielder merges into the Cheviot Hills to the north. Kielderhead is rugged and varied (see page 151). Gentle walks are plentiful around the reservoir and many routes encompass Kielder's public art works. A couple of recommended trails include the lakeside path to the Belling peninsula on the north shore of Kielder Water, and the riverside walk from the picnic area at Matthew's Linn.

Back-country camping is permitted by the Forestry Commission on 17 sites around Kielder, including at Plashetts – a peninsula overlooking Kielder Water. No facilities whatsoever, just a rough patch of grass to pitch up for a night. Campers must dig latrines. Those requiring more facilities should try the campsite near Kielder village (see page 144). There are also eight **bothies**. For locations, go to the Kielder Castle Information Centre or call the Forestry Commission on 01434 221012. You should phone ahead anyway to book the campsites and bothies and check that none are closed.

Kielder Observatory

Kielder Water, signed off the main road a third of a mile south of Kielder Castle; from the turn off, it's 2 miles to the observatory. ① 07805 638469
Ⓦ www.kielderobservatory.org; parking at the observatory; toilets.

No need to be an astronomy buff to come here: the enthusiasm of the staff and volunteers at the observatory will soon have you hooked, including those with no interest in star-gazing. Even without the astronomy bit, the experience of travelling to this remote place in the dark, the hill-top view of Kielder Forest and water, and the building itself are worthy of the trek alone.

The Northern Lights

'When can you see the Northern Lights at Kielder?' is a question the director of Kielder Observatory, Gary Fildes, is asked a lot. 'It all depends what ingredients you put into the mix – and having an active sun,' he responds. Kielder is the best place in England to watch the phenomenon because of the dark skies and relative closeness to the North Pole. The A69 corridor is also good, says Gary, as long as you can see the northern horizon and you're away from city lights. If the conditions are right (clear skies and a strong solar storm) you may see curtains of flickering green light across the sky. Powerful storms peak every 11 years (in 2014, for example).

The strength of the sun's flares are indicated by something called the KP index: the higher the number, the more spectacular the light show will be. Go to www. spaceweather.com to find out the KP index for a given night. 'KP5 and above is what you're looking for,' advises Gary. 'If you get a KP9,' he says animatedly, 'drop the baby.'

The striking timber structure juts out of the hillside on stilts; inside there are no windows, except for two roof shutters that become 'your eye into the universe' when they open to reveal a deathly dark sky dusted with millions of stars. Two huge telescopes crank into gear as soon as the shutters open. They turn automatically on a room-sized circular track like sunflowers searching for the sun, except they are seeking planets of course.

Gary Fildes, the director of the observatory, gives gripping evening talks. He began the event I attended with this taster: 'We grow ambivalent to how violent the universe can be. About half an hour ago, a meteor the size of a double-decker bus passed us just 45,000 miles away.' That was followed by a fascinating talk on the Northern Lights peppered with facts and awe-inspiring stories about the solar system. About 30 of us (mostly people with no knowledge of astronomy) packed into the cosy lecture room heated by a wood-burning stove. We ooh-ed and ah-ed at slides depicting various phenomenal astro events while Gary talked enthusiastically of solar winds, sun spots and chromal mass ejections. At one point he showed a film clip of the sun emitting flares. He paused it on a particularly violent flare and said casually: 'There's enough energy in that flare to power the USA for 100 million years.'

For all the latest on solar activity at Kielder and for information on talks and the hugely popular **star camps** in spring and autumn, visit www.kielderobservatory.org. As we were going to press, I read an update on the website reporting an astonishing meteor passing over Kielder that was so big and bright, it cast a shadow on the ground.

Food and drink

You'll find **cafés** at all three visitor centres in Kielder. Leaplish also has the **Boat Inn Restaurant** (*01434 250294*) which serves standard pub lunches and dinners and caters to holiday-makers. The **Angler's Arms** in Kielder Village is more of a locals' pub. There's a small **grocery store** in Kielder Village but it's not particularly well stocked with fresh foods (you're better off shopping at the deli in Bellingham).

Old School Tearoom Falstone NE48 1AA ① 01434 240459
Ⓦ www.falstonetearoom.co.uk. Open Easter–end Oct. Former Victorian school selling freshly prepared lunches. The tearoom doubles as a small shop, craft gallery and information point with free Wi-Fi.
Pheasant Inn Stannersburn NE48 1DD ① 01434 240382
Ⓦ www.thepheasantinn.com. One of the best pubs for Sunday lunch or dinner in Northumberland. Hearty traditional British mains and puddings made with local produce (roast Northumberland lamb is particularly good). Great selection of local ales served in an unpretentious 400-year-old farmhouse with much rustic appeal (low beams, wooden furniture and old photographs of Redesdale life hanging on the walls).

② Forest Drive

This pot-holed track traverses the upland landscape north of Kielder Water from Kielder Castle to Blakehopeburnhaugh in 12 slow-going miles. If you're in a hurry to reach the A68, this is not the best route; but if you're happy to trundle along enjoying the moorland and forest scenery and perhaps stopping for lunch or a walk, Forest Drive is for you. Halfway along, the Sitka spruce trees open up permitting a long view into the hills with Kielderhead to the north and Emblehope Moor to the south.

Short walks around Blakehopeburnhaugh

Not the longest place name in England in case you are wondering (that is Cottonshopeburnfoot a mile north). A distinctive name by itself is not a good enough reason to enter the pages of this book, but one with a magical waterfall hidden in a wooded dene certainly is. **Hindhope Linn** is reached from the picnic and parking area near the eastern entrance to Forest Drive in just over a mile by following Blakehope Burn.

Walking north from the car park, you can make a circuit to **The Three Kings**, a stone circle thought to be between 3,000 and 4,000 years old. Return by following the Pennine Way along the River Rede.

③ Falstone, Greenhaugh and the Tarset Valley

Kielder village is largely a modern settlement and of little appeal to visitors, but at the eastern end of the reservoir there are a couple of hamlets with good pubs, eateries and guesthouses.

Falstone stands out for its tea room, peaceful setting by a burn and children's playground. The enclosed green by the river is a tranquil spot with picnic benches. If you wander along the riverbank, you'll come to a sheepfold which is actually a contemporary sculpture called the Stell (a local word for sheepfold) where you can take a seat on one of two stone 'sofas'.

In the sheep-grazed hills a couple of miles northeast of Falstone, you come to **Greenhaugh**. It's not really on the way to anywhere, unless you're visiting nearby Black Middens bastle, so generally this hamlet comprised of a stone street, rustic pub with a wood-burning range (Holly Bush Inn *01434 240391; www.hollybushinn.net*) and farm selling fresh eggs by the roadside goes unappreciated by visitors in Redesdale/Kielder.

There are some lovely **walks** around Greenhaugh and the buttercup-filled **Tarset Valley**, including a short trail to the Tarset Burn which passes a glorious upland hay meadow stuffed with great burnet, sweet-vernal grass, wood crane's-bill, eyebright, pignut and self-heal. To get there, follow a track just south of the village and off the main road (look out for the national park sign). You can make it a longer walk by continuing south along the burn to Lanehead and then turning northwest and hiking past Thorneyburn Fell and through **Sidwood** (beautiful mixed woodland with lots of red squirrels). Re-enter Greenhaugh from the north.

Wildlife-watching

Kielder is well known for its birds of prey including ospreys, goshawks and tawny owls. They do well here because of the remoteness of the forest and protection from persecution afforded by the Forestry Commission. There's an organised osprey viewing station at Leaplish.

Wading birds breed on the moors, and you'll see all the usual water birds in the lake (including ospreys fishing if you are lucky). Tits and flocks of siskins flit along the burns where there are willows, birches and alders. Also look out for crossbills perched on the uppermost branches of trees.

In this conifer-dominated upland environment, **red squirrels** have the upper hand over greys, making Kielder the last stronghold for our native squirrel in England (70% of the red squirrel population). They are not infrequently seen around the entrance to Forest Drive where there are feeding stations. Chewed pine cones on footpaths are a sign that squirrels are about.

The Forestry Commission rangers and wildlife experts lead a number of excellent **wildlife-watching trips** throughout the year, including dawn deer safaris, owl hunts, fungi forays, goshawk walks, and badger and osprey watching. See the events pages on their website or phone for details (*01434 250209; www.forestry.gov.uk*).

The high road from Greenhaugh to Otterburn

If heading east out of Kielder in the direction of Otterburn, you could take the track signed for 'High Green' on approaching the junction at Gatehouse Farm (1½ miles north of Greenhaugh). The quiet paved lane ascends quickly into remote countryside making for a spectacular journey across some of Northumberland's finest moorland countryside. It's perfect for cycling, but you'll need good leg and lung muscles for the climb to 1,000 feet. Once you're at the highest point, which is roughly where the Pennine Way crosses the road, the terrain flattens out allowing you to enjoy the view of the Cheviots before descending into the lowland farmland around Otterburn.

Otterburn, Bellingham and the hills

Rough are Redesdale's fells, rough are the grasslands and old fortified farmhouses, and rough is Redesdale's history. The scenery is desolate at times with only the occasional farm surrounded by fells and tussocky grasslands, a scattering of towns and hamlets and a few settlements guarding the Roman road into Scotland (the A68). As you head north towards the Scottish border at Carter Bar, the landscape becomes particularly moody and typically Cheviot-like with bulky hills muscling into one another and views for many miles around. Snow posts appear on roadside verges.

Further south around the Woodburns and Ridsdale, the sheep-grazed grasslands are interspersed with the odd heather slope, field of buttercups and Forestry Commission woodland. Lapwings tumble above damp meadows and the pitiful cry of curlews is always in earshot in spring. I once broke down on the road between Bellingham and West Woodburn and spent a very enjoyable hour watching a meadow filled with courting curlews. Other good places to break down on a sunny day in spring would be the lanes around Ridsdale and Elsdon and the high road over Whitley Pike from Greenhaugh to Otterburn (see opposite). Cyclists and Pennine Way walkers will enjoy many a bird-filled sky hereabouts.

④ Kielderhead National Nature Reserve

A wide, black upland region, which looks wintry even in the sunshine … The song of the lark would be out of place here; the curlew's cry harmonises with the scene.
Walter White *Northumberland and the Border*, 1859

North of Kielder reservoir, an extensive area of moorland stretches north to the Scottish border. Thigh-high heather, bracken and dwarf shrubs like bilberry cover the slopes, but as with the Cheviot landscape elsewhere, there are also plenty of peat bogs, gullies and squelching moss-covered hummocks to trip up, over and down. I once read a description of a 13-mile hike through this rough terrain likened to 'a week in the Burmese jungle'. I wouldn't say the walking was quite that arduous, but you'll certainly want sturdy waterproof boots and gaiters.

I should add that the terrain, while rough underfoot, is also dramatic and beautiful: all those swelling hills creating endless coloured folds, clouds rolling fast across big skies and the sun picking out individual slopes to bathe in light.

Though undeniably lonesome (don't expect to meet many – if any – fellow walkers up here) these moors are full of wildlife surprises: the sudden appearance of a merlin pursuing a meadow pipit, a wild Cheviot goat, exquisite day-flying emperor moths skimming the heather, and an expanse of cloudberries, their orange fruits ripe to eat.

Much of Kielderhead is designated a Site of Special Scientific Interest (SSSI) for its moorland flora and breeding birds which include golden plover, dunlin, red grouse, curlew and even ring ouzel. Cottongrasses, sphagnum mosses, bog asphodel and mountainous shrubs like bilberry and cloudberry grow in abundance. Also look out for the insectivorous sundew where it's mossy and wet. Downy birch and rowan trees crowd the sides of secluded waterways hidden in ravines.

Border Reivers

They were cruel, coarse savages, slaying each other as the beasts of the forest; and yet they were also poets who could express in the grand style the inexorable fate of the individual man and woman, and infinite pity for all the cruel things which they none the less perpetually inflicted upon one another. It was not one ballad-maker alone, but the whole cut-throat population who felt this magnanimous sorrow, and the consoling charm of the highest poetry.

G M Trevelyan *The Middle Marches*, 1914

The border country from the late medieval period until the mid 17th century was the Wild West of Britain: a violent place marked by clashes between rival kinship groups in Scotland, Northumbria and parts of Cumbria who had greater ties to family groups than to country. These allegiances provided a level of security to the border people who had suffered centuries of Anglo-Scottish warfare.

Some of the most notorious families were the Armstrongs, Elliots, Forsters, Dodds, Milburns and Robsons – surnames which remain some of the most common in the North East today. Reivers rode on horseback wearing steel bonnets and armed with swords and travelled across the Cheviot Hills, raiding farmsteads, stealing livestock from one another and seeking retribution. Incidentally, It is because of the Border Reivers that we have the words 'bereaved' and 'blackmail'. The former speaks for itself but the etymology of 'blackmail' is not so clear. The word is thought to originate in the border region (also used further north) where payments and goods were offered in return for immunity from raids.

A culture of story telling developed in the hills in which tragic love stories, raids and clashes were recalled in song. Recital of the melancholic border ballads died out during more peaceful times in the latter half of the 17th century, but some were recorded before they were lost completely; most famously by Sir Walter Scott in his *The Minstrelsy of the Scottish Border*. There's an extract of *The Battle of Otterbourne* on page 157.

⑤ Whitelee Moor National Nature Reserve and Catcleugh Reservoir

Heather slopes, wooded cleughs, peat bogs and tussocky pastures characterise the hilly ground all the way to the Scottish border. Burns run off the fells feeding Catcleugh Reservoir and the River Rede that winds its way through the grasslands. Otters swim here as they do in many rivers within Northumberland National Park.

Catcleugh's sheet of water enclosed by trees provides an eye-catching vista. The reservoir was created in the late 19th century to supply water to Tyneside and as with Sweethope Loughs further south, ospreys sometimes help themselves to trout. There is public access across the dam: from the southern end, you can follow Chattlehope Burn up to Girdle Fell and Chattlehope Spout. It's hard-going with so much wiry heather under foot, but the view of Catcleugh Reservoir and surrounding forests at the top will stay in the memory.

⑥ Carter Bar

Scotland bursts upon the traveller coming over the brow of the hill at Carter Bar. From the lofty vantage point at 1,400 feet above sea level you can see the Lammermuir Hills to the north and the Cheviots cupping the landscape to the east. There's a large parking area where many people stop to take in the view and stretch their legs. A path to the west winds up boggy Carter Fell and into Whitelee Moor National Nature Reserve. From here, Catcleugh Reservoir comes into sight.

⑦ Bellingham

Land Rovers parked outside Bellingham's (pronounced 'Belling-jum') Country Store and wagons passing with livestock should tell you that this small, unassuming town caters for the farming community. It's a pleasant enough place to stop for lunch and a good base for exploring Kielder Forest (ten miles away) and Redesdale's lonesome hills (behind you).

St Cuthbert's Church is at the western end of the High Street and just past the town hall (the building with a distinctive green clock tower). It dates in part from the 13th century and has a highly unusual stone roof. It survived the lawless centuries that followed its construction unlike many other medieval buildings that burned down when reivers were in town. Inside, you'll see the barrel vaulted roof spanning the nave in 15 stone ribs.

A curious curved tomb in the churchyard called the **Lang Pack** is associated with a legend set in nearby Lee Hall. In 1723 the manor was left in charge of servants who were visited by a pedlar who wanted to stay overnight. Permission was refused but the servants agreed that he could store his large, heavy pack inside. After the pedlar left, they were alarmed to see the bag moving so they shot at it with a pistol (as was the way in Redesdale back then). On opening the bag they found the body of a man wearing a whistle. Suspecting a raid, the servants armed themselves before blowing the whistle to lure the dead man's accomplices. Sure enough, the gang appeared and were swiftly shot dead. Come morning their bodies had disappeared. The body in the pack was buried in the churchyard.

Nearby is **St Cuthbert's Well** – another distinctive stone structure. The stout, octagonal pant is not as old as it looks (probably 18th century) though the cover may be medieval.

One of the oldest and largest **agricultural shows** (*www.bellinghamshow.com*) in Northumberland is held just outside Bellingham on the bank holiday at the end of August. Expect all the usual traditional events including sheep and dog shows, horse jumping, vintage vehicle parades, stalls selling food, face-painting, archery and so on.

Bastles houses and towers

Murder, theft and arson were enough of a persistent threat in the borderlands during the 16th and 17th centuries to necessitate the construction of defensive farmhouses. These bastle houses are dotted all over Northumbria and the Scottish Borders, providing a visual reminder of the centuries of reiver raids.

Bastles are essentially two-storey dwellings with hugely thick walls and tiny upstairs windows. If an attack was feared, livestock were rounded up and locked in the ground floor before families climbed onto the second storey, sometimes by ladder or rope which was then pulled inside.

Tower houses (sometimes called pele towers) are generally understood in Northumbria to be tall, fortified structures of several storeys and often with a battlement. Unlike bastle houses they are associated with the estates of prominent landowners. As well as protecting inhabitants, towers served as lookout points and warning stations where beacons would be lit to alert locals of approaching invaders.

Hareshaw Linn

Bellingham town centre, reached by following the riverside path/road opposite the police station; car park at the trail entrance.

The walk to this 30-foot high waterfall in Bellingham is one of the most picturesque in Northumberland National Park. After an unremarkable first half mile to a picnic spot by the river (passing an old ironworks dam), the trail delves deeper into woodland, criss-crossing Hareshaw Burn many times. Continuing upriver, the trees become older and more heavily clothed in luxuriant mosses; jingling streams fall off the steep-sided gorge, and huge boulders pile in the river. When I last walked this trail in spring, all the usual woodland plants including primroses, wood sorrel and dense patches of wild garlic were in flower. Nuthatches, wrens and tree-creepers hid behind the trunks of oaks as I passed and I caught sight of a buzzard navigating through the trees.

The waterfall is one of the most pleasing kind, not a tunnel of water, but a cascade spraying in every direction on hitting rocks before entering a dark plunge pool.

It takes a couple of hours to walk to Hareshaw Linn and back but it's easy to navigate (no map needed) and very family friendly. You can't walk beyond the falls, so no chance of going too far. Children can be willed onwards by the promise of a money tree. Perhaps that's building it up too much, it's actually a stump decorated with coins, guarded by a huge fir next to one of the bridges.

Bellingham Heritage Centre

Woodburn Rd, NE48 2DG ℗ 01434 220050 Ⓦ www.bellingham-heritage.org.uk. Open daily in summer and Mon, Wed and Fri from autumn half-term to Easter; café.

In Bellingham's old train station yard is this unexpected museum that chronicles the upland industries and communities of bygone years. It houses displays on the Border Reivers and relics from the days of coal mining and traditional upland farming. There's also a photographic exhibition and large display of old cameras (quite random but intriguing nonetheless). The old smithy dates to 1834 and comes from nearby Stannersburn. It was formerly the workshop of an elderly man who had worked as a blacksmith for many decades. One afternoon in the 1970s, he locked up and decided not to return. Those who run the museum did a commendable job of rebuilding it exactly how he left it, still with a couple of unopened bottles of beer among his tools of which there are around 500.

Food and drink

At the time of writing, the **railway carriage tearoom** at the Heritage Centre was not yet open, but it's sure to be a special place to stop for a cup of tea and slice of cake when renovations are completed in 2012. By the memorial in Bellingham's town centre, you could try the **Rocky Road Café**. On the main street, the **Village Bakery** sells inexpensive average sandwiches, pasties and cakes. Between Bellingham and Kielder, there's a pleasant bistro off the main road at **Boe Rigg** campsite (see page 143).

⑧ Otterburn

Otterburn's medieval tower, coaching inns, historic mill and convenient location near the junction of two major roads (the A696 and A68) make it an obvious stopping place for travellers heading into Northumberland National Park, but if I'm honest, it's one of those places that sounds a bit better than it actually is. A clear highlight in summer is the **Otterburn Village Festival** (*www.otterburnvillagefestival.co.uk*). Vintage cars, buses and tractors come out in force and there's always a dog show, bird of prey display and so on.

The most prominent historic attraction is **Otterburn Tower** (now a hotel but not to be confused with the Otterburn Hall hotel), a hugely impressive castellated manor house founded in the years after the Norman Conquest. The oldest part is the 14th-century tower which is incorporated into the 19th-century manor and is now an elegant wood panelled dining room.

The Otterburn Trail (pick up a leaflet in the

Redesdale's bastles

Some of Northumberland's historic fortified farmhouses – or 'bastles' – have been converted into barns or more cheerful-looking cottages; a few stand on the loneliest of fells all ragged and ruinous and instilling a tremendous sense of the region's lawless past. Many of the best examples of the latter kind are found in Redesdale, an area made even more atmospheric by the occasional sound of artillery fire from Otterburn's army training camp.

There are several clusters of bastles in the countryside between Kielder and Elsdon. Two of the best preserved are **Woodhouses** (see page 187) and **Black Middens**. The latter is found near Kielder's Tarset Burn (signposted off the quiet lane from Greenhaugh to Comb). Black Middens is memorable for its external stone steps leading to the first floor entrance and holes in the doorway where a drawbar used to secure the opening. You'll find a good few bastles around here (an English Heritage board by the roadsides shows you their locations). Continuing north up the Tarset Burn, you come to **Boghead Bastle** which has a duct above the doorway that enabled those sheltering on the first floor to douse the entrance in water if it was set alight by raiders.

On the road between Bellingham and West Woodburn, there are a couple of restored bastles among farm buildings at **Hole** and **Low Leam**. A pull-in area just east of Low Leam farm promotes access to the isolated bastle of the same name.

The striking ruin of **Shittleheugh Bastle** stands in open countryside marked by medieval ridge and furrow fields a couple of miles north of Otterburn. Only the original ground-floor doorway and gable ends remain intact. The walls stand to full height and look sculptural against the sky.

Otterburn Mill) is a fairly easy **walk** (just a few miles) that takes you in a loop around the hills north of the village and encompasses the **Iron Age hillfort** at Fawdon Hill. You'll enter the wooded banks of Otter Burn (which does indeed provide a home to otters).

Otterburn Mill

Otterburn NE19 1JT ⑦ 01830 520225 ⑩ www.otterburnmill.co.uk. Open daily.
'The Queen has now made a selection from the patterns of Otterburn Tweed, which you kindly sent … ' So began a letter from Buckingham Palace penned to the Otterburn Mill in 1939 pertaining to blankets for the young princesses, Margaret and Elizabeth. Since then orders for Otterburn Pram Rugs from the 18th-century mill have not stopped. The main difference now is that the chequered fabric (pastel pink, yellow and blue) is no longer produced at Otterburn, production having ceased in 1976. Today, alongside woollen goods, you'll find budget outdoor clothing in the large former weaving sheds, a café and displays of old machinery.

The Battle of Otterburn

Cowards had no place there, but heroism reigned with goodly feats of arms; for knights and squires were so joined together at hand strokes, that archers had no place on either party.
J Froissart *The Ancient Chronicles*, 1388

One of the most well-recorded of all the Anglo-Scottish clashes in Northumberland is the Battle of Otterburn, famously fought by moonlight on the 19 August 1388. It ended with a victory for the Scottish army, despite the death of their leader, the Earl of Douglas, and the capture of the legendary Henry 'Hotspur' Percy and his sibling, of Alnwick Castle. The battle is immortalised in a couple of ballads, one English, *The Ballad of Chevy Chase*, the other Scottish. *The Battle of Otterbourne* contains the following verses:

It fell about the Lammas tide,
When the muir-men win their hay,
The doughty Douglas bound him to ride
Into England, to drive a prey ...
When Percy wi' the Douglas met,
I wat he was fu' fain;
They swakked their swords till sair they swat,
And the blood ran down like rain.

The location of the battlefield is not precisely known but the best consensus is that it took place just west of Otterburn, an area that still retains its open character. **Percy's Cross** stands in a small plantation by the side of the A696 and is thought to mark the spot where the Earl of Douglas was killed. It was already of some age when it was moved a couple of hundred yards in 1777.

Food and drink
Otterburn's pubs are rather tired-looking so if you're looking for somewhere to eat and drink, I suggest the **Tower Inn and Stable Bar** (*01830 520620; www.towerinn. co.uk*) annexed to Otterburn Tower Hotel. The courtyard is very pleasant and it's not too expensive to eat here, unlike the restaurant inside the main building and that at the nearby **Otterburn Hall Country House Hotel** (*01830 520663; www. otterburnhall.com*). You could also try the café at **Otterburn Mill**.

⑨ Otterburn Ranges
Forget for a moment that this open moorland is England's second largest live firing range, and focus instead on the fact that it is also one of the most unspoilt stretches of countryside in Northumberland covering 90 square miles and one fifth of the national park. The ranges are often closed to the public (during training exercises) but the rest of the time (when red flags are not

Access on the Otterburn Ranges

The Controlled Access Area is roughly southwest of the River Coquet to the River Rede/A68 at Byrness and as far south as Otterburn. When red flags are flying it means you must not enter the zone. Firing Times are published on the Ministry of Defence's website (*01830 520569; www.otterburnranges.co.uk*). When red flags are not flying (usually one weekend a month and mid-April to mid-May), visitors must keep to the military roads and way-marked paths. There are no access restrictions on Ministry of Defence land north of the River Coquet.

flying) you can enjoy some of the most remote moors and roads in England (access permitted for cars). This is great cycling country with open views all around and dead quiet roads.

It's fitting that this military training camp should be sited in an area once well-known to Roman soldiers. There are no longer Roman forts here but you can visit the earthworks which mark where **Roman camps** housed squads during the construction of the Roman road, Dere Street. The most easily accessible is **Brigantium** at High Rochester (take track from Rochester, on the A68) where Roman masonry remains in situ. The earthen walls of **Chew Green camp** are seen where the Roman road crosses the Scottish border.

Archaeological remains also include prehistoric burial cairns, lost medieval villages, bastle houses and lime kilns. One of the most interesting of the 75 Scheduled Monuments on the ranges is the **World War I practice trench** near Silloans which brings to mind those at Ypres and the Somme (OS grid reference NT836027; site not marked on Ordnance Survey maps). Access is from Bushman's Road but you must be escorted to the site (groups should speak to the Ministry of Defence on the number above to arrange a visit). Armchair travellers may like to take a trip on Google Earth to see an impressive birds-eye view of the trenches which appear as deep zig-zagging fissures in the ground.

This vast area has not been improved or farmed since it came under the management of the Ministry of Defence in 1911, which explains why the waterways and grassland habitats are in such good condition. Otters, black grouse and merlin are some of the more unusual upland inhabitants. Curlews, lapwings and skylarks will certainly accompany walkers in spring.

⑩ Elsdon

It's hard to find in Redesdale, or anywhere in Northumberland National Park, a more appealing village with such an intriguing past. Descending into Elsdon, your first impression is of a very old settlement hiding away below hills rippled with the tell-tale signs of medieval farming. At its centre, Elsdon boasts a large, open green surrounded by 18th-century cottages, three inns and a church of great antiquity. Two of the pubs have changed use but still retain interesting features like the rustic sculpture of Bacchus sitting on a barrel above the doorway of the old Bacchus Inn (east side of the green).

Guarding the village to the north is one of Northumberland's most intact medieval **towers**, once the residence of successive church vicars. It dates from the 14th century. There's no public access, but visitors are permitted to walk some way up the drive to inspect its mighty walls.

The other notable defensive structure in Elsdon is a Norman **motte and bailey castle** comprised of two large earthen ramparts that rear over the northeast corner of the village. Architectural writer Pevsner describes it as the best example of its type in Northumberland.

Cock-fighting, bear-baiting and pagan traditions

'In consequence of the long isolation of the village amid moors and morasses, remote from the enlightening influences of civilisation', wrote Tomlinson in his 1888 *Comprehensive Guide to Northumberland*, 'many pagan customs and superstitions were observed till within a very short time ago. The Midsummer bonfires, through which cattle were driven to protect them from disease were burning only a few years ago on Elsdon green – their origin, in the worship of Baal, being forgotten.'

Other bygone traditions include cock-fighting and bull-baiting. At the southern end of the green is a pinfold which looks similar to a sheepfold but was used to house stray livestock until their owners paid a fee for their release. My Victorian guidebook notes that Elsdon's **village fête** at the end of August has 'long been obsolete'. Well, the tradition has been revived since 1888; it's once again a popular family event drawing crowds to the bunting-decorated green during the August Bank Holiday.

St Cuthbert's Church

There are two churches really worth visiting in Redesdale: one at Bellingham (see page 153), the other in Elsdon. Both reflect in their walls those unstable times of cross-border fighting. As you enter Elsdon's 14th-century church, notice the deep grooves in the pillar on the left; they are said by Tomlinson in his aforementioned guide to have been made 'by the fierce bowmen of Redesdale in sharpening their arrows before leaving church'. It's an evocative image and intriguing tale that seems to have endured. At least, the church-going locals I spoke to had heard the story.

A more shocking discovery was made in the 19th century when a **mass grave** containing a large number of human skeletons was unearthed by the north wall of the nave. The skeletons were all young men and boys and were thought to be Englishmen who fell during in the notorious Battle of Otterburn in 1388 (see page 157).

St Cuthbert's contains a number of intriguing **tombstones** including one in memory of 'Thos. Wilson, officer for the duty of salt' who died in 1778. Inside, you'll see a Roman officer's tombstone and a funereal stone of the same period built into the chancel. 'Julia Lucilla had this erected to her husband well deserving. He lived forty-eight years, six months and twenty-five days' – and not a day longer.

Look in the vestry and you'll see a cabinet containing **three horse skulls**. They were discovered in the spire above the bell turret during restoration work in the late 19th century. The animals may have been sacrificed as part of a pagan ceremony during the construction of an early sacred building, but whatever the reason they ended up in the belfry, they are certainly a very unusual feature in an English church.

Elsdon's grim side

Besides horses heads, bull-baiting, cock-fighting and a mass grave of fallen warriors, Elsdon's darker past is revealed just outside of the village on a lonely hillside by the side of an unclassified road to Morpeth. At Steng Cross stands **Winter's Gibbet** (or 'Winter's Stob' as Northumbrians used to call it) – a gibbet with a wooden head hanging from its post. My aunt, who lives nearby, tells me the head periodically goes missing. It marks the spot (the gibbet is not original) where the body of William Winter was hanged in chains following his execution in Newcastle in 1791 for the murder of a local woman. Incidentally, she was killed at The Raw, an unmistakable bastle house on a farm three miles north of Elsdon (viewable from the farm track).

The superstitious folk of Elsdon are said to have rubbed wood chips from the gibbet on their teeth as a cure for toothache in the 19th century.

Food and drink

The only thing lacking in this otherwise perfect Northumbrian village is a really good pub serving food, but it does have a couple of cafés around its green including the lovely **Coach House** (an old inn with a gallery upstairs; closed Monday and Friday) and the Impromptu Café highlighted opposite.

A road with a view: Kirkwhelpington to Elsdon

If travelling into Redesdale from the south by car, you'll probably take the A68 or the A696. The latter is initially unremarkable – a straight passage north with green fields all around – but after Kirkwhelpington, you gain altitude and the scenery becomes more typical of the Northumberland uplands with heather moors, forests and a sense of remoteness. Five miles on and the road reaches its highest point at around 1,000 feet before descending towards the Elsdon turn-off. From here, you gain an unbeatable view of the Simonside Hills and distant Cheviots. If making this journey in August, you will be blown away by the colour of the hills when the heather comes into flower transforming the landscape from green and yellow to shocking pink.

Impromptu Café Elsdon NE19 1AA ℗ 01830 520389. Closed Thu. You can be sure of a cheerful welcome in this great little cyclists' café (also a visitor information point) that has been run by the same couple since 1980. It's housed in the old school house near the tower and is identified by the bicycles stacked outside.

A dip in Darden Lough

Choose a hot day in August to do this four-mile circular walk and enjoy the heather slopes in flower and a plunge in the mountain tarn at the top. The key is to strip off (there's rarely anyone around) as soon as you reach the lough and before you've cooled down, which doesn't take long on this hillside. You'll be accompanied by mountain bumblebees (black with a red bum), meadow pipits and red grouse the whole way.

It's a stiff ascent but the route is fairly easy to navigate by following wooden marker posts. Allow around 2½ hours. You'll need stout waterproof boots as the terrain is very uneven and boggy in parts.

Set foot from the Grasslees lay-by three miles northeast of Elsdon on the B6341 (OS grid reference NY958981). Follow the signpost downhill to Grasslees Burn and then begin your ascent through bracken and heather. There are a couple of sections where the path leads away from the fence line, but for the most part, follow it continuously to Darden Lough.

Squelch on through Miller's Moss with its large cushion mosses and head for the post on top of a hillock to your right. The heather is deep and bushy and reaches the top of my thighs in places.

The ground flattens as you approach the lough – a dark, remote mountain lake (there's a smaller tarn nearby which also makes a good plunge pool).

After your swim, turn your back to the lough and follow a fence line uphill to Darden Pike cairn where you can see the craggy Simonside Hills and the distant Cheviots. Follow the marker posts downhill. The trail swings eastwards before rejoining the path you climbed on the outward walk.

⑪ Sweethope Loughs and the Wanney Crags

Sweethope Loughs – essentially one large trout-filled lake west of Knowesgate – is largely hidden out of sight by a ring of conifer trees, but a public right of way around the lake's southern edge affords views of the blue expanse. Ospreys occasionally help themselves to fish on their way to Africa in September but humans must obtain a **fishing** permit to take advantage of one of the best trout lakes in Northumberland (*01830 540349*).

Of most interest to walkers, climbers and birdwatchers will be the nearby Wanney Crags rising above Sweethope Loughs to the north. At the top of **Great Wanney**, find yourself a rock to sit on and enjoy Redesdale's countryside unfolded before you with the Simonsides and Cheviots both in sight.

'High o'er wild Wanny's lofty crest, where the raven cleaves the cloud', begins an old local ballad. Ravens inhabit the crags here to this day. They try and nest every year but often give up when rock climbers take advantage of the first fine days of the year in early spring. For this reason, choose where you sit carefully so as not to disturb the birds (and wait until later on in summer to go climbing if you can). You may see their acrobatic courtship display during which the male rolls onto his back mid-flight to impress his mate. Peregrines sometimes swoop by, and goshawks and other birds of prey are not uncommon.

North of Great Wanney, a wide track winds through heather and woodlands on the Forestry Commission site called **Fourlaws**. Keep to the track as it passes between Aid Moss and Aid Crag and avoid the rough public footpaths from March to August so as not to disturb nesting birds. On summer's evenings you can sometimes hear nightjars close to the track.

Along the River Wansbeck: Kirkwhelpington to Morpeth

Welcome to Capability Brown country. The celebrated garden designer was born at Kirkharle and lived here until he was 23. The landscape for miles around is at times like a vignette of an 18th-century country estate where undulating meadows, waterways, ponds and ancient broad-leaved trees come together to picturesque effect as if planned by Brown himself.

The River Wansbeck flows off Redesdale's craggy hills and into lowland farmland around the rose-filled village of **Kirkwhelpington** before passing through the National Trust's **Wallington** estate. Good cycling lanes thronged with wildflowers lead to **Middleton** and **Hartburn**. The former has a pub, the Ox Inn; the latter is just a very picturesque hamlet of stone about a cross and church.

From **Mitford** to **Morpeth**, road and river intertwine through woodland making for a memorable journey with the Wansbeck dancing through the trees. The B6343 crosses the river several times by way of old stone bridges, the last being particularly eye-catching with its huge sandstone blocks.

⑫ Kirkharle Courtyard

NE19 2PE, midway between Ponteland and Otterburn and just off the A696
① 01830 540362 ⑳ www.kirkharlecourtyard.co.uk; open daily.

The main reason visitors come to Kirkharle is to wander around the stone barns that have been sensitively converted into workshops. You'll find jewellery and furniture makers, sculptors and painters based here as well as a café, displays relating to Capability Brown's garden designs and the headquarters of Shepherds Walks (see page ix). You can book guided trips here or buy trail guides. Their mohair hiking socks come highly recommended by this writer.

Lancelot 'Capability' Brown (1716–83)

The great 18th-century landscape gardener lived at Kirkharle until in his twenties and went to school in nearby Cambo. A plan for the landscaping of Kirkharle was found in the 1980s and is almost certainly Brown's work. The design was never realised – until 2010. It will be some years before the trees around the pond mature, but already the lakeside trail is a pleasant place for a wander where you can watch house martins catching airborne insects. Brown went on to create many of the great country estates in England, including Hulne Park at Alnwick Castle.

It's a short stroll from Kirkharle to the 14th-century St Wilfrid's Church. If you want to walk further, take the cross-country route to Kirkwhelpington, a pretty village two miles north. The walk starts from the **Loraine Monument** next to Kirkharle Courtyard and is described on a nearby board. The memorial stone and information panel will tell you everything you might (not) want to know about how Robert Loraine met his death in this field in 1483.

⑬ Wallington

Cambo NE61 4AR ⓣ 01670 773600 Ⓦ www.nationaltrust.org.uk/wallington.
Gardens and café open all year, house open early Mar–early Nov, Wed–Mon 12.00–17.00; National Trust.

Four grinning dragon heads greet you on the approach to Wallington – one of the great country houses of Northumberland. You could easily spend most of a day at this National Trust property exploring the rooms, gardens and woodlands, and playing games on the grassy courtyard. Next to the Palladian clock tower is a café with outside tables, a shop selling plants and herbs and a large enclosed green where children can freely run around while parents watch from the terrace.

The late 17th-century house is reached from the courtyard. There are many memorable rooms and features: the Italianate plasterwork of the drawing and dining rooms, the fine collection of Victorian dolls' houses, a cabinet containing 3,000 toy soldiers, wall tapestries and a complete kitchen dating to the 1900s with the largest dresser you'll see anywhere.

The **Central Hall** was styled on an Italian Renaissance *palazzo* and is arranged over two levels with arcades painted with ferns and flowers. Guests used to enjoy high tea here. They were surrounded by eight large pre-Raphaelite paintings still hanging today and which were all created by William Bell Scott in the mid 19th century. His brief was to 'illuminate the history and worthies of Northumbria' and so we see depictions of the Industrial Revolution on Tyneside, the construction of Hadrian's Wall, and Danes invading from the sea. In some, the action in the background tells the story, as in the *Grace Darling* painting.

Wallington's **walled garden** is reached at the end of a short walk through woodland and past an ornamental pond. A thin stream trickles through the green oasis landscaped with terraces of plants and shrubs. A kiosk serves ice cream and drinks at the far end of the garden.

A longer walk is enjoyed by descending through woodland to the River Wansbeck (native white clawed crayfish live in the water and red squirrels in the trees). The river eventually flows under Northumberland's most elegant bridge – a Palladian crossing on the southern edge of the estate. Wait until you see it bathed in evening light.

Cambo

Cambo, the old estate village of Wallington, lies a short distance north of the manor whiling away the years at the top of a hill. It boasts nothing more than a couple of rows of stone houses, a 16th-century pele tower, a church and a hill-top view of tumbling farmland, but a hamlet quainter than this is hard to find. Ox-eye daisies, roses and sweet peas fill the cottage gardens and herbs drape over the stone walls adding to Cambo's English country village appeal.

There is one particularly curious object here: a gaudy **drinking fountain** in the form of a fierce-looking dolphin. It was built on the order of Sir Charles Trevelyan (of Wallington Hall) as part of the reconstruction of the hamlet. The Latin inscription translates as: 'not unmindful of future generations'.

At the north end of the village is the parish **church** – a 19th-century building with a clock tower, decorative door, some well-preserved medieval coffin covers and a churchyard offering expansive views of mature parkland. A young Lancelot 'Capability' Brown used to walk across these fields (those to the west of the village) every day on his three-mile journey from Kirkharle to Cambo's school house. Apparently one former schoolmaster (after Brown's time) kept an annotated record of former alumni which is decoded by the following rhyme:

> *The names distinguish'd by a star*
> *Were the most docile by far;*
> *And those with equi-distant strokes*
> *Were secondhanded sort of folks;*
> *But where you find the letter B*
> *A humdrum booby you will see;*
> *And where an exclamation's set,*
> *The rascals went away in debt.*

Herterton Gardens

Cambo NE61 4BN ℗ 01670 774278. Open Apr–30 Sep.

In 1976 Marjorie and Frank Lawley began creating out of derelict farmland five distinctive gardens in the grounds of their 16th-century house. They have not stopped digging, cultivating and clipping topiary bushes since.

When I visited one evening in summer just after the advertised closing time, they allowed me to quickly wander around while they quietly pottered in the flower beds. I caught the last sun rays creeping over the tops of the hedges and took pleasure in the saturated colour of the cottage flowers bursting through the deep green and gold foliage.

Interestingly, the Lawleys decided to bring back the formal gardens once seen in many country estates before the trend for open landscaped parklands. To that end, they consulted Elizabethan gardening books including William Lawson's *A Country Housewife's Garden* (1619), written with domestic gardeners in the North East in mind.

Among the five plots are a formal, physic, flower and nursery garden. Memorable stone features include a huge urn thought to be Roman and the old arches of a granary which shelter two statues (a falconer and a Viking) said to have come from Alnwick Castle.

⑭ Bide-a-Wee Cottage Garden and Nursery

Stanton, near Netherwitton, Morpeth NE65 8PR ℡ 01670 772238 Ⓦ www. bideawee.co.uk. Open beginning of May–end Aug, Sat–Wed 13.30–17.00.

Bide-a-Wee is hidden away off a road to nowhere roughly between Morpeth and Longhorsley. Undulating meadows grazed by sheep surround the gardens which were formed out of an old sandstone quarry over two decades ago. Paths snake up and down and through the quarry where ferns drape from the rock walls and over ponds crowded with more shade-loving, moisture-licking plants. Elsewhere, you'll find colourful herbaceous borders, swathes of cornflowers (this being the home of the national collection of *Centaurea*) and a row of beehives.

⑮ Mitford

Mitford is nestled in woodland by the River Wansbeck a few miles west of Morpeth. For those staying in Morpeth, I'd recommend taking the car for a walk along the B6343, simply to enjoy the scenery along the riverside and all the humpback bridges crossed *en route*. The hamlet itself is nothing hugely special though it does have a pub, old mill and a lone thatched cottage (one of only a handful of thatched buildings remaining in Northumberland). Undoubtedly, Mitford's greatest appeal is the pastoral setting, church and ruined castle.

St Mary Magdalene Church (*open Jun–Aug, Tue and Thu, 14.00–16.00*) faces the ruin of Mitford Castle about half a mile west of Mitford. Both are reached by way of a lane off the main Mitford to Morpeth road (signed for Mitford Church). You can also **walk** here from Morpeth (just a few miles) across meadows and along the wooded riverside. The church's oldest stonework dates from the 12th century and includes the priest's door and south arcade, but for the most part it has the appearance of a solidly Victorian edifice with a steeple and tall spire. Like the castle opposite, the church was destroyed by fire several times, notably in 1216 during King John's northern rampage.

Mitford Castle appears in a field guarded by crows and jackdaws and looks arresting on its green knoll even in its crumbling state. As you can believe, it has been ransacked many times since its construction in the mid 12th century.

⑯ Morpeth and Carlisle Park

This busy working town off the A1 is cocooned in a loop of the River Wansbeck. South of the waterway is Carlisle Park, which is easily one of the town's most attractive features with its gardens, castle and riverside footpath. To the north is Morpeth's centre. A steady stream of cars continually passing through the market town detracts somewhat from Morpeth's appeal; but overlook the traffic and you'll find a number of historic streets and buildings.

Bridges and bagpipes

The dainty **Chantry Footbridge** dates to 1869 and rests on the hefty piers of a 13th-century crossing. Many people linger mid-way to admire the river scenery. The three-arched **road bridge** opposite was designed by Thomas Telford and built in 1831. Walkers also have the choice of crossing further upriver by way of stepping stones (reached from Abbey View).

On the north side of the river the 13th-century **All Saints Chantry** (*01670 535200; open daily*) crouches between the footbridge and road bridge. It once operated as a toll house for the crossing but it's now the **tourist information centre** and a wonderful **Bagpipe Museum**. Visitors are urged to come to this free museum to hear the distinctive soft notes of the Northumbrian smallpipes. The museum also serves as a meeting place for bagpipe players and enthusiasts and you may well find local musicians playing as you wander around the cabinets displaying instruments. Unlike Scottish bagpipes, the Northumbrian pipes are bellows blown. The instrument requires much concentration to play; hence musicians often have a far-away look as they perform.

Market Place

At the western end of Bridge Street, you'll hit the **Market Place** by a small roundabout and crossroads. Vanbrugh designed the **Town Hall** which was built in 1714 and rebuilt following a fire in the late 1800s. The reception is in the old butter market. If you're passing, it's well worth having a peek inside, especially to see the grand staircase, which the receptionist will allow you to view if you ask.

Morpeth's landmark **clock tower** stands alone at the entrance to Oldgate on the other side of the roundabout. Its irregular-shaped stones (recycled from a medieval building) give the appearance of a building much older than its early 17th-century construction. A curfew bell is tolled every day at 20.00 except on

Alleyways and yards

As you wander around Morpeth's streets, you'll notice a number of narrow passageways between buildings. They take us back to the days when the town was a stopping point for horse-drawn coaches travelling from Edinburgh to London on the Great North Road. Inns provided shelter to travellers, and adjoining blacksmiths and stables, reached via alleys, took care of the coach horses.

Wednesdays when the bell ringers are practising. Richard Major, the Tower Captain (how's that for a job title?) told me the tradition goes back to 1706.

Facing the clock tower is a wonderful **cheese shop** (see below).

Carlisle Park, Morpeth Castle and the riverside

Rowing boats and swans glide along the River Wansbeck, enhancing the setting of **Carlisle Park** on the southern edge of Morpeth. There's a paved riverside towpath here (suitable for wheelchairs), a bowling green and paddling pool. Near the park's formal flower-beds is the **William Turner Garden** (*01670 535203; open daily until dusk*) which celebrates the 'father of English botany' in a series of eye-catching gardens containing medicinal herbs.

It's a bit of a steep hike up **Ha' Hill**, where once stood an 11th-century motte and bailey castle until it was destroyed by King John in 1216. The reward for the climb is a view over Morpeth's red-tiled rooftops, the imposing early 19th-century **Court House** (once the old gaol and sometimes mistaken for the castle) and the surrounding countryside. When the Ha' Hill castle was razed, it was replaced by **Morpeth Castle** (now a Landmark Trust holiday property) to the south above Postern Burn. Although not a complete castle (only the old 14th-century gatehouse survives) it is nonetheless impressive.

Food and drink

Picnickers will find plenty of places in **Carlisle Park** to enjoy sandwiches. In the town centre, try the tranquil **Millennium Green** – a pretty garden tucked away down an alley (Old Bakehouse Yard) off Newgate Street. Opposite is the snug **Old Bakehouse Tea Rooms**.

Cheese Shop 6 Oldgate, NE61 1LX ① 01670 504434 Ⓦ www.thecheeseshopmorpeth.co.uk. Facing the clock tower is this fine specialist shop stocking over 150 varieties of cheese from Northumberland and further afield.
PepperPot 5 Oldgate, NE61 1PY ① 01670 514666 Ⓦ www.pepper-pots.co.uk. This cosy, friendly Italian by the clock tower uses many local ingredients in its pizza and pasta dishes, including regional cheeses from Morpeth's Cheese Shop across the road and seafood from the North Sea. Great value, laid-back and child friendly (kids can make their own pizza).

Great Morpethians

Collingwood is a name you hear a lot in the North East: on street signs, monuments and pubs from Tynemouth to the Scottish Borders. The Admiral is largely unheard of outside of the North despite leading the British armada to victory in the Battle of Trafalgar after Nelson was killed. Before the famous 1805 battle, Collingwood lived with his wife in the Georgian brick house bearing his name on Oldgate. His fondness for his family home is expressed in the following lines quoted on a plaque above the doorway: 'Whenever I think how I am to be happy again, my thoughts carry me back to Morpeth.'

If you wander through Carlisle Park, you'll likely come across the **William Turner Garden** which celebrates one of the country's greatest botanists who was born in Morpeth in the early 16th century. In his most celebrated work, *A New Herball*, Turner provided the first systematic account of plants and their medicinal properties in English which helped to popularise common names such as daffodil and primrose.

On the southern outskirts of Morpeth is the medieval parish church of St Mary where the suffragette, **Emily Davison**, is buried. She famously stepped out in front of George V's racehorse during the Epsom Derby in 1913 and later died of her injuries. Huge crowds gathered for her funeral. Her gravestone bears the epitaph of the Women's Social and Political Union slogan: 'deeds not words'.

⑰ Bothal

The River Wansbeck continues merrily from Morpeth becoming more wooded and dreamy on its final coast-bound journey. About 3½ miles east of Morpeth, it meanders past Bothal Castle and its neat 19th-century estate village which ranks alongside the likes of Ford as one of the most pristine in Northumberland. You can make this journey on foot by following the riverbank trail the whole way.

Bothal's medieval church and uniform honey-coloured houses with their distinctive metal-patterned windows and maroon paintwork, are hidden in a hollow, and the village as a whole feels very much cut off. Mature broadleaved trees (stunning in autumn) rise on a steep bank above Bothal, increasing this sense of seclusion. There's no visual link from the village to the river, but it is easily accessed by following a grassy lane from the memorial cross and St Andrew's Church (note the distinctive bell cote). Those wishing to cross the Wansbeck have the choice of stepping stones or a wire bridge. It's beautiful down here and a nice spot for a swim.

Bothal Castle, which dates to 1343, is a beast with huge curtain walls, tower and gateway, but because of its isolation few people seek it out – or even know of its existence. Unfortunately, it's not open to the public, but striking views are had when approached from the west by road (also from the riverside and the aforementioned track).

Around Ponteland

Well-to-do villages dot the countryside around Ponteland. They include Darras Hall where many Newcastle United football players live. Matfen, Great Whittington, Whalton and Stamfordham have a Cotswolds-like appeal, and some pubs get very busy at Sunday lunchtimes. Like the countryside around Kirkwhelpington and Morpeth, this area continues the sheep-grazed, rolling grassland theme where a potter around a stately home followed by a cream tea are the order of the day. The quieter country lanes are similarly popular with cyclists and those enjoying a motor in the countryside. I've spent some very memorable afternoons with my grandmother around here, dawdling along byways, getting in the way of tractors, stopping to chat to cyclists, drinking cups of tea, going to fêtes and so on.

⑱ Ponteland and Darras Hall

Ponteland was once a quaint old village. It still retains some of its old roots by the ornamental bridge over the River Pont. Here stands St Mary's Church with its Norman tower, and the Blackbird Inn, a manor house which started life as a fortified tower built in the 14th century before it became incorporated into the 17th-century manor. There's a vicar's pele tower on Main Street (opposite Waitrose).

Further mention must be made of **Darras Hall**'s houses; not the Dallas mansions, but the original 1950s and 1960s dwellings which formed part of this utopian suburb, dubbed the 'Garden City of the North'. Cherry trees, ornamental conifers and rose bushes edge the manicured lawns and driveways of these buildings which all have features that distinguish them from the house next door. Think *Stepford Wives* … in rural Northumberland. Parklands and Avondale Road have some interesting 1960s houses with severely sloping roofs and almost floor-to-ceiling windows. They are not listed and gaping holes appear every few hundred yards on some streets where buyers have demolished the original houses in order to build lavish mansions from scratch.

Food and drink
New Rendezvous 3–5 Bell Villas (opposite the Diamond Inn), NE20 9BD ☏ 01661821775. Very good Chinese food in the old Blacksmiths; popular with locals (including Alan Shearer).

⑲ Milkhope Centre
Blagdon NE13 6DA (just off the A1, 9 miles north of Newcastle). Open daily.
This rural retail 'park' shares similarities with Kirkharle further north. The concept is similar: small local businesses brought together in converted farm buildings in a rural setting. You'll find a few furniture shops, an art gallery and a busy coffee shop. Good luck getting a table on a Saturday lunchtime.

The highlight for many will be the **Blagdon Farm Shop** (*01670 789924; www.theblagdonfarmshop.co.uk*), which is superbly well-stocked with local produce. The meat and cheese counters are particularly generous and they only sell food 'produced by farms that are either organic or follow traditional farming methods that are kind to the natural environment.' All the big name regional producers are represented as well as meats from the Blagdon estate and vegetables grown in their walled garden.

Northumberland Cheese Company farm

Green Lane, Blagdon (nr Horton Grange) NE13 6BZ ℗ 01670 789798 ℗ www.northumberland-cheese.co.uk. Open daily.

If you take the car for a wander around the country lanes northeast of Ponteland, you may stumble upon this cheese farm and café. A more direct route would be to turn off the A1 at Seaton Burn.

Foodies will have spotted Cheviot, Kielder and Hadrian cheeses in pretty much every good deli in the North East. Well, this is where they are made. The stone farm buildings include a viewing window where you can see the cheese-making machinery at work.

Upstairs (no wheelchair access) a café offers quiches, cheese flans, cheese scones, cheese soup and, of course, the full range of Blagdon's cheeses. Having spoken to lots of local retailers during the research for this book, it would seem the most popular are the nettle and Cheviot varieties. The latter is a good, sharp cheese.

⑳ Whalton

Well-to-do Whalton is considered a very desirable village: a broad sweep of neat stone cottages with a manor house, pub, ancient church and community spirit in bucket loads. When funds were needed for repairs to the church in the early noughties, a local penned this report: 'Whaltonians thrive on adversity. Grants, loans, donations, flower festivals, fêtes, concerts and coffee mornings have helped to provide and we now look to the future with confidence.'

Expect all the usual gala attractions at the annual **Whalton fête** in September (birds of prey demonstrations, Morris dancing, local craft stalls, vintage cars, traditional Northumbrian music and so on) as well as extremely entertaining sheep races, in which the animals compete with a doll made out of a pair of stuffed tights strapped to their backs.

Traditional festivals also include the **Ba'al Fire** on old Midsummer's evening (4 July) during which school children dance around a bonfire lit next to the Beresford Arms. At one time people used to leap through the flames. The event has Pagan origins and is historically a sun-worshipping festival.

As with many churches, it's not until you step inside that they reveal their antiquity. This is true of **St Mary Magdalene Church** which externally has the appearance of a 19th-century place of worship, but is almost solidly 13th century inside.

At the eastern end of the village just before you head back out into the open countryside, you'll come to **Whalton Manor** (*01670 775205; www. whaltonmanor.co.uk; holiday cottage accommodation*), which looks like a continuation of the fine stone houses it follows. It is claimed that the mansion is the longest manor house in England, but it is really just four dwellings merged into one. Parts date from the 17th century but most of what you see today was altered by Sir Edwin Lutyens in the early 20th century. The archway seen from the road is his doing. If you get the chance to wander through the arch, you'll see the old stable (still in use) about a cobbled courtyard. It's wonderfully unchanged. Most people who book a tour come to see the **gardens** which were laid out by Gertrude Jekyll in 1908 and contain beautiful herbaceous borders set around a lawn.

Country lanes around Belsay

The unclassified roads winding through Whalton, Ogle, Berwick Hill and Bolam Lake are a cyclist's delight. You'll see the odd car and tractor, but mostly it's quiet enough to dawdle along, do a spot of birdwatching, stop for sandwiches and so on. There are no dramatic vistas, just meadows bound by hedgerows, the odd farm and a couple of old hogback bridges including **Bellasis Bridge**, a 400- to 500-year-old stone crossing over the River Blyth (just north of the Cheese Farm at Horton Grange). It has two arches, a triangular cutwater and, curiously, fragments of shell in its grouting.

You could make a trip to **Kirkley Hall** (*north of Berwick Hill; 01670 841235; www.kirkleyhallzoo.co.uk*), an agricultural college that also houses a small zoo with emus, marmosets, meerkats, wallabies and farm animals. Children can hold rabbits and newly hatched chicks.

㉑ Bolam Lake Country Park

Near Belsay NE20 0EU ℗ 01661 881234. Café and visitor centre open weekends and during school holidays; lakeside path is supposedly wheelchair accessible but the ground is quite muddy and rough in places.

Bolam Lake and woods are conveniently situated next to a couple of country lanes popular with cyclists and day-trippers, making it a good stopping point for picnickers and those dreaming of a soft drink and slice of cake (there's a little café here and another up the road: the Stable Coffee Shop). The lakeside path (three quarters of a mile, partly on a boardwalk) is very pleasant with views of swans and ducks in the large manmade lagoon with trees all around. Red squirrels are sometimes seen in the woods around the café and visitor centre.

Food and drink

Stable Coffee Shop Bolam West House Farm NE61 4DZ ℗ 01661 881244; open
Friday–Monday. Pleasant café in farmland setting near Bolam Lake. Most food
baked on site. Tables outside next to a hay barn.

㉒ Belsay Hall

Belsay NE20 0DX ℗ 01661 881636 ⓦ www.english-heritage.org.uk; open daily from
1 Apr–early Nov and during school holidays, weekends only at other times; café;
English Heritage.

Work began on Belsay Hall in 1806 when the owners returned from a year and
a half-long honeymoon travelling around Europe. The design of the villa is
what architectural historians call Classical Greek Revival. Belsay is raised like a
Grecian temple on a platform above three steps and is distinguished by its plain
façade with almost no decorative masonry except for two huge Doric columns
either side of the doorway. Some would say it's austere; others see beauty in
those clean lines and smooth sandstone blocks. Incidentally, the stone was
quarried from the garden. The Greek temple theme continues in the Pillar
Hall – a square reception room surrounded by colonnades on two storeys.

The absence of furniture, ornaments and paintings might come as a
disappointment to antiques enthusiasts, but others will find it enjoyable
enough just to wander around the light-filled rooms, take in the view of the
open parkland and imagine what the interior might have once looked like.
Note, the faded original William Morris wallpaper in the upstairs rooms.
English Heritage has staged some superb contemporary art exhibitions here in
the past (check online for upcoming events).

Garden lovers are in for a treat. Formal terraces planted with shrubs and
perennials fall away from the south side of the Hall. Walking away from the
house with the terraces on your left, you enter a series of green walkways
that lead past magnolia trees, a croquet lawn (you can watch croquet here in
summer) and the winter garden until you reach the wooded **quarry gardens**.
This is the most distinctive and romantic of all the gardens at Belsay and
clearly fashioned in the Picturesque style with plenty of intentionally rustic
features. The air is cool and fresh and all around exotic ferns, rhododendrons,
trees and creepers hang, sprout and climb over the roughly cut rock faces. At
one point you pass under a giant rock arch. After the darkness and seclusion
of the quarry, the path opens into the sun-filled parkland around the castle.

Some visitors don't make it past the Hall and gardens and so miss out
on one of the finest fortified towers in Northumberland. As with many of
Northumberland's embattled manors, **Belsay Castle** is formed of a mansion
house (built in 1614 and now largely in ruins) with an earlier tower at one
corner. As far as children are concerned, the 14th-century tower is an all-
singing, all-dancing 'proper castle' with parapets, arrow slits and heavy,
castellated stonework. Access to the top is from the Great Hall. Great views
from here.

Food and drink

You have two good choices for lunch at Belsay, either the **English Heritage café** inside the grounds of the Hall, or the **Blacksmiths Coffee Shop** (*01661 881024*) at the estate entrance. An outdoor table at the Blacksmiths is just the ticket on a sunny day. You can watch swallows flying around the surrounding meadow as you enjoy a bowl of soup.

If you're looking for a traditional pub lunch, the **Waggon Inn** (*01661 881872; www.waggoninn.co.uk*) on the main Ponteland to Belsay road (A696) is a popular choice, especially on Sundays.

㉓ Matfen and around

A jaunt into the hinterlands west of Ponteland reveals more old villages and tranquil lanes suitable for touring by bicycle. It's hilly in places, especially as you climb northwards to Ryal. Cyclists can expect some exhilarating downward plunges, but plenty of stiff ascents too. Around Stamfordham, the countryside is pretty tame and most walking routes make good use of footpaths across fields, bridleways and country lanes.

Heading west from Ponteland, you'll pass **Dissington Hall**, a complete Georgian estate you can walk through (or innocently cruise past), and **Dalton** with its long row of well-kept houses and quaint chapel.

Stamfordham looks pretty ordinary at first as you head up Grange Road but you'll soon reach a large open green with its 1735 market cross (the covered building with four open arches) and two neat terraces, mostly in stone. St Mary's Church dates from the 13th century though it was largely rebuilt in the mid-1800s but plenty of old features survive including the chancel arch.

If you're approaching Matfen from the south, look out for Hope Lane where there's a prominent castellated house and prehistoric **standing stone**. It stands seven feet tall and has circular depressions (known as cup marks) at its base. Northumberland's rich stone 'art' is well documented but the reason for these indentations is not known.

Matfen Hall (*01661 886500; www.primahotels.co.uk*) is glimpsed between trees as you head through parkland pitted with sand bunkers on your way to Matfen village. The early 19th-century hall is now a spa hotel with a large golf course. A bistro in the conservatory overlooks the 300-acre landscaped parkland; you can enjoy cream teas in the grand surroundings of the drawing room (an upmarket restaurant in evenings). In the wider estate is a **Go Ape** tree-top adventure centre (*0845 0948634*) open to those not staying at Matfen Hall.

Matfen is what many people would say is a perfect English village with its unaltered stone terraces set around a broad green lined with mature trees. A burn traverses the length of the village, passing under a couple of sweet bridges in its own time. The church dates from the mid-1800s and is not of huge architectural interest but its 117-foot tall spire rises above the rooftops completing the model village scene (that and the red telephone box).

It should come as no surprise that Matfen is a favourite lunch stop for ramblers, cyclists and Sunday day-trippers who make good use of the welcoming green and **village store** which doubles as a **café** serving light lunches. A take-away tea, wedge of brie, some tomatoes, a couple of rolls and a grassy spot under a tree made my afternoon one sunny day in September. If you want something more substantial, you're out of luck, unless passing through on a Friday in which case it's fish and chip night at the **Black Bull**. Otherwise, the pub only offers bar snacks (and good Northumbrian ales).

Continuing westwards across fields dotted with hay bales and tractors, **Great Whittingham** is soon upon you. The village rises on a sloping hill and by now you should be aware that the terrain is becoming rather more undulating than around Stamfordham.

A plaque in the village reads: 'Best kept village 1977'. Not that it has gone downhill since then: the gardens of Great Whittingham's stone cottages are quite a sight in summer and the village has won various Britain in Bloom awards (in recent decades). The Queens Head Inn has an outside beer garden; (since I visited it's changed ownership but had not re-opened at the time of writing).

There's not a lot to see in the hamlet of **Ryal**, due north of Great Whittingham, but it does have wonderful views and a lovely little hill-top church, originally built in the 12th century but much changed since. Two hands are needed to turn the door ring. Inside, you'll find a large number of medieval cross slabs built into the wall. As is commonplace, they are carved with shears representing a woman and a sword for a man. Beyond the churchyard walls, lemon and green fields bound by hedgerows and blocks of forests stretch far into the distance.

Cyclists heading west on NCN Route 10 can expect a few thrilling rollercoaster miles ahead through a beautiful pastoral landscape. A mile east in the other direction, **Ingoe** sits amid prehistoric monuments including a burial mound and the **Warrior Stone**, a similar standing stone to the one at Matfen.

∽∽∽

Food and drink

High Farm House Brewery Southeast of Matfen NE20 0RG ℡ 01661 886192 ⓦ www.highhousefarmbrewery.co.uk. Poorly signposted unless your approach is from the Military Road (B6318). This is a great middle-of-nowhere place to eat (and drink). The owners of the 200-acre 19th-century working farm branched out into beer-making in 2003. Since then they've developed an excellent reputation for their real ales (Nel's Best is a good golden bitter) and brewery tours. They now also operate a small shop and café (*open for lunch every day except Wed; evening meals Thu, Fri and Sat only*). Outside, you'll find tables in an open hay barn, a children's play area and gentle 3-mile walk devised by the farm. **Matfen High House** (*01661 886592; www.matfenhighhouse.co.uk*) is a good B&B next door.

㉔ Chollerton

Many visitors on their way to Hexham must have put on their brakes at Chollerton on seeing its old church and scenic position overlooking a lush vale. One of the first features you'll notice about **St Giles's Church** is the irregular-shaped building by the road. The stone horse mount by the doorway is a clue as to its former use. It dates from the 19th century and is the old stable and hearse house.

Inside the church, the most intriguing stones are the pillars: round on one side of the nave and octagonal on the other. The former are Roman and no doubt came from one of the nearby forts. Also dating to this period is the old font on the right as you enter the church which was a Roman altar in a previous life.

Uphill from Chollerton is a wonderfully complete and unchanged **19th-century farm**. It still retains its old windmill, blacksmith's forge, carriage house, farmhouse, and a row of cottages (described by English Heritage as an important example of industrial farm housing). There's no public access but you can take in the assemblage of buildings by pulling over by the side of the A6079.

In the other direction, towards Hexham, is **Cocklaw Tower** – a medieval tower house standing among sprawling farm buildings. It's a beast of a structure despite its ruinous walls. To reach Cocklaw, head south from Chollerton on the A6079 and take the first lane on your left after the old viaduct; no public access, but it is partially visible from the road.

㉕ Barrasford and nearby castles

Haughton Castle hides behind a bank of mature trees only revealing itself for the briefest of moments as you pass through the quiet settlement of Barrasford, a couple of miles north of Chesters Roman Fort. The village has a very good pub that draws in Sunday lunch parties, and a pleasant riverside **walk** offering a rare glimpse of Haughton Castle's exposed turrets.

To reach the river and see the medieval manor house, cross the stile by the bridge at the eastern end of the village and follow the merry burn to the River North Tyne. It's a bit brambly and the long dew-laden grasses tend to be trouser-dampening, but it's worth the tramp along the footpath for the views when you reach the wide, rapid-surfing North Tyne. At the riverbank, turn right by an old oak and follow the trail until you reach a cottage. A rope ferry, licensed under Henry II, once carried passengers to the other side of the river. The best view of the castle is from this point. Take your sandwiches but remember a mat as the ground is rarely bone dry.

Haughton Castle (no public access but a right of way goes through the grounds) stands on the west side of the River North Tyne not far from Humshaugh looking rather stern with its formidable embattlements and small cheerless windows. It was fortified in the 14th century and survived the next few hundred years of cross-border conflict before being altered somewhat to become a more comfortable 19th-century country house.

If you continue northwest of Barrasford on the road to **Wark** (an attractive large village), you'll come to **Chipchase Castle**, next in the line of the great Northumbrian country houses in the North Tyne Valley (*01434 230203; www. chipchasecastle.com; house open to the public Jun only, gardens open all summer*). Chipchase is a hugely impressive part-Jacobean, part-Georgian manor house with a medieval tower set within landscaped parkland. It forms the centrepiece of an estate that encompasses a stretch of the best salmon river in England and Wales (fly-fishing arranged through the castle). A small chapel stands alone in the grounds of the castle and on the other side of the manor is a walled garden and nursery.

Food and drink

Barrasford Arms Barrasford NE48 4AA ☏ 01434 681237 ⓦ barrasfordarms. co.uk. Hunting paraphernalia fills the bar of this 19th-century inn that has built up an excellent reputation for its food. It's always busy at weekends so you might want to book a table in advance. Meats are sourced from Northumbrian farms and there's always a local ale on tap. On the walls in the corridor hang black and white photographs showing Barrasford when it was a railway village.

㉖ Wark-on-Tyne

Wark is a large village facing the verdant banks of the North Tyne and is most memorably approached from the east across a slim metal bridge. It's pleasant enough with a green bound by well-kept stone cottages and a pub. The inn everyone talks about (Battlesteads) is a short walk south of the village on the Hexham Road (B6320).

Food and drink

Battlesteads Hotel & Restaurant Wark NE48 3LS ☏ 01434 230209 ⓦ www. battlesteads.com. Many people visit Wark just to come to this 18th-century farmhouse which has won numerous national awards, mainly on account of its green ethos, home-grown produce and dinner menu. Most ingredients are sourced within a 25-mile radius including all the meats. Even their inexpensive sandwiches are that little bit special (crayfish tails with lemon mayonnaise, for example). It's hard to find steak and fish dishes as good and reasonably priced as this in Northumberland.

㉗ Simonburn

Simonburn is up there with the likes of Cambo and Bothal as one of Northumberland's quaintest hamlets. There's not a lot here of course; just some rustic terraced cottages facing a large green and 19th-century St Mungo's Church. The lanes leading to Simonburn meander through tranquil Northumbrian countryside – all fields bound by drystone walls and crossed by wooded burns. What Simonburn has that Cambo and Bothal don't is a place to eat.

Simonburn Castle sits on a wooded mound half a mile northwest of the hamlet. Only fragments of masonry remain from the castle which was built in 1766 as an eye-catcher from Nunwick Hall to replace an earlier 13th-century tower.

The same distance in the other direction (northeast), you'll reach **Nunwick** – another flower-filled hamlet of stone. **Nunwick Hall** dates from 1760 but is only occasionally open to the public.

Food and drink

Simonburn Tea Room The Mains, NE48 3AW ☏ 01434 681321 ⓦ www. simonburntearooms.com. It's a real treat to chance upon this lovely tea room and B&B which serves hot dishes as well as sandwiches, scones, cakes and so on. When it's sunny, you can sit in the enclosed garden.

Local words

Burn stream
Cleugh gully (pronounced 'clook')
Cuddy small horse or pony
Haar sea mist (sometimes called 'fret')
Haugh flat land by water (pronounced 'hoff')
Heugh jagged hill
Hope sheltered valley eg: Linhope, Harthope
Kirk often seen in place names eg: Kirknewton, Kirk Yetholm (Old Norse origins, meaning 'church')
Knowe small hill
Law hill
Linn waterfall
Lonnen lane
Lough mountain lake (Northumbrian equivalent of 'loch', prounounced 'loff')
Muckle big
Northumbrian 'burr' used to describe the local pronunciation of 'r'
Shiel shepherds' or fishermen's huts
Stell sheep fold (round, stone enclosure)
Tup ram
Whaup curlew (somewhat onomatopoeic if you've ever heard curlews in the breeding season)
Yon that
Yow ewe (sheep)

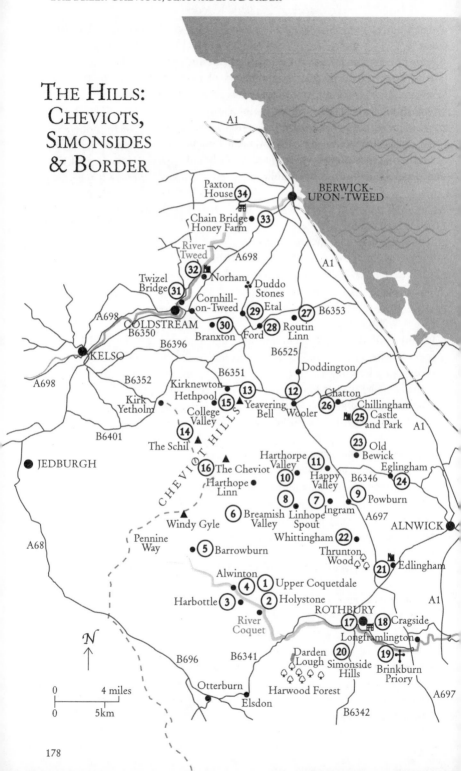

THE HILLS:
CHEVIOTS,
SIMONSIDES
& BORDER

A1

Paxton House (34)

BERWICK-
UPON-TWEED

Chain Bridge •
Honey Farm (33)

River
Tweed

A698

A1

(32) Norham

Twizel
Bridge (31)

Cornhill-
on-Tweed

Duddo
Stones

(29) Etal

(27) B6353

A698

COLDSTREAM (30)

(28) Ford

Routin
Linn

B6350

Branxton

B6396

B6352

KELSO

B6396

A698

B6352

Kirk
Yetholm

Kirknewton
Hethpool

B6351

Doddington

B6525

College
Valley

(15)

(13)

Yeavering
Bell

(12)

Wooler

Chatton

(26)

Chillingham
Castle
and Park

A1

B6401

The Schil (14)

Harthorpe
Valley

(11)

(25)

(23) Old
Bewick

JEDBURGH

The Cheviot (16)

(10)

Happy
Valley

Eglingham

(24)

Harthope
Linn

(8)

(7)

Ingram

B6346

(9) Powburn

A697

ALNWICK

Windy Gyle

(6)

Breamish
Valley

Linhope
Spout

A68

Pennine
Way

(5)

Barrowburn

Whittingham (22)

Thrunton
Wood

(21)

Edlingham

Alwinton

(4) (1)

Upper Coquetdale

Harbottle (3)

(2)

Holystone

ROTHBURY

(17)

(18) Cragside

A1

River
Coquet

Longframlington

(19)

N

Darden
Lough

(20)

Simonside
Hills

Brinkburn
Priory

A697

0   4 miles

0   5km

B696

B6341

Otterburn

Harwood Forest

Elsdon

B6342

5. THE HILLS: CHEVIOTS, SIMONSIDES & BORDER

This is where outdoor enthusiasts come to get away from it all. Solitude and big landscapes are guaranteed in the northern reaches of Northumberland National Park on the Scottish border. There's a lot pack in: hiking through valleys to waterfalls, watching the salmon run, searching for prehistoric rock art, cycling old drovers' trails, waiting for otters, climbing heather-covered crags and exploring ruined castles.

The **Cheviots** can seem desolate with their largely tree-less slopes and covering of sub-montane grasses and shrubs, but between their folds are deep glacial valleys, trout-filled rivers, waterfalls and remote farmsteads. On many summits are remains of ancient **hillforts** and **Bronze Age cairns**. I have suggested a couple of walks and cycle rides here and there, and hinted at the wildlife you may see on your way, but you'll need to come prepared with Ordnance Survey Explorer maps OL16 and OL42 to follow all the routes outlined in these pages.

Between the coast and Cheviot foothills, and extending for almost the entire length of Northumberland, is a long arc of craggy hills and moors hiding prehistoric rock carvings, castles, hillforts and an ancient wild cattle park. The best known area is the **Simonside Hills** near Rothbury which should not be missed in August when the heather flowers turn the ridge deep pink.

The **River Tweed** marks the boundary with Scotland and is explored here along with places along its tributary, the **River Till**. Those who take a leisurely jaunt along these rivers will find a scattering of ruined castles and towers and a couple of old-world villages.

To access the national park and its hinterlands you can either shoot along the A697 or take a more meandering route (as described in this chapter) along old drovers' trackways and unclassified roads that criss-cross the moors and hills and hug the courses of rivers. By tootling along country lanes you encounter quite a few hamlets, farms and 19th-century villages. Rothbury and Wooler are the largest settlements.

Getting around

A car or touring bicycle is going to really help you explore the hills. Some towns and villages on the eastern edge of Northumberland National Park and the border area can be reached by bus, but if you're heading deeper into the Cheviots without a car, you'll need to hire a bike, saddle up on horseback or hitch a ride along one of the tracks that runs through the larger Cheviot valleys. The only **train stations** of help are at Morpeth and Berwick-upon-Tweed.

Bus

From **Berwick-upon-Tweed**, there's a fairly useful service along the **River Tweed** and another to **Wooler** via **Ford** and **Etal**. Both have around seven buses a day (fewer on Sundays). Between Wooler and **Alnwick**, you'll find occasional buses to **Chillingham**, **Whittingham** and **Powburn** (for Ingram and the Breamish Valley). For the **Simonside Hills** and **Rothbury**, there are several services a day from Morpeth (from Newcastle, take the X14).

Cycling

Heading into the **Cheviot valleys** on a touring bike cannot be recommended enough. Upper Coquetdale, Breamish Valley, Harthope Valley and College Valley all have paved tracks that follow their respective rivers through the brooding hills. If that's not an invitation enough to cyclists, because these roads are all dead ends, they are almost free of cars. College Valley is particularly quiet because motorists are not permitted to enter without a permit. Also consider the old drove roads that cross the Cheviot Hills, especially Salter's Road from Alnham, which is paved.

The **sandstone hills** on the eastern edge of the National Park may not be as high as many of the Cheviot summits, but many of the quieter tracks and lanes rollercoaster across country from Rothbury to Coldstream and over the moors to the coast involving some seriously steep ascents. Distant views of the Cheviots are guaranteed almost the whole way.

Mountain bikers are particularly well-catered for in the Rothbury and Upper Coquetdale area thanks to the Forestry Commission-managed conifer woods including: Harbottle, Thrunton and Harwood (collectively known as the Rothbury Forests).

Also consider touring the **River Till**. The roads around here are fairly quiet and you'll dip in and out of a string of old villages with pubs and cafés.

The **Pennine Cycleway** (355 miles from Berwick to the Peak District) follows the River Tweed before turning south along the eastern edge of the National Park via Alwinton and Elsdon and onwards to Hadrian's Wall.

Walking

Multi-day walks in the Cheviot Hills are made possible by holiday cottages in the valleys and a couple of well-placed bunkhouses, notably at Mounthooley in College Valley and Barrowburn (see accommodation listings opposite).

Good walks in the valleys, hills and towns in and around Northumberland National Park are suggested throughout this chapter. I've only provided synopses of the routes so you'll need Ordnance Survey Explorer maps OL16 The Cheviot Hills and OL42 Kielder Water & Forest.

Horseriding

Bridleways (many of which are on ancient drove roads) cross the Cheviots linking the valleys and making this a superb place to visit on horseback.

Northumberland National Park has a number of excellent maps detailing circular routes by horse. For more information, contact one of the National Park Centres (see page 185) or see the horseriding section of the National Park's website where you can download route maps (*01665 578885; www. northumberlandnationalpark.org.uk*).

For guided horseriding trips in the Cheviots, try **Kimmerston Riding Centre** at Wooler (*01668 216283; www.kimmerston.com*).

Taxi

If you are walking linear routes across the Cheviots or Simonside Hills it's useful to know there are a couple of local taxi firms that will collect you from far-flung places.

Ron's Taxis ℗ 01668 281281/0777 8543907. For north Northumberland eg: College Valley and the Wooler area.
Coquetdale Taxis ℗ 01669 620820/07823 776109. Collect from in and around Rothbury including the Simonside Hills.

Accommodation

Alnham Farmhouse B&B and cottages Alnham, near Rothbury NE66 4TJ ℗ 01669 630210 ⓦ www.alnhamfarm.co.uk ⓔ stay@alnhamfarm.co.uk. Out-of-the-way stone farmhouse in the foothills of the Cheviots offering reasonably priced B&B in smart rooms with pristine linen and contemporary bathrooms (one room has a roll-top bath). Locally sourced breakfast ingredients. Good value self-catering cottages also available. Alnham is a hamlet surrounded by farm buildings and rolling fields, but it's close to many tourist destinations including Rothbury (10 miles south). Salter's Road – an old drove track – goes through Alnham and straight into the Cheviot Hills making for a memorable cycle ride. If you happen to be touring on horseback, there's room for five horses in the adjoining stables.
Barrowburn Camping Barn, Cottage and B&B Barrowburn, near Alwinton (Upper Coquetdale) NE65 7BP ℗ 01669 621176 ⓦ www.barrowburn.com ⓔ stay@barrowburn.com. Walkers seeking a rustic, remote place to stay in the Cheviot Hills will love it here. The camping barn sleeps 17 and can be booked out in its entirety. It costs about the same as a campsite to stay here and is cheap even for smaller groups, but you'll need to bring everything bar the kitchen sink (including bedding, a camping mat, matches for the coal fire, etc). The late 19th-century building was once a school for shepherds' children (see page 190). The green timber-clad building next door (the Deer Hut) is a basic holiday cottage charging little more than youth hostel prices.
Chatton Park House Chatton NE66 5RA ℗ 01668 215507 ⓦ www.chattonpark. com ⓔ enquiries@chattonpark.com. No children. The driveway is lit with little

lights giving this Georgian country house the appearance of a luxury hotel the moment you turn off the main road. You'll be greeted at the front door by Michelle with a big smile. She is the perfect host (helpful, friendly and discreet). For well above average prices, you get plenty of extras: furnishings are plush (heavy curtains, leather armchairs, super king-sized beds) and your high ceiling room comes with a view of the four-acre parkland surrounding the manor. On cold nights, you can sit by the wood fire in the living room listening to jazz and sipping an aperitif before heading out for dinner. There's only really one very good place to eat in the area and that's the White Swan at Warenford (see page 213). Breakfasts at Chatton Park House are up there with the very best in Northumberland with local kippers and smoked salmon and scrambled egg on the menu alongside classic full English and continental offerings. There's also a small holiday cottage in the grounds of Chatton Park House.

Cheviot Holiday Cottages Ingram NE66 4LT ① 01665 578236 ⓦ www.cheviotholidaycottages.co.uk. The setting of these cottages in the hamlet of Ingram couldn't be more tranquil with a medieval church to the rear and farmland and the Cheviot Hills to the front. Most cottages sleep two or four people and are arranged around a courtyard (great for large family gatherings). They are extremely well-appointed (hence the above-average price) and decorated in a contemporary farmhouse style (wooden furniture painted shades of grey, cream and duck-egg blue, exposed beams, range cookers, wood-burning stoves, etc). The River Breamish flows past Ingram; Linhope Spout is a short car or bike ride away.

College Valley Estates cottages Hethpool, College Valley ① 01890 830302 ⓦ www.college-valley.co.uk ⓔ holidays@college-valley.co.uk. Four quite different average-priced stone holiday cottages dotted around the valley; all furnished to a very good standard (contemporary, farmhouse styling with solid pine furniture, wood-burning stoves/fires). The biggest draw is the location with some of the best hill walks in Northumberland straight from the door. Dunsdale (sleeps eight) is the most remote, tucked away along the Lambden Burn under heather hills and crags. Hethpool Mill, at the entrance to the valley in a hamlet, is the most accessible and one of the best appointed. Southern Knowe (a former schoolhouse though you'd never guess) is more basic than the others and is set in a farm quite far down the valley.

Collingwood Arms Main St, Cornhill-on-Tweed TD12 4UH ① 01890 882424 ⓦ www.collingwoodarms.com ⓔ enquiries@collingwoodarms.com. One of the plushest inns offering B&B accommodation in Northumberland. Inside the Georgian hotel, the rooms are immaculate and decorated to an extremely high standard with polished hard-wood furniture, soft greys and tartan fabrics, one or two antiques and contemporary bathrooms that could be straight out of a Farrow & Ball catalogue (Molton & Brown handwash complete the upmarket look). Bedrooms are named after ships under the command of Admiral Collingwood during the Battle of Trafalgar. The hotel's restaurant is superb (see page 219) and there's a sunny courtyard and garden to the rear.

Linhope House Walby Hill, Rothbury NE65 7NT ① 01669 622843
Ⓦ www.linhopehouse.co.uk. On the edge of Rothbury and just a few minutes on foot from the town centre is this Edwardian townhouse set back from the road, offering upmarket B&B accommodation (slightly above average prices). A real fire was warming the living room when I visited and Joanne gave me a very friendly welcome. The bedrooms are sparkling and have large sleigh beds, goose-down duvets and a contemporary feel but with a touch of the old. Local sausages, bacon and smoked fish served at breakfast.

Mounthooley YHA Bunkhouse College Valley, Kirknewton NE71 6TX ① 01668 216358 Ⓦ www.yha.org.uk Ⓔ paulineatthetop@hotmail.com. I can't think of a more remote place to stay than at this old stone shepherd's cottage deep in College Valley. Some of the finest Cheviot hill walks straight from the front door. The warden, Pauline, lives next door and is very friendly and cooks a mean full English breakfast. Inside, there are two dormitories and a couple of family rooms. The living room has a fire and there's a BBQ area outside. You don't need a College Valley permit to drive into the valley if you are staying at the bunkhouse.

Orchard House High St, Rothbury NE65 7TL ① 01669 620684
Ⓦ www.orchardhouserothbury.com Ⓔ info@orchardhouserothbury.com. Georgian townhouse in the centre of Rothbury with sumptuous furnishings, immaculate rooms and much period appeal. Breakfasts are a treat with locally sourced produce, as you would expect from a top-end B&B.

Tosson Tower Farm Great Tosson, near Rothbury NE65 7NW ① 01669 620228
Ⓦ www.tossontowerfarm.com Ⓔ stay@tossontowerfarm.com. Friendly former drovers' inn dating to the 18th century on a working farm offering slightly above average-priced B&B accommodation and good value self-catering cottages in converted farm buildings. The Simonside Hills loom over the pretty hamlet which is a short drive or cycle ride from Rothbury. The ruins of a medieval pele tower, from which the hamlet gets its name, stands opposite the farmhouse. Rooms are very clean and furnished in a traditional farmhouse style with patterned fabrics, solid wood furniture and the odd antique. Breakfast is served in a light-filled conservatory with views of the Coquet Valley. This is a great base for walkers (hike to the top of Simonside straight from the front door).

Wild camping

Camping in the hills is not permitted, but you are unlikely to be bothered if you're walking with a bivvy bag or backpacking tent and stay above the tree line (1,500 feet or higher) and out of farmland and Forestry Commission woodlands. Take all rubbish out, don't light fires and stay only one night; this applies especially if you pitch late and leave early the next morning. Camping at high altitudes is inherently risky and you'll need good kit and winter clothes year round. There are very few official campsites in the Cheviots except for a couple of caravan sites at Wooler and further south in the Kielder and Redesdale area (see *Chapter 4*).

The Cheviot valleys and hills

Wherever you wander in north Northumberland, the Cheviots are almost always brooding in the distance, guarding the frontier with Scotland with purpose. There's no mistaking this stonking corridor of smooth humps down the western edge of the county which are strikingly rounded and unlike all the other hill ranges in northern England.

The slopes of these long-extinct volcanoes are dominated by dwarf shrubs and grasses and, except for a few plantation woodlands, the Cheviots appear at first quite featureless. It's not until you set foot that the character of individual hills and valleys becomes apparent with their wooded ravines, ancient trackways, Iron Age hillforts and waterfalls. In terms of altitude, you'll find some of the highest hills in England here with six summits over 2,000 feet.

Though seemingly desolate, the vegetation covering the Cheviot plateaux forms an internationally important habitat characterised by sphagnum mosses, cotton grasses, sedges, cloudberry, bilberry and heather. In ravines, you may see alpine flowering plants including rose root, dwarf cornel and alpine willow herb.

Deep valleys radiate away from highest peak, **The Cheviot**, which marks roughly the centre of the range. Coquet, Breamish, Harthope and College valleys are named after their respective rivers which rush eagerly off the hillsides. In glacial valleys like College and Harthope, the burns form wide straight channels through the hills; other rivers, like the Coquet, are of the meandering, oxbow-lake forming type. For the most part, they are all rocky and fairly shallow with shingle banks and rapids and the odd pool suitable for bathing.

Horseriders, cyclists, walkers and back-country hikers will find miles of lonely footpaths and bridleways in the Cheviots and a handful of quiet paved tracks that will take you deep into remote countryside, with no through roads.

Midges

Midges can be a bother in summer, but they are not as vicious as the infamous Highland midges. You'll probably still want to take repellent, though, especially if camping. As soon as there's the faintest gust, they're not a problem so you should be fine on the hills; even the breeze created by walking is usually enough to keep them away. The best repellent I've tried is Avon's Skin So Soft – dry oil body spray. Yes, it's a beauty product but midges hate this stuff. It's occasionally stocked in some campsite and outdoor shops; otherwise order it online (*www. avonshop.co.uk*).

This is not the Cotswolds and you won't find quaint villages strung along valley basins or many places to pick up supplies so you'll need to come prepared. Isolation and remoteness is what will draw you here. Those day-trippers who came looking for cream teas and gift shops quickly turned around and headed back out.

① Upper Coquetdale

Seasoned travellers to Northumberland National Park go dreamy-eyed when you mention Coquetdale. It's a much sung valley that oozes lush scenery and has parts that feel wonderfully remote. I'm talking really about Upper Coquetdale – roughly the extent of the River Coquet from its jingly beginnings in the southwestern corner of the Cheviots at Chew Green, past Barrowburn, Alwinton, Harbottle and on to Rothbury, 30 miles from its source.

The upper reaches are classically Cheviot-like: big heavy moors, sparkling burns and the occasional stand of conifer trees and hay meadow; but further south around Holystone, the landscape becomes wooded (now with ancient broadleaved trees) before entering the open flood plains at Hepple.

Accessing Upper Coquetdale

A paved road extends for 12 lonely miles from Alwinton to the Roman camp, Chew Green, on the Scottish border, making for a memorable **cycling** trip.

Northumberland National Park

With some 2,200 residents in total, Northumberland National Park is the least populated of all the national parks in the UK by quite some way. It borders Scotland in the west and extends as far south as Hadrian's Wall, encompassing the whole of the Cheviot range and the Simonside Hills.

You'll find a huge amount of information online (*www.northumberland nationalpark.org.uk*) and at the three excellent **National Park Centres** in Rothbury, Ingram and Once Brewed (Hadrian's Wall). As well as all the usual tourist information, they stock Ordnance Survey maps, walking guidebooks and Northumbrian hiking socks (Capricorn Mohair Socks are a local brand that live up to their slogan: 'probably the best socks you will ever buy'). Details of the two centres covering the northern end of the National Park are below.

Rothbury National Park Centre Church St, Rothbury NE65 7UP ① 01669 620887. This is the main office for the National Park. Open 1 Apr–31 Oct, daily 10.00–18.00 and weekends in winter, 10.00–15.00.
Ingram National Park Centre Near Powburn NE66 4LT ① 01665 578890. All the usual information and advice plus an exhibition about prehistoric archaeology in Breamish Valley. Open 1 Apr–31 Oct, daily 10.00–17.00.

Wildlife in the valleys

Classic **upland bird species** like ring ouzel (also known as the 'mountain blackbird'), wheatear and whinchat inhabit the sheltered slopes of burns. Higher up, particularly where there are crags, look out for peregrine falcons and ravens (the Hen Hole in College Valley is a good place). Red grouse are frequently seen (and heard) flying out of heather, particularly in the Simonsides.

Along the fast-flowing rivers, dippers are easy to spot bobbing up and down on rocks (similar size and colour of a blackbird but with a prominent white 'bib'). The other bobbing bird you are likely to see on the shinglebanks is the grey wagtail (slate-coloured back and yellow chest). Look out for rarer yellow wagtails as well (almost completely yellow). **Breeding waders** include common sandpipers, oystercatchers, redshank, lapwing and curlew – or 'whaup' to give it its local name.

Northumberland boasts some of the best **salmon and trout rivers** in England, notably the rivers Tweed, Till and Tyne. Salmon and sea trout spawn in Cheviot burns. Find a bridge in autumn from which to watch them leaping over rapids.

Good places to look out for **goosanders** and **otters** are in the lower reaches of some rivers such as the Coquet (in the Rothbury and Brinkburn Priory area, for example) and River Breamish around Ingram. Otters are famously elusive but you never know if you have the patience to sit quietly in a secluded riverside spot at dusk or early in the morning. You're unlikely to chance upon one while out walking (they'll be aware of your presence and move on); you're much better off staying in one place and allowing them to come to you. Otter spraint (poo) on rocks will indicate they are around. Even if you don't see one, plenty of other birds (kingfishers, dippers, herons) and mammals (particularly bats in wooded stretches of rivers) will no doubt make an appearance.

For much of the way it follows the River Coquet through the valley passing farmsteads like Barrowburn.

Walkers who have come by car will find several parking areas off this main track which mark the start point of popular hikes into the hills, including Windy Gyle (see page 191) and a number of trails from Alwinton. You don't have to walk far before you feel the swelling moors enclosing you; every time you turn back, the hills seem to have shuffled in that bit closer.

The River Coquet forms the northern boundary of the **Otterburn military training area** (also see page 158) which covers the southern moors in the Cheviot range. Countryside and hills north of the river are yours to explore at any time; south of the river, there are restrictions. Red flags indicate the ranges are closed to the public. In reality, most visitors explore the hills to the north anyway because the signed walking trails are on that side. If you want to experience the desolate moors to the south, you'll need to check access restrictions first by going to www.otterburnranges.co.uk or calling 01830

520569. Usually, the ranges are open one weekend a month and for four weeks during the lambing season from mid-April to mid-May.

② Holystone's woods, moors and well

Plantation forest dominates the hilly ground between Holystone and Harbottle, but amid the conifer trees is a remnant patch of ancient oak woodland. The dawn chorus here in spring is quite something. As well as all the common woodland birds, you may hear wood warblers or see flycatchers; look out, too, for red squirrels.

In recent years, an astonishing discovery was made on **Holystone Common** (just south of Holystone Burn): a six-foot-high skyscraper ants' nest. The conical structure is made of pine and spruce needles and constructed by the uncommon hairy northern wood ant. There are other nests around here, just be careful not to disturb them – they are rare and take years to build.

You can explore Holystone Woods from the Forestry Commission car park and picnic area west of the village. A longer hike could incorporate **Harbottle Crags** (open heather moorland northwest of the forested slopes).

Closer to the village centre is **Lady's Well** (signed) – a secluded pool with a cross in the middle. The rectangular stone basin is thought to be Roman. There are no obvious remains of the Augustinian nunnery that once stood in Holystone.

Woodhouses Bastle

2 miles south of Holystone, reached by a grassy track from the Hepple to Harbottle road.

Wild Cheviot goats

Goats have been a feature of the British countryside for as long as the land has been farmed. In England, our native goats almost completely died out in the 19th century when exotic breeds from overseas were introduced to the UK. However, some native breeds – escapees and the like – survived in a handful of remote corners – places like College Valley for instance.

The shaggy, long-horned goats you may come across today in the Cheviots are descendants of the earliest primitive goats that were domesticated over thousands of years successively from the time of Neolithic farmers onwards. These scarce animals are not as timid as you might imagine but still have a wariness that is to be expected of a breed that has run wild in the hills for a very long time. Occasionally walkers come across a kid that looks as if it's been abandoned. It hasn't of course and its mother will return soon enough.

Four herds are found in the National Park: at Kielderhead, Upper Coquetdale, and Yeavering Bell and Newton Tors near College Valley. Each herd is directed to the best grazing grounds by an old nanny who knows the hills well.

One of the best examples of a border fortified farmhouse stands at the top of a grassy vale keeping watch over the Coquet river basin and distant Simonside Hills. It probably dates from the 16th century but has been re-roofed in relatively recent times. As is typical of bastle houses (see page 154), the walls are hugely thick and the windows are small holes and slits. You can see into the ground floor which has a stone vaulted ceiling.

③ Harbottle

This sleepy hamlet along the River Coquet is best known for its 12th-century **castle** (originally a motte and bailey) which teeters on the edge of a grassy summit above the main street. Built as a defence against the Scots, it now lies completely ruined, with crumbling walls and scattered stones everywhere; the view of the forests, craggy hills and houses and church below makes the climb to the top very worthwhile.

For a short, stiff **walk**, take the footpath from the car park at the western end of the Harbottle (beyond the parking area for the castle) and climb for half a mile up the craggy, heather-covered hills opposite the village to **Drake Stone** – a huge rock (said to have healing properties) near an icy tarn. You can return in a loop via West Wood by following the trail along the northern shore of the lake. The circular route is around two miles.

Food and drink

Star Inn Harbottle NE65 7DG ① 01669 650221. Pub and information point with a craft shop.

④ Alwinton

Alwinton lies at the meeting of two good trout rivers – the Coquet and Alwin – and route of the ancient drove road, Clennell Street, that once extended from Morpeth to Kelso. Like Harbottle, Alwinton is another quiet hamlet of stone (with a couple of pubs), but the scenery is more open and you feel as though you are at the doorway to the Cheviots rather than at the garden gate.

Several highly worthwhile **walks** start from Alwinton, including a five-mile route to **Kidland Forest** that begins along Clennell Street for nearly a mile. Where the drove road bends to the left near the top of the hill, strike off right and go through a couple of gates before making your way around the hillside and descending to the corner of the forest. Return to Alwinton by following the River Alwin the whole way. You can visit **Clennell Hall** (*01669 650376*) on your way back – a country house (now a hotel serving food) that goes back many centuries and still retains its ancient defensive tower. Another option for refreshments is the **Rose and Thistle** (*01669 650226*) in Alwinton.

St Michael and All Angels Church is half a mile south of the village. It dates from the Norman period and is curious for two reasons: the footpath made from old gravestones (including one with a very prominent skull and

Old drove roads

Footpaths, cart-tracks, packhorse routes and livestock trails have crossed the Cheviots for as long as these moors and valleys have been farmed. The Romans created highways through Northumberland's hills, notably Dere Street that crosses high ground in the southwest corner of the Cheviot range. Drove routes expanded in the late medieval period and especially after the Union of the Crowns when relatively peaceful times promoted cross-border trade. During the 18th and early 19th centuries, tens of thousands of animals (mainly cattle) were seasonally driven across the border.

Some drovers travelling from Scotland also traded in illicit goods, especially whisky (duties on the liquor were higher in England thus promoting an illicit trade). Whisky stills were hidden in rocky outcrops in a number of places. A mile or so west of Barrowburn where Rowhope Burn meets the Coquet, there was once an 18th-century inn (evocatively named Slymefoot) that was notorious for receiving smuggled spirits.

Clennel Street, Salter's Road and The Street are some of the best-known drove routes that are still used by farmers. Nowadays, ramblers and cyclists also make good use of them. They are largely wide tracks (grassy, dirt or paved) that tend to take a drier route over the hills, avoiding bogs.

A popular walk is the stretch of Clennel Street that runs north of Alwinton above the River Alwin, and The Street to Windy Gyle.

crossbones carving), and the flight of steps from the nave to the chancel. Not much masonry survives from the 11th and 12th centuries, but you will find some Early English features dating from the 13th century; the rest is Victorian.

The annual **Alwinton Border Shepherds' Show** (*www.alwintonshow.co.uk*) is early in October and traditionally the last of the season in Northumberland. It's also one of the largest fairs in the county where you'll see all the usual displays such as sheep dog trials, craft tents, food stalls, Westmorland wrestling and bagpipe music.

⑤ Barrowburn

Barrowburn farmstead stands by the River Coquet deep within the valley, six miles upriver from Alwinton and reached along a paved road. The hills and flower meadows hereabouts are some of the most beautiful in the whole of the Cheviot range and walkers will find plenty of options for hikes, which are made all the more enjoyable by the promise of a cuppa and slice of cake at the tea room (surely one of the most remote cafés in Northumberland). Barrowburn also has a

fascinating history, best recounted by Ian Tait, a sheep farmer who has lived here all his life.

The meadow behind the farm buildings is a blaze of yellow, green and purple in June and July when yellow rattle, buttercups, eyebright, clovers, wood crane's-bill and knapweed come into flower. Mountain bumblebees (see page 208) rather like this field. Heading up the track are two buildings that can be hired: the Deer Hut and a camping barn. The latter is the old school which was opened by one of the famous Kirk Yetholm gypsies in the late 19th century.

Food and drink

Barrowburn tea room NE65 7BP ① 01669 621176 ⑩ www.barrowburn.com. A real fire (lit most of the year), friendly welcome by the Tait family and inexpensive tea, cakes, scones and sandwiches, lure walkers and cyclists off the hills. Up the farm track is a camping barn and basic self-catering cottage run by the farm (see *accommodation*, page 181).

Gypsy Kings and Presidents

The following tale was told to me one winter's afternoon at the Barrowburn tea room. It concerns a poacher in the mid-19th century who was chased by a couple of gamekeepers to his home. The story goes that the poacher hid his shotgun in his son's crib but the gun accidentally went off, shooting the child through the arm. On hearing the story – and realising the child would never be able to work on the land – the landlord's wife rather kindly paid for the child to receive an education. His name was Andrew Blythe (the Blythes were a famous gypsy family in Kirk Yetholm just over the Scottish border) and he eventually made a living travelling the Cheviot Hills teaching shepherds' children how to read and write. He opened the schoolhouse at Barrowburn and was the schoolmaster there for 50 years, as his gravestone in Kirk Yetholm describes.

If that wasn't a good enough story in itself, there's another tale about the Blythes which sounds a bit too good to be true but is intriguing nonetheless. The Blythes were related to the gypsy royal family, whose kings and queens lived in the Gypsy Palace at Kirk Yetholm (a cottage with a fascinating history). The last king, incidentally, was Charles Faa Blythe whose coronation in 1898 was watched by 10,000 spectators.

Back in 1752, 18 gypsies from Northumberland (including members of the illustrious Blythe clan) were transported to South Carolina from Morpeth Gaol. A man named William Blythe, who was said to be a relative of one of these Northumberland gypsies in South Carolina, died in a car crash in 1946, three months before the birth of his son, William Jefferson Blythe. After his mother remarried, the boy changed his name to William Jefferson Clinton, better known as Bill Clinton.

Hill farming and community life in Barrowburn

Ian Tait is a fifth generation hill farmer at Barrowburn and has lived here since birth. His flocks of Cheviot sheep are the white-faced ewes you'll see in the hills around the farm. 'They're the wildest domestic sheep in the world', says Ian. 'Skittish, but intelligent and very protective of their young.' Their mothering instinct is so strong in fact that they sometimes 'steal' another ewe's lamb. 'It's not unusual to see two ewes claiming one lamb as their own'.

There are not many buildings at Barrowburn except for the farm, old school house, and community hall. Over a cup of tea and scone one winter's day, Ian told me about how the community once centred around these scattered buildings. 'The building downriver used to be a dance hall. It's used for storage now and is full of hay, but if you were to look under the hay, you'd see a beautiful sprung wooden floor.' It was here that the local farmers and their families used to dance to border folk songs, including the Barrowburn Reel.

'The school was the focus of the community,' Ian says. It was opened by a gypsy in the late 19th century (see box opposite) and closed in the 1970s. Ian now runs the old schoolhouse as a camping barn but he remembers how farmers' children (including himself) used to travel from all around to the simple stone building on the hillside. 'There was only one teacher and all ages were taught in the same room: big kids at the back and younger kids at the front. If the weather was bad in winter and most children couldn't get to school, we used to sit in front of the fire in the teacher's house next door, drinking hot Ribena and doing our maths.'

'School trips were not just for the children,' Ian recalls. 'The whole community would join us and we'd all go off to the beach at Tynemouth for the day.'

Walks around Barrowburn

The classic **Barrowburn hike** is the five-mile moorland and burn route northwards to **Murder Cleugh**. From the tea room, take the farm track away from the Coquet that passes the green Deer Hut and old schoolhouse (marked as a bunkhouse on Ordnance Survey maps) and follows the course of Hepdon Burn to Middle Hill forest. Go through the dark, lifeless woods and then follow a narrow path around the side of a steep hill with views of the Usway Burn below. Murder Cleugh is not far ahead and is approached from the northeast after crossing the burn. The perimeter fence leads all the way to the southwest corner of Murder Cleugh where you go through a farm gate. Just around the corner on the left, a memorial stone in the copse reads: 'Here in 1610 Robert Lumsden killed Isabella Sudden'. The return route over Barrow Law is special, with the humps of several summits all around and a far-reaching view of the River Coquet channelling a silvery course through the valley.

A popular eight-mile **circuit of Windy Gyle** begins and ends a mile west of Barrowburn where Rowhope Burn meets the Coquet. Follow the old drove route, The Street, northwest round Swineside Law and over the summit of

Black Braes before joining the Pennine Way on the Scottish border for the eastward hike to Windy Gyle. The return is made by following a track along a ridge with Trows Burn on one side and Wardlaw Burn on the other. The stretch back to the paved road is along Rowhope Burn.

A recommended short hike (just over three miles), with hill-top views and swimming opportunities, begins from **Buckham's Bridge**, four miles up the Coquet from Barrowburn. Within a few hundred yards of following Buckham's Walls Burn northwest (away from the road), you'll come to the first pool where you could take a dip. They become more generous as you press on. On reaching a junction of two burns by a sheepfold, you change course and head west, though still following the same burn. A few hundred boggy yards later, there's another sheepfold and a track leading up Deel's Hill. The view at the top of hills sloping into one another deserves a few moments to be taken in before you descend back to the car park.

⑥ Breamish Valley

Breamish Valley (a continuation of Ingram Valley) is one of the big four valleys in the English Cheviots. It's quite different from the U-shaped Harthope and College valleys further north in that its shallow river takes a more roundabout route through the steep-sided bracken hills on its way east. For that reason it doesn't have quite the same tunnel views, but it's not the valley basin that visitors really come to see. A major draw for many day-trippers are the hillforts and Linhope's waterfall.

A paved track takes you up and down the hills and alongside the river for several miles into the core of the valley. You can drive as far as Hartside and there are various pull-in areas and official parking bays all the way from Ingram.

If walking over the hills, you may well notice ancient cultivation terraces on many slopes. This whole area has been farmed for thousands of years; the evidence of which is all about you. There are Bronze Age burial cairns dotted in a number of places, the odd abandoned medieval village and an impressive concentration of hillforts built some 2,300 years ago. At Wether Hill and Brough Law near Ingram you can even see the outlines of Iron Age roundhouses.

⑦ Ingram

This sweet hamlet is the first you come to on taking the paved track through Breamish Valley. Tucked away at the end of a side lane, it is worth seeking out for the **church,** which dates in part to the early Norman period. The tower and tower arch are some of the oldest structures. Early in the year the churchyard is covered in snowdrops. Look out for a small headstone a few feet high which has a stone carving of a man and woman holding hands, and a couple of headstones with skull and crossbones near the porch door.

An archaeological exhibition at the **National Park Centre** (*01665 578890; open daily 1 Apr–31 Oct*) features artefacts discovered during digs at the Iron Age hillforts in the valley.

Northumbrian folk music traditions

Geoff Heslop, record producer who has recorded many of the most influential North East musicians over the last 40 years. He plays with his wife, Brenda, herself a songwriter, in their band, Ribbon Road (www.ribbonroadmusic.com).

The North East of England is rich in music, both in songs and tunes and we are fortunate that this music is very much still alive with an increasing number of musicians performing and writing.

The history of music in the area probably begins for us in the Border Ballads, many of which were collected by Sir Walter Scott in the late 18th century. These songs tell the tales of great events and foul deeds from the region's bloody past. Many reflect the activities of the infamous Border Reiver families during the hundreds of years of troubles until around the mid 17th century. These were collected together in the volumes of the Child Ballads (those collected by Francis James Child in the 19th century). Many of these ballads are still sung today, including *The Fair Flower of Northumberland* and *Johnnie Armstrong* – which tells the story of one of the most notorious Border Reivers.

We have our own instrument, the Northumbrian smallpipes, which is bellows blown and has a distinctive sweet tone. There's been a revival in the instrument since the mid 20th century, largely due to the increase in the number of pipe-makers; there are now a large number of players of all ages, both in the North East and throughout the world and many modern tunes are being written.

The two other contributors to the music of the area are the songs which came out of the area's industrial heritage of mining, shipbuilding and fishing and the music hall songs of the 19th century. Many fine songs were written reflecting the often hard life of the workers and their families, but also the Geordie sense of humour in the face of it, such as *Keep Your Feet Still Geordie Hinnie* and *Cushie Butterfield*, which has the following lines:

> *I'm a broken-hearted keelman*
> *and I'm o'er head in love*
> *With a young lass from Gateshead*
> *And I call her my dove*
> *. . . Her eyes is like two holes*
> *In a blanket burnt through*
> *And her breath in the mornin'*
> *Would scare a young coo*

Food and drink

The **National Park Centre** has a hot drinks machine and sells snacks. The nearest place for hot food is the **Plough Inn** at Powburn (*01665 578259*).

Ingram hillforts walk

Following a circular walk of just 4½ miles from Ingram, you will encounter five hillforts and a sprinkling of Bronze Age burial cairns. The National Park Centre in Ingram has a leaflet with a basic map showing the location of the hillforts (also marked on Ordnance Survey Explorer map OL16).

The route is basically this: set foot from the car park half a mile west from Ingram. On the other side of the road, a track leads steeply up **Brough Law**. For many visitors, this is the most impressive of all the local Iron Age forts because of its ruined stone walls and ramparts, remains of roundhouses – and view of the valley below. The other forts are reached by skirting round the side of Ewe Hill and down to Middledean Burn (a ravine with a hillfort on the side) and then up to the summit of Cochrane Pike, which has great views of Coquetdale. The return walk is via Wether Hill (note the outlines of roundhouses), Turf Knowe with its terraces, and Ingram Hill.

⑧ Linhope and Linhope Spout waterfall

Tucked below conical Ritto Hill and surrounded by some hefty summits, is the secluded hamlet of **Linhope** which hides under trees by the meeting of the River Breamish and Linhope Burn. The walk to the waterfall, a mile or so from Linhope, is straightforward with a short ascent and descent at either end but nothing that should put off families. Follow the farm track along the edge of a stand of conifers and then a well-trodden path round the side of a hill and down into a wooded ravine where **Linhope Spout** plunges 60 feet through a secluded rock cleft into a dark pool. In winter half the fall may be frozen solid, with icicles the size of swords hanging from the rocks.

⑨ Powburn Antiques shop

Hedgeley Service Station (A697), Powburn NE66 4HU ☎ 01665 578303. Open Wed–Mon from 11.00.

This is a great affordable antiques emporium by the side of the A697. I've seen furniture and architectural items in here that would sell for more on eBay. There's quite a lot to rummage through and some corners are better than others, but you'll generally find rustic wooden furniture (church pews, trunks, chest of drawers – that kind of thing), as well as linen, antique prints, secondhand books, china and oddments.

⑩ Harthope Valley

Behold a letter from the mountains, for I am very snugly settled here, in a farmer's house, about six miles from Wooler, in the very centre of the Cheviot Hills, in one of the wildest and most romantic situations . . . All the day we shoot, fish, walk, and ride; dine and sup upon fish struggling from the stream, and the most delicious heath-fed mutton, barn-door fowls, poys, milkcheese, etc . . .

Sir Walter Scott in a letter to his friend, William Clerk, 26th August 1791

The house from which Scott penned the above letter was Langleeford – a remote farmstead by Harthope Burn which is regularly passed by walkers exploring this glacial valley. Three of the highest peaks in the Cheviot range are within reach of the day hiker from here: The Cheviot, Hedgehope Hill and Comb Fell. Even those out for a gentle cycle ride along the valley bottom or potter under trees by the river will find Harthope Valley every bit as enchanting as Scott discovered over 200 years ago, with river birds and trout in abundance, sheep and grouse on the slopes and small waterfalls here and there.

Harthope Linn and walks from Langleeford

Harthope Burn is wooded for much of its course and plenty of grassy areas invite a picnic and paddle. Those who can tolerate the icy waters flowing off the hillside will find bathing holes every so often including the magical Harthope Linn – a secluded plunge pool where the brave shower under a small fall overhung with mountain shrubs, trees and ferns.

Langleeford farmhouse is a popular starting point for the well-trodden footpath to **Harthope Linn** (and The Cheviot), for it lies at the end of the paved track into the valley; use the parking area not far from the farm (close to where Hawsen Burn meets Harthope Burn). If you continue on the farm track past Langleeford (don't cross the river but go through a kissing gate), you'll come to the waterfall (two miles upriver from the parking area). It's easy to navigate but feels longer than two miles because it's uphill the whole way.

If continuing upriver from the waterfall to **The Cheviot**, you will need a compass, map and good outdoor clothing. The stream bubbles in peaty hollows as it becomes narrower and quieter until Harthope Burn disappears altogether. Looking down the valley, you can see the yellow, lime and deep green slopes folding into each other, the North Sea in the distance and clouds sailing dangerously close to the hill-tops. This is a wonderful place to be on a sunny afternoon. The Cheviot is reached after a stiff hike following a fence line to the Pennine Way (stone slabs lead the way to the summit at 2,674 feet). Return via **Scald Hill** – The Cheviot's shoulder.

The other major walk from the Langleeford parking area is to **Hedgehope Hill** (the perfectly rounded massif you see poking up higher than all the other hills on the approach through the valley). You'll pass the impressive **Housey Crags** (a destination in themselves) from where there are great views of all the major summits peering down through the valley, including The Cheviot and Comb Fell.

⑪ Happy Valley

2 miles south of Wooler; there's a rough parking area of sorts either end of Happy Valley: at Carey Burn Bridge and Coldgate Mill (reached by following Cheviot Street from Wooler town centre to a ford); Middleton Hall has an official parking area but you'll need to make your way on foot to the river.

So the burning question will be: is Happy Valley as idyllic as it sounds? In an

Fell racing

On the last Sunday in June, runners make the climb over Black Braes to the summit of Windy Gyle during the annual **Windy Gyle Fell Race** – a nine-mile course with 1,500 feet of ascent. The current record holder completed the route in a breath-taking 58 minutes and (an all important) five seconds; see www.northumberlandfellrunners.co.uk. In comparison to the **Chevy Chase**, however, the Windy Gyle run is just a warm-up. The most arduous of all fell races in Northumberland is this 20-mile circuit from Wooler to the top of the highest peak in Northumberland (The Cheviot) involving 4,000 feet of ascent. Those up for the challenge should visit www.woolerrunningclub.co.uk.

area with so many wooded glens and jazzy burns, Happy Valley has a lot of competition, but it is certainly a gem and easy to reach from Wooler. It's not on the scale of Harthope Valley (a continuation of Happy Valley) or Breamish Valley, but it has its own charms and can be walked in under an hour.

From Coldgate Mill, a footpath follows Coldgate Water upriver through woodland for a mile or so before the scenery opens into rough grazing pastures with gorse bushes and shrubs. Look out for hares and small birds. The final stretch to the junction with Harthope Burn is picturesque with heavily wooded slopes rising from the valley bottom and glimpses of the river which flows leisurely round shingle banks and boulders – and appears at its happiest.

⑫ Wooler

Wooler is promoted as the 'Gateway to the Cheviots' and if you are heading for the hills, it will be your last opportunity to pick up supplies. It's a fairly large market town surrounded by green hills and fields where you'll find plenty of food shops, an antiques emporium, gift shops and a café or three scattered along its principal street.

Gear for Girls (*01668 283300*) is halfway along the High Street and sells a large range of outdoor clothes and boots (no corresponding shop for men in the area). For tourist information, maps, hiking socks and walking books, head to the **Cheviot Centre** on Padgepool Place (*01668 282123; open 10.00–14.00 May–Oct, daily and Nov–Apr, Mon–Sat*), reached from the far end of the High Street (opposite end to the marketplace) where there's a car park.

Food and drink

Breeze High St, NE71 6BU ℗ 01668 283333 Ⓦ www.breezewooler.com. Popular café-cum-art gallery serving soups, filled baguettes and quiches.
The Good Life Shop High St, NE71 6BG ℗ 01668 281700. Deli with everything you'll need for a picnic, including many local cheeses. Coffees to take away.
Milan Restaurant High St, NE71 6BY ℗ 01668 283692 Ⓦ www.milan-restaurant.

co.uk. Ask any local where the best restaurant is in town and they'll point you to this modern Italian set back off the High Street (go under the arch by the Black Bull). It's not cheap but the food's good and there's nowhere else really worth eating at in Wooler.

⑬ Yeavering Bell

South side of the B6351 between Akeld and Kirknewton; grid reference NT928293.

Northumberland's largest Iron Age hillfort (pronounced 'Yevering') crowns the top of a double-peaked conical hill over 1,000 feet high near the entrance to College Valley. Apart from a superb view across the Cheviot tops in one direction and out to the North Sea in the other, you'll see scatterings of rocks and the signs of where over a hundred roundhouses used to stand within the protective walls of the huge stone rampart. This perimeter wall would have once stood up to eight feet tall.

North of the B6351 in the field beyond the lay-by is the site of an Anglo-Saxon royal palace, **Gefrin** (the old name of Yeavering, derived from the Welsh for goat ('gafr') which is nice because wild goats roam Yeavering Bell to this day).

If you continue northwards on the same road, you'll come to a picturesque church at **Kirknewton** dating from the 13th century. St Gregory's was mostly rebuilt in the latter half of the 19th century but its chancel is very old and it houses a 900-year-old stone relief of the Adoration of the Magi.

⑭ College Valley

Access from Westnewton (near Kirknewton on the B6351); permits for driving into the valley are issued by Sale and Partners on Glendale Rd in Wooler on behalf of College Valley Estates; no permits are issued during the lambing season in Apr–May; cost £10 ℡ 01668 281611.

This long glacial valley is the most isolated, tranquil – and some would say spectacular – of all the major valleys in the Cheviot range. Its seclusion is helped by the fact that only 12 permits a day are issued for access by car. Those without a permit must leave their car in the designated parking area just beyond Hethpool, and hike in. Sheep rule this road.

The paved riverside road into College Valley from Hethpool makes for a wonderfully scenic cycle ride or drive with views through the tunnel-straight valley, which is blocked at the southern end by a wall

Adders

Britain's only venomous snake loves nothing more than a sunny clearing on a heather or bracken slope. Adders will quickly slip away into the vegetation if you get too close (usually before you've spotted it) and will move so fast that their distinctive black zigzag appears as a thick straight line. Sometimes, they will coil and give you an angry hiss before making their exit. It's their way of saying 'back off' – and you should do just that. Anyone who is bitten should seek urgent medical help. Bites can be fatal to pets, though such occurrences are very rare. Few people would be stupid enough to approach an adder, but I did hear a tale about a soldier on the Otterburn Ranges who thought it would be funny to pee on a basking adder. Well, you can guess what happened.

of cloud-nudging summits protecting the frontier with Scotland. You'll pass the odd plantation woodland and thick patch of gorse; a few old shepherds' houses, now mostly converted into holiday cottages (see accommodation, pages 182–3), a bunkhouse, a load of sheep and an isolated village hall about halfway through the valley.

Cuddystone Hall is a plain 1960s building with a nice big bell. It's occasionally the scene of a night of dancing and celebration, this being the most remote place to legally tie the knot in Northumberland. If you get the chance to look inside (the door is sometimes left open) the notice boards have some information about the planes that crashed into the surrounding hills during World War II and the famous rescue of American airmen from the B17 Flying Fortress by the shepherd at Dunsdale and his collie dog, Sheila (see box opposite). Outside the hall is a **memorial** to those who lost their lives which shows the locations of crash sites. If you hike to any of these places, you'll find debris from the planes still lying in situ.

⑮ Hethpool

Hethpool is an eye-catching hamlet at the entrance to College Valley with a country house and row of attractive cottages with roofs far longer than their walls are high. They were built in the Arts and Crafts style in the early 20th century.

Behind Hethpool House is a stand of mature oaks (no public access) called the **Collingwood Oaks** which are named after Admiral Collingwood (Nelson's right-hand man at the Battle of Trafalgar) who is said to have walked around the countryside pushing acorns into the ground believing the trees would supply timber for the battleships of the future. Little did he know that metal would replace wood by the time his oaks matured. The Collingwood Oaks at Hethpool were actually planted by his wife while Collingwood was at sea. He was supposedly very pleased to hear about her project, but sadly Collingwood never saw these trees as he died in 1810 on his return to England. To mark the bicentenary of his death, a new oak woodland was planted near the road on the approach into Hethpool.

Wanderings from Hethpool

Stunning views of College Valley are experienced on a number of shortish walks from Hethpool. Of particular interest are the hillfort trails, of which there are quite a few around the entrance to the valley, including to Yeavering Bell (see page 197) and the strenuous climb to the top of **Great Hetha** – a great route where you'll see the ramparts of a hillfort, as well as a stupendous view of the tops of many peaks. Also consider following St Cuthbert's Way along Elsdon Burn to **Ring Chesters** – another fort reached after a steep ascent (a slightly longer route this one).

Less strenuous and of no distance is the circuit to **Hethpool Linn** (under two miles), which gushes in a wooded gorge not far from the hamlet and is reached by following St Cuthbert's Way which strikes away from the row of cottages by the sharp bend in the road. From the waterfall you can access **Hethpool Lake** – a manmade pool with a boat house.

Exploring deeper into College Valley

Walkers are spoilt in College Valley though you must pay with an initial four-mile walk in if you don't have a car pass. Luckily there's a well-situated youth hostel at the end where you can stay overnight enabling an ascent of The Cheviot at first light the next day. You could of course take the high path via

Sheila and the Flying Fortress

A snowstorm was battering the Cheviots on 14 December 1944 when nine US airmen were flying back to their base following an aborted bombing raid. They were flying low over the hills to avoid the plane icing when they crashed into West Hill near the Braydon Crags. Two of the airmen were killed instantly and three managed to make their way to Mounthooley – now the bunkhouse at the head of College Valley.

Shepherds John Dagg and Frank Moscrop from Dunsdale and Southern Knowe cottages heard the plane come down. They went into the hills with John's border collie, Sheila, which managed to sniff out the four other remaining survivors found huddled together in a peat gully.

The two shepherds each received a British Empire Medal. As for Sheila, she was awarded the animal equivalent of the Victoria Cross, the Dickin Medal, the first ever civilian dog to receive the medal.

The dying wish of the pilot of the B-17, who passed away in 2005 at his home in Fort Lauderdale, was that his ashes be scattered at the site of the plane crash where fragments of the wreckage still lie. The request was fulfilled by relatives later that year.

St Cuthbert's Way and the Pennine Way (a day hike in itself) rather than the road.

Mounthooley YHA Bunkhouse is situated in a prime spot for exploring some of the most memorable hills and crags in the Cheviot range, including the Hen Hole, Bizzle Crags and the awesome whale-back Schil. A favourite view is from **Auchope Cairn** looking across to Scotland in one direction and down over the Hen Hole and the head of the valley in the other. Incidentally, if you were to get stuck up here in inclement weather, there's a basic refuge between the Schil and The Cheviot on the Pennine Way.

Hop over The Cheviot and you'll be in the neighbouring valley (Harthope) where an enchanting small waterfall awaits on the other side (see page 195). The following **two-day circuit** is highly recommended: Langleeford (Harthope Valley) – Harpthope Linn – The Cheviot – the Schil – overnight at Mounthooley YHA – Lambden Burn – Hawsen Burn – Langleeford.

⑯ The Cheviot

If it weren't for the excellent Pennine Way footpath made of stone slabs, you'd really struggle to make your way across the table-flat squelchy quagmire that is the summit of Northumberland's highest mountain (2,676 feet). The gullies and peat bogs are so deep in places that to go off-piste means jumping from one island of coarse grass to another.

Perhaps I've just been unlucky, but pretty much every time I've been up to the top of The Cheviot, I find it sulking under a swirling smoke machine-like fog. If you happen to be here when The Cheviot is having a good day, you can see all the mountain ranges from Cumbria to the Lothians. Northeast of the stone monument, marking the highest point, are the fragmentary remains of a B-17 bomber that crashed into the mountain during World War II.

Despite the fog and desolation, there's still something quite captivating about The Cheviot, partly because of its height and partly because it is located right bang in the middle of the Cheviot range with beautiful valleys and many other summits nearby. And, I suppose, there is a certain draw about a brooding hill like this that holds onto its cap of snow into summer.

Hen Hole

This rocky, ice-sculpted chasm hides around the corner at the head of College Valley luring walkers into its deep cleft. It's well-known to ravens, peregrine falcons and in years gone by, golden eagles.

The demanding route criss-crosses College Burn the whole way to Auchope Cairn and requires hands and feet at times – and good lungs. Many an unsuspecting (and unprepared) hiker has scrambled too far through the chasm to turn back. The burn splashes from ledge to ledge for 1,500 feet until it reaches the valley floor, and at one point forms a trio of small waterfalls called the Three Sisters. A less strenuous route to the Cheviot is up and along the Schil (you can peer down the Hen Hole when you get to the mountain hut).

Windy Gyle

The summit of Windy Gyle on the Scottish border tops 2,000 feet making it one of the highest in the Cheviot range and for that reason one of the best-known to hikers. For many Pennine Way walkers, crossing the peak is one of the most memorable moments on the entire long-distance path down the spine of England.

As its name suggests, the summit is a windswept place and one of the most remote corners in the Cheviots. All the major hills are in view from here: Shillhope Law, Hedgehope Hill, the Schil and The Cheviot. In the 15th and 16th centuries, wardens appointed by the King to control the lawless border country, used to meet in the Cocklawfoot/Windy Gyle area to settle disputes. These rendezvous sometimes ended in bloodshed, including one meeting in 1585 during which Lord Francis Russell, son-in-law of the English warden, John Forster, was murdered. Russell's Cairn, a Bronze Age burial cairn at the summit, is named in his memory.

The many routes on foot to the summit of Windy Gyle include that from the River Coquet (see page 191), along the Pennine Way, and from Cocklawfoot in Scotland.

Rothbury and around

From Hepple to Rothbury, luxuriant grasslands lie sheet-flat to the River Coquet which has carved a heavily ribboned course through the lowland meadows and created oxbow lakes under the gaze of the Simonside Hills. Beyond Rothbury – a prosperous town with a celebrated National Trust house nearby – the river curls around Brinkburn Priory before continuing on its journey to the sea at Warkworth.

⑰ Rothbury

Forested hills to the north and east shelter the capital of Coquetdale from the boisterous winds that punish the fell tops. To the south, beyond the River Coquet, green vales slope gently upwards until they come to an abrupt halt by the foot of the Simonside Hills. You can see why Rothbury makes an excellent base for walkers and you'll find a number of good walks direct from the town centre (see below).

Rothbury itself is popular with visitors and has a couple of galleries and cafés and one of the most celebrated of all National Trust houses on its doorstep (Cragside), but mostly it's a busy rural town going about its business. The **National Park Centre** on Church Street (see page 185) stocks maps, hiking socks and the usual tourist information bumph. Rangers are always coming and going, this being the HQ of Northumberland National Park.

The **town centre** holds much visual appeal: two rows of stone townhouses and traditional market town shops arranged either side of a green bank and a small triangular green with a cross (dedicated to Lord Armstrong of nearby Cragside). A good number of **shops** around here go back several generations. They include a hardware and ironmongery established in 1888, a deli selling local produce, Otterburn Mill (an offshoot of the well-known clothes and country store in Redesdale), a bakery, a quaint toy shop that has been in the same family for 100 years (toy tractors seem to be their speciality), a traditional leather shoe-shop and a superb butcher. Many rural towns must have once been like this.

All Saints Church is a few paces away from the cross on the green and is worth visiting for its Anglo-Saxon font alone. The present-day church was largely rebuilt by the Victorians but the chancel still contains 13th-century masonry. It's the 1,200-year-old rectangular font pedestal that warrants a closer look (the bowl is 17th century). Considering its age, the stone carvings are remarkably bold and clear. On one side what looks like a tiger is carved walking through a forest, and on another, the haunting faces of the apostles looking up to Christ.

Heading west along the upward sloping High Street, you'll come to two art galleries. **Coquetdale Arts Centre** (*01669 621557*) on Front Street displays painting, drawings and crafts made by local people. The **Congregational Art Gallery** (see below) is housed in an old church on the High Street. Inside, there's a bright, contemporary art space with an excellent café and paintings by some of the most highly regarded artists and photographers in the North East.

Food and drink

Rothbury has several very good local food shops clustered around the centre. Sandwiches to take away and food for holiday cottages, BBQs, etc are best sourced from **Tully's of Rothbury** (deli and pantry stocked with local produce), the **Rothbury Bakery** or **Rothbury Family Butchers**.

Congregational Art Gallery High St, NE65 7TL ☏ 01669 621900 ⓦ www.thecongregational.org.uk. Open Mar to Dec but closed Mon and Wed. Bright, contemporary café with a wood-burning stove and cosy settee in a converted church. Superb homemade soups and scones.

Goats on the Roof Fontburn NE61 4PL ☏ 01669 621896. Overlooking Fontburn Reservoir (7 miles south of Rothbury), is this unusual café in a timber hut on a rare-breeds farm. There literally are goats on the roof.

Harleys Tea Room 9 Bridge St, NE65 7SE ☏ 01669 620240 ⓦ www.harleystearoom.co.uk. Cosy tea room and gift shop not far from the river selling sandwiches and baked potatoes as well as more substantial lunches (burgers, fishcakes and the like).

Tomlinson's Café and Bunkhouse Bridge St, NE65 7SF ☏ 01669 621979 ⓦ www.tomlinsonsrothbury.co.uk. Pleasant café serving good light lunches in a youth hostel. You can hire bikes here.

Sundews

On open ground where there's a covering of moss and it's squelchy under foot, look out for the meat-eating round-leaved sundew – a tiny insectivorous plant about the size of a baby's hand with disk-like projections covered in pink hairs. In really wet bogs, you may see the great sundew (long, tapered leaves but otherwise similar to its more widespread relative). On the tip of each hair is a drop of what looks like dew which is sugary and irresistible to insects, but also sticky. Once stuck, the plant digests its prey over a couple of days.

Hill walks from Rothbury

Breamish Valley, Harwood Forest and Thrunton Woods (Forestry Commission) are a short drive from Rothbury, but there are also good places for walks right from the town centre. Two miles south along St Oswald's Way on a hillside overlooking the town are prehistoric rock carvings at **Lordenshaws** (see page 207). Good views of Rothbury and the Coquet from here. Keep on the same trail and you'll be into the Simonside Hills proper.

Another recommended **walk** (around five miles) climbs steeply above the **Rothbury Terraces** (north of the town). Even if you don't fancy the ascent onto the heather moors, it's worth walking the first quarter mile from the town centre, just to enjoy the expansive view of the river valley and Simonside Hills; a leaflet in the National Park Centre on Church Street describes the route in full. To start, head uphill away from the town centre and turn right up a lane by the Catholic church. It's a bit steep, but you gain good views after a few hundred yards. For the hill walk, you'll need Ordnance Survey Explorer map OL42. After another 500 yards or so, take a concealed path that runs alongside a house just after a cottage called Roding (stone steps and a handrail help you over the garden wall). Once past the quarry, there's a trail that takes you in a long loop under sandstone crags, across a heather plateau (sundews (see above) grow rampantly in localised areas up here) and through an old mixed woodland called Primrose Woods before re-entering Rothbury in the town centre.

Riverside walk to Thrum Mill

A short walk east from Rothbury along the River Coquet brings you to Thrum Mill. It's not so much the old flour mill (now converted into a house) that is of interest; more the dreamy river setting hidden from view by broadleaved trees. The Coquet is forced through a narrow stone gully and over rapids where anglers and herons fish by the water's edge, and the occasional kingfisher and dipper darts by; otters sometimes appear when it's quiet. In recent years, I saw a young osprey catching trout by the rapids. It was a very unusual sight, but in September when ospreys migrate, you never know where they might show up.

To reach Thrum Mill from Rothbury on foot, walk to the end of Bridge

Street and take the footpath that leads to the riverbank (don't cross the bridge). Turn left and follow the path with the Coquet on your right for just under a mile. Cyclists or drivers should approach along on the B6344 east out of town. There's a pull-in parking area by the river. Take care when walking along the road.

Old bridges across the River Coquet

Three striking multi-arched bridges span the Coquet from Rothbury to just beyond Brinkburn Priory. The oldest is in **Rothbury** town centre, parts of which are thought to be 15th century. East of Brinkburn, the mid 19th-century **Pauperhaugh Bridge** crosses the Coquet in five graceful arches. This is a good bridge from which to watch trout and salmon leaping over the rapids below in the autumn. Look out for goosanders and dippers from here to **Weldon Bridge** – the last crossing in the trio, which is best viewed from the riverside path. It dates to 1760 and has the added attraction of an inn (the Angler's Arms) with a dining area in an old train carriage. Rothbury's bridges and riverside are best appreciated on foot by following St Oswald's Way, along the south side of the river.

Scenic route: Rothbury to Alnwick

A high road over the hills to the coast connects two of the most popular market towns in Northumberland. From Rothbury, the B6341 climbs steeply past Cragside and through Debdon Woods before reaching open heather moors. There are several pull-in places along the road from where you can take in the view of the Cheviot Hills. Don't miss Edlingham church and castle (see page 209).

Scenic route: Rothbury to Breamish Valley

From Rothbury, follow the B6341 for a couple of miles to Thropton and then take an undulating road due north through the old-world villages of Whittingham and Glanton, to Powburn – the gateway to Ingram and the Breamish Valley. The roads round here climb quite high offering a tremendous view of the Cheviots rising above a timeless pastoral landscape: field upon field divided by hedgerows, old stone farm buildings, horses in paddocks, hares sprinting across pastures, foraging partridges and so on. This is a great bike ride. Early mornings are particularly memorable, especially in winter when the Cheviots are covered in snow and the lowlands look silvery green under a covering of frost.

⑱ Cragside

Rothbury NE65 7PX ① 01669 620333 ⓦ www.nationaltrust.org.uk/cragside. Open early Mar–Nov, 11.00–17.00 during school holidays (gardens open until later; check website for opening hours at other times of year). Café and adventure playground; National Trust.

The electric light has been introduced into the house by the distinguished owner, who has utilised the power of a neighbouring burn to work the generating machine . . . Words are inadequate to describe the wonderful transformation which Lord Armstrong has made on the barren hillside as it existed prior to 1863. Every natural advantage has been utilised by the great magician.

W W Tomlinson *Comprehensive Guide to Northumberland,* 1888

Tyneside industrialist and innovator, William Armstrong, was way ahead of his time when he set about filling his 19th-century country house on the outskirts of Rothbury with ingenious electrical gadgets. Cragside lays claim to being the first house in the world to be lit by electricity. Water was used to generate the electricity that lit Joseph Swan's novel filament lightbulbs. Armstrong had his own electrical room where he conducted experiments and developed his latest contraptions, including lifts for servants to transport coal through the house, electric gongs announcing dinner and an automatic pig spit.

Externally, Cragside is particularly eye-catching: part Gothic, part Tudor with many gables, tall chimney stacks, high-pitched roofs and timber additions. When viewed through a parting in the trees from the Debdon Burn, the house looks majestic crowded by so many lean conifers and thrust skywards like a Bavarian castle.

Armstrong (and his house) was famous in this lifetime and he hosted many dignitaries at Cragside, including the Prince of Wales and his family in August 1884 who came to inspect the intriguing new technologies. The **Drawing Room** was completed just in time for the royal visit. It's the grandest room in the house with a huge intricately carved marble fireplace, ornate plaster work and a number of important paintings including a Turner watercolour. The rest of the house is by no means stately, but it's fascinating for other reasons and rich in Arts and Crafts detailing, including William Morris stained glass and wallpapers, and extensive oak furnishings.

The grounds

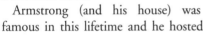

Some people visit Cragside just for the **gardens** and **woodland walks**. As its name suggests, the house is built into the craggy sandstone hillside and makes use of the rocks and varying heights to create romantic vistas. The wider landscape is very much part of Cragside's appeal and there are no walls shutting out the moors, burns and crags. The lakes are manmade and all the Scots pines, firs, redwoods, azaleas and rhododendrons were planted by Armstrong – well, technically by some 150 gardeners. They are said to have dug in seven million trees and bushes. Closer to the house are formal terraces, a fine glasshouse, picturesque bridges, an intricate bedding carpet and one of the largest **rock gardens** in Europe. Narrow paths below the house wind through heathers and alpine plants and past a couple of cascades.

Armstrong's Victorian enthusiasm for efficiency, order and punctuality is not just reflected inside the house. The Gothic **clock tower** near the formal gardens helped regulate the working hours of estate workers – all 300 of them at one time. It has two mechanisms: one to operate the clock and the other to chime a bell that sounded at meal times and at the start and end of every working day.

Within the wider grounds, there are 40 miles of way-marked **footpaths** as well as a scenic **carriage drive** that circumnavigates the whole estate via a couple of lakes.

Back at the Tumbleton Lake by the Visitor Centre, there's a good **café** with all the usual National Trust offerings: scones, sandwiches and a handful of hot dishes made with seasonal produce. Around the peaceful lagoon are sought after picnic tables.

⑲ Brinkburn Priory

Near Longframlington (5 miles east of Rothbury) NE65 8AR ① 01665 570628 Ⓦ www. english-heritage.org.uk. Open 1 Apr–30 Sep, Thu–Mon; English Heritage.

At the bottom of a wooded track, the doorway to the priory church appears through a parting in the trees making for an enchanting first glimpse of Brinkburn. The 12th-century building, once inhabited by Augustinian monks, is otherwise completely hidden from view in a loop of the River Coquet. Late in the afternoon, sunlight pours through the stained glass windows of the church bringing out the colour and patterns in the sandstone walls. You can hear the river, and thrushes singing outside, but on some weekend afternoons in summer, Brinkburn's string quartet or the local choir fills the priory. A summer music concert here is not to be missed.

Architecturally, Brinkburn is celebrated for its Transitional style which blends Norman and Early English and dates from the end of the 12th century to the beginning of the 13th. A good example is the aforementioned entrance seen on the approach, which shows chevron detailing typical of the Norman style, and above, an arcade of three Gothic arches of the Early English style.

Inside the church – the only intact building in the monastic complex – there are no screens or obstructions to distract from the elegant tiers of lancet windows and towering pointed arches. Outside are a few remains of ruined priory buildings, but mostly your attention will be drawn to the manor house which was built out of the ruined monastic buildings and reconstructed in the 19th century. You can go inside, but it's in a terrible state ('awaiting restoration', says English Heritage). Some decorative plasterwork remains intact and features such as the elegant floor-to-ceiling doors that open into the garden. Its very emptiness has a deeply evocative quality, however.

Northumberland's sandstone hills

Most visitors in Northumbria have heard of the Pennines and Cheviot Hills, but few people know of the sandstone hills sandwiched between the Cheviot foothills and the coastal plains that form a long arc from Berwick to Otterburn (roughly the area between the A697 and the A1).

The Simonside Hills near Rothbury are much-walked; the rest is largely unheard of. Places like Bewick Moor, Hepburn Crags, Doddington Moor, Kyloe Woods and the Bowden Doors crags are appreciated only really by rock climbers, locals and archaeology enthusiasts. Unlike the rounded humps of the Cheviots, these hills are craggy and boulder-strewn and don't form quite such a pleasing panorama, but they do offer some of the most expansive views in the whole of the county: of the Cheviots on one side and the coast on the other. In a few places, you can see both on a clear day. Here, I've described the Simonside Hills and touched on some of the unsung crags, villages and moors further north between Rothbury and Doddington.

⑳ The Simonside Hills

A ramble along this whale-backed sandstone massif between Harwood Forest (on the outskirts of Elsdon) and Rothbury is a favourite with hill walkers from Northumberland and Tyneside. The views are magnificent: miles of grasslands and forests stretching all the way to the North Sea, and the blue humps of

Prehistoric rock art

Northumberland is particularly renowned for its numerous 5,000-year-old **cup-and-ring grooves and marks** carved into stone slabs. They are usually hand-size with a series of concentric circles formed around a central depression, and many are astonishingly well defined. Their preservation depends on visitors refraining from walking on the stones and on farmers keeping the area clear of cattle. Good examples are found at **Weetwood Moor** (east of Wooler), **Chatton Park** and **Doddington Moor** and Lordenshaws's rocks on the hillside south of Rothbury.

The most visited cup-and-ring marked stones in Northumberland are scattered in grassland close to **Lordenshaws** car park, but are quite well hidden from view among tussocky grasses (children may enjoy a rock art hunt). These grooves and depressions look particularly impressive when the sun is low in the sky and the lines really stand out. The remains of a medieval deer park wall, and ridge and furrow ripples in the fields indicate where medieval farmers ploughed the land. Hang on until its dusk and you might see a barn owl quartering over the vole-rich grasslands. Rare brightly coloured waxcap toadstools and peculiar brown projections called earthtongues (a type of fungus) emerge in autumn.

Lordenshaws car park is four miles south of Rothbury and reached off an unclassified paved lane off the B6342.

the Cheviots in the distance. To the south, if the light is favourable, you can see Tyneside. I met a local walker up on Simonside who said you could once make out the red glow from Consett's furnaces in the days when the County Durham town manufactured steel.

What makes the Simonsides so distinctive, apart from the striking profile against the sky and famous prehistoric rock carvings at Lordenshaws, are its rocky outcrops. For the most part, however, the hills are covered in an expanse of heather with patches of bracken, cowberry, bilberry and the occasional peaty bowl and gully. Red grouse are easily startled in the heather and will take off with their characteristic 'go back, go back' call. In August, the Simonsides turn fuchsia when the heather flowers. Good views, apart from on the hills themselves, are had from Elsdon and Rothbury and northbound on the A696 (between Kirkwhelpington and Elsdon).

Walking in the Simonside Hills

You can traverse the Simonsides in a day – a hike made very manageable by the fact that once you reach the top of the escarpment, you stay at pretty much the same altitude the whole way (discounting the stiff climb to the summit of Simonside). A recommended seven-mile linear route starts from above the River Coquet at Hepple Whitefield Farm (by the unclassified road to Great Tosson) and crosses the highest points on the Simonsides (Tosson Hill and Simonside) before descending to Lordenshaws. The route is pretty lonesome for the first few miles, but gets busier with hikers around Simonside. If you don't want to walk the return route, Coquetdale Taxi (*01669 620820*) will meet you at Lordenshaws car park if booked in advance.

The most popular linear route is from the cup-and-ring marked stones near the Lordenshaws (see box, page 207) car park to the top of Simonside and back down again (four miles). Many people also walk up through woodland from Great Tosson – a stone hamlet with old farm buildings and a crumbling pele tower at the foot of the escarpment.

Superstitious walkers should take care around Caudhole Moss on the southern side of Simonside. Club-wielding dwarfs are said to lure travellers into the deep bogs.

Further east towards Elsdon, walkers will come to a couple of mountain tarns, including **Darden Lough** (page 161), on the edge of Harwood Forest.

Mountain bumblebees

Bombus monticola likes gorging on bilberry nectar in spring and heather in late summer which makes Northumberland National Park a good place to see this distinctive bee with its black body, yellow mane and bright orange-red tail. It has declined massively in recent decades, but it's not too difficult to find in upland areas like the Simonside Hills.

㉑ Edlingham

'Eadwulfingham' to give the hamlet its Anglo-Saxon name, lies equidistant between Rothbury and Alnwick (not to be confused with Eglingham further north). It's not so much the hill-top hamlet that is of interest; more its distinctive church and castle that are hidden somewhat from view at the end of a lane (reached from the B6341).

If the tower of **St John the Baptist Church** looks more like a defensive building, that's because it was built during the 14th century when invasions from the north were feared. Villagers and the priest may have sheltered from the Scots in here. It has no belfry openings (you might as well open the door to attackers) and the windows are really just slits. Overall, the tower makes the church look plain and very serious and provides a strong visual reminder of how dangerous the countryside around here once was. It shares similarities with Ancroft's parish church, six miles from Berwick-upon-Tweed, which also has a rather squat, defensive tower dating to roughly the same period. The earliest masonry visible is Norman, seen in the south porch doorway (and its barrel-vaulted ceiling), nave and chancel arch.

Edlingham Castle stands in a striking position on a hillside close to the church with ragged moors and the viaduct of the defunct Alnwick–Cornhill railway as its backdrop. All that remains of the mid 12th-century house, that once had a moat and barbican, are its foundations, a few walls and part of its defensive tower, built in 1340. A severe chasm has formed in one of the walls, giving the structure a dramatic profile.

㉒ Whittingham

Are you going to Whittingham Fair?
Parsley, sage, rosemary and thyme.
Remember me to one who lives there,
For once she was a true love of mine.

Those who have wandered north of Thropton (which is west of Rothbury) on the quiet back lanes may chance upon this peaceful village on the edge of the national park. There's a traditional **summer show** held on the third Saturday in August, which was immortalised in the above ballad – at least it was until Simon and Garfunkel sang the now more famous Scarborough Fair version.

The village itself is very attractive with a good number of well-kept stone houses either side of a green bank studded with trees. The fountain at the top of the slope bears travellers in mind: 'May this pure fount perpetual streams supply to every thirsty soul that passeth by and may its crystal waters ever run unchanged by winter's frost, or summer's sun.'

Whittingham Tower, near the centre, is an impressive 14th-century fortified house constructed with huge sandstone blocks that was remodelled somewhat in the 19th century. Now a family home it was once a refuge for villagers during the centuries of cross-border fighting before it became an almshouse ('for the use and benefit of the deserving poor', as the inscription above the doorway informs us).

Following the River Aln westwards to Little Ryle, you'll see **St Bartholomew's Church** by the side of the road. The interior is notable for its surviving Early English architecture, but the most remarkable feature of the church is its tower, the lower part of which is Saxon. If only the Victorians had left the top section alone.

㉓ Old Bewick

Most people whizz past Old Bewick on the A697 but for those taking a meandering route through the countryside or the high road to the coast, you might want to stop here. The hamlet itself is quaint enough with its old farm buildings and cottages, and there's a **hillfort** just behind the settlement, but it's the **Holy Trinity Church** tucked away up a lane half a mile north of Old Bewick that you should really see. Its hugely thick walls, slit windows and Romanesque chancel arch are clear giveaways as to its status as one of the oldest churches in Northumbria; it is Saxon in origin with enough of its structure surviving from the 11th century to describe it as Norman. One of the most interesting features is the carvings on the capitals of the chancel arch: the tree and two mean-looking heads at the top of each pillar may be a representation of the pre-Christian green man.

The ancient churchyard, enclosed by a burn and many firs and broadleaved trees, makes a wonderful sanctuary for animals and plants; snowdrops put on a dazzling display in February.

㉔ Eglingham

Eglingham's stone houses stand either side of a sloping through-road. There's not a huge amount to see from a visitor's perspective, but what it lacks in attractions it makes up for with its pub which is one of the best for miles around (see below).

St Maurice Church has been much restored over the centuries, but it does have a Norman chancel arch. Its font dates to 1667 and bears the words 'wash and be clen' [sic]. One of the bells in the tower is called Anthony. It is apparently inscribed in German with the following words: 'Anthony is my name. I was made in the year 1489.'

Food and drink

Tankerville Arms Eglingham NE66 2TX ① 01665 578444 ⑩ www.tankervillearms. com. Downstairs this is a smart stone inn with low beams, wooden furniture, a fire and local ales; upstairs the rooms (B&B) are modern and decorated to a good standard. The best thing about this cosy pub is the food, which is reasonably priced and extremely good (many locally sourced ingredients).

㉕ Chillingham Castle & Park

Chillingham (2 miles south of Chatton) NE66 5NJ ① 01668 215359 Ⓦ www. chillingham-castle.com; open 1 Apr–31 Oct, daily from 12.00, usually closed Sat; café.

Forgive any disorder by thinking and knowing that I rescued a roofless, floorless wreck of a castle, with a jungle having taken over the garden and grounds.
Sir Humphry Wakefield Bt 2002

Chillingham is one of the eeriest and most atmospheric castles you'll come across on your travels in Northumberland. It was besieged on numerous occasions during medieval times and many a captured Scot and Border Reiver were executed here. You certainly won't forget visiting the medieval fortress; a word of caution though, this is not Alnwick or Bamburgh Castle and you won't find polished cabinets displaying rare porcelain, dining rooms dripping in crystal and gold and immaculately laid out rooms. I find it enthralling because it is not all of those things.

Many kings were entertained here, including Edward I who stopped off on his way north in 1298 to capture William Wallace (better known to Hollywood film enthusiasts as Braveheart). It wasn't until 1348 that Chillingham became a fully fortified castle. It's formed of four square-angled towers enclosing a central courtyard. The walls are embattled and the whole edifice looks pretty intimidating. You'll get the idea as soon as you step into the courtyard with its stern, grey walls, dark windows and ominous staircase leading to the Great Hall.

Cruel things have happened to prisoners held in the dungeons at Chillingham. 'If you were a Scot back in the 14th century and you were caught and brought to Chillingham Castle, it was a death sentence', the curator, Bobby Fairbairn, told me. Bobby opened the door to the dungeon where you can see the lines prisoners carved on the walls representing the number of days they had been in captivity. The re-created torture room contains skeletons in cages and various authentic medieval torture devices including an iron maiden and executioner's block. It's chilling stuff, and children (and adults) might find it too harrowing for a family day out, but you can just bypass that area of course.

Perhaps not surprisingly, Chillingham Castle is much frequented by ghost-hunters: many apparitions and strange goings on have been reported by visitors and guests. 'I've experienced so many things that can't be explained – objects being thrown around the rooms and that', says Bobby.

Many of the rooms are furnished in a medieval or Tudor style with wall tapestries, banners, armoury and the heads of various beasts hanging from the walls. You are unlikely to have seen antlers as big as those in the Minstrels' Hall: they once belonged to an elk that lived half a million years ago. When I visited the state rooms, it was winter time when the property is usually closed to visitors; Bobby pointed to the yellow drapes over the windows which I can only describe as looking full. 'If I drew those curtains, hundreds of bats would fall out', he said. Time for a walk in the Italianate gardens.

Chillingham Park and cattle
Chillingham NE66 5NP ① 01668 215250 ⓦ www.chillinghamwildcattle.com. Open Easter–Oct, Sun–Fri; tours on the hour; no wheelchair access.

> At the first appearance of any person, they set off in a full gallop; and, at the distance of two or three hundred yards, make a wheel round, and come boldly up again, tossing their heads in a menacing manner: On a sudden they make a full stop, at the distance of forty or fifty yards, looking wildly at the object of their surprise . . .
> Ralph Bailey describing a Chillingham bull in Thomas Bewick's *History of Quadrupeds*, 1792

The history of this ancient 365-acre parkland goes back to the founding of the Chillingham estate in the 13th century. When the wooded parkland was enclosed, its population of wild white cattle also became cut off; they have remained isolated from the outside world ever since.

Chillingham cattle are thought to be the last surviving native wild herd in Britain and are descended from the wild ox that used to inhabit the forests that covered much of the British Isles in prehistoric times. They certainly have a wild look with their unruly-looking woolly coat and fierce horns.

The herd is currently around a hundred animals strong but the population fluctuates from year to year. Over the hard winter of 1946 numbers plummeted to just 13 individuals. To prevent their near extinction again, hay is provided during the winter; otherwise they are completely left to fend for themselves. 'They live and die by their own strengths as they have done for hundreds of years,' says Richard Marsh, the park warden.

The best way of seeing the cattle is to join an hour-long tour with Richard through the beautiful parkland which also encloses many ancient trees. You may see a bull fight, which is quite a spectacle. Because the animals are potentially dangerous, you can't visit the park without joining a tour. However, you can sometimes see the cattle from a permitted 6½-mile footpath (the Forest Walk) that runs around the perimeter of the parkland; take binoculars, and also look out for red squirrels.

㉖ Chatton and around
There's not a huge amount to see in Chatton, pleasant enough as it is, but the village does have a superb art gallery at the eastern end of the main road. The **Chatton Gallery** (*01668 215494; www.chatton-gallery.co.uk*) showcases

Seven castles

Close to Chillingham Castle and Park is a prominent earthwork where on a clear day you can see seven of Northumberland's castles: Warkworth, Alnwick, Dunstanburgh, Bamburgh, Lindisfarne, Ford and Chillingham. Known as Ros Castle, this vantage point (above the Hepburn Crags) also provides an unparalleled panoramic vista of the Cheviots – catch them at first light for a truly memorable sight.

Ros Castle is a double-ramparted earthwork about 3,000 years old and over 1,000 feet above sea level; you can reach it on foot from the Chillingham Park perimeter path (see facing page). If travelling by road, you'll need to zigzag a little bit on the lanes east of the A697 (between Powburn and Wooler). You want the steeply ascending road between Hepburn and North Charlton (incidentally, this is a highly scenic route to the coast which goes over heather moorland). Before you reach the moors, there's a parking area from where you can walk to Ros Castle. Nearby and closer to the parking area is a hillfort.

Ros Castle 1 mile east of Hepburn; OS grid reference NU080253.

the paintings of the celebrated landscape artist, Robert Turnbull, and other selected artists and sculptors. The surrounding craggy hills are dotted with prehistoric sites, including **Chatton Park Hill** with its cup-and-ring marked stones.

If you are heading to the coast, I recommend the scenic B6349 which bypasses Chatton but does take you across a memorable bridge and over Belford Moor. **Weetwood Bridge** spans the River Till and is one of the most elegant medieval bridges in Northumberland with a wide arch made of blushed sandstone. It stands a couple of miles east of Wooler on the B6348 (the best views are actually *en route* to Wooler). There are a few old metal lattice and stone bridges around here including the early 19th-century **Fowberry Bridge**, set in woodland by **Fowberry Tower** (once a 15th-century towerhouse but now chiefly a late 18th-century manor).

Halfway between Wooler and Belford, but still on the right side of the hills to gain a good view of the Cheviots, are the **Bowden Doors** rocks, known to climbers for their dramatic sandstone outcrops.

Food and drink

White Swan Warenford NE70 7HY ☏ 01668 213453. 'The beautiful county of Northumberland has great produce which we are proud to purchase from local suppliers and prepare in-house.' This old, unpretentious inn (no gastro pub styling in here) just off the A1 and 4 miles south of Belford is not well known outside of the local area, but it should be on the radar of foodies in north Northumberland.

I liked the fact the provenance of the meat and fish is stated on the menu. Traditional meat dishes served with imaginative sauces and sides (lamb with a date couscous, for example).

㉗ Routin Linn: prehistoric rock art and a waterfall

Grid reference NT982367, between Doddington and Ford and just under 2 miles east of Kimmerston on an unclassified road to Lowick.

Although few visit this gem of a waterfall, possibly because of its obscure location, it deserves seeking out should you find yourself taking a cross-country route to Berwick-upon-Tweed or the coast. Its nearby prehistoric rock carvings are also well worth seeing.

Routin Linn (sometimes called Roughting Linn) can be walked by following a wooded farm track off the Lowick to Kimmerston road. After about 100 yards, follow a footpath on the left down to the secluded **waterfall**, which drops 50 feet over jagged rocks into a pool.

Return to the farm track and continue on your way to **Goatscrag Hill** following a fence-line and passing a farm. Climb to the top of the craggy massif for a spectacular view of the Cheviots on one side and the coast on the other. A clear grassy track runs around the side of the hill whose south-facing rocky overhangs functioned in prehistoric times as a shelter and burial site. Take a closer look at the walls: what appear to be carvings of deer are etched into the sandstone.

More prehistoric rock carvings are found back at the crossroads (grid reference NT983367). About 25 yards north of the road and reached by a path through woods, is a huge stone slab in a clearing which is covered in **cup-and-ring** motifs of differing shapes. It is said to be the most decorated stone in Northumberland and the largest panel of prehistoric rock art in England.

The Rivers Tweed and Till

Scotland's second largest river, the Tweed, forms the border with England from Coldstream to Berwick-upon-Tweed. One of the best salmon and trout rivers in Britain, it is wooded for much of its length making it popular with anglers, canoeists and walkers. Along its banks are stone huts called shiels which were once extensively used by salmon fishermen; some have been converted in to holiday cottages. There are several places worth stopping for, especially in and around Norham with its castle, old bridges and nearby honey farm.

The River Till (a tributary of the Tweed) flows north–south along the eastern edge of Northumberland National Park and eventually merges with the River Breamish. You'll find a cluster of quaint villages and historic sites along its northern reaches, notably Ford and Etal villages, Heatherslaw Mill and places associated with the Battle of Flodden in 1513 (now all part of the Joicey family's huge estate).

㉘ Ford

A sweeter little village than Ford could hardly be imagined outside of Arcadia.
W W Tomlinson *Comprehensive Guide to Northumberland*, 1888

Ford stays in the memory: its immaculate main street with an old fountain at one end (now a planter but wouldn't it be fabulous if it spouted water again?) is a picture of rural peace and has remained unchanged for well over a hundred years. The Victorian-styled lanterns are not original, but let's not get too picky.

Few cars – and usually none at all – park on the street (apparently residents park at the back) so it really feels like you are stepping back in time. This could be the set of a BBC period drama; all it lacks is a carriage, and a bonnet for the lady behind the post office counter. The estate office told me: 'some visitors arrive at the village and it looks so perfect that they think it is private and they can't go in.' You can enter and parking is permitted on the main street, but do you dare pollute the view with your modern machinery?

Lady Waterford Hall (*01890 820503/07790 457580; open daily mid Mar– end Oct*) was a school until the 1950s. The building – and the rest of the village – was commissioned by Louisa Anne, Marchioness of Waterford, who became the sole owner of the Ford estate on her husband's death. She was an

Doddington Ice Cream

At some point on your travels around Northumberland, you've probably come across Doddington Ice Cream. It's produced in the village of the same name under Doddington Moor near Wooler (well known to archaeologists for its prehistoric rock art) and is stocked in many good cafés and farm shops in Northumberland. If you're passing through, there's a refrigerator stocked with pots of ice cream by the side of the road (look out for the huge model cow). Put your money in the honesty box.

Originally a traditional dairy farm, Doddington farm began producing cheese in the 1980s and branched out into ice cream production in 2000 at a time when many dairy farms were closing. The family is proud of its heritage and product. Jackie told me: 'The ice creams sell themselves because they are quality products. There is nothing artificial in them; if it tastes of strawberries, that's because it is made with real fruit and nothing that is not natural.'

Northumbrian-inspired ices include Heather Honey made with produce from Chain Bridge Honey Farm in the Tweed Valley, Alnwick Rum Truffle and the legendary Newcastle Brown Ale.

Doddington NE71 6AN (a few miles north of Wooler) ① 01668 283010
Ⓦ www.doddingtonicecream.co.uk.

accomplished painter and spent 22 years creating the striking pre-Raphaelite-esque frescoes inside the hall. The paintings depict biblical stories but the figures are all local people who sat for Lady Waterford.

At the top of the street (opposite end to the fountain) a ceramic relief of Queen Victoria bears down on the village from above the doorway of Jubilee Cottage. Turning left, you'll come to a curious cottage with a giant stone horseshoe over its doorway. It was once a blacksmith's but is now an **antiques shop** (*01890 820521*). Further down the same lane, is a quaint **secondhand bookshop** (*01890 820500/01361 850692*) squeezed into the two front rooms of the old estate Drawing Office.

St Michael's and All Angels Church stands by the side of Ford Castle facing the Cheviot Hills. The building goes back to medieval times but was restored in the mid 19th century. It has some curious features including the two faces either end of the arcades. The little man with a beard near the porch is medieval; his facing friend is Victorian. Outside, looking at the porch, you'll see more stone heads including two creepy faces to the right of the entranceway. At the back of the church (inside) are a few medieval memorial stones on the ground. One is said to show the Northumbrian bagpipes complete with a chanter and bellows but as much as I stared at the stone, I couldn't make it out (not helped by the table on top of it). Perhaps you'll have better luck. In the churchyard are a number of very old gravestones from the early 18th century and a tiny memorial stone dated 1641. In the sloping field is the ruin of a vicar's pele tower.

Opposite the church is the Old Dairy, an **architectural antiques emporium** with craft workshops (*01289 302658; open Wed–Sun 11.00–17.00*) selling an assortment of period furniture, fixtures, fireplaces, old garden tools, brassware and more; its **coffee shop** has an outside seating area (teas served on vintage china).

Ford Castle is a staggering 13th-century fortified mansion which is more impressive than Chillingham Castle in some ways, with its three-surviving corner towers and imposing gateway and curtain wall. Unfortunately it's not only closed to the public but mostly hidden by trees; the best views are from St Michael's churchyard. In the weeks before the Battle of Flodden in 1513 (see box on page 220), James IV of Scotland is said to have spent a few nights with Lady Heron in the fortress (her husband having been previously captured by the Scots). As the king took his leave, he set the place alight. Today the building is leased by the council and used as an outdoor education centre.

Ford Moss Nature Reserve

Near Ford village, reached from the B6353; grid reference NT970375; ⓦ www.nwt.org. uk. Northumberland Wildlife Trust.

Enclosed by a thick band of pine trees a mile east of Ford village is this rich lowland peat bog. Don't let those last two words put you off – it's a tranquil reserve inhabited by many birds and plants, and makes a very pleasant place for a walk. The central area lies in a hollow (once a lake formed after the last Ice Age) and is covered by heather, thick *Sphagnum* mosses, hare's tail cottongrass and patches of cranberry and bog myrtle. The insectivorous round-leaved sundew grows here (see box on page 203). The most prominent feature is a tall brick chimney that marks where a coal mine once operated. A path (part bridleway, part permissive footpath) runs around the perimeter of this basin. In autumn, the thorn trees lining the uphill track from the car park are full of migrant thrushes.

㉙ Etal

Your first glimpse of Etal's single street, which connects the manor at one end with the castle at the other, is quite a surprise: the row of whitewashed stone cottages and thatched inn (the only thatched pub in Northumberland) looks more like Suffolk than Northumberland. The village was laid out in the mid 18th century (though some of the houses have since been rebuilt) and it draws a similar reaction as Ford because of its old-world character. These two villages must be some of the most photographed places in north Northumberland.

Just south of Etal and visible from the B-road, is a **cricket ground** where matches are held on weekends in summer. There's even a women's team that plays on Saturdays.

English Heritage care for **Etal Castle** (*01890 820332; www.english-heritage. org.uk; open, 1 Apr–Nov daily and Dec–Mar, Sat–Sun*) which is not exactly the most intact fortress in Northumberland, but still retains its gatehouse and keep. Inside, there's an interesting exhibition explaining the history of the Battle of Flodden fought in 1513 at nearby Branxton.

The castle stands above the **River Till** and the disembarking point for the Heatherslaw Light Railway. A footpath runs north along the wooded riverbank, which is studded with old oak and willow trees and makes for a pleasant stroll. The old cornmill by the river is now the workshop of furniture makers, Taylor and Green of Etal.

Opposite Etal's main street on the other side of the B6354, **St Mary's Chapel** stands in the grounds of Etal Manor. The gated driveway gives the appearance that the parkland is private, but you are permitted to walk to the chapel. The building dates to the mid 19th century and was constructed in memory of Lord Frederick Fitz-Clarence, the one-time Lord of the manor (and illegitimate son of the Duke of Clarence, later William IV). He is interred below a prominent tomb carved with a sword and foliated cross (reached via a small door to the left of the organ).

Food and drink

For really good hot food and smart dining, the **Collingwood Arms** in Cornhill-on-Tweed is your best bet for miles around (see page 219).

Lavender Tearooms Etal TD12 4TN. Open daily but closed Fri Nov–Apr).
Sweet café in the post office, selling sandwiches, scones and baked potatoes,
coffees, etc.

Heatherslaw Mill

Near Cornhill-on-Tweed TD12 4TJ (between Ford and Etal) ℗ 01890 820488
Ⓦ www.ford-and-etal.co.uk. Open Easter–Nov; café.
Heatherslaw is the only working water-powered cornmill in Northumberland.
Information boards inside explain that a mill has stood here since the 13th
century, although the present structure is 19th century. You'll also find out
about the milling process and social history of the area and see the millstones
and water wheel in action. The shop sells biscuits, cakes and bags of rye,
wholemeal and spelt flour produced on site. The bakery opposite the cornmill
was cooking Swiss rolls when I visited and the smell of chocolate was wafting
along the riverside – it was enough to lure me off my bike anyway.

Heatherslaw Light Railway

Near Cornhill-on-Tweed TD12 4TJ (between Ford and Etal) ℗ 01890 820317 Ⓦ www.
heatherslawlightrailway.co.uk. Hourly service between 11.00 and 15.00, 1 Apr–31 Oct.
Small carriages clank along behind the 15-inch-gauge steam engine for the
four-mile journey from Heatherslaw Mill to Etal village. It's very much aimed
at families with children and costs just a few pounds. You can walk the return
journey from Etal by way of a path running parallel to the B-road at the top
of the village.

Duddo Stones

1 mile northwest of Duddo village (between Norham and Ford); grid reference
NT931437.
This Bronze Age stone circle dates from around 2,000BC and is prominently
situated on top of a flat hill in an arable field. The five stones, which stand
between five and ten feet tall, are pretty arresting (like giant hands and fists
thrust from the ground). They look most striking late in the afternoon when
the sun picks out the grooves and ancient cup marks in the stones. Human
remains were excavated from the central area in the late 19th century suggesting
the site had mythical or sacred value, as is common with stone circles elsewhere.
    Duddo Farm permits access to the stone circle which is signposted from the
village and takes about half an hour to reach.

㉚ Branxton

This unassuming hillside village is mostly of interest for its proximity to the
Flodden battlefield (see box on page 220), but it does have a wonderful little
church and one of the quirkiest visitor attractions in the region: the Cement
Menagerie (see opposite). On the side of the village green is a red telephone
box that Branxton proudly claims is the smallest tourist information 'centre'

in the world. Inside you'll find leaflets and details of places of interest nearby, as well as this notice: 'The Scottish Government recently gave £5 million to refurbish the Bannockburn Visitor Centre at Stirling. Not having access to similar funds, this phone box was bought for £1 by Branxton Parish Council'. A short walk or drive west out of Branxton on your way to the Flodden Field battle site is the parish **church of St Paul**, situated on a breezy hill with views of undulating hills (if travelling from the village, go left when you reach a fork in the road). The oldest part is the chancel arch which dates from the 12th century. Wounded soldiers were brought here following the 1513 battle fought on the nearby hillside, and it's said that the body of James IV of Scotland, wrapped in the Royal Standard, lay here before being taken to London. Inside St Paul's a booklet on sale tells you all about the Battle of Flodden and the surrounding area.

If you continue away from the church for a third of a mile up the road, there's a parking area from where a footpath leads steeply up Branxton Hill (site of the Battle of Flodden) to a memorial cross, overlooking the village and dedicated 'to the brave of both nations'.

The Cement Menagerie

Branxton village, opposite the telephone box and next to the fountain. Free entry but please leave a donation to ensure its survival for the future pleasure of others.

This is one of the most curious of museums – if you can call it that – in Northumberland and deserves to be better known. Between the shrubs, trees and water features in the back garden of an ordinary house in Branxton village are colourful life-sized animals made of cement. There's a giraffe, panda, deer and hippo; a man on a horse and another on a camel; and many small animals and birds hiding in bushes. It was built over several decades in the 20th century by a retired joiner for the enjoyment of his disabled son.

Since the death of its creator in 1981, the wonderful garden and its menagerie has been passed down through the family who, thankfully, have kept it open to the public.

Food and drink

Collingwood Arms Main St, Cornhill-on-Tweed TD12 4UH ℡ 01890 882424 ⓦ www.collingwoodarms.com. This old coaching inn above the River Tweed is one of the best small hotels and restaurants in north Northumberland (also see accommodation page 182). The dining room is chic (muted colours, wooden floors, contemporary tableware) but not pretentious. Service is excellent (friendly, attentive) and the food a hit with those who appreciate traditional British dishes with a northern twist, such as Border lamb with black pudding and parsnips for example. Local ingredients include red meat from Norham, fish from Eyemouth, bakery items from Heatherslaw Mill and vegetables from the kitchen garden; all puddings are made in-house. Light lunches are served in the brasserie.

㉛ Twizel Bridge and Castle

Close to where the River Till breaks away from the Tweed (halfway between Cornhill-on-Tweed and Norham on the A698) is one of Northumberland's most striking medieval bridges.

Twizel has five arched ribs on its underside supporting a single-span that curves in an arch above the lazy River Till which meanders through woodland below. The trees rise on a steep bank and you can just make out Twizel Castle peeping above the treetops. In the days leading up to the Battle of Flodden in 1513, both the English and Scottish armies would have crossed this newly constructed bridge on their way to battle.

From the parking area, go through a gate and either take the track to the riverside (very pleasant place for a wander) or go steeply uphill to the medieval ruin of Twizel Castle. The crumbling fortress stands high above the river and bridge, draped in ivy. It's made of the pinky grey sandstone you find quite a lot round here. Some of the stones from the castle were used in the 1882 rebuilding of nearby Tillmouth Park country house (now an expensive hotel that has lost some of its shine but none of its grandeur).

Battle of Flodden

The last medieval battle in England – and the most significant in Northumberland – was fought on a hillside just outside of Branxton village, four miles southeast of Coldstream on the Scottish border.

The 1513 clash between the Scots and the English was sparked by Henry VIII's attack on France which put James IV of Scotland in the difficult position of renewing the 'auld alliance' between France and Scotland at the request of the Queen of France. And so a huge Scottish army left Edinburgh for northern England in mid-August, lead by the king. They crossed the River Till over Twizel Bridge and took Norham after a siege lasting six days.

By the end of August, the Earl of Surrey, whom Henry VIII had left in charge of defending England, arrived in Newcastle and proceeded north with an army of equal size to the Scottish force – around 30,000 men.

The two sides came together on 9 September 1513, at Branxton Hill: standards flying, knights in armour and men with arrows, swords and long spears (pikes) at the ready. The Scots had the most advantageous position at the top of the hill bearing down on the English along Pallin's Burn, but they missed a prime opportunity to advance. In the end, the English archers were devastating in their precision and the Scots with their cumbersome pikes were slaughtered in their many thousands – perhaps 9,000 men. The battle lasted just a couple of hours, resulting in victory for the English army. By dusk, the King of Scotland, many noblemen and thousands of men on both sides lay strewn across the hillside.

㉜ Norham

The ancient small border town of Norham is best known for its castle that rises above the River Tweed on a rocky eminence looking every bit as ragged and romantic as when William Turner painted the scene in the late 18th century. This fortress once kept a watchful eye of Scotland on the other side of the Tweed, and Norham town, nestled in a loop of the river half a mile to the west.

The history of Norham starts with the founding of a monastic centre in the 7th century. A church has stood here since at least AD830 though the present St Cuthbert's is of Norman origin. The town grew around the castle from the 12th century but pretty much everything you see today, except for the medieval layout, market cross and parts of the church, dates from the 19th century.

Broad streets lead to a large **green** surrounded by stone houses where farmers and fishermen used to live. Round the corner on West Street a gun makers service the thriving country sport industry in these parts. Many of the houses are built of the same reddish sandstone used in the construction of the castle and other buildings in and around the Tweed valley. The stone **market cross** is quite an eye-catcher, the lower part of which dates to the medieval period (Norham was granted a licence for markets in 1293).

Even to the lay eye, **St Cuthbert's Church** has a strikingly long nave and chancel. The building has been much restored over the centuries since its construction in Norman times but there is stonework from the 12th century that survives, notably the chancel arches. Pevsner in his *Buildings of England* series describes the south arcade as 'truly majestic'.

On the outskirts of the town (on the A698) is Norham's **old train station** (*TD15 2LW; 01289 382217; open to tours and on bank holidays*) that has been lovingly restored and still retains its platforms, booking office and signal box.

On the other side of the Tweed, reached by crossing Norham's stone arched bridge and turning right at the cross roads, is **Ladykirk Church** – a fine example of Scottish Gothic architecture in the village of the same name. It was built (on quite some scale) in the late 15th century on the order of James IV of Scotland after he saw a vision of the Virgin Mary on falling from his horse in the nearby river.

Norham Castle

Norham TD15 2JY ℡ 0870 333 1181 Ⓦ www.english-heritage.org.uk. Open daily 1 Apr–30 Sep; English Heritage.

In medieval times, the Bishops of Durham ruled Norham and the castle, which started life in 1121 as a timber building, was their northern stronghold. It was rebuilt in stone towards the end of the same century with a keep and curtain wall and thereafter underwent many changes and additions. Much of what remains today dates from the 16th century, though fragments of the early stone walls and arches survive. Situated as it is on the border with Scotland, it was besieged many times (13 to be more precise) from its construction until it succumbed to James IV of Scotland in the days before the Battle of Flodden in 1513. Since then it has been left to the elements and is now a ruin. Nevertheless, it's still an impressive fortresses with a brute of a keep, moat (now dry), vaults and crumbling walls.

Food and drink

Norham has a couple of pubs, including the **Victoria Hotel** (Sunday lunches only) and a 200-year-old butcher's shop, **Foreman & Son**, which sells rare-breed meats and pies. Both face the green. The nearest café is probably at the Honey Farm (see below).

㉝ Chain Bridge Honey Farm

Horncliffe, Berwick-upon-Tweed TD15 2XT Ⓣ 01289 386362 Ⓦ www.chainbridgehoney.co.uk. Open Apr–Oct daily and Nov–Mar, Mon–Fri; free entry; café, (closed in winter) .

Chain Bridge Honey is as ubiquitous in Northumberland as Craster kippers, Doddington Ice Cream, and the Northumberland Cheese Company, and no doubt you will have already come across their pots of liquid gold in farm shops, B&Bs and delis across the North East. Fenwick's of Newcastle sells it and I've seen it on the shelves in London's Fortnum & Masons.

You can buy (and try) all their different honeys and various beauty products from the friendly visitor centre at the farm. The Flower Comb Honey has a particularly strong taste and scent (I've never found a flower honey as good as this anywhere in England). In the shop you'll see a working hive with an observation glass panel where you can watch the honey bees doing their thing. An exhibition room next door tells you everything you want to know about bees and bee-keeping. The vintage double-decker bus outside serves as a café.

The flavours of honey vary depending on where the hives are situated: on heather moors or in flower meadows. If you've come across bee hives on hillsides during your travels in north Northumberland, chances are they are involved in producing Chain Bridge honey.

The famous Union Chain Bridge spanning the Tweed is a short walk from the honey farm (hidden by trees).

Union Chain Bridge

Connecting the Honey Farm with Paxton House, this magnificent 449-foot long iron suspension bridge spans the Tweed. When it opened in 1820, hundreds turned up to watch its designer, Captain Samuel Brown, cross the bridge with horses pulling carts laden with an estimated 20 tons. Among those in the audience was the great Scottish engineer, Robert Stevenson (of lighthouses fame). A young Isambard Kingdom Brunel accompanied by one of France's esteemed engineers, Charles Navier, visited a few years later. Clearly, this was a bridge causing quite a stir among the engineering giants of Europe

– and rightly so: at the time it was the largest iron suspension bridge in the world. Captain Brown knew a thing or two about structures made with decking that are designed to move, from his time in the Royal Navy. His flexible chain links are said to have been based on a ship's rigging blocks.

To find out more about the bridge, see the exhibit at the Chain Bridge Honey Farm.

㉞ Paxton House

Near Berwick-upon-Tweed TD15 1SZ ☏ 01289 386291 ⓦ www.paxtonhouse.co.uk. Open 1 Apr–31 Oct daily; café.

On the Scottish side of the River Tweed (and reached quite marvellously from England by crossing the suspension bridge at Horncliffe) is this celebrated country house built in the Palladian style by James Adam in 1758. In 80 acres of landscaped parkland, it looks down through trees to the river below. Much of the interior and its furnishings date to when the house was constructed, including the Chippendale furniture, French wallpapers and Rococo plasterwork. Many of the paintings and antiques were amassed during the first owner's Grand Tour of Europe; the Picture Gallery contains works on loan from the National Galleries of Scotland. Particularly memorable is the **Georgian kitchen**, impressively restored and operational on certain days.

The **gardens** encompass a playground for children and croquet lawn (mallets for hire inside). Housed in the old boathouse, which still has its underground fish store, is a tiny **museum** dedicated to the fishing heritage on the Tweed.

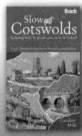

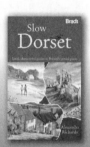

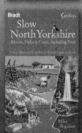

6. DURHAM CITY, COAST AND AROUND

'Where are you from?'
'Everington. County Durham.'
'Durham? Isn't there an amazing cathedral?'
'Dunno, I've never been.'
From the film *Billy Elliot*

The dialogue between the son of a Durham miner and a middle-class boy from the south of England in the film, *Billy Elliot*, may make you cringe, but it hints at a division in County Durham that remains partly true: the prosperous cathedral city with its acclaimed university, and outlying colliery villages like the fictitious Everington in *Billy Elliot* (set in Easington). In reality, the region is more mixed, and not every settlement beyond the city has its roots in heavy industry. Despite this, if you ask an outsider what they associate with Durham, they may well reply: 'coal and a cathedral'. Those who have explored Durham, may add to that: a dramatic coastline, flower meadows and heather moors, castles, wooded gorges, old waggonways, railway heritage, Roman forts and Beamish Museum – one of the most popular attractions in the North.

The boom in coal mining and expansion of colliery villages during the 19th and early 20th centuries had a long-lasting impact on the landscape and local people. Mining reached its peak in 1921 when there were 160,000 miners in the region (up from 15,000 a hundred years earlier). After the last Durham coal pit closed in 1994, unemployment rocketed and some places fell into decline; others were redeveloped and reinvented. The winding wheels and chimneys that once loomed over the uniform terraces are gone though many settlements retain elements of their colliery-town character (plain brick terraces with back lanes, working men's clubs and colliery brass bands) and strong mining identity, as witnessed at the annual Durham Miners' Gala (see page 233).

A number of **ex-colliery villages** are found at the coast – an area blighted for many decades by the routine dumping of pit waste on the beaches and in the sea. Today, the landscape is very different following an intensive clean-up operation launched at the turn of this century. Since the removal of 1.3 million tons of debris, Durham's **coastline** has been transformed into one of the greatest natural attractions the county has to offer visitors and matches many stretches of the North Yorkshire and Northumberland coasts in its rugged beauty.

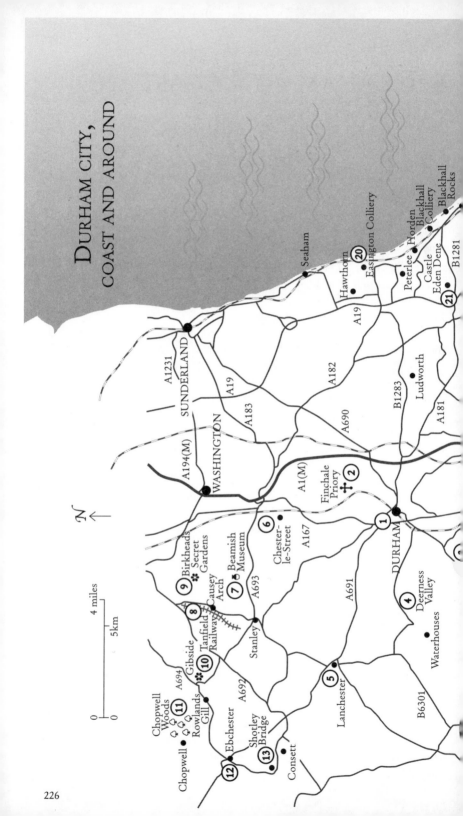

DURHAM CITY,
COAST AND AROUND

N

226

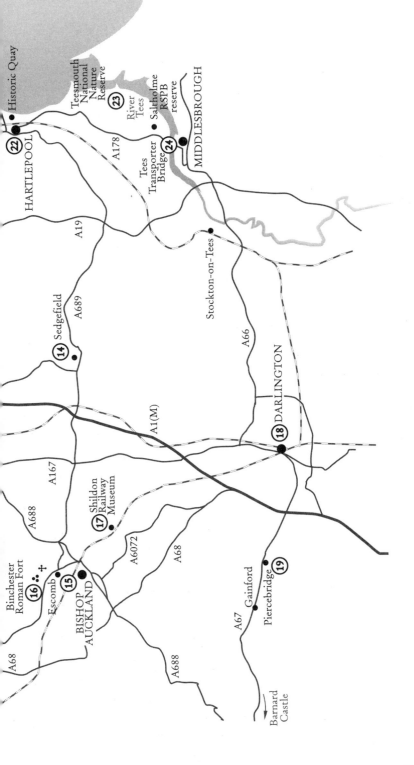

But what of the jewel in Durham's crown? Much of this chapter is devoted to the most celebrated **Romanesque cathedral** in Europe, and guiding visitors through the cobbled streets of Durham city. The River Wear ribbons around the wooded outcrop on which the cathedral stands adding to the appeal of the city – and offering a good few miles of pleasant riverside walks.

The Durham Dales are covered in *Chapter 7*.

Getting around

Bus

Durham's many **countryside** and **coastal villages** are well-connected by bus. Services are not always frequent, especially in remote parts, but there are few settlements you can't reach on the network. See the Durham County Council website for a bus map (*www.durham.gov.uk*).

Train

The East Coast Main Line from London to Edinburgh makes frequent stops at **Darlington** and **Durham**, while slower trains stop at **Chester-le-Street**. The **Durham coast** is serviced by train between Sunderland and Stockton, with stations at Seaham and Hartlepool.

Cycling and walking

Rail trails

When the coal mines closed, so did many of the railway lines that snake through the region connecting pit to port. Miles of wide trackbeds run alongside riverbanks and farmland, through woods and over stone bridges. They are thoroughly used by cyclists, walkers, horseriders and wheelchair users. It's an exceptionally extensive network; for instance, my uncle often walks from his house in Washington to Beamish (a distance of some eight miles through a very urbanised landscape) and only crosses two roads, mostly by accessing the old railway lines.

The trails conveniently link up at a number of places, principally at Broompark (west of Durham) and Lydgetts Junction (south of Consett). You could walk, for example, from Bishop Auckland to Gateshead (almost the length of the county) pretty much on railway paths the whole way (Brandon–Bishop Auckland Way, the Lanchester Valley Way and Derwent Walk).

At the coast, **National Cycle Network routes 1** and **14** traverse the length of Durham on what is sometimes referred to as the **Mineral Railway Line**, which linked collieries between Sunderland and Hartlepool. A branch line runs from South Hetton to Seaham. The main line does not hug the coastline (that railway is still in use), but takes cyclists a few miles inland.

Durham Coast Path

The 11-mile clifftop footpath from Crimdon to Seaham (see page 258) is an exhilarating trail and highly recommended. There's no corresponding path for bikes, but sections can be cycled a little way inland using tracks and lanes, for example between Hartlepool and Easington Colliery. See www.durhamheritagecoast.org.

Accommodation

Finding a low-cost guesthouse or luxury hotel in Durham is not difficult; excellent mid-range B&Bs are not as plentiful. Below I've picked out some of the best.

Gadds Townhouse 34 Old Elvet, Durham DH1 3HN ☎0191 384 1037 Ⓦ www.gaddstownhouse.com Ⓔ info@gaddstownhouse.com. One of the more expensive places to stay in Durham. Recently refurbished (formally known as the Fallen Angel) and offering boutique-style B&B accommodation in opulent rooms, most of which are themed. The Edwardian Express evokes the era of luxury train travel, while the Ruby room could almost be in a Tudor mansion. The upmarket restaurant specialises in steaks and fish dishes.

Hedley Hall B&B Hedley Lane, near Sunniside NE16 5EH ☎01207 231835 Ⓦ www.hedleyhall.com Ⓔ hedleyhall@aol.com. Very pleasant stone-built guesthouse conveniently situated a few miles from Beamish Museum in a farmland setting. Clean and comfortable average-priced rooms; self-catering bungalows (wheelchair accessible). Dinners on request (bring your own bottle).

Moor End Guesthouse 7–8 Moor End Terrace, Durham DH1 1BJ ☎0191 384 2796 Ⓦ www.moorendguesthouse.com Ⓔ stay@moorendguesthouse.com. A couple of miles east of Durham city is this homely B&B decorated in a modern cottage style with stripped pine furniture and floors. Prices are a little above average, but so is the standard of accommodation.

South Causey Inn Beamish Burn Rd, Stanley DH9 0LS ☎01207 235555 Ⓦ www.southcausey.co.uk Ⓔ southcausey@hotmail.com. Plush, rather pricey rooms with modern bathrooms and some antique furnishings, set in over 100 acres of farmland with a lake, equestrian centre and outdoor activities area (archery, horseriding, etc). Tanfield Railway and Beamish Museum are close by. Rooms outside of the main inn are quieter. Cosy restaurant serving good pub food.

University colleges Durham ☎0800 289970 Ⓦ www.dur.ac.uk Ⓔ event@durham.ac.uk. During Easter, summer and Christmas, low-cost B&B accommodation is offered in many university colleges, and year-round in some including the historic College of St Hild and St Bede ('Hild Bede'). As you would expect, the rooms are basic (and not always en suite), but the surroundings are full of character and may include access to secluded gardens normally closed to the public. In some colleges, breakfast is served on long dining tables in grand halls (think *Harry Potter*). To stay centrally, try Hatfield College or, most dramatic of all, University College at the castle where some rooms offer direct views of the cathedral.

Victorian Townhouse 2 Victoria Terrace, Durham DH1 4RW ①0191 370 9963 Ⓦ www.durhambedandbreakfast.com Ⓔ stay@durhambedandbreakfast.com. Contemporary furnishings, wallpapers and lighting in spacious rooms with some period furniture and original features such as fire surrounds, ceiling roses, etc. The Victorian terraced house offers glimpses of the cathedral.

West Wood Yurts Cut Thorn Farm, Burnopfield NE16 6AA ①07823334910 Ⓦ www.westwoodyurts.co.uk Ⓔ yurts@westwoodyurts.co.uk. Within the grounds of the National Trust's Gibside estate (close to Gateshead and Newcastle) is one of very few 'glampsites' in the North East. The six Mongolian yurts are traditionally styled but have Ikea furnishings and modern wood-burning stoves. The farm also welcomes caravans and those with tents. Elsewhere on the estate is a small, unusual-looking **Banqueting House** that dates to the mid 18th century and is now a holiday cottage with two rooms (*01628 825925; www.landmarktrust.org.uk*).

① Durham city

As the London to Edinburgh train approaches Durham station, all heads in the carriage turn to the right to take in the view of Durham's cathedral standing halfway to heaven on a rocky eminence above the River Wear. In the late afternoon sun the Norman masterpiece lights up, golden and magnificent.

Durham grew around the cathedral after its completion in the 1130s, but expansion was limited in a place perched on a natural cul-de-sac and bound by the River Wear on three sides. For that reason, Durham is not somewhere one chances upon or passes through; it must be sought out. Millions of pilgrims over the centuries have done just that, ever since the body of St Cuthbert came to rest here in AD995.

The city was, however, able to expand northwards and on the other side of the river. Near the railway viaduct, you'll find uniform blocks of Victorian brick terraces which contrast with the medieval streets and Georgian houses radiating away from the cathedral.

Orientation

Durham city is not easily reached by car; the streets are cramped and a congestion charge operates on the peninsula to deter motorists (*0191 384 6633; Mon–Sat 10.00–16.00, excluding bank holidays*). Most people wouldn't want to anyway as the approach on foot is so enjoyable. It's a straightforward walk from the train station following the pedestrian signposts. Alternatively, the Durham **Cathedral Bus** runs a couple of times an hour every day except Sunday, public holidays and during the Durham Miners' Gala. It connects the cathedral and city centre with the train

The origins of Durham

The history of Durham cannot be told without reference to the secluded isle of Lindisfarne off the north Northumberland coast and the most famous bishop of Lindisfarne, Cuthbert. When St Cuthbert died in AD687 he was initially buried on the island, but 11 years later his body (reportedly undecayed) was moved to the mainland when the monastic community were driven out by Viking invaders. For seven years the monks wandered around northern England with Cuthbert's coffin (and the Lindisfarne Gospels) until they came to Chester-le-Street at the end of the 9th century. Here they stayed for over a hundred years until Cuthbert was moved one last time.

The story goes that on nearing the wooded peninsula, today known as Durham, the cart carrying Cuthbert's coffin, stopped and could not be budged. This was interpreted as a sign from the saint, and so a shrine was built on the rocky mound above the River Wear, referred to by a passing milk maid searching for her lost cow as 'Dun Holm'. The name explains the name Dun Cow Lane off Palace Green and the stone relief of two maids and a cow on the northwest tower of the cathedral.

station and coach park (tickets are very cheap and valid all day).

The historic core of the city is the area around Palace Green where you'll find the cathedral and castle. The centre is small and you can easily wander through the streets and see most of the renowned buildings within an hour or two, but you should allow longer to visit the museums and explore the riverside and outlying areas.

Durham city centre on foot

A well-trodden route to Palace Green is across the medieval Framwelgate Bridge (from where you gain a tremendous view of the castle walls and cathedral towers) and up Silver Street and Saddler Street. Below I've described a more roundabout route along the tranquil riverside (the map shows where it goes).

Framwelgate Bridge and Prebends Bridge

On crossing **Framwelgate Bridge** into the centre of Durham, descend the steps to the banks of the Wear. The riverside is thick with trees on both sides making for a very pleasant stroll on the paved path to where the waterway

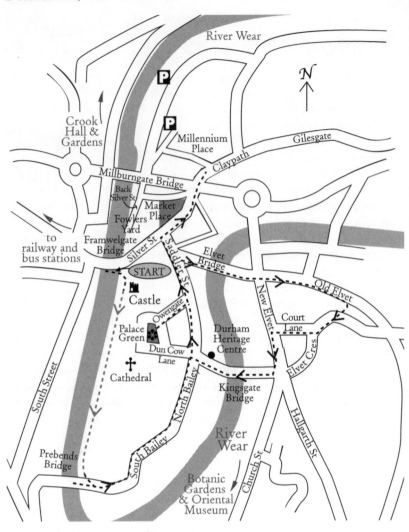

forms a tight bend (under half a mile away). On reaching the three-arched late 18th-century **Prebends Bridge**, turn up the bank, cross the bridge halfway, and drink in the most famous view of the cathedral thrusting skywards through the trees. Turner famously painted this romantic scene bathed in yellow light in 1835, though he tilted the cathedral to include more of the towers. Another wonderful view is from **South Street** on the west side of the river (the cobbled lane connects with Prebends and Framwelgate bridges). The cathedral glints through the trees in the evening light.

South Bailey and North Bailey

Durham's historic centre is reached by following a path from Prebends Bridge under a stone archway which opens onto **South Bailey**. The sinuous road of

Durham Miners' Gala

On the second Saturday in July, the streets of Durham are filled with the sound of brass instruments, drums and rousing speeches during the annual miners' parade, which remembers the country's coal mining heritage. The Gala (pronounced 'Gayla') is also an opportunity for trade unions and Labour Party representatives to raise pressing political issues. At times there's a carnival-like atmosphere with folk dancers and musicians in costume (one band dressed as nuns in 2011) but most of the parade is formed of brass bands marching with their colourful banners. A special service is held in the cathedral.

cobbles lined with Georgian houses and lit by old lamps brings to mind streets in Oxford and Cambridge. Many of the buildings here belong to St John's and St Chad's colleges, including the **church of St Mary the Less**. Inside is a memorial to a famous local **Polish dwarf** who was honoured in death by being buried in 1837 near the entrance to the cathedral. The gravestone of the three-foot tall man is suitably diminutive, marked only with his initials 'JB'. A statue stands in the Town Hall (Market Place) with some of his belongings including a suit, cane and violin.

South Bailey becomes **North Bailey** where glimpses of the cathedral come into view from behind the street wall. The rose window on the east face of the cathedral soon appears right in front of you. On the other side of the road is a church housing the **Durham Heritage Centre and Museum** (*0191 384 5589; www.durhamheritagecentre.org.uk*) which gives background information on the development of Durham City, local industries and daily life under the control of the ruling bishops. The cobbled street on the left (Dun Cow Lane) recalls how the city became known as Durham (see box on page 231).

Avoid the temptation to walk directly to the cathedral via Dun Cow Lane; instead, enjoy the more spectacular approach from the north end of Palace Green by continuing ahead and turning left up **Owengate**. The winding lane passes a 19th-century almshouse, now the World Heritage Site Visitor Centre (*0191 334 3805*), which is your best bet for **tourist information** now that the tourist information centre at Millennium Place is a telephone-only service (*03000 262626*). Owengate opens onto the wide green where the length of the magnificent **cathedral** is seen in its entirety. Turn around and you'll see the **castle**.

Palace Green

Palace Green is enticing with its intriguing mix of old buildings. Standing close to the red telephone box on the corner of Owengate is **Moneyer's Garth**. Where now stands a 19th-century university building, until 1536 this was the site of the bishops' mint. Next door is the grand 21 bay-window façade of **Cosin's Hall** (now the university's Institute of Advanced Study), which is clearly Georgian. Note the decorative doorway with its ornamental columns and leaf-carved frieze. Contrasting with the splendour of Cosin's Hall is a modest row of **almshouses** built in 1666 (a **café** inside sells sandwiches, cakes and soups). Tucked away out of sight at the end of the row is a plain Georgian building (**Abbey House**), once also known as 'The Dovecote' by male students when in 1899 it became a hostel for the first female undergraduates. It is now the Department of Theology and Religion. On the side of Dun Cow Lane, you'll see an exposed section of a medieval wall which was integrated into the current building.

On the **west side** of Palace Green is the Tudor-styled **Pemberton Building**, which looks much older than its early 1930s construction. It is home to one of the earliest university debating societies in the world, founded in 1842. The medieval-looking **Palace Green Library** buildings adjoining it are as old as they appear, dating to the mid 15th century onwards. Also here, inside the **Treasures of Durham University** exhibition (*0191 334 2972; www.dur. ac.uk*), is a small number of objects from the university's extensive collection of antiques. The centrepiece is a rare 1623 first edition book of Shakespeare's works which was famously stolen in 1998. The gripping story of the theft – and the book's recovery – is told in the museum. At the end of the row is the **Exchequer Building**, which was built under the rule of the Prince Bishops for administrative purposes.

Saddler Street and the Market Place

Leaving Palace Green, head back down Owengate and turn left onto **Saddler Street** – once famed for the production of … mustard. In 1720, a local woman called Mrs Clements developed the process of grinding mustard seeds in a mill to produce a distinctly hot powder. Her mustard became legendary and was said to be enjoyed by King George I. Durham Mustard was later produced by a number of local firms until the last was absorbed into Colman's of Norwich.

The Shakespeare tavern claims to be the most haunted pub in England. To the side of the pub is a secluded alley that winds under the castle walls and eventually opens near Framwelgate Bridge. For now, press on to the **Market Place** – a wide square with mostly Victorian frontages and dominated by the spire of **St Nicholas' Church** (mid 19th century), the **Town Hall** and the statue of the **3rd Marquess of Londonderry**. The restored Victorian **Durham Indoor Markets** (*www.durhammarkets.co.uk; open Mon–Sat*) shelters rows of stalls including a secondhand bookshop, delicatessen, old sweet shop and a pipe and tobacco stall. Near a block of six red phone boxes in the square is a

Boating on the river

On sunny days there can be few activities more pleasurable in Durham city than messing about in a wooden rowing boat. Whichever direction you travel from the boat hire station at Elvet Bridge, you'll pass under three of Durham's bridges and enjoy views of the River Wear tugging gently on overhanging branches as it meanders lazily around the city.

Browns Rowing Boats Elvet Bridge ⓣ0191 386 3779 ⓦ www.princebishoprc. co.uk. Easter–Oct charged per hour; sightseeing motorboat cruises also available.

statue of **Neptune** who stands baring his muscles, buttocks and tumbling locks above a doomed sea creature. The figure is ten miles from the sea but he keeps alive the memory of an unrealised plan in the 1720s to connect Durham city with the coast by canal and river.

The steps between the church and the flyover lead to **Fowlers Yard** art and craft workshops (*www.fowlersyarddurham.co.uk*) in Back Silver Street, where you'll find an embroiderer, jeweller, painter and textile artist among other craft workers, as well as a microbrewery and coffee house.

Claypath and Gilesgate

Beyond the church and flyover is **Claypath**, a long, busy road that, though not hugely attractive at first, is flanked by pretty, pastel-coloured houses where it becomes **Gilesgate** (particularly by the green). For now, turn left into the **Millennium Place** (in front of the Gala Theatre) to see a moving bronze **sculpture** of six life-sized monks carrying St Cuthbert's coffin.

A detour to Old Elvet

Retrace your steps to Saddler Street and take the lane on your left leading to **Elvet Bridge**, which dates in part to the 12th century. Below the stone arches, wooden rowing boats gather like ducks to bread; many postcards of the city picture this scene. On the other side of the Wear is **Old Elvet** – a wide road with many Georgian façades, including the grand **Royal County Hotel** where left-wing dignitaries and Labour Party representatives traditionally watch the Miners' Gala parade from the balcony. The Victorian **Old Shire Hall** (now a university building) is an imposing red-brick building that is somewhat incongruous on this elegant street. A little further uphill is the **Dun Cow Inn**, an old, squat pub serving Black Sheep and Castle Eden beers.

Cross the small triangle green opposite and veer right, passing the **Old Assize Courts** on your left and **St Cuthbert's Church**. Turn right at the end of the street onto **Court Lane** and walk towards the cathedral which is in full view ahead. Turn left onto **New Elvet** and take a footpath on the right just beyond the traffic lights. Cross over **Kingsgate Bridge** and return to North Bailey and the cathedral along a cobbled lane.

Durham Cathedral

Palace Green ⓘ 0191 386 4266 ⓦ www.durhamcathedral.co.uk. Open daily until 18.00 (17.30 Sun); extended opening until 20.00 between mid–Jul and end Aug.

'Half church of God, half castle 'gainst the Scot' wrote Sir Walter Scott of Durham Cathedral. The much quoted line is inscribed on **Prebends Bridge**, from which the visitor gains one of the most romantic views of the Norman building. Scott's words refer to the construction of Durham cathedral as a shrine to St Cuthbert *and* as a display of power, signalling to potential invaders from the north the might of the medieval kings, and ruling Prince Bishops (who until 1836 had powers to raise an army, mint their own coins, levy taxes and make laws).

Initially a church was built to house Cuthbert's coffin but nothing remains today of that Saxon edifice. The foundation stone of the cathedral was laid in 1093 and the building mostly completed 40 years later, though it now has later additions. Cuthbert's body has lain here ever since, but not without disturbance. The coffin has been opened three times since it came to Durham, first in 1537 when the Dissolution commissioners paid a visit. On finding Cuthbert's body still 'fresh, safe and not consumed' they left it alone, but not before taking the gold and jewels that decorated his shrine. In the 19th century, more treasures were taken – those items are now on display in the Treasures of St Cuthbert exhibition.

The cathedral is entered through the north door under three zigzag-patterned arches. Note the large replica **sanctuary knocker** with its wild eyes and locks (the 12th-century original is on display in the cathedral Treasures exhibition). Until the early 17th century, criminals were offered temporary immunity from prosecution in the cathedral by knocking on the door. After 37 days of receiving shelter, they had to leave the country or turn themselves in.

From the marble font, the full impact of the Norman **nave** reveals itself. The immediate impression is one of great strength and might as the eye scans the carved geometric patterns on the seven-foot wide piers. Between each is a column that soars past the arcades and galleries forming a series of elegant arches spanning the ceiling. The combination of rounded ribs and pointed arches gives the ceiling formidable strength. Before Durham, no stonemason had attempted to create a vaulted ceiling like this on such a scale.

The huge **rose window** at the eastern end of the cathedral is 15th century but was reconstructed in the 19th century with new glass. At its centre, it depicts Christ surrounded by the 12 apostles.

At the **crossing**, look up into the 15th-century interior of the 155-foot **tower** which can be climbed from the south transept. A mere 325 steps later and you'll be taking in the view of fields and settlements beyond Durham and the river below. Also in the **south transept** is a highly decorative **medieval**

clock painted turquoise and gold. Beyond the choir stalls, bishop's throne and finely painted organ pipes, is the **sanctuary** where one of the most celebrated and intricate stone structures in Durham cathedral is found. The 1380 Gothic **Neville Screen** rises all spears and spikes from behind the altar; it is still magnificent despite having lost its bright paintwork and the alabaster angels and saints that once stood in its 107 niches. The figures are said to have been buried by monks fearing their destruction during the Reformation, and have never been recovered.

Before the King's commissioners stripped the cathedral of its riches, **St Cuthbert's shrine**, which lies in a tranquil space beyond the altar, was, according to medieval records, lavishly decorated with gold and green marble. Today, a plain stone slab engraved 'CVTHBERTVS' marks the saint's final resting place. The statue of Cuthbert holding the head of King Oswald reminds us that the Northumbrian ruler's head was buried with the saint.

The shrine area once marked the east end of the cathedral but an extension was added in the mid to late 13th century to accommodate the increasing number of pilgrims. The elegant lancet windows and tall, slender columns in the **Chapel of the Nine Altars** create vertical lift like nowhere else in the cathedral.

The walk back along the nave to the western end of the cathedral allows you again to take in the tremendous power of the nave and the 14th-century west window. Crossing the line by the font, you enter the only area of the cathedral that women were permitted in when there was a Benedictine community resident. The **Galilee Chapel** – once the 'Lady Chapel' – is at the westernmost end of the building. Another of the most distinguished parts of the cathedral, it has many arches decorated with chevrons, medieval stained glass and wall paintings, and tomb of the Venerable Bede (see page 53). The great Anglo-Saxon scholar who died in 735 is one of a small number of men buried in the cathedral. Bede wrote about St Cuthbert's life and was an important figure during the cultural flowering of Northumbria (roughly from the mid 7th to the early 9th centuries). Like Cuthbert, his body hasn't always lain in Durham: Bede was first buried in his home town of Jarrow on Tyneside before being moved to the cathedral by a monk in 1022.

More striking stone vaulted ceilings are found in the restaurant and cathedral shop, both of which are reached from near the Galilee Chapel. The **cloisters** are also entered from the south aisle. The **Monks' Dormitory**, now a library, is well worth visiting for its long oak beamed roof (completed in 1404).

Treasures of St Cuthbert exhibition

Northumbria's golden Anglo-Saxon era is celebrated in this fascinating cathedral museum where you'll find objects taken from St Cuthbert's coffin including his pectoral cross and silk garments – as well as the wood case itself (now in fragments). Rare manuscripts and a facsimile of the Lindisfarne Gospels are also on display.

Durham Castle

Palace Green Ⓣ 0191 334 3805 Ⓦ www.dur.ac.uk; open to visitors on afternoon guided tours (term time) and mornings, and some afternoons during university holidays.

On the orders of William the Conqueror, a fortress was built at Durham in 1072 as a show of strength and to keep Scottish invaders at bay. Until 1836 it was occupied by successive bishops of Durham and then came into the ownership of the university. Architectural writer Nikolaus Pevsner describes it as 'one of the most completely preserved and most easily appreciated Norman strongholds in the county.'

The most prominent building is the octagonal **keep** which stands on a mound looking tremendously serious and ancient but actually only dates to the mid-19th century, when it was reconstructed from ruins. The keep now provides accommodation for students – and visitors in summer (see accommodation page 229). The oldest parts of the castle are the Norman chapel and gallery.

The fortress is entered through a gatehouse from Palace Green which shows signs of Norman stonemasonry with bands of zigzags crowning the archway. The courtyard is enclosed by medieval buildings including the **Great Hall** which contains a huge dining table similar to those found in the older Oxbridge colleges. Meals are still prepared in the medieval kitchen. Also memorable is the mighty **Black Staircase**, built in 1662 from wood, and the exquisitely carved 12th-century doorway into Tunstall's Gallery.

Outside the city centre

Set in 18 acres of woodlands and wildflower meadows to the south of the city is the University **Botanic Garden** (*South Rd, DH1 3TN; 0191 334 5521; www.dur.ac.uk/botanic.garden*). Glasshouses contain tropical plants and an extensive cactus collection. On the other side of South Road, visitors will find a large collection of antiques and artworks at the **Oriental Museum** (*Elvet Hill, DH1 3TH; 0191 334 5694; www.dur.ac.uk/oriental.museum*). The Chinese objects alone amount to over 10,000 items including ancient earthenware, silk robes and an ornate early 19th-century bed.

The **Victorian terraces** south of the railway station and 1857 stone **viaduct** (a stompingly huge bridge of many arches and great height) are worth wondering around if you time before your train. The likes of Hawthorn Terrace, Mistletoe Street and Lawson Terrace are some of the most unspoilt traditional terraces in the county. You'll also find an inviting old pub called **Colpitts Hotel** on Hawthorn Terrace (see page 239).

A couple of miles southeast of Durham is the affluent village of **Shincliffe**, reached by following the **Weardale Way** east from Prebends Bridge along the river. Walk through Shincliffe until you come to a very pretty run of houses lining the leafy High Street. At the east end of the street is the **Seven Stars Inn** (*0191 384 8454; www.sevenstarsinn.co.uk*) where you can enjoy a bite to eat and a drink in the sun. Alternatively, there's a **coffee shop** in the garden centre.

Crook Hall & Gardens

Sidegate DH1 5SZ ① 0191 3848028 Ⓦ www.crookhallgardens.co.uk; open mid Apr–end Sep, daily 11.00–17.00 and selected days at other times of the year; café and plant sales; 10-min walk from Durham city centre.

When Keith and Maggie Bell bought Crook Hall in the 1990s, they almost grassed over the unkempt walled gardens. Visitors to Durham will be pleased they decided instead to restore the grounds as traditional English gardens and open the property to the public. Many artefacts were uncovered during the restoration including old smoking pipes, Victorian hair pins, fragments of pottery and a gunpowder pouch – all of which are on display here.

Crook Hall is really three historic buildings: a Georgian mansion, a Jacobean house and an 800-year-old banqueting hall. They huddle together on a low hill gazing at Durham Cathedral in the distance. Inside are architectural details like the 400-year-old staircase and Jacobean timber-framed roof. An upstairs gallery showcases paintings by local artists.

A dozen or so distinctive gardens surround the buildings including Elizabethan and Georgian walled gardens overflowing with rambling roses, bossy lupins, oriental poppies and oxeye daisies. Children will love the box-hedge maze. There are few places in the North East that can offer a more traditional English garden experience than at Crook Hall where you can take a seat on a cast-iron chair in a historic walled garden and over a cream tea admire the cathedral.

Food and drink

Inexpensive Italian restaurants in Durham are plentiful. **Capriccio Ristorante Italiano** (*0191 370 9550; www.capriccioristoranteitaliano.co.uk*) is authentically Italian and offers a range of pizza, pasta and fish dishes. **La Spaghettata** (*0191 383 9290; www.fabiosdurham.com*) is a lively, low-cost eatery serving decent, predictable pizza and pasta dishes. Both places are popular with locals (particularly students) and are in Saddler Street.

Colpitts Hotel Hawthorn Terrace, DH1 4EL ① 0191 386 9913. No longer a hotel, just an understated, old-world pub with Victorian fireplaces, simple furnishings and full of local chatter.

Finbarr's Restaurant Waddington St, Flass Vale DH1 4BG (10 minutes' walk west of Framwelgate Bridge) ① 0191 370 9999 Ⓦ www.finbarrsrestaurant.co.uk. Upmarket, contemporary restaurant serving modern British dishes using some locally sourced ingredients including venison from Kielder and fish from the North Sea. Sunday lunches.

Flat White 21a Elvet Bridge, DH1 3AA. Come here for good, inexpensive coffee. Quirky with a student vibe. Light lunches, cakes, etc.

Leonard's Coffee House Fowlers Yard, Back Silver St, DH1 3RA ⓣ0191 3840647 Ⓦ www.leonardscoffeehouse.co.uk. Good breakfasts, lunches and coffee situated in Durham's cultural hub among craft workshops.

Vennel's Café Saddlers Yard, 71 Saddler St, DH1 3NP. The words: 'Everything baked on premises' will catch the eye of visitors looking for a healthy lunch. This gem of a café is hidden away in a 16th-century courtyard just off Saddler Street and sells quiches, soups and sandwiches.

The Victoria 86 Hallgarth St, DH1 3AS ⓣ0191 386 5269 Ⓦ www.victoriainn-durhamcity.co.uk. East of the river and the historic centre of Durham on a long road of Victorian and Georgian houses, this traditional tavern has stayed true to its 19th-century heritage. The wood-panelled interior, Victorian fire surrounds, bare floorboards, open fire and selection of real ales make the Victoria a favourite with 'proper pub' devotees. The period theme is continued upstairs in the guest rooms which have period-styled bed frames and wallpaper.

Around Durham city

The ruins of a priory, old pit villages and hamlets that interest with little more than a church and quaint row of cottages await the visitor who explores the farmland outside Durham city.

② Finchale Priory

Five miles north of Durham DH1 5SH ⓣ0191 386 3828 Ⓦ www.english-heritage.org. uk. Open daily; English Heritage.

The sight of the 13th-century priory ruins enclosed by a loop in the River Wear and a thick bank of trees would be jaw-dropping if it weren't for the nearby caravan site and car park-style barrier at the entrance. Overlook the modern intrusion and you'll find the buildings and grounds quite captivating, as enough arcades and towering walls still stand to make quite an impression.

The priory's origins go back to the early 12th century when St Godric, a retired pedlar and later a sea captain and pilgrim, founded a hermitage in the sheltered spot by the riverside where he lived in seclusion. St Godric was laid to rest in a chapel, of which little remains. On his death, the priors of the monastery at Durham Cathedral took over the site and founded the Benedictine priory you see today.

③ Brancepeth

Though missing a bustling village hub, the leafy surroundings and long, wide avenue of stone-built houses leading away from Brancepeth Castle make this one of the most distinctive and attractive places in the county. An old photograph of this street (The Village) from the turn of the 19th century shows the Georgian cottages covered in ivy and looking a little run down. It's easy to identify the location because all the houses have remained the same, except they are smarter. The Village is capped at its southern end by the pillared driveway to the castle. To the north, beyond the crossroads, the houses are more imposing and have Tudor styling.

Some say the name 'Brancepeth' is a corruption of 'Braunspath' which recalls a fearsome boar (a 'braun') that was said to roam the area many hundreds of years ago. If you pass the **Brancepeth Castle Golf Club** (set in the castle's old deer park), you'll see the boar motif.

Hidden along a quiet lane just off The Village is **St Brandon's Church**, which goes back 1,000 years though very little remains of the oldest parts. In 1998, a fire gutted the church and destroyed precious woodwork, but once the flames were extinguished, over a hundred medieval stone coffin covers were revealed in the damaged walls. The collection is thought to be the largest in the North East. Some of the cross slabs are on display in the restored church interior. Of great interest are the unusual engravings of cross heads with multiple points and shafts carved as a Tree of Life with sprouting foliage.

The two massive round gate towers and high curtain wall of **Brancepeth Castle** (*www.brancepethcastle.org.uk; not generally open to the public*) give the appearance of a mighty Norman fortress. If you have the chance to get up close – perhaps at one of a handful of public events such as craft fairs or outdoor plays – you'll find the stonework is a little too neat and pristine to be so old. Indeed, though a Norman castle did once stand here, most of what you see today dates to the early and mid 19th century.

The castle played a role in the 1569 Rising of the North involving the then owner, Charles Neville, the Earl of Westmorland, and, from nearby Raby Castle, Thomas Percy, the Earl of Northumberland. The unsuccessful attempt to depose Queen Elizabeth I and place Mary, Queen of Scots, on the throne resulted in the execution of Percy and the ousting of Neville from his castle. He fled, to Holland and the crown took over Brancepeth. Over the following 400 years, the castle changed hands several times and is now in private ownership.

④ Deerness Valley

The River Deerness flows eagerly towards Durham through woods and pastures and below a number of ex-colliery villages before merging several miles later with the River Wear. Following the waterway for much of the route is a line of an old railway, which makes a very pleasant walk (see under Waterhouses, below).

The hills above the wooded valley are divided into horse paddocks and grazing fields. If you're walking hereabouts in March and make the climb out of the valley, you may be greeted with the sound of curlews announcing the onset of spring.

Waterhouses

Coal lorries make regular rounds to the old miners' cottages standing side by side on a hill above the River Deerness, where for much of the year the smell of burning coal and wood wafts through the hillside terraces that make up the village. To the rear of cottages on Hedley Hill Terrace are back lanes with vegetable plots, coal bunkers and a pigeon cree. If this sounds like a caricature of an old Durham pit village, it's not intentional; it's just that Waterhouses really is like this. That said, the community is more mixed today and in recent years, a lawyer, doctor and university lecturer have moved into the area, so it's not altogether like stepping back in time.

The main reason you may visit Waterhouses and neighbouring **East Hedleyhope** – another ex-mining village, noted for its Victorian brick terraces and wildflower meadow – is to walk the **Deerness Valley Railway Path**. Coal wagons used to trundle along the 8½-mile line from Crook to Broompark via the above-mentioned colliery villages and on to Esh Winning and Ushaw Moor. The wide wooded path follows the river under stone bridges, past fields and the sites of old open-cast mines. A local told me that when Queen Victoria visited Durham, the royal train was parked at the end of the line near East Hedleyhope. It must have been quite a sight for residents who were used to seeing coal wagons rattling past their houses.

The Wizard of Esh

When I met Robert Liddle, an elderly man from the ex-colliery village of Esh Winning in the Deerness Valley, he told me about his knowledge, acquired from his grandmother who used to live in nearby Waterhouses, of medicinal herbs. She used to treat locals for common ailments in the days before the National Health Service and modern healthcare. On her death, Robert, aged nine, took over the 'practice' and ran it from his living room. He would often return from school to find a queue of people outside his front door.

'I'd use herbs collected from hedgerows, fields, woodland edges and the beck. Most were ordinary plants like foxgloves, dandelions, clovers, nettles and watercress,' he explained. Robert treated miners' boils, colds, rashes, infections and so on. During the course of our conversation it became clear that he also learned about what some once called witchcraft.

'My gran told me water could hold a wish. If you can magnetise water for a short period, which should be impossible, why can't it hold a wish?'

He mentioned that she was the local witch doctor or 'wise woman'. Once common in many rural areas for several centuries, the 'profession' had almost completely died out by the early 20th century.

With great sadness. I report that Robert passed away just before this book went to print.

⑤ Lanchester

University lecturers and professionals commute from Lanchester to work in Durham and Newcastle. You only have to look at the smart Georgian cottages around the large green to see why they like it here. For visitors, the busy village, which could be described as a small town, makes a pleasant stopping point.

The medieval **church of All Saints** has a tall Norman chancel arch with three bands of chevrons. It's not the oldest stonework in the church, though: some of the masonry used in the construction of the building (and in nearby houses) came from the nearby Roman fort. A Roman altar, still clearly etched with lettering stands in the south porch. The curious chest in the chancel dates to the 16th century and once contained parish documents and records.

Heading west out of Lanchester up Cadger Bank (the B6296), the trees soon give way to open farmland. At the top of the hill on the left (half a mile from Lanchester), is a **Roman fort** (*no public access, but you can view it from the lay-by*). The perimeter walls of Longovicium are almost completely grassed over. A Roman village lies outside of the fort and may one day be excavated. It's certainly worth stopping at the fort, as much to enjoy the expansive view of meadows and the wooded slopes of hills as the historic site.

Lanchester Valley Railway Path

Download Heritage Walks leaflets at ⓦ www.lanchesterparish.info.

The 12-mile trail from Consett to Durham runs through the centre of Lanchester passing old station houses and platforms, open farmland and the ruins of **Beaurepaire**, a 13th-century manor house and one time retreat for monks. The trail follows the River Browney for much of the way to Durham (look out for sand martins nesting in the riverbank, and kingfishers).

Westwards from Lanchester are the foothills of the heather-clad Pennines where the trail connects with the **Waskerley Way** railway path at **Hownsgill Viaduct**, one of a handful of awesomely high railway viaducts in the county. The trail continues through upland farmland and onto the moors until it comes to an end at Stanhope.

A pleasant short walk from Lanchester follows the railway path for a mile or so east to **Malton nature reserve** and picnic site. Where now you see a pond, woodland, lush wetland vegetation and many dragonflies, butterflies and amphibians, there once stood a colliery.

Food and drink

A number of eateries are found on Front Street; most are take-aways. They include **Yannis**, which serves excellent Greek food to take out or eat in.

Hall Hill Farm

Lanchester DH7 0TA ① 01388 731333 ⓦ www.hallhillfarm.co.uk; open daily Apr–Sep and weekends at other times of the year.

Tractor rides, adventure play areas, close contact with farm animals and a café make this large farm four miles southwest of Lanchester popular with families. Children can bottle feed lambs, hold chicks, ride a donkey or simply run around in the acres of green farmland. Holiday cottages a mile from the farm can be rented.

⑥ Chester-le-Street

A tall railway viaduct with 11 arches strides across this busy town halfway between Durham and Newcastle, best known for its church, castle and cricket ground. Chester-le-Street has Roman origins (once known as Concangis), but nothing remains from that period. In the years following Danish raids on the Northumberland isle of Lindisfarne in the 9th century, the monks from the priory travelled around the North East for seven years with the body of St Cuthbert (and the Lindisfarne Gospels) before settling at Chester-le-Street in AD883 for 112 years. A wooden shrine was built on the site of the present **church of St Mary and St Cuthbert** (on Church Chare), which was rebuilt in stone in the mid 11th century. You can find Saxon stonework in the sanctuary and chancel, but the rest of the building is mostly medieval and Victorian. A facsimile of the celebrated **Lindisfarne Gospels** is on display. Adjoining the church is an **anchorage** which was built in the latter half of the 14th century and housed a religious recluse. It is now a small **museum** *(0191 388 3295).*

Lumley Castle is an imposing medieval fortress that looms over Chester-le-Street. It provides a wonderful backdrop to the International Cricket Ground, home of **Durham County Cricket Club** (the newest of the county cricket clubs). If you're just passing and want to see the pitch, you can access the outside areas of the stadium from Austin's Bar and Bistro *(0191 388 3335; www.durhamccc.co.uk).*

Lumley Castle

Chester-le-Street DH3 4NX
Ⓣ 0191 389 1111 Ⓦ www.lumleycastle.com.

The one-time seat of the Lumley family stands on a prominent hill east of Chester-le-Street. It is a complete castle with four square turrets marking the four corners of a quadrangle and largely dates to the late 1300s. The arresting mansion is now an expensive **hotel** (rooms are sumptuously furnished in medieval style: four-poster beds, red and green drapes, dark oak furniture, etc) with a golf course and posh **restaurant** (the Black Knight). **Elizabethan banquets** are held throughout the year. **Cream teas** are served between 15.00 and 17.00.

Along the River Derwent

The River Derwent flows off the Pennine hills, past Consett and through a wooded vale on the border between Northumberland and Durham before meeting the River Tyne at Gateshead. The highest upland stretches are covered in *Chapter 7*. Here I describe the countryside south of Gateshead. Despite their proximity to the urban landscape, a walk along the old railway line (Derwent Walk), through Chopwell Woods or Gibside detaches you from city life no less so than in parts of the Pennines or Northumberland National Park. Elsewhere in Derwentside, the countryside is mainly sloping farmland and grazing pastures offering far-reaching views. The area is not short of heritage attractions, including Tanfield Railway and the much-praised Beamish Museum.

⑦ Beamish Museum

Beamish DH9 0RG ⓣ0191 370 4000 ⓦ www.beamish.org.uk; open daily in summer, closed Mon and Fri 31 Oct–Easter; last admission 15.00; period cafés, fish and chip shop and pub on site.

Beamish is one of those rare museums that blurs reality and theatre so convincingly that you feel the centuries have rolled back when you step into the museum's recreated period streets. The 300-acre open-air museum tells the story of the local area in Georgian, Victorian and Edwardian times, and is superlative on so many levels: for its authenticity, variety of buildings and experiences (such as ice-skating in winter, tram and train rides, brass band concerts and a walk down a real mine).

Entire buildings and cobbled streets were taken from elsewhere in Durham, brought to the pastoral landscape at Beamish and reconstructed brick by brick.

No Place

A hamlet off the A693 called No Place was too intriguing to overlook while researching this book. I had a good feeling about the settlement west of Stanley after reading that in the 1980s residents had hotly objected to council plans to change the name of the village to 'Co-operative Villas' (the road sign now uses both names). I hoped it wouldn't disappoint like Pity Me – a suburb of Durham which is terribly ordinary and, I discovered, doing just fine.

But, what about No Place? The row of bungalows with immaculate lawns and hedges just outside the hamlet could be Any Place. But, the centre of No Place turns out to be a very neat block of miners' houses arranged along three long terraces with back lanes between each row; a plain Victorian school and a good pub, the Beamish Mary Inn (see page 246).

The village was built in the late 1800s for workers at nearby Beamish Mary colliery and once had a jazz band that formed during the general miners' strike of 1926.

Other features and buildings were already here, including the drift mine, farm and Georgian manor house.

You won't find many interpretation boards or 'do not touch' signs at Beamish; instead you'll see staff in costume working in the fields, making hay, ploughing farmland with heavy horses, chatting in the street, tending to the Georgian garden, changing barrels in the Victorian pub, feeding pigs and making bread.

It is hard to get round Beamish in one day, so make sure you come early. The Victorian/Edwardian town is where most people alight first on taking the tram (which offers a 'hop on, hop off' service around the whole site) from the entrance hall. Here you'll find a dentist, bank, solicitor's office, printers, pub, sweet shop, garage and, many people's favourite, the Co-operative Store.

Food and drink

Beamish Mary Inn No Place, Stanley DH9 0AQ ℗0191 370 0237. Real ales and a crackling fire lure those in the know out of Beamish Museum after a full day in the 19th century. This old pub continues the heritage theme with rustic wooden benches, antique prints, a factory punch-card clock and an old bicycle hanging from the ceiling.

Shepherd & Shepherdess Inn Beamish DH9 0RS ℗0191 3700 349 ⓦ www.shepherdbeamish.co.uk. The sharp-eyed will notice that the child-sized figures above the old doorway of this traditional 18th-century pub are the wrong way round (either that or the pub should be renamed the 'Shepherdess and Shepherd'). The friendly landlady will tell you that one day the young couple ran off into the woods and when they returned, they stood in the other's position by mistake. Sunday lunches and a wide selection of steak, fish and chicken dishes (all reasonably priced); beer garden and location right next to the entrance to Beamish museum.

The Stables Beamish Hall, Stanley DH9 0YB ℗01207 233 733 ⓦ www.beamish-hall.co.uk. An excellent choice for lunch. Dishes are made with ingredients from local farms and the ale is brewed on site. If it's a bright day, you'll probably want to eat outside in the sun-filled courtyard (this being the old stable block for Beamish Hall). A path out the back of the contemporary restaurant leads to a large adventure playground where there's also a café. Beamish Hall is a grand, early 19th-century villa set in glorious parkland and now an expensive hotel. It's a popular wedding venue so keep that in mind if booking a room during weekends in summer.

⑧ Tanfield Railway

Marley Hill, Gateshead NE16 5ET ℗0845 463 4938 ⓦ www.tanfieldrailway.co.uk. Trains run four times every Sunday and at special events throughout the year (see website for timetable); café at Andrews House Station.

The golden age of the railways is relived on the world's oldest operating line in a wooded valley just south of Gateshead. Train rides along the six-mile track

The Pitman Poet

Me aad sangs hev kept me in beer an' the floor o' the public bar hes bin me stage for forty years. Aw'd sing, we'd drink, aw'd sing, we'd drink agen, sangs wi'oot end, amen.'
Tommy Armstrong (with the permission of the *Tommy Armstrong Society*)

Songwriter and pit worker Tommy Armstrong (1848–1920) was born in Shotley Bridge but lived for most his life in the Tanfield area where he wrote songs about the lives of miners. His ballads recall mining disasters, strikes and daily life in colliery towns. He achieved fame in his lifetime but died penniless.

One of his famous songs, *The Sooth Medomsley Strike*, tells the story of how miners were evicted from their homes by oppressive colliery owners and managers. The opening verse includes these lines:

The miners of South Medomsley they never will forget
Fisick and his tyranny and how they have been tret;
For in the midst of danger, these hardy sons did toil,
For te earn their daily bread se far beneath the soil.
Te make an honest livelihood each miner did contrive,
But ye shall hear how they were served in eighteen eighty-five.

from Sunniside to East Tanfield operate year round, stopping at a couple of stations.

The rural setting, period station architecture and steeply wooded Causey Valley with its much-photographed stone bridge are hugely atmospheric, enhanced by the sound of hissing steam, screeching carriages and engine whistles. But, Tanfield is much more than just a trip on a steam train. My lasting impression when I visited as a young child was the **Marley Hill Engine Shed** (the oldest working engine house in Europe, built in 1854). I remember the thrill of touching the large wheels of a steam engine; the oil, soot and smell of coal; and men in overalls working on the bellies of locomotives. It's still the same today.

Tanfield Railway was built in 1725 to transport coal from Stanley and Marley Hill to the River Tyne. Back then, horses pulled wagons on wooden tracks, but they were replaced by locomotives and metal rails in the 19th century. The line closed in 1962 but work soon began on the restoration of locomotives by a group of friends; to date some 20 locos have been brought back to life. Tanfield Railway is still manned by devoted volunteers.

Causey Arch

Built in 1727 to carry coal wagons across the steep Causey gorge, this 105-foot wide stone arch is the oldest railway bridge in the world and was once the largest single span arch in Britain. Today it stands as a monument to the region's great railway past – and makes an eye-catching focus for a walk along the Tanfield Railway Path or Causey Burn. There's a picnic spot near Causey Arch Station.

Food and drink

South Causey Inn Beamish Burn Rd, Stanley DH9 OLS ℡01207 235555 Ⓦ www.southcausey.co.uk. Good traditional pub food using local produce grown in a large vegetable garden. The interior is inviting with dark furniture, stripped oak floors and an open fire. Extensive outdoor grounds make the inn popular with families. Good standard of B&B accommodation.

⑨ Birkheads Secret Gardens

Near Hedley Wood, Sunniside NE16 5EL ℡01207 232262 Ⓦ www.birkheadssecretgardens.co.uk; open Mar–end Sep, Wed–Sun; some areas wheelchair accessible; café.

Today visitors stroll through topiary avenues, enjoy a coffee in the sun, buy plants and admire the profusion of shrubs and flowering plants in Birkheads' stunning three-acre site. Rewind to 1987 and this was just another field in open farmland near Causey Arch. Over the years, Christine and Mike Liddle have created a series of linked gardens including a meditation garden, a small arboretum and a sanctuary for bees and butterflies.

⑩ Gibside

Near Rowlands Gill, Gateshead NE16 6BG ℡01207 541820 Ⓦ www.nationaltrust. org.uk. Parkland and tearooms open daily (check website for chapel opening times); music events and concerts in summer; National Trust.

Once you set foot in this historic landscape garden on the outskirts of Gateshead, you'll feel as cut off from the 21st century as you would in any large, remote National Trust estate. The grounds have all the grandeur you would expect of a 18th-century landscaped parkland with eye-catchers, wooded walkways, and classical architecture. A stroll along the wide avenue of mature oaks from the famous Palladian chapel to the 140-foot Column of Liberty is wonderfully romantic, especially in autumn when the intensity of light and colour is spectacular.

The ruins of an **orangery** and old **mansion house** lie halfway between the column and chapel so by the time visitors make it to the end of the avenue, most are happy to turn back. But, you may want to enjoy a longer **walk**, in which case take one of the footpaths through the woods and farmland or down to the River Derwent. Walk uphill from the Column of Liberty and you'll reach the **stables** where panels explain the history of Gibside. Here a **coffee shop** in a cobbled courtyard sells snacks and secondhand books.

Work began in 1760 on the **chapel**, originally designed as a mausoleum for the Bowes family, but it was several decades later before the building was complete. This outstanding example of Georgian church architecture is the main focal point in the parkland. Its interior is decorated with arches and columns rising to a domed ceiling; the pews are cherry wood, as is the unusual three-tiered pulpit.

A small **farmers' market** is held on the first and third Saturday of every month. Close by, a productive **walled kitchen garden** with decorative flower-beds supplies ingredients to all the eateries on the estate, including the popular **tea room** (no entrance ticket required to eat here). On Friday evenings from 18.00 to 21.00 throughout the year it becomes a **pub** and beer garden where you can enjoy real ale from Wylam Brewery in the evening sun or cosy up beside log fire braziers.

Walk to Gibside

A recommended family-friendly walk or cycle ride to Gibside from Tyneside is through the **Derwent Walk Country Park** and along the **Derwent Walk railway path** (I usually walk from Winlaton Mill or Thornley Wood where there are car parks). It's flat, wide, safe and offers glimpses of Gibside's orangery, house and column and the river twinkling through the leaves of birch and oak trees in the vale below. The view from the viaduct is tremendously expansive and you'd be very unlucky not to see a red kite (with prominent forked tail). These semi-urban birds of prey were reintroduced to the Derwent Valley in 2004 and are now a frequent sight above Gateshead.

When you reach a busy road, either follow the road signs to Gibside or take the fiddly, though more off-road route, by crossing the A694 and following a grassy footpath through houses (you'll need an OS map for this route).

⑪ Chopwell Woods

The main access points are from High Spen and Chopwell

The Friends of Chopwell Woods group was one of the most vocal opponents of the Government's unsuccessful proposal to sell off state-owned woodlands in England in 2011. It shows just how well used (and loved) this 900-acre plantation woodland is by the surrounding communities who have easy access to the miles of footpaths and mountain bike trails that criss-cross the forest. The landscape is hilly in places, but you gain plunging views of the Derwent Valley.

The Forestry Commission is gradually thinning out the conifers and replacing them with broadleaved trees such as oak, beech and ash so that the landscape better resembles the forest that once covered the valley. This should increase the diversity of wildlife seen in the woods; but despite the dominance of conifer trees at the moment, you are never far from deer, red kites and bats. Red squirrels used to live here but are a very rare sight today. The ponds were created when a German plane dropped three bombs over the woods in 1941. Over the years, the craters have filled with water and newts and dragonflies have moved in.

Derwentcote Steel Furnace

Forge Lane, NE39 1BA; between Rowlands Gill and Hamsterley, 1½ miles west of Lintzford, off A694; open at all times; free access (outside only); English Heritage.

From the early 18th century, the Derwent Valley was at the heart of the British steel-making industry until Sheffield became more dominant in the following century. The furnace on the southern edge of Chopwell Woods, built in the 1720s, is the earliest and best example of its type in Britain and very distinctive. There's no general public access inside the building but you can walk up to it.

Steel was produced in two stone chests located below the beehive chimney that stands between two stone sheds. Iron bars imported from Sweden were packed into these cavities with charcoal and then heated to 1,000°C until the charcoal diffused into the iron, making steel. To do this, the furnace had to be fed with coal every few hours for a whole week. Ten tons of steel were manufactured here every month. The raw steel was then taken to a forge to be worked, after which the furnace is said to have taken a week to cool down.

Chopwell

The brick terraces in this ex-mining village are stacked one above the other on a hillside overlooking the Derwent Valley. At the top of the village, extending away from Hall Road, they run in long uniform lines, divided by back lanes or greens. Encroaching new housing threatens the vernacular architecture, but for now, many of the streets stay true to their original Victorian form.

Marx Terrace and Lenin Terrace keep alive the memory of when Chopwell was nicknamed 'Little Moscow' in the early 20th century for its support of the Communist Party. During the General Strike of 1926, the Union Jack was removed from council offices and replaced with the Soviet flag. The miners' union banner famously displays the faces of Marx, Lenin and Keir Hardie (the first leader of the British Labour Party) and is paraded through the streets during the Durham Miners' Gala (see box on page 233) in July. The town's mining past is also remembered on Derwent Street where the old colliery wheel now stands as a monument.

Food and drink

Feathers Inn Hedley on the Hill, Stocksfield NE43 7SW ℡ 01661 843607 Ⓦ www.thefeathers.net. A few miles northwest of Chopwell Woods (and in Northumberland) is a gastro pub that has bagged more prestigious awards in recent years than any other in the North East. The Feathers Inn stands on the main thoroughfare of Hedley on the Hill – a pleasant village of stone about a green. The pared-down interior has whitewashed and exposed stone walls, simple wood furniture and an open fire. There's also a beer garden where you can enjoy one of four regional ales on tap. The food is as local and ethical as you'll find anywhere. The menu changes frequently depending on what produce is in season and the availability of meat and fish from local suppliers. Beef from the

The Shotley Bridge sword makers

Some say the sword-making families from Solingen in Germany that settled in the Derwent Valley in the late 17th century were fleeing religious persecution and were attracted to the secluded location; others say it was the soft water, good for tempering steel that lured them here. Whatever the reason, it was an unlikely beginning for a Durham village. Oley and Mole families (anglicised from Ohlig and Mohl), became known for producing some of the finest weapons in the country; these were used by the English army during the Napoleonic wars.

The trade died out in the mid 19th century when Sheffield and Birmingham developed stronger steel industries than in the Shotley Bridge/Consett area. The Moles moved to Birmingham and continued in business, eventually becoming part of the razor-making firm now known as Wilkinson Sword.

Tyne Valley, local roe deer, wood cock, and turbot from the North Sea were being served up, when I visited in late autumn.

⑫ Ebchester

Roman stones (and even the remains of a bath house) have been found in the gardens of this small, unassuming village on a main thoroughfare three miles north of Consett. Such finds reveal Ebchester was built on a Roman fort (Vindomora).

If you do pause on your travels, there's a pleasant run of old stone cottages leading away from the post office and a very old church (**St Ebba's**) built in part using recycled Roman stone. The oldest walls date to around 1100 and include the Norman chancel arch, while the base of the font is thought to be an old millstone, which could be Roman. You can see ramparts of the Roman fort in the southern edge of the churchyard as well as the headstone of 'Jos. Oley', the inscription of which tells you Joseph was 'the last of the Shotley Bridge sword makers' (see box above) and died in 1896.

⑬ Shotley Bridge

Sandstone houses line the long, sloping streets that curl away from the wooded River Derwent and its 1838 bridge, but despite the hillside aspect, this pleasant village is fairly well concealed by trees. If you've travelled here via neighbouring Consett, once known for its steel works, it's quite a surprise to come across such tall, affluent-looking houses and shops.

The history of Shotley Bridge is tied to the sword-making industry that flourished here from the late 17th century for over 150 years (see box above). There are few reminders of this intriguing past since modern-day officials authorised the demolition of the sword makers' houses on Wood Street that used to have German inscriptions on their door mantles, though the legacy lives on in the name of the pub, the Crown and Crossed Swords, the street name, Oley Meadows, and the recently built Swordmakers Apartments.

South Durham

From Durham city, green pastures and farmland roll south towards Darlington and North Yorkshire. Some of this area is technically outside of County Durham but I've included an overview here and paid particular attention to the area around Bishop Auckland, known for its palace, Roman fort, and superb railway museums. Barnard Castle is covered in *Chapter 7*.

⑭ Sedgefield

Even without its famous racecourse, historic parkland and rural traditions, the town's Georgian centre, large green and medieval church make Sedgefield conspicuously appealing.

St Edmund's Church dates in part to the 13th century and is notable for its 17th-century interior woodwork. You can walk to **Hardwick Hall Country Park** from the town centre by following a footpath through the Hardwick Arms Hotel archway on North End. The grounds were laid out in 1750 with a temple and follies positioned around an ornamental lake facing what is now the plush **Hardwick Hall Hotel** (*01740 620253; www.hardwickhallhotel.co.uk*).

On Shrove Tuesday, a notoriously fierce game of **mob football** begins at 13.00 from the village green. A small leather ball is passed through the bull ring opposite the Black Lion pub and then tossed into the rowdy crowd of men who spend the next few hours kicking and throwing the ball (and each other) about town until at 16.00 someone wins the ball by returning it to the bull ring. The origins of the game go back several centuries, possibly a millennium. Traditionally it was played between countrymen and tradesmen but now anyone joins in.

Food and drink
Dun Cow Inn 43 Front St, TS21 3AT ☏01740 620894. Tony Blair's choice of pub when the then US president, George Bush, was visiting his constituency in the early noughties. Traditional pub dishes and real ales.

⑮ Bishop Auckland

Although one of the largest and most historic market towns in Durham, Bishop Auckland is not on the mainstream tourist map. The spacious market square with its mix of old buildings lies in the northeast corner of the town.

At the end of two neat rows of whitewashed Georgian cottages is the dramatic entrance archway to Auckland Castle (sometimes known as Bishop's Palace). The buildings and its parkland are not to be missed on a trip to south Durham.

Auckland Castle

Bishop Auckland DL14 7NR ⓣ01388 602576 ⓦ www.auckland-castle.co.uk; parkland open daily; castle open Easter–Jun and late Sep, Sun and Mon 14.00–17.00. Jul and Aug, Sun 14.00–17.00, Mon and Wed 11.00–17.00.

The powerful Prince Bishops of Durham established a hunting lodge here some 800 years ago but it wasn't until 1832, when Durham Castle was given to the university, that the estate became the main residence of the Bishops of Durham.

You reach the impressive buildings through the gateway of a castellated screen wall. Interior highlights are the **State Rooms**, including the Long Dining Room with its collection of Francisco de Zurbaran portraits, and the Throne Room decorated with portraits of the Prince Bishops from centuries past and containing the original bishop's throne. The **chapel** was converted from a huge 12th-century banqueting hall in the 1660s. Its interior is much celebrated on account of its size, height and beautiful arcades made of marble and sandstone.

Continuing past the castle buildings on the main drive, a gateway opens into an 800-acre wooded parkland which falls away from the castle to the River Gaunless. It's free to enter and very popular with families and walkers. An 18th-century stone bridge spans the water but the most celebrated feature in the grounds is an unusual **deer shelter** dating to 1767. Part folly, part animal shelter, the arcaded enclosure also seems to catch the eye of passing children. 'It's very giant', I overheard an impressed three-year-old remark. He later asked his mother why there are so many castles here. I think what he rightly observed is the extensive castellated walls and towers seen throughout the estate, which seem to fire the imagination of youngsters and add to the adventure playground appeal of the parkland.

Escomb Church

Escomb, 3 miles west of Bishop Auckland DL14 7ST ⓣ01388 602860.

'One of the most important and most moving survivals of the architecture of the times of Bede', says the Pevsner architectural guide of the 7th-century church which stands in the centre of Escomb village ringed by 1960s houses. Unless you're walking the Weardale Way, you'll probably have to go out of your way to see one of Britain's most complete Saxon churches as there is little else to entice visitors to the village. But, it is a detour well worth making. Those who care for the building have done a superb job explaining all its wonderful curiosities and narrating its significance and place in history. The porch alone is a mini-exhibition space containing stone crosses and various artefacts – all from the Saxon period.

Your visit starts at number 26 Saxon Green, where you will find the keys to the church hanging outside the front door. On entering the churchyard (which contains some good examples of medieval gravestones) even those without an interest in church architecture will immediately appreciate that Escomb Church is special with its strikingly high walls, box shape and small windows. Experts say it is distinctively northern (Saxon churches in the south of England are wider and shorter).

What is also extraordinary is that this little church has remained almost without change for over 1,300 years. The church booklet explains how the building has survived through love and the conservation efforts of villagers and because the Prince Bishops of Durham 'had other things to do than build anew in a little outlying village'.

Inside the simple limewashed building, the eye is immediately drawn to the tall, hairpin **chancel arch** (and the **medieval fresco** painted on its underside) which probably came from the Roman fort at Binchester. Roman stones have been widely recycled in the walls and there are many examples of **diamond broaching** (cross hatches carved into stones). One piece of masonry near the sanctuary on the North wall (to the left of the small window) has the sideways inscription 'BONO REI PUBLICAE NATO' ('to the man born for the good of the state'). The barely visible letters may have been carved on a Roman plinth. On hot days, listen carefully and you may hear the resident whiskered bats shuffling around in the timber-framed roof.

A black Frosterly marble **grave cover** encrusted with hundreds of fossilised corals lies in front of the altar. On the wall behind the altar, a **stone cross** may have been a 'preaching cross' used by missionaries in the early days of Anglo-Saxon Christianity and before this church was built.

Outside, many **irregular stones** are found in the church walls. Look for a horse mount, Roman altar stones and a grooved slab possibly carved by chariot wheels. Their origins are not altogether clear but it is certainly enjoyable looking for these curious stones and pondering their former life. Before you lock up, look back at the wonderful **Saxon sundial** (not the one above the porch but to the right on the south wall). It has three markings indicating the time of services when Escomb Church was in regular use as a place of worship.

⑯ Binchester Roman Fort

North of Bishop Auckland DL14 8DJ Ⓣ 01388 663089 Ⓦ www.durham.gov.uk/ binchester. Open daily from Easter-end Sep .

The largest Roman fort in the county is found above the River Wear in farmland north of Bishop Auckland. Like the forts at Lanchester and Ebchester, Binchester stands on the **Roman road**, Dere Street, which ran from York to Corbridge, across Hadrian's Wall and into Scotland; unlike those less prominent forts, Binchester actually has a visible a stretch of this ancient route. Excavations are ongoing at Binchester and archaeologists are unearthing new structures every year. Recent digs revealed what they think is a Roman barrack block and, under pasture outside of the fort is a busy civilian settlement on which excavations have recently started.

If you went to Binchester today, you'd see the foundations of a number of buildings including the commandant's house and the fort ramparts (like earth mounds). Most striking is the commandant's **private bath house**, said to be the best example in Britain. Close up viewing of the hypocaust is provided inside a museum that stands over the bath house to protect it. You can clearly appreciate how hot air circulated through the brick stacks, heating the floor tiles above.

⑰ National Railway Museum at Shildon

Shildon DL4 1PQ ☏01388 777999 ⓦ www.nrm.org.uk; open daily except over Christmas; free entry.

Shildon, just southeast of Bishop Auckland, is not exactly on the tourist trail, but its superb railway museum is one of the most popular heritage attractions in Durham. Over 70 historic engines are housed mostly indoors within a huge modern engine shed. **Steam train rides** take visitors along a short track, and special events are held throughout the year. I was lucky enough to visit when all the surviving Deltic locomotives were driven into the museum for a special weekend-long event. I didn't need to know much about trains to be awestruck

Rainhill Trials

The date was October 1829; the location: Rainhill, Lancashire. The objective: to convince the directors of the new Liverpool and Manchester Railway of the best locomotive design to pull trains on the new passenger line. The prize was £500 – and guaranteed prestige. There were five competitors: a horse-powered machine and four steam engines.

Timothy Hackworth and George and Robert Stephenson knew each other well from their days at Wylam in Northumberland and had worked together on engineering projects, but for the nine-day competition at Rainhill, they were rivals. The event was witnessed by thousands of people (which must have pleased the railway's bosses who gained valuable PR for their new venture). Problems with Hackworth's engine, *Sans Pareil*, ensured a win for the Stephensons' *Rocket* which powered into the pages of newspapers and history books thereafter.

The potential for steam engines to revolutionise passenger transport and drive the Industrial Revolution was realised from this moment on. Robert Stephenson observed, 'The trials at Rainhill seem to have sent people railway mad'. Timothy Hackworth was also driven to distraction when he discovered a crack in *Sans Pareil's* cylinder casting which had been built at the Stephensons' Newcastle workshop. This led some to charge the Stephensons with foul play, though there was no evidence of this.

by the fleet which included the resident *Deltic Prototype* – a beast of an engine painted sky blue with 1960s styling.

At the historic end of the site, is **Timothy Hackworth's cottage** which explores the development of Shildon as a pioneering railway town and celebrates the famous Stockton and Darlington Railway engineer whose name is stamped all over Shildon (I counted three streets named 'Hackworth' as well as the local park, school, pub and various other buildings). Mention the name Stephenson to the staff in the museum and they'll give you a good-humoured grumble. During the famous Rainhill Trials engine competition of 1829, Hackworth's engine *Sans Pareil* (which is housed in the museum) lost to the Stephensons' *Rocket*, and some locals haven't forgotten this – or the reason why they think his engine exited the race early (see box on page 255).

⑱ Darlington

A newly pedestrianised centre has greatly improved the appeal of this large market town on the southern edge of County Durham. Darlington is still a little rough around the edges (I saw these two signs in a tapas bar window: 'No caps, tracksuits or vests' and 'tops to be worn at all times') but for the most part it is a perfectly pleasant (and wonderfully car-free) place. Most of the buildings date to the 18th and 19th century and include the restored Victorian **market hall**, and tall **clock tower** (1864) that bears a resemblance to Big Ben; even the bells were made by the same company. An outdoor market is held on Monday and Saturday.

Head of Steam railway museum

North Road Station, Darlington DL3 6ST

① 01325 460532 ⑩ www.head-of-steam.co.uk; open Apr–Sep, Tue–Sun and Oct–Mar, Wed–Sun; call for times; café and outdoor picnic area.

North of the town centre, is this gem of a museum that celebrates the region's railway heritage on the route of the historic Stockton and Darlington railway – the first passenger railway in the world. The building is actually an old station, still with its original footbridge, Victorian loos, booking office and platform, and now houses several steam engines. Authentic railway posters, leather suitcases on trolleys and old signs are wonderfully evocative of the early days of railway travel.

For many train enthusiasts, the highlight will be George Stephenson's *Locomotion No. 1*, built for the opening of the railway and the first steam engine to pull a train carrying people. The image of Stephenson driving his locomotive on its inaugural trip on 27 September 1825 with a few hundred passengers crammed into coal wagons is terrifically romantic. A local newspaper (quoted at the museum) recorded the event: 'Astonishment was not confined to the human species, for the beasts of the field and the fowls in the air seemed to view with wonder and awe at the machine ... The whole population of the towns and villages within a few miles of the railway seem to have turned out, and we believe we speak within the limits of truth, when we say that not fewer than 40,000 or 50,000 persons were assembled to witness the proceedings of the day.'

Near the A66 is the startlingly odd Darlington **brick train** – a sculpture of a puffing *Mallard* steam engine unveiled in 1997 to celebrate the town's railway heritage. It is made with 182,000 bricks (including some special 'bat bricks' which allow pipistrelles to enter the hollow interior). Access is from Morrisons supermarket in the Morton Park Industrial Estate.

Food and drink

A couple of bistros and restaurants merit a try in Darlington's town centre. **Cantina Street Food** on Skinnergate (*01325 467555*) has rustic, Latin American appeal and serves lunches and dinners as well as coffees and alcoholic drinks. On the same street is **Barnacles fish and chip take away**. At the time of publishing they sold cod and chips for the bargain price of £3 (a Wednesday special). Just round the corner on Blackwellgate is **Uno Momento** (*01325 381910*), a contemporary Italian and alternative to nearby Pizza Express.

⑲ Piercebridge and Gainford

West of Darlington, two attractive villages by the River Tees are reached in quick succession (by road or along the riverside footpath). Piercebridge and **Gainford** both have large, tree-studded greens with old churches and are surrounded by stone cottages.

Piercebridge lies on the route of the Roman road, Dere Street, which crossed the River Tees here. The foundation stones of the Roman bridge are still visible in a field a few hundred yards east of the village and south of the Tees (the river having changed its course since the 2nd or 3rd century when the bridge was constructed). The three-arched bridge that spans the water today dates to 1789.

Also on the south side of the river is the **George Hotel** (*01325 374576; www.georgeontees.co.uk*), whose tall antique clock inspired the nursery rhyme 'Grandfather's Clock' (actually written in 1876 as a marching song by Henry Clay Work), and is the reason we call tall, case-clocks by this name. A visit to the bar might bring those lyrics to mind: 'but it stopped short, never to go again when the old man died'. North of the river is the village green and an organic farm with a **café** and well-stocked shop (*01325 374251; www. piercebridgefarm.co.uk*).

Walking and exploring the beaches along the Durham Coast Path

Both the start and end points on the coastal trail, as well as the villages in between, are serviced by buses from Hartlepool, Durham and Sunderland.

The well-signposted **Durham Coast Path** from Crimdon to Seaham runs along a grassy headland for 11 windswept miles. You can see the cranes, buildings and piers of Sunderland and Hartlepool silhouetted through the sea fret to the north and south, and rock stacks, pebble beaches and wooded inlets in the bays below. What remains with you the whole route are the views of the wave-carved cliff walls and the glinting sea stretching to the horizon like a sheet of aluminium. The path is up and down much of the way on account of all the rivulets and wooded gorges that characterise the Durham coast. Some you can skirt around, but others involve a hike down to the shore and back up the other side.

Crimdon's dunes slope gently to the beige beach, which is mostly sandy and one of the child-friendliest along the Durham coast. As you walk north, the beach becomes rockier (good for searching for sea creatures in the many pools).

Around the **Blackall Rocks Nature Reserve**, the base of the cliff walls have been eroded by the sea into many pits and caves. If you've seen the 1960s Michael Caine film *Get Carter*, you might know that the closing scenes were filmed hereabouts. Back then, mounds of colliery waste filled the inlets and a thick black sludge covered the beach; there were no skylarks singing in the background and the sea-facing slopes were not dotted with cowslips and primroses as they are today. The last time I walked this path, a barn owl flew out from one of the folds in the headland and began scouring the meadow behind me for voles.

The path continues past some allotments and descends to **Denemouth** beach at the opening of the **Castle Eden Dene National Nature Reserve** (see page

Along the coast

For much of the 20th century, Durham's coast was not the sort of place you'd visit with a beach towel and bucket and spade. Colliery waste was routinely dumped in the sea which turned the sand and water black and the entire coastline from Hartlepool to Sunderland into a no-go area. Some locals did venture onto the beaches, but only to collect fragments of coal to heat their houses.

Today, the sea is blue, and white waves break onto the sandy shores and pebble beaches following a ten year clean-up operation. The bays are not as pristine as those in Northumberland, and some still show signs of past abuse, but the coastline as a whole is wonderfully rugged. Solitude is virtually guaranteed along much of the 11-mile clifftop path which offers wide sea views and wildlife-watching opportunities.

261). A walkway leads across the mouth of the gorge by a reedbed and under the gaze of a viaduct (early 20th century). The beach here is not so appealing as elsewhere on the Durham coast and you'll notice if you walk to the shore that a solid shelf of colliery stones and debris runs the length of the bay. Coal fragments and bricks with the names of nearby collieries such as Eldon and Lumley protrude from the bank, reminding visitors of the industrial past. Over time, this manmade barrier is being eroded away and the sea water will reach further inland, restoring the marshland habitat.

Climb back on to the headland and press on to **Horden** – once a popular spot for bathers and day-trippers in the early 20th century before one of the biggest coal pits in the country was sunk here. There are some beautiful wildflower grasslands close to the coastal footpath.

Many of the scenes in *Billy Elliot* were filmed in **Easington Colliery** (see page 260), a couple of miles ahead. If you detour off the coastal path to the village, you may recognise the terraces and back lanes from the film (though they could have been in a number of old mining villages in these parts).

Hawthorn's dene is partly ancient and contains many old ash and oak trees, as well as two lime kilns. In spring the ground below the railway viaduct is covered with ramsons that scent the air with garlic as you walk.

The final leg of the coast path continues along the clifftop past **Dawdon** and **Blast Beach** (an evocative name for a place that has witnessed so much industrial activity over the years). Rock stacks are the last pleasing coastal feature before you walk into **Seaham**, past its large, empty harbour where just a couple of vessels are moored. The town has been spruced up in recent years with new homes and a revamped promenade (at the northern end of Seaham), which is a pleasant place to sit with a bag of chips.

Glacial meltwater eroded a number of finger-like channels in the limestone escarpment that stretches from Hartlepool to Sunderland. These steeply sided **denes** are secluded and overgrown in places and you can sometimes hear the sea echoing through the mouth of the ravines (especially at Hawthorn where the brick viaduct amplifies the sound); the rivulets that flow along them are know as gills. Castle Eden Dene (see page 261) and Hawthorn Dene are the best examples, but you'll also find ravines at Crimdon, Easington Colliery (Fox Holes Dene), Horden, Dawdon and Seaham.

Plants along the Durham coast grow on magnesian limestone, which is found in just a handful of locations in England and nowhere else by the sea. Orchids, salad burnet, rock rose and blue moor-grass flourish where mowing regimes allow and support a number of invertebrates including glow worms and the northern brown Argus butterfly (sometimes called the Durham Argus butterfly). The species is chocolate brown with white edging and orange spots. If you walk the Durham Coast Path between May and August, you'll come across some excellent examples of this flower-rich habitat at **Beacon Hill** (near Easington) and **Blackhall**. Further inland is **Thrislington National Nature Reserve** (seven miles southeast of Durham, between the villages of West Cornforth and Mainsford), a fantastically rich magnesian limestone grassland known for its show of dark red helleborine, mountain everlasting and 11 species of orchids.

⑳ Easington Colliery and around

Set back from the coast are a number of old pit villages, including **Blackhall Colliery**, **Horden** and **Easington Colliery** (the setting for the film *Billy Elliot*). Some of the Victorian streets have been demolished, but you can still find blocks of traditional red brick terraces with their distinctive back lanes elsewhere.

Colliery wheels stand in most villages as monuments to the mining past. On a hill outside Easington Colliery is the village's original **pit shaft cage**, which transported miners some 500 yards below the ground. It stands alone facing the sea on the site of the old mine shaft and is one of the most poignant memorials I've come across, marking where 3,000 men worked at the colliery's peak in the 1930s until its closure in 1993. The cage is reached along a grassy footpath from the car park just off Tower Street (on the northern edge of the village and west of the railway line; on Ordnance Survey maps it is found north of where the shafts are marked).

One time I visited **Blackhall Colliery**, an elderly man stopped to chat while I looked at the colliery wheel. He was happy to tell me about conditions in the mines: working in water up to his knees every day and so on. I asked what he did after the mine closed in 1981, to which he replied with a laugh, 'I took early retirement'. Thousands were made unemployed all over Durham when the mines shut one by one during the latter half of the 20th century; they had little chance of finding new work.

There is more to nose around in the coastal villages than mining memorials and vernacular architecture, though. If you are travelling through **Easington Village**, for example, you'll find a medieval **church** (St Mary's on Hall Walks) with a Norman tower. Opposite is a striking limewashed manor house called **Seaton Holme** (*0191 527 3333; open during the week all year plus weekends 1 Apr–30 Sep*), the former retirement home of a Durham bishop and also medieval in origin.

∞∞∞

Food and drink

There's not a great selection of eateries in the area, but I can vouch for **Bradley's Fish Shop & Restaurant** on the Coast Road at Blackhall Colliery (*0191 5872055*). Bradley's is easily reached from the coast path, making it an ideal place to stop for lunch on your walk. You could also try the **Half Moon Inn** on the Stockton Road in Easington Village (*0191 527 0203*).

㉑ Castle Eden Dene

Stanhope Chase, Peterlee SR8 1NJ ⓦ www.naturalengland.org.uk; main access from the Natural England car park at Oakerside Dene Lodge also reached from the Durham Coast Path.

This under-celebrated National Nature Reserve extending to the Durham coast is not somewhere you are likely to stumble across, hidden away as it is in a deep ravine by the sea. Out of all the wooded gorges from Sunderland to Hartlepool, it is the richest in wildlife, the longest (three miles) and, many would say, the most beautiful. It also contains the largest area of semi-natural woodland in the North East and a tremendously tall brick railway viaduct that crosses the mouth of the inlet.

The steep banks descend a hundred feet to a river and are thick with yews. These venerable trees have inhabited Castle Eden since at least Saxon times. We know this because the Saxons called the gorge 'Yoden' meaning Yew Dene (a word that lives on in many local street names and as a Fish and Chip shop in Peterlee).

Elsewhere, oak, ash, beech, dense patches of rhododendron and the occasional larch or pine tree grow, and ivy and ferns drape the vertical limestone walls above the burn. The lush vegetation makes the dene dark and secluded in places, and ripe for folklore. If you're imagining a romantic 18th-century woodland garden, you're on the right lines. The gorge was privately owned for 250 years (until the 1940s) by the Burdon family who lived in the nearby manor house and used the dene to entertain visitors. That explains the grottos, ornamental shrubs, old footbridges and the wide paths once used by carriages carrying finely dressed day-trippers.

Castle Eden is well-regarded for its flowering plants, of which there are around 300 varieties in the reserve (as well as some 150 mosses and liverworts). Spring is a good time to visit when all the usual yellow woodland plants are in flower, followed by a display of bluebells. Three colonies of the uncommon herb paris are found here (look for a low-lying plant with a purple centre and long pointed green petals). A single specimen of Britain's rarest plant, the lady's slipper orchid, grew at Castle Eden until one day in 1926 when a policeman plucked its only flower and gave it to a young woman studying botany.

Food and drink

Castle Eden Inn TS27 4SD ⓣ01429 835137 ⓦ www.castleedeninn.com.
Upmarket old coaching inn serving regionally sourced meat and fish dishes including 'locally shot roe deer'. Expensive but the best food you'll find in the area.

㉒ Hartlepool

Don't be put off by the sprawling layout of Hartlepool and the dual carriageway running through its centre; the town has many fine civic buildings, a superbly reconstructed old quay, sandy beaches and a marina crowded with sailing boats and eateries. The historic Headland (the coastal peninsula) wraps around a working dock and is considered quite separate from the rest of Hartlepool. Together with the marina and heritage quay, this is where you'll probably want to spend most of your day.

If arriving by train, the **tourist information centre** (*01429 869706; open Tue–Sat*) is just round the corner on Church Square in a peculiar-looking church. There's an art gallery here and you can climb the 164 steps to the top of the tower and see the whole of Hartlepool and its coastline (a good way to orientate yourself in this complex town). Architectural historian Nikolaus Pevsner described the creators of Christ Church as 'the naughtiest of mid-Victorian architects'. Indeed, the short, wide building, tall tower and adjoining parapet (that looks a little bit like a bayonet) are most unusual.

Hartlepool Headland

This windswept peninsula is the historic centre of Hartlepool where you'll find period houses facing the sea and a number of landmarks including piers, a lighthouse and the 19th-century coastal battery. The sandy beach continues north for 1½ miles all the way to Crimdon. Just south of the golf course is **Spion Kop Cemetery** – a burial ground and a really important site for wildflowers. Orchids and lime-loving species flourish in the nature reserve.

Birders will know that the headland is an excellent place to visit after high winds during the migration seasons when birds travelling over the North Sea are often blown onto the peninsula. Unusual species turn up every year sending the twitcher community into a frenzy. The trees outside Verrills fish and chip shop on the High Street (next to St Hilda's Church) are so important that they are known as the 'fish shop trees' among birders.

Heugh Gun Battery (*01429 270746; www.heughbattery.com; open Thu–Sun*), on the nose of the peninsula, was reconstructed in the early 1900s and played a role in defending Hartlepool from the German navy. A plaque on the

Who hanged the monkey?

If you've seen Hartlepool United's monkey mascot, heard about the Mayor dressed in a monkey costume who was elected in 2002 on the promise of 'free bananas for school children', or walked around the marina and come across the statue of a monkey, you may think the town is, ahem, going bananas.

Hartlepool's monkey obsession is linked to the wreck of a French warship during the Napoleonic wars. The sole survivor was a soggy pet monkey which local fishermen believed was a French spy. Legend has it that, being reasonable folk, they gave the monkey a fair trial after which he was found guilty, sentenced to death for treason and hanged from a boat's mast. The story explains the football team's mascot, H'Angus, and the jibe 'monkey hangers' used to describe Hartlepudlians.

promenade outside the battery commemorates the death of the first soldier to die on British soil during the Great War when a German shell exploded on the headland on 16 December 1914. Inside the museum, you'll find a number of armoured vehicles, original guns, the workings of an underground magazine and a recreated Somme trench.

Close by on Church Walk is **St Hilda's Church** (*01429 267030; www. hartlepool-sthilda.org.uk; open for services and 14.00–16.00 on Sat in winter and the same time on Wed, Sat and Sun Easter–Sep*), a large and very impressive Early English building constructed in the 12th century on the site of an Anglo-Saxon monastery. Besides the nave and its many arches, visitors cannot fail to be impressed by the monster buttresses supporting the tower. A visitor centre details the history of the church and surrounding area.

Hartlepool Marina and Historic Quay

Maritime Experience Museum, Maritime Ave, TS24 0XZ Ⓣ 01429 860077
Ⓦ www.hartlepoolsmaritimeexperience.com. Open daily.

On summer days, a stroll along the yacht-filled waterfront is one of the highlights of a visit to Hartlepool. The other major draw is the recreated 18th-century port. If you've been to Beamish Museum, you might feel this is the maritime equivalent.

Enclosing the quay on three sides are period shops built and furnished as they may well have looked back in the days of the Napoleonic wars. Around the cobbled quay you'll find a gunmaker, naval tailor and a nautical instrument maker – as well as a water-facing café. The centrepiece is the huge HMS *Trincomalee*, the oldest British warship still afloat, built in 1817. Period re-enactments and canon fire displays are a hit with families. On board there are four decks to explore and you should allow around an hour just to see the ship.

Food and drink

With a busy fishing fleet operating out of Hartlepool, you'd expect the fish and chips to be pretty good, and that is largely the case. Two of the most popular by the coast are **Verrills** on the headland's High Street (*01429 267756; open Tue–Sat*) and **Surfside Fish Bar & Restaurant** (perfect thin and crispy batter) on the promenade just north of Seaton Carew (*01429 861150*). There's a selection of bistros at Navigation Point next to the marina and you'll also find an Italian and a modern pub serving traditional meat dishes on the historic quay next to the Maritime Experience.

㉓ Teesmouth National Nature Reserve

Teesside's Seal Sands, Greatham Creek and Saltholme are up there with the best wetland birdwatching sites in the North East. Together they form part of the Teesmouth NNR – one of the most extraordinary landscapes and nature reserves you will find anywhere. If you're thinking of coming here, keep in mind that power station chimneys, cranes and an army of electricity pylons form the backdrop to the grasslands and waterways. This futuristic skyline was the inspiration for the opening shot of Ridley Scott's film, *Blade Runner*. It's not for everyone, but it is wild in its own way and fantastically sculptural. I'm not being diplomatic; this is genuinely one of my favourite wetland landscapes. Love it or hate it, you will be impressed that the seals, hares, lapwings, orchids and owls are thriving in this seemingly brutal, yet strangely serene, environment.

Those intimidated by all the pipes and towers should head to the RSPB-managed pools, reedbeds and grasslands at **Saltholme** (*01642 546625; www. rspb.org.uk; open every day except Dec 25; visitor centre and café*). The reserve has been tinkered with to make it bird (and family) friendly – and to take the edge off hard surroundings.

North of Saltholme on the A178 and before you reach the bridge over Greatham Creek (where you'll see common seals at low tide and lots of waders), there's a pull-in area on your left signposted for the Teesmouth NNR where you can birdwatch.

㉔ Tees Transporter Bridge

One of three remaining transporter bridges in Britain, the longest of the 11 surviving bridges of its type in the world and one of the great experiences of a jaunt into the industrial North, the Transporter Bridge just had to be mentioned in this book, despite being located in Middlesbrough. It is, however, very much a part of the landscape of Teesside and the aforementioned nature reserves. If you are travelling north on the A1, the structure is a half hour drive east of Darlington, or a 15-minute walk north of Middlesbrough railway station.

The blue bridge has the appearance of two cranes facing each other with their arms meeting in the middle. Its cantilever construction allows a platform suspended by steel cables to efficiently cross the river without really restricting the movement of boats. The journey is over too quickly (in just two minutes 30 seconds) but for 70p (£1.30 for those with cars) it is what you might call a cheap thrill.

In 1931, in the days before strict safety controls, my grandmother, aged 11, walked across the top of the bridge with her father. 'It was quite an event and I was very excited', she told me. 'We climbed the staircase up the tower and then followed the walkway across the length of the bridge. When the platform below started moving across, the whole bridge shook and I thought I'd fall!' On reaching the other side, they returned to Middlesbrough in the conventional way which cost, she remembers, a penny.

7. NORTH PENNINES

I t's mining that's responsible for the pitted fells, terraces of stone cottages, Methodist chapels, schools and reading rooms; the way the meadows rising out of the valleys are boxed into 'allotments' where miner-farmers toiled to support their families in lean times; the smelt mill flues, mine entrances and chimneys; the railway lines, workshops, blacksmiths and mine agents' houses. Relics from the 18th- and 19th-century lead mining and quarrying industries lie scattered in every hamlet and on every hillside in the North Pennine valleys, and occasionally the rich minerals in this European Geopark reveal themselves above ground; but to the casual visitor, with the exception of the odd striking chimney, lime kiln and water wheel, it's far from obvious that this was once the biggest lead mining region in the world.

For the most part, the North Pennines Area of Outstanding Natural Beauty (AONB) – the second largest AONB in the UK covering 770 square miles and spanning four counties and six prominent valleys (the South Tyne, East and West Allen, Derwent, Wear and Tees) – is characterised by wooded gorges, heather moors, flower-filled meadows, unusual rock formations, whisky-coloured burns, waterfalls and a pastoral landscape reminiscent of the Yorkshire Dales.

But what really draws visitors is the sense of remoteness and wilderness. Nowhere in England is truly wild of course and even the most desolate-looking Pennine moors are managed, but, nonetheless, the feeling you get when setting foot across Stanhope Common, coming across Alpine plants left over from the last Ice Age, hearing the drumming of snipe and the courtship display of black grouse, or looking down through the glacial valley at the top of High Cup Nick is one of supreme detachment and isolation.

This chapter takes in those valleys and fells within Northumberland and Durham, though occasionally I've strayed over the border into Cumbria.

Getting around

With such an extensive network of cycling trails and footpaths, this is a feasible place to holiday without a car if, for example, you tackle the long-distance routes. But, public transport is scarce outside of the fringe towns like Barnard Castle, Wolsingham and Hexham so travelling around by this method is not really viable, but if it's just a question of getting into the dales, you have a couple of options.

In **Weardale**, the Weardale Railway (see page 287) steam and diesel engines will take you (in style) from Bishop Auckland West as far as Stanhope. In **Teesdale**, a couple of buses operate, one from Barnard Castle to Middleton-in-Teesdale (the 95/96) which connects with some Darlington services and goes

NORTH PENNINES

HALTWHISTLE

Haydon
Bridge
A69
B6305
HEXHAM

River
Tyne
River
Allen
Langley
④
Langley Castle
Allen Banks &
Staward Gorge
B6306
A68
River
Tyne
③

Allendale
⑤
B6295
Slayley
Forest
Derwent
Gorge &
Reservoir

River Ninebanks
South Tyne
⑥
Dryburn
Moor
Blanchland
⑨
⑧
Edmundbyers

A689
South Tynedale Railway
Alston
①
⑦
Allenheads
B6278

Nenthead
⑬
Killhope
Lead Mining
Museum
Stanhope
Common
A68

Garrigill
②
⑭
Cowshill
Rookhope
Stanhope
⑫
Wolsingham
Harperley
POW Cam
B6277
Ireshopburn
River Wear
A689
⑩
A689

Burnhope
Reservoir
St John's
Chapel
WEARDALE
Weardale Railway
A68

Cross
Fell ▲
Cow Green
Reservoir
A6278
Hamsterley Forest

N
Langdon
Beck
Newbiggin-
in-Teesdale

②④ Cauldron
Snout
②③
②②
Middleton-
in-Teesdale
⑪

High Force
and Low Force
②⓪
⑲
Raby
Castle
⑯

UPPER TEESDALE
Grassholme
Reservoir
⑱
Egglestone
Staindrop

0   4 miles
Selset
Reservoir
②①
Romaldkirk
Cotherstone
⑮
BARNARD
CASTLE

0   5km
B6276
Hannah's Meadow
Hury
Resevoir
⑰

Balderhead
Reservoir
TEESDALE
Egglestone Abbey

Brough
Blackton
Reservoir
A67
River Tees

A685
A66
Bowes
Rokeby
Park

via Romaldkirk, Cotherstone and a few other places (*Mon–Sat; www.arrivabus. co.uk*); and a very infrequent minibus from Middleton to Upper Teesdale (see page 301) which stops at High Force and Langdon Beck. For **Allendale** and **Allenheads**, take the 688 from Hexham (*Mon–Sat; www.simplygo.com*) and for the **South Tyne Valley**, the 680 Nenthead to Carlisle service via Alston, Slaggyford and Lambley (*Mon–Sat; www.cumbria.gov.uk*).

The nearest non-heritage **train stations** are at Darlington, Hexham and Haltwhistle.

Cycling

Thigh-busting moors and long exhilarating downhill stretches abound in the North Pennines. Hundreds of cyclists take on the **Coast-to-Coast** and the north–south NCN **Route 68** every summer and you'll find excellent facilities along the way. There are plenty of day rides of course: around the reservoirs and along disued railway lines (notably the **Waskerley Way** and **South Tyne Valley trail**) and country lanes above the valley basins.

Hamsterley Forest (see page 286) caters exceptionally well for all grades of mountain bikers (cycle hire available).

Besides **WoodnWheels** in Hamsterley Forest, you can also hire bikes at **North Pennine Cycles** in Nenthead (*01434 381324; www.northpenninecycles. co.uk*).

Walking

The North Pennines presents some of the best opportunities for moorland, waterfall and valley walks in England. I've peppered the following pages with suggestions of routes which will lead you through some of the finest wooded gorges and hill-top tracks in the AONB along packhorse trails, footpaths and disued railway lines, but this is not a walking guide and you'll need Ordnance Survey maps OL43 and OL31 to follow routes.

Four well-established, waymarked trails cut across the countryside: the **Teesdale Way** and **Weardale Way** traverse the AONB following their respective rivers from west to east; the **Pennine Way** takes the remote north–south route across the highest fells; and **Isaac's Tea Trail** makes a circuit of the Allen valleys. The latter 37-mile circular trail (marked on Ordnance Survey maps) follows in the footsteps of Isaac Holden, a devout Methodist who travelled the Pennine moors in the mid 19th century selling tea and raising money for good causes.

Packhorse trails

The helpful people at the North Pennines AONB office have put together a series of guides for mountain bikers and horseriders following 18th-century packhorse trails over the moors at Alston, Hamsterley, Hartside, Blanchland and at Teesdale's Hury and Blackton reservoirs. There's an inexpensive set of routes for cyclists and another for horseriders (*01388 528801; www. northpennines.org.uk*), on sale at tourist information offices.

Information

Apart from prominent **tourist information centres** in Barnard Castle, Middleton-in-Teesdale, Alston and Bowlees, the **Durham Dales Centre** in Stanhope (see page 286) is well resourced. Online, the **North Pennines AONB** website (*01388 528801; www.northpennines.org.uk*) holds a huge amount of information about the landscapes, geology and wildlife of the region. The AONB also produces many high-quality guides, booklets and leaflets on sale online or by phone and at tourist information centres. **Natural England** rangers are on hand to help you enjoy and access the Moor House and Upper Teesdale National Nature Reserves; the reserve office is at Widdybank Farm, Forest-in-Teesdale (*01833 622374*).

Accommodation

Carrs Farm Wolsingham DL13 3BQ ℗ 01388 527373 ⓦ www.carrsfarm.co.uk Ⓔ joy.henderson@carrsfarm.co.uk. Eco bunkhouse in newly converted barn powered by the sun and wind. Hillside location south of Wolsingham surrounded by meadows and with views of Weardale. Excellent choice for walkers and cyclists.

High Keenley Fell Allendale NE47 9NU ℗01434 618344/07765 001005 ⓦ www.highkeenleyfarm.co.uk Ⓔ stay@highkeenleyfarm.co.uk. With Allen Banks woodland and Hadrian's Wall within (fairly) easy reach plus expansive hill-top views, the location couldn't be better for cyclists and walkers. This being a working livestock farm, the friendly owner welcomes horseriders. Very good-value, inexpensive accommodation in a converted barn and set around a courtyard. All three contemporary rooms of a high standard – nothing too fancy, just simply decorated with modern bathrooms. Locally sourced produce used in breakfasts.

Langdon Beck YHA Forest-in-Teesdale DL12 0XN ℗ 0845 371 9027 ⓦ www.yha. org.uk/hostel/langdon-beck. Superbly located for walking and cycling in Upper Teesdale, this exceptionally welcoming eco YHA on the B6277 which has solar panels and a wind turbine is also very well kept and has a spacious dining area with views of the surrounding hills and meadows. Curlews, lapwings and lambs in abundance right outside the window. Dinners (should you not want to make your own) are really good, for example mushroom and wild garlic soup followed by bolognese. 'I used wild garlic growing in the garden,' says the manager casually. I really liked the fact that he also remembered everyone's name and was happy to help with planning walks.

Langley Castle Near Hexham NE47 5LU ℗ 01434 688888 ⓦ www.langleycastle. com Ⓔ manager@langleycastle.com. Hugely impressive and lavishly decorated medieval towerhouse castle and one of the most exclusive hotels in the region; situated in woods on the edge of the North Pennine moors. The medieval theme continues throughout the interior. Feature rooms have four-poster beds, luxurious curtains and wallpapers, window seats, dark wood furniture and exposed stone walls. 'Castle View' rooms in converted buildings within the grounds of Langley Castle are reasonably priced. Hotel restaurant is similarly upmarket (see page 279). Beware of wedding parties most weekends in summer.

Ninebanks YHA Mohope, West Allen Valley NE47 8DQ ① 01434 345288 Ⓦ www. ninebanks.org.uk Ⓔ ninebanks@yha.org.uk. Originally a mineshop built to house leadminers in the 18th century and still with many old features like stone flag flooring and timber beams, this remote and very 'green' youth hostel 1½ miles south of Ninebanks on a hillside is a great base from which to explore the Allen valleys. Family–friendly with en-suite rooms that would make a very low-cost option for a family of four or six, or a party of walkers/cyclists.

Old Barn 12 Market Pl, Middleton-in-Teesdale DL12 0QG ① 01833 640258/07813 697906 Ⓦ www.theoldbarn-teesdale.co.uk Ⓔ lynda@theoldbarn-teesdale.co.uk. Converted barn on Middleton's main street and next to the tourist information centre, this neutrally decorated B&B with three very comfortable en suites with feather duvets and modern bathrooms offers very good-value accommodation considering the superior standard of rooms. Excellent choice for walkers and cyclists, with a drying room, bike storage and pick up/drop off service from the head of trails and Barnard Castle.

Rose & Crown Romaldkirk, Barnard Castle, Co. Durham, DL12 9EB ① 01833 650213 Ⓦ www.rose-and-crown.co.uk Ⓔ hotel@rose-and-crown.co.uk. Romaldkirk village and its characterful 18th-century inn (low beams, open fires, dark wooden furniture and wonderfully snug) ooze old-world charm and offer some of the very best dining and high-end accommodation in the North Pennines. The rural setting is hugely picturesque with meadows, hills and a leafy riverside all within walking distance. The Rose & Crown ticks every box for location and quality, but to stay in one of the very comfortable rooms (heavy fabrics, Molton & Brown soaps, traditional styling but modern) expect to pay well above average prices.

On the wilder side

Aside from the larger caravan parks, campers looking for small, no-frills places to pitch up have a couple of choices.

In **Upper Teesdale**, try **East Underhurth Farm** behind Langdon Beck YHA (*01833 6222062*); **High Side Farm** (see below) and **Low Way Farm** (*Holwick DL12 0NS, opposite the pub; 01833 640506*).

In **Weardale**, walkers and cyclists can camp in Rookhope at a small paddock with a shower and toilet in the **Old Vicarage** (*DL13 2AE; 01388 517375; walkers and cyclists only - strictly no cars or caravans; open Mar–Oct*) and the **Barrington Bunkhouse** (*DL13 2BG; 01388 517656; www.barrington-bunkhouse-rookhope. com*) which has a lawn for tents (facilities in the bunkhouse).

It's always worth asking at some of the more remote **pubs** that have land and take campers such as the **Strathmore Arms** (*Holwick DL12 0NJ; 01833 640362; www.strathmorearms.co.uk*) 3 miles west of Middleton-in-Teesdale (no facilities).

Disused shepherds' huts and **bothies** are scattered in the most inhospitable places in the North Pennines. Some are informally used by hikers caught out in bad weather; others, like **Greg's Hut** near Cross Fell summit on the Pennine Way (*grid reference NY691355; Mountain Bothy Association-run*) have flooring and even a wood-burning stove, but can fill up quickly (you can't book).

Wild campers should seek permission from landowners – but that's not always straightforward if you're trekking over remote terrain. Generally speaking, as long as you're out of farmland and on the highest fells, pitch up late and leave early, it's unlikely you'll be troubled. In Upper Teesdale, you could call the helpful Natural England rangers at Widdybank Farm (*01833 622374*) who may be able to advise.

High Side Farm Bowbank (near Grassholme Reservoir) Middleton-in-Teesdale DL12 0NT ℗ 01833 640135 ⓦ www.highsidefarm.co.uk. Open from around Easter to end of Sep. Small, hillside campsite (maximum of ten people) on smallholding at 1,000 feet, with toilets and showers and plenty of free-range chickens around. Buy steak, lamb, pork and eggs direct from the farm to cook on your barbecue.

Rye Hill Farm Slaley near Hexham NE47 0AH ℗ 01434 673259 ⓦ www. ryehillfarm.co.uk Ⓔ info@ryehillfarm.co.uk. Sheltered by trees, the camping field at Rye Hill Farm is quiet and a good choice for tent campers (though they also take caravans) in the Hexhamshire/Upper Derwent Valley area. Gentle farmland surrounds the site which is close to Slaley Forest.

South Tyne Valley and Alston

Scenically, the northern reaches of the South Tyne Valley are typical of the wider Tyne Valley and Hexhamshire countryside: green pastures carved by drystone walls and hedgerows, parkland studded with mature oaks, broadleaved woodland and the odd stone hamlet here and there; but the landscape steps up a gear quite quickly on heading south, and certainly by the time you reach Lambley, the Pennine moors are looming tantalisingly close.

Alston, England's highest market town, is particularly popular with cyclists, railway aficionados and walkers. At Garrigill, some of the most alluring riverside scenery awaits, topped off with a waterfall and plenty of bathing pools.

South Tyne Valley: Haltwhistle to Alston Moor

The mixed-use waymarked 23-mile South Tyne Trail makes the ideal way of discovering the valley and some of the best river, woodland and hill country in the North Pennines. I've described the route in brief here – you'll need the OS Explorer maps OL43 and 31. For the most part it follows the railway path (as far as Alston). Cyclists have the option of diverting onto the road in a few places where the route becomes tricky for bikes. From Alston to Garrigill and onto the source of the Tyne, walkers stay close to the riverside; cyclists take a quiet hilly lane via Leadgate.

Haltwhistle to Lambley

Pick up the disused railway line south of the A69, and enter thickets of birch and oak and gentle countryside from the second mile. At the Featherstone crossroads, continue straight ahead on the railway path; or for a pit stop, turn left and continue up a lane to the inviting **Wallace Arms** (*01434 321872*) – a cosy real ale pub with a log fire, restaurant and sun-filled beer garden. Turning right along the lane will take you to the riverside and **Featherstone Castle** – an imposing 13th-century embattled manor with turrets, a gatehouse and pele tower. There's no general public access to the castle but it appears quite impressively across parkland from the banks of the River South Tyne (lovely riverside path for walkers here).

Lambley Viaduct causes cyclists and less so walkers a bit of trouble. Physically, the towering arches of the 1852 railway viaduct are spectacular, but there is no access to the 100-yard stretch in front of the old train station (now a private house) so walkers and cyclists must descend steeply to the river, pass under the viaduct and come back up the other side. To do this, cross the viaduct first and enjoy the plunging view of the wooded gorge; then, turn right down the steps at the end. You'll need to carry your bicycle – some task, and you might prefer to follow the re-directed road route signed just under a mile back at Thorneyhole Wood car park that passes above Lambley village (be prepared for a heck of a climb from river to moor level).

Slaggyford to Alston

Once you're back on the railway line, the temperature drops as you enter the North Pennine moors proper where heather covers the highest plateaux and woods and fields descend to the river. **Slaggyford** and its quaint old railway buildings and platform make a pleasant place to stop for sandwiches. A gate here sternly pronounces: 'Any person who omits to shut and fasten this gate is liable to a penalty not exceeding forty shillings'.

The South Tyne Trail continues straight ahead on the disused railway line but it gets pretty boggy and almost impossible to cycle (fine for walkers with gaiters) so you might want to take the road route by turning left and heading for the river via Slaggyford village. Note that the South Tynedale Railway is being extended from Kirkhaugh to Slaggyford, so this route may become more passable in the future. You can take bikes on the train for a small fee.

If you're **cycling** along the road route to Alston via Slaggyford, you pass a converted chapel with a dovecote before reaching the A689 where you turn right. After a mile or so, NCN Route 68 signs lead you off the main road, over the river and onto a quiet country lane for the last five miles to Alston. This is wonderful cycling. It's quiet with some challenging ascents and descents and glorious river and countryside scenery: pastures divided by dry stone walls, old farm buildings, an unusual church (see Kirkhaugh on page 274) and farmers rounding up sheep with their Border collies.

Walkers continuing on the railway line from Slaggyford find the trail becomes squelchy under foot and then very stony, though that may change in the future when the railway is extended. The last leg from Kirkhaugh to Alston follows the **South Tynedale Railway** where the odd narrow gauge steam engine puffs by. There's a small viaduct between Kirkhaugh and Alston that spans Gilderdale Burn. Below is a secluded swimming pool.

The market town of **Alston** and its painstakingly restored Victorian station are ahead. Of the many pubs here, one of the most inviting (the Cumberland Hotel in Townfoot; see page 273) is found without having to climb the hill into the town centre.

Alston to the source of the Tyne via Garrigill

Classic North Pennine scenery stays with the walker or cyclist the whole way: heavy moors looming over pastures dotted with sheep and shingly rivers crowded with trees. **Garrigill** is a welcome resting point with a freehouse inn on the green.

For the final few miles, **walkers** stay close to the rocky South Tyne as it jingles through fields and old woodland offering a few places to take a dip. **Ashgill Force** is the highlight – a curtain waterfall you can walk behind.

Undulating meadows and open landscapes accompany **cyclists** along the quiet lane to Garrigill via Leadgate; moody purple hills draw closer with every pedal push.

Cyclists and walkers take the same final paved track to reach the **source of the Tyne**. It's surprising how quickly the river becomes thin enough to leap across and then just a foot wide until at last it is a mere bathroom tap dribbling off the hillside that you can dam with your foot. A contemporary sculpture marks the source.

① Alston

The main cobbled street through England's highest market town climbs steeply up a hillside and pauses at a bend in the road, before continuing up and out of town. In the past, horses and carts would rest at this landing by the market place; today it's the coast-to-coast cyclists who stop for a breather.

The view of the old stone houses dropping away along the winding road, and the hills rising on the other side of this Cumbrian valley has Hovis advert charm and there are even a few people pushing their bicycles up the hill just to complete the picture. Now imagine this scene after a snowfall and you can hardly imagine a more step-back-in-time place in the Pennines except for Blanchland in the Derwent Valley.

For all Alston's old worldly appeal and run of early 17th-century houses built during the growth of the lead-mining industry, it's still a working town, albeit one that caters reasonably well for visitors, with cafés, food stores, pubs, craft shops and an **outdoor clothing shop** (*Hi-Pennine Outdoor, Market Pl; 01434 381389*). The **tourist information centre** (*01434 382244; open daily in summer and 10.00–15.00, Mon–Sat Oct–Mar*) is in the Town Hall at the foot of Front Street.

Gallery 1611 (*open Easter–Oct*) is a lovely little shop opposite the marketplace showcasing ceramics by leading craftsmen and women in the region, including Syl Macro whose vases and plates made with different clays reflect the geology and colours of the Pennine hills. Next door, **Just Glass** sells antique jugs and vases, while the **Cane Workshop** opposite specialises in restored antique cane and rush chairs.

St Augustine Church was rebuilt a few times, notably in 1770 to a design by Smeaton (of Eddystone Lighthouse fame) and 100 years later – the building standing today. Its most striking feature is its 17th-century single-handed clock which came from Dilston Hall (along with a bell) in 1767 in the decades after the execution of Lord Derwentwater for his part in the Jacobite Rebellion. Only the bell was installed; the clock forgotten about for 200 years until restoration in 1977. Its single hand operates with the assistance of stone counterweights hanging in leather slings from pulley wheels. In the churchyard, look for the epitaph on the gravestone of a cobbler which includes these lines:

> *My cutting-board's to pieces split,*
> *My size-stick will no measures mete,*
> *My rotten last's turn'd into holes,*
> *My blunted knife cuts no more soles . . .*
> *My lapstone's broke, my colour's o'er,*
> *My gum-glass froze, my paste's no more,*
> *My heels sew'd on, my pegs are driven, –*
> *I hope I'm on the road to heaven!*

Food and drink

Alston's Front Street, has a couple of cafés, including the friendly **Cumbrian Pantry** which sells inexpensive scones and sandwiches, and the tea room at Alston Station. For something more substantial, try the **Alston House Hotel** (*Townfoot; 01434 382200; www.alstonhousehotel.co.uk*) – a bistro and restaurant serving traditional British dishes and Sunday lunches.

Cumberland Hotel Townfoot ① 01434 381875 ⑩ www.cumberlandinalston.com. I counted six pubs in Alston (a town with a population of around 1,000 people) and found this freehouse offered something different to the others with bookcases, pew benches, real ales, an open fire and convivial atmosphere with walkers and cyclists coming and going. Very good value hearty pub food.

South Tynedale Railway

Alston CA9 3JB ① 01434 381696 ⑩ www.strps.org.uk; four departures daily during summer holidays (check website for operating days at other times of the year); café.

Steam engines trundle through the wooded South Tyne Valley four times a day in summer, offering glimpses of moorland scenery and passing over the Tyne Viaduct. The return journey takes around an hour but you might want to hop off at Kirkhaugh Station and take a wander up to Whitley Castle or down to the river.

Originally a branch of the Newcastle to Carlisle railway, the Alston to Haltwhistle line opened in 1852 and closed in the 1970s only to reopen a decade later under the care of the local railway preservation society. Trackbeds were replaced and the station buildings restored allowing the first narrow-gauge steam engines to enter passenger service in 1983. Though just a few miles of the line were originally opened, it keeps getting longer and by the time you read this, it may have reached Slaggyford where plans are underway to restore the platform and timber station house.

The Hub museum

Station Yard, Alston CA9 3HN ① 01434 381609 ⑩ www.alston-hub.org.uk; open Jun–end Sep daily and weekends Easter–Christmas.

Round the back of Alston's restored train station is this fantastic little museum in an old goods shed dedicated to transport heritage. Filling every space inside The Hub are vintage motorbikes and a few cars, as well as a large collection of bicycles showcasing in a roundabout way the evolution of this most enduring form of transport from the penny-farthing to a 1972 Raleigh Chopper. A mass of memorabilia hangs from the walls and ceilings: model aeroplanes, black and white photographs, road signs and vintage advertisements.

Kirkhaugh Church and around

Unusually dedicated to the Holy Paraclete (in other words, the Holy Ghost), this secluded Victorian church with a distinctive needle-like spire (apparently the rector was influenced by churches he'd seen in Germany's Black Forest) stands in farmland by the River South Tyne and adjacent to a grand villa with shuttered windows. A stone cross in the churchyard dates to before the Norman invasion reminding visitors of the Anglo-Saxon church that once stood here. Internally, a hammerbeam roof and chairs instead of pews will catch your attention, but the thing that will strike you first when entering the church is the wood-burning fire which shows just how cold it gets up here in the winter.

The countryside around Kirkaugh Church is extremely pretty: fields with mature trees leading to the river, a scattering of old farm buildings, 17th-century bastle houses and a pele tower at Randalholm. Quiet lanes connect the places of interest, and the church – within walking distance from Alston – can be incorporated into a circular jaunt via the Roman fort at Whitley Castle.

A walk to Whitley Castle

Britain's highest built Roman fort (*grid reference: NY694486*) is reached by following the Pennine Way north out of Alston for 2½ miles. If you time your walk well, you can return by steam train on the South Tynedale Railway from Kirkhaugh; alternatively cross over the railway line at Kirkhaugh and walk back along the east side of the River South Tyne by way of quiet country lanes and a waterfront footpath. All that remains of the Roman fort that once housed a garrison of 500 men (and was probably connected with lead- and silver-mining) are its impressive earthen ramparts and the faint outline of the foundations of barrack blocks (now turfed over). Roman altar stones, masonry from a bathhouse hypocaust and smaller finds have been recovered over the centuries although no major excavation has ever taken place.

② Garrigill

Cyclists tracing the source of the Tyne, and the local farmer seeing to his livestock are really the only people that continue on the lane south of Garrigill, and with no motor traffic permitted a few miles ahead, this compact stone village stands somewhat at a dead end: all the better for those enjoying a quiet drink on the green outside the pub. Other than the George and Dragon, there's a church, 1950s-style post office which doubles as a village store and, surprisingly, an indoor **swimming pool** and sauna next door to the pub which is available to hire by the hour for a reasonable fee (*01434 382537; www. stjohnspool.co.uk*).

Waterfall walk

One of the Pennine's great waterfalls, **Ashgill Force** is reached on foot from Garrigill (for those with OS Explorer map OL31) by following a three-mile circular trail. The outward journey is across meadows; on the return, you follow the River South Tyne which flows sprightly over a series of waterfalls and through rocky chasms where on a sunny day families picnic by the water and the keen strip off and take the plunge. Birdwatchers will see curlews galore on the hillsides and goosanders, dippers, wagtails and common sandpipers along the South Tyne. Look upwards now and then on the off chance of seeing a bird of prey: I once saw a peregrine entering a stoop from high above the river here.

Cross the road bridge in Garrigill as if heading out of the village, and take the steep stony lane that strikes off uphill on the corner. A hundred yards up, turn right (signed for 'Pasture Houses'), passing in front of a cottage. Ahead, meadows crossed with drystone walls trail downhill to Garrigill tucked away in the valley below. Continue through an old farm with buildings dating to the 18th century (note the stone roof slabs).

The trail soon veers uphill to meet the B6277 which you follow for no distance to **Ashgill Bridge** – a high stone road crossing that merges seamlessly into the walls either side of the road to form a sweeping curve. Cross the bridge and take a path on the right down through conifer trees. A splinter path to the right squeezes through rocks (those who don't fancy this route to the waterfall can continue on the main trail) and opens with a view of Ash Gill burn tipping over a high precipice into a deep pool.

To return to Garrigill follow the riverside trail by crossing a footbridge and following the signs for 'Low Crossgill'. Keep the river (which joins the South Tyne) on your left the whole way. Ahead, ignore a bridge with a farm gate and cross a stone bridge signed for Garrigill, returning to the village along a quiet lane.

The Allen valleys

The rivers East and West Allen run off the central moors and flow through farmland and woodland until they converge south of Haydon Bridge, forming the River Allen. **Cupola Bridge** – a magnificent trio of arches built in 1778 – spans the confluence of the Allens and marks the head of Allen Banks and Staward Gorge (one of the region's most beautiful woodlands).

Upriver into the heart of the North Pennines, the scenery in both the east and west valleys becomes increasingly remote with meadows becoming rough grasslands and ramshackle barns replacing cottages. Snow markers appear by the sides of the highest roads and a ski-tow appears above Allenheads.

Compared to the western dale, the East Allen Valley is more populated owing to two sizeable settlements: Allendale and Allenheads. The former, a medieval market town, claims (slightly more convincingly than nearby Haltwhistle) to be the geographical centre of Britain.

On the higher slopes, evidence of the mining industries are glimpsed here and there, and many buildings associated with the industry are found in the now quiet settlements, particularly at Allenheads. You might well spot the odd bastle house and defensive tower, evidence that farmers and landowners in the late medieval period once feared the appearance of Border Reivers riding over the hills on horseback to steal their livestock – and worse.

③ Allen Banks and Staward Gorge
Under the boughs of oak trees and around boulders and shingle banks where herons stand by the river's edge and dippers jump from rocks into the water, the River Allen (north of the convergence of the West Allen and East Allen) flows lazily through a steep-sided, wooded gorge on its way to the Tyne. In spring, the familiar tunes of woodland birds are occasionally interrupted by a more exotic song: the rhythmic notes of a pied flycatcher or the coin-spinning song of a wood warbler, both birds newly returned from Africa and infrequently heard elsewhere in Northumberland. In wood clearings look out for wild pansies – this area is well known for them – and, in the conifer trees, red squirrels.

Allen Banks is a precious broadleaved woodland – ancient in places – and utterly enchanting: visit on a balmy summer's evening when swifts are gliding high above the canopy and the first bats have emerged to catch insects by the river, and you'll see what I mean; glimpsing an otter on an evening like this would not be unheard of.

Walking the length of the gorge from the National Trust car park near Ridley Hall past Plankey Mill to Staward Peel and back is fairly straightforward and takes a couple of hours. A recommended route is to keep the river on your left and ignore the first suspension bridge, but cross the Allen at Plankey Mill and then continue to the ruined pele tower on the other side of the river. On the return, walk past Plankey Mill, keeping the river on your left and cross at the suspension bridge close to the car park.

Ninebanks and around

The quiet meadows, parkland and steep wooded slopes of the West Allen Valley are sparsely populated. **Whitfield** is scattered about a bit with a pub an unusually grand church out on a limb by the river (a nice place for a wander or picnic), a fist of houses and village shop-cum-café and crafts workshop on the main road (A686). If you turn uphill here, you'll eventually reach a stone school and tiny 18th-century church high above the lapwing-populated valley.

One conspicuous building in the hamlet of **Ninebanks** stands out from the 18th-century miners' houses and farm buildings: a defensive pele tower dating to the times of the Border Reiver conflicts in the 16th century. The church, half a mile south, is notable for its hearse house (a stone building that once housed the village's horse-drawn funeral cart), built in the 19th century with money raised by local philanthropist and tea peddler, Issac Holden.

~~~~~~~~~~~~~~

Food and drink

Whitfield Village Pantry Whitfield NE47 8HA ℗ 01434 345709 ⓦ www.
whitfieldvillagepantry.co.uk; open daily Tue–Sat and until midday on Mon
and Sun. Café, village store, gallery and workshop all in one. Upstairs is MAKE
(*www.makerecycledcraftworkshop.com*) where recycled haberdashery items
are 'waiting to be recycled into new things' by visitors sitting by the log stove
knitting and sewing with a cup of tea and slice of cake. Open workshop sessions
on Thursdays; on other days you must book courses (felting, patchwork, making
clothes) in advance.

④ Langley Castle and some mining heritage

Places of interest around **Langley**, not far from Hexham, must be hunted out – some more than others. Langley Castle is signposted off the A686, as is the charming railway station café, but finding the old lead smelt mill, flue and one of the most complete (and now sadly abandoned) 19th-century collieries in England, requires a bit of detective work with an Ordnance Survey map.

Medieval **Langley Castle** is somewhat hidden in woods a couple of miles south of Haydon Bridge. It's one of the most impressive defensive towerhouses in Northumberland with embattled turrets on each corner of a central block (picture a sandcastle) and immediate wow factor. Though restored in the 19th century, much of what you see is the original 1350 building with seven-foot thick walls, huge fireplaces, a chapel and some of the best preserved medieval garderobes you will find anywhere.

Now an upmarket hotel (see accommodation, page 268), Langley is sumptuously decorated with rich red fabrics and dark wooden furniture to reflect its medieval origins. Non-guests can dine here or take afternoon tea in the opulent drawing room heated by open fires and lit with medieval style wrought-iron chandeliers. Ask to visit the roof terrace which offers views for miles around (apparently to Hadrian's Wall, though I couldn't make it out).

Like many manmade pools in the North Pennines, **Langley Reservoir** was built to power the now-demolished **smelt mills**, but you can walk up to a surviving **chimney** by taking the B6305 away from the reservoir in the direction of Hexham. You can't miss it at the top of the hill, but you might overlook its **flue** – a 'horizontal chimney' that runs across the fields for nearly a mile (now cut by the B6305) connecting the mill to the vertical chimney. Like those elsewhere in the Pennines, it was designed to release harmful lead and silver vapours and particles away from human habitation and farmland. You can see the grassy mound from the road (*grid reference NY838611*) and its opening at the Garden Station (see below).

Most remarkable of all the industrial buildings and structures remaining in this area is the **Stublick Colliery** (500 yards south of the B6295/B6304 crossroads on the road to Allendale), that once extracted coal to power the smelt mills. It retains its engine houses and chimneys and, though there's no public access to the derelict site, you can view the group of buildings from the road.

The Garden Station

For details see opposite.

The creators of this inspired café near Hexham have restored the Victorian railway station buildings and platform and transformed the whole site into wooded gardens. It's wonderfully secluded, along an old railway line with high banks thickly planted with shrubs and shade-loving species, and you can walk on the woodchip path and under stone bridges arching over the line. Look for sculptures in the bushes and an old smelt flue that connects with Stublick Chimney (see above). Vegetarian lunches and cakes are served inside but you can sit at one of the outside tables on the old platform.

The list of activities keeps growing and now includes beekeeping, bookbinding, breadmaking, willow-weaving garden design and fungi forays. A small museum in a shed tells the story of the railway that opened in 1867 and the nearby lead-mining industries.

Food and drink

The Garden Station Langley (near Hexham) NE47 5LA ① 01434 684391; open daily 10.00–17.00 Mar–Oct. Enchanting café in an old railway station surrounded by trees, bushes and potted plants (see opposite). Children can run down the disused railway line or play on the lawn. Mainly vegetarian lunch dishes, soups and sandwiches made with organic seasonal produce. Inexpensive cakes and breakfasts too.

Langley Castle Near Hexham NE47 5LU ① 01434 688888 ⓦ www.langleycastle. com. Intimate evening tables in a medieval towerhouse and not as expensive as you might expect for five excellent courses. Two- and three-course dinners on weekdays from 12.00–18.00 are good value. Example dishes are monkfish with pancetta, and duckling in a plum sauce. Scones and afternoon teas are served in the sumptuous drawing room for those just wanting to pop in and savour the medieval surroundings.

⑤ Allendale

The remote market town of Allendale is the kind of place where walking into a pub during the week sometimes draws a few stares from regulars. I read this account by a Victorian visitor who was frustrated at having been refused accommodation at every inn: 'What did it mean? I wondered. Is a man with a knapsack on his shoulder taken for a rogue here?' He visits the Allendale Smelting Mill and tells the manager of his experience. 'Ay; they're cautious folk up there,' he replies. Allendale's far more welcoming these days but that word 'cautious' rings a little bit true – in some of the pubs at least.

A tangle of streets at the heart of Allendale reveals its medieval origins but most of the buildings date to the 19th century. Squeezed among them are a scattering of 18th-century houses, a couple of Methodist chapels, a reading room, an old pharmacy, a village hall, an original Co-operative food store, a savings bank and a handful of venerable inns – many buildings still with their original lettering and frontages.

Artsy places worth visiting include the **Allendale Forge Studios** (*01434 683975; open daily*), an artists' co-operative on the site of an old blacksmiths in the marketplace. Besides working studios, there's a gallery, café and craft

Allendale Ba'al Festival

New Year's Eve in Allendale is a spectacle of fire, light, ceremony and drunkenness which begins with local men dressed in costume called 'Guisers' (a hereditary position) parading in a circuit around the village centre with flaming tar barrels on their heads, and ends in a raucous celebration in the streets and pubs. The procession, thought to have Pagan origins, is timed so that the men return to the centre of town and tip their barrels into the huge bonfire in the Market Place, setting it alight on the stroke of midnight.

shop selling knitted Alpaca clothes, handmade soaps and jewellery. A mile upriver (reached on foot by following the riverside path just down from the Hare and Hounds pub) or by taking the B6295, you'll come to the **Allen Mill** (*NE47 9EQ; 01434 683953; www.allenmillregeneration.co.uk*) still with its 19th-century workshops, now converted into a couple of craft shops, a traditional printing room and the excellent Allendale Bakery & Café (see below). Allendale Brewery is also based here – the company that produces the popular Golden Plover ale served in local pubs.

Food and drink

Allendale Bakery Allen Mill NE47 9EQ; 01434 618879; www.allendalebakery.com; open daily; closed Tue Nov–Apr. Excellent homemade food: hearty soups with warm rye bread, ploughman's sandwiches, salads, scones – or simply fresh bread with pâté. Expect above average prices for excellent food. All good Northumbrian fare including 'game from local hunters'. Family-friendly with wooden games for children (and adults).

Allendale Tearooms 01434 683575; open Tue–Sun. Friendly tea shop in the centre of Allendale serving light inexpensive lunches, Sunday lunches, scones and delicious cakes. A small selection of tourist information and guidebooks.

The Crown Catton NE47 9QS ℗ 01434 683447. 'All our meats sourced from local farms', will catch the eye of those dining in this unpretentious hillside country pub a few miles north of Allendale. Paired back interior with stripped wooden floors, exposed stone walls and a log fire. Allendale Brewery ales and traditional British dishes (steaks, fish and chips, lamb chops), Sunday lunches and sandwiches.

⑥ Dryburn Moor and the Chimneys

Crossing the high moors between the East and West Allen valleys is a memorable journey by road or across country following old packhorse routes. A blanket of heather and windswept cotton grasses dominate the plateau and you can see for many miles around and down into the valleys. It's pretty desolate, which is Dryburn's greatest appeal, but it's not featureless or without wildlife. The skylark can always be relied upon up here and occasionally walkers may hear the plaintive 'pu-pee-oo' cry of the golden plover. Two prominent lead-mining chimneys punctuate the skyline 2½ mile southwest of Allendale (grid reference NY807537) and below them, a raised turf mound shoots across the landscape – one of the old 'horizontal chimneys' so prevalent in these parts.

⑦ Allenheads

Strong veins of lead ore made Allenheads the most important lead-mining area in Britain at one time. Today, the village centre at least seems to hide away from the world in a hollow by the river, but those who take the slip road off

Lead-mining communities

The two big lead-mining companies operating in the North Pennines (W B Lead in the Allendales and Weardale, and the London Lead Company in Teesdale and Alston area) had a profound impact on the character of settlements through their promotion of obedience, discipline and education, which is partly why you see so many chapels, schools, reading rooms and mine agents' houses in the mining settlements.

Miners received paltry recompense for the lead ore they dug and for their reduced life expectancy due to breathing in dangerous dust, so it became commonplace in the 18th and 19th centuries to supplement their income by farming (hence the description 'miner-farmer'). Small houses and enclosed fields, known as 'allotments', are still seen all over the hillsides.

the B6295 will find it's really a very welcoming place with much old-world character.

A sense of order pervades the buildings at Allenheads with its neat rows of miners' houses, workshops and estate offices, many of which were constructed under the instruction of Victorian engineer and mine agent, Thomas Sopwith, who was fixated with rules, punctuality and self-improvement. He built the school on the hillside in 1849 which he could see from his riverside house using a telescope. Any pupil caught arriving just a few seconds late would be reprimanded.

Allenheads Inn catches the eye with its vintage bicycles, road signs and wagon wheels in the beer garden and stocks under the trees. Built in 1770, it was the former home of the Beaumont family – one of the biggest mine owners in the North Pennines. Opposite is a small **Heritage Centre** – giving an introduction to the village, its mining heritage and community life.

Food and drink

The **Allenheads Inn** (*01434 685200*) is fine for a pint of Black Sheep but for lunch, try the cosy **Hemmel Café** (*01434 685568; open daily in summer and Thu–Sun in winter*), a favourite with cyclists.

Blanchland and the Derwent Valley

The Upper Derwent Valley on the edge of Consett is well known to outdoor enthusiasts in Durham and Tyneside. Beyond the **reservoir**, the Derwent continues on its journey to the Tyne, passing Shotley Bridge, the National Trust's Gibside estate and the Tyne Riverside Country Park (all described in *Chapter 6*).

Here, we stay with the upper reaches of the valley and take in the moorland and woodland scenery, and the ancient settlement of **Blanchland** with its 12th-century abbey.

⑧ Derwent Gorge and Reservoir

The main car park where there's a shop and café is reached by turning off the B6278 a mile east of Edmundbyers, birdwatchers might want to park up at Powhill Country Park on the south shore.

The River Derwent's journey from the Pennine moors to the Tyne is halted by the three-mile-long **Derwent Reservoir** – the second largest reservoir in Northumberland, frequented by birdwatchers, anglers, picnicking families, windsurfers and dinghy sailors. You can cycle along the mixed-use path that encircles the lake in an hour and a half or so, gaining views of the moors, fields and woods rising above its shore; much of the route is wheelchair accessible, and there's a scattering of picnic tables. By the car park and loos near the dam, a well-stocked shop (and tuck shop) has everything you need to go fishing – you can also book fishing lessons here (*01207 255250*).

Mixed woodland and scrub along the southern shore of the reservoir attracts finches and tits as well as the odd red squirrel, but the best place for woodland birds is the ancient oak woodland of **Derwent Gorge**, east of the reservoir and Muggleswick, that cloaks the tightly ribboned Derwent. Redstarts and wood warblers are recorded as breeding species here. Also look for plants associated with undisturbed woods such as sweet woodruff, wood sorrel and wild garlic in spring.

⑨ Blanchland

Hunkered down in a hollow by the wooded River Derwent and seemingly unchanged for hundreds of years, Blanchland is more historically alluring and tranquil than any village in the region. Walking over its humpbacked bridge on a summer's evening when the 18th-century sandstone houses are soaked in orange light is pretty hard to beat, but for me Blanchland is at its most timeless in winter when the smell of coal seeps into the surrounding countryside, leading ramblers down off the heather slopes and towards the yellow glow from the Lord Crewe Arms.

The village almost certainly gets its name from the French white-robed Premonstratensian Canons who established an abbey here in 1165. Everything else you see grew around the abbey – and in some cases from its venerable walls, including the pub which was once the Abbot's lodge, kitchen and guesthouses and still has its priest's hole.

St Mary's Church, hidden by trees just beyond the embattled gatehouse, is hugely atmospheric inside and clearly built out of the ruined abbey with a soaring archway and lancet windows of the Early English style; the rest was reconstructed in the 18th century. A medieval stained-glass panel near the altar shows a white-robed monk, the folds of his cloak just still visible.

According to folklore, during the turbulent centuries of cross-border fighting, the monastery almost evaded plundering by the Scots who had lost their way on the fells in heavy fog. Unfortunately, the untimely ringing of the bells announcing it was safe to come out of hiding, revealed the abbey's whereabouts to the invaders. Blanchland later suffered under Henry VIII and eventually came into the ownership of Lord Crewe, Bishop of Durham.

Once you've wandered around the centre and admired the stone square of cottages, visited the church, tea rooms and fetching post office (note the stone cheese press outside and the white post box), you might consider taking a stroll down the river.

Blanchland riverside walk

Though muddy in places, this is an easy 1½-mile riverside trail through gentle wooded countryside. There's a lovely bathing pool with a shingle bank for children to play on not far after leaving Blanchland.

To reach the start, with your back to the Lord Crewe Arms, walk towards the river turning right just before the bridge onto a lane. Go through an opening in the wall, taking the grassy footpath that leads to the water's edge where you turn right. Keep the bubbling Derwent on your left, looking out for dippers and goosanders and a little waterfall streaming down the opposite bank. You'll pass a drystone wall with an eye-catching run of very large coping stones. After a boardwalk, cross a bridge onto the far side of the river. Continue a short way up the road before turning into woodland by the footpath sign (this may be hidden by trees). Follow the trail back to Blanchland through dark Sitka spruce and then brighter oak and birch woodland. The village appears quite wonderfully in a hollow below as you emerge from the trees. Return to the village centre by crossing the humpbacked bridge.

Food and drink

The old school facing down the main street is now the **White Monk Tearoom** (*01434 675044; open daily*) which serves sandwiches, soups, hotpots and cakes. There's only one pub (also a B&B), the **Lord Crewe Arms**, which is under new management (due to reopen in 2013 with a refurbished interior) so I can't comment on the food, but the interior is unlikely to lose its historic appeal (stone archways and staircases, oil paintings on the walls, a bar with a vaulted ceiling and logs crackling in huge fireplaces).

Punch Bowl Edmunbyers DH8 9NL ① 01207 255545 ⓦ www.thepunchbowlinn. info. Friendly, tastefully decorated pub (tartan seat covers, brown leather armchairs) in an old hill-top village with a big green, serving very good pub dinners (steak and ale pies, steaks, sausage and mash and Sunday lunches). Beer garden, three local ales, adjoining tea room and decent average-priced B&B accommodation.

Weardale

From the top of the next enormous mountain we had a view of Weardale. It is a lovely prospect.
The green, gently-rising meadows and fields on both sides of the little river, clear as crystal, were
sprinkled over with innumerable little houses; three in four of which (if not nine in ten) are
sprung up since the Methodists came hither. Since that time, the beasts are turned into men,
and the wilderness into a fruitful field.
John Wesley, founder of Methodism, writing in his journal, June 1772

The landscape and character of Weardale changed immensely in the centuries following Wesley's missionary trips in the late 18th century as lead mining took off and workers flooded into the valley; today, the mines have gone and the population is a fraction of what it once was and in many ways the landscape has reverted to something like it was in Wesley's day. It's by no means pristine, however, and the scars of lead mining are noticeable in places, and some villages, while they tell a fascinating story about the social history of this area, are somewhat bleak.

Attractions include the outdoor lead mining museum at Killhope, one of the largest recreational forests in the North East (Hamsterley), a heritage steam railway line and historic settlements of Wolsingham and Stanhope. Away from the valley basin, put your hiking boots on – there are some great walks up onto the old hunting forests of the Prince Bishops of Durham behind Stanhope (now moorland), and through flower meadows, particularly in Upper Weardale around St John's Chapel and Ireshopburn.

⑩ Wolsingham

One of the most appealing old market towns in the North Pennines, Wolsingham is found on the eastern edge of the Durham Dales quietly welcoming visitors to Weardale. The marketplace and Town Hall stand amid a web of well-kept streets lined with 18th- and 19th-century houses and a scattering of earlier dwellings (see those next to the three-storey Georgian-looking Whitfield House on Front Street) and four churches. Cafés and pubs are peppered around the marketplace and Front Street where you'll also find the odd antiques shop.

During the first weekend in September, cattle, sheep dogs, musicians, falconers, traditional dancers and food producers head to Scotch Isle Park at the eastern edge of the town for one of the oldest **agricultural shows** (*www.wolsinghamshow.com*) in England.

The River Wear and the Weardale Railway run largely undetected along the southern edge of the village. You can catch a steam or diesel train on the **Weardale Railway** (see page 287) from the station here or wander along the wooded riverside path. Aside from the Weardale Way, you could also walk uphill along the **Waskerley Beck** and across fields to the Victorian **Tunstall Reservoir** – a tranquil lake (and nature reserve) enclosed by broadleaved woods where there are picnic tables. Set foot a few hundred yards north of the town centre, from the Demesne Mill Picnic Area car park signed off the road bridge on Angate Street (a continuation of Market Place). A shorter route follows the river for under a mile to some stepping stones.

Food and drink

Black Bull Inn Frosterley DL13 2SL ℡ 01388 527784 ⓦ www.blackbullfrosterley.com. Close to the locos puffing their way along the Weardale Railway line is this old pub with bags of old-world character (grandfather clock, iron range fire, stone slab flooring, wooden benches and a peal of 12 bells). Traditional British dishes produced with local, seasonal ingredients (such as local lamb served with an apricot and walnut stuffing and pork and black pudding) including Sunday lunches. All puddings made in house. 'Our dedicated chefs often catch fish and shoot rabbits and wood pigeon for the menu.' Neither ales nor food are cheap. Occasional live music and theatre events.

No 10 10 Market Place, Wolsingham ℡ 01388 528344 ⓦ www.no10thecoffeeshop.co.uk. Contemporary bistro serving coffees, breakfasts and lunches including casseroles, salads and pasta dishes as well as soups and sandwiches – all at restaurant prices.

Harperley Prisoner of War Camp

Grid reference NZ126355; by the side of the A689 between Wolsingham and Crook about 600 yards west of the A68 roundabout on your right if travelling from Wolsingham.

Still with its canteen, theatre and 49 derelict huts and German landscapes painted on its walls, this rare survival from World War II between Wolsingham and Crook narrowly escaped being lost to the elements and is now undergoing restoration with money from English Heritage. It's not currently open to

Frosterley marble

Quarried in its namesake Weardale village for centuries, this black marble distinctively patterned with white fossilised sea creatures that lived in tropical waters 325 million years ago, appears in a number of important buildings in the North Pennines and further afield. It's actually a limestone, polished to great effect and it features in the fonts at Stanhope and Frosterley, at the Anglo-Saxon Escomb Church near Bishop Auckland and in Auckland Castle, but most spectacularly in the 13th-century Chapel of the Nine Altars in Durham Cathedral.

Bollihope Burn contains the stone in its natural state. A good place to see it is at **Harehope Quarry** environment education centre (signposted off the A689 on the eastern fringes of Frosterley, itself between Stanhope and Wolsingham). Follow the public footpath and look down from the bridge.

the public, but you can peer through the wall of conifer trees and just make out the huts. On the refectory walls, the paintings of mountains and a boy in lederhosen playing the pipe would have once evoked happy memories of home. The purpose-built theatre even has an orchestra pit. Prisoners worked as farm labourers and some never left Weardale after the war ended, hence the occasional German surname around these parts.

⑪ Mountain biking in Hamsterley Forest

Hamsterley, 5 miles south of Wolsingham DL13 3NL (signposted off main roads) ① 01388 488312 ⑩ www.forestry.gov.uk; visitor centre with tea room, shop and information area; Forestry Commission.

Hamsterley is best known for its long-established mountain biking trails. They range from three-mile long green routes suitable for young children and families to an 18-mile red and black challenging circuit where a technical bike and helmet are needed. The Forestry Commission manage the predominantly coniferous woods, and the trails are well-maintained and facilities within the forest (signage, information centre, equipment hire) are excellent.

You can hire bikes at **WoodnWheels** (*near the visitor centre; 01388 488222; www.woodnwheels.org.uk; open daily Easter–end Oct and weekends in winter*) which stocks tandems, standard cross-country bikes and 'dirt jump trail bikes' – just the ticket for those technical routes. You can even hire powerful lamps for night rides in winter. Expect to pay upwards of £25 for an adult's bike for the day.

⑫ Stanhope

Weardale's largest settlement is a busy town with a similar pace to Middleton-in-Teesdale and a couple of historic buildings and streets of note. The parish of Stanhope was hugely wealthy in the 19th century because of a tithe on lead ore claimed by the church; the **old rectory** (Georgian mansion on Front Street) is evidence of those heady days.

Stanhope Castle – a late 18th-century castellated manor (now divided into private houses) – stands at the western end of the main road looking down **The Butts**, a street with much period charm. Opposite, **St Thomas's Church** has a 320-million-year-old fossil tree stump in its churchyard; fossilised creatures are also seen in the font which is made of black Frosterley marble. The oldest part of the church is the tower, the base of which is Norman and contains medieval stained glass. A Roman altar stone stands at the other end of the church and inside the chancel are two 17th-century Flemish wood carvings. Close by the church, the **Durham Dales Centre** (*01388 527650; www.durhamdalescentre. co.uk; open daily Apr–Oct*) has craft shops, gardens and a tea room as well as a tourist information shop selling maps and books.

Stanhope's **outdoor heated swimming pool** is open from June until the end of September (*Castle Park, on the junction of the A689 and B6278; 01388 528466*).

Weardale Railway

Bondisle Way (eastern edge of Stanhope) ℗ 01388 526203 Ⓦ www.weardale-railway.
org.uk; trains run at weekends from early Apr–end Oct with additional days in Aug, at
Easter and over Christmas.

Opened in 1847 during the boom years of mineral extraction, this branch line
of the Stockton and Darlington Railway was eventually extended to Stanhope
and Wearhead but by the time it reached the end of the line in 1895, the lead
mining industry was on the wane. The line closed in 1993 but reopened soon
later as a heritage railway with stations at Bishop Auckland West, Wolsingham,
Frosterley and Stanhope. Steam and diesel engines run along the line twice
daily when operational, taking in unspoilt valley scenery as they chug above
the wooded River Wear. The old station buildings and arched iron bridge at
Stanhope are particularly eye-catching.

Food and drink

A good few cafés, a bakery and a couple of pubs strung along Stanhope's main
street include the cosy **Weardale Tea Room** (the one with two life-size toy soldiers
guarding the entrance doorway) which has tables upstairs and sells all the usual
scones, sandwiches and teas to eat in, and cakes, biscuits and pies to take out. Also
try the café in the restored **Stanhope station**.

Into Upper Weardale

Road and river stay close together all the way through Weardale. After
Stanhope, the fellfoot hamlets and villages come every few miles: Eastgate,
Westgate, Daddry Shield, St John's Chapel, Wearhead. Diversions off the main
road along trails and country lanes will reveal the miner-farmer landscape of
the 19th century. Even just a short climb out of the valley offers superb views
of the facing vales all pleasingly divided into small meadows in the traditional
way with drystone walls (a far cry from the large Northumberland farms) and
dotted with stone cottages and huts.

Hay meadows around here brim with wild flowers and wading birds all
summer long. The unclassified lane on the south side of the River Wear
between Stanhope and Daddry Shield and the north side between Daddry
Shield and Cowshill makes a memorably scenic cycle ride or drive.

Rookhope and Stanhope Common

For spectacular views of Weardale and walks over grouse-filled heather moors,
climb steeply out of the hamlet of Eastgate (a few miles west of Stanhope) by
foot along the Rookhope Burn or by taking one of several lanes ascending out
of the valley. Here the old mining village of **Rookhope** was visited many times
by the poet W H Auden who found much inspiration from the juxtaposition
of the natural and manmade landscapes. In his day there were more visible
signs of industry, but relics still dot the hillsides, notably Jeffrey's Chimney and

the trackway of the steepest incline railway in England. Perhaps most striking is **Rookhope Arch** – a fragment of a smelt flue that once carried fumes away from farmland. It's seen by the burn *en route* to Lintzgarth.

As you leave Rookhope behind and climb higher still onto **Stanhope Common** (once the Prince Bishops' medieval hunting ground), the grassy slopes become dominated by heather and soon there are hardly any signs of human habitation and you find yourself surrounded by some of the most spectacularly desolate upland countryside in England. At **Bolts Law** you can see five counties on a clear day.

Food and drink

Parkhead Station Stanhope Moor, Stanhope DL13 2ES ① 01388 526434 Ⓦ www.parkheadstation.co.uk; open daily. Cyclists fall into this remote café and B&B above Crawleyside. It used to be the station master's house for a railway (now the Waskerley Way) that ran through the Durham Dales transporting limestone and coal.

Rookhope Inn Rookhope DL13 2BG ① 01388 517215. A traditional inn serving typical pub dishes (lamb, steak, pies). Friendly welcome to walkers and cyclists.

St John's Chapel

The centre of this small village with its post office and cobbled square could almost be straight out of the Edwardian town at Beamish Museum; it is named after its mid 18th-century church (the one with a clock tower). If you turn up Harthope Road (signed for Langdon Beck), you'll soon reach a footpath on the far side of a bridge which takes you on a very pretty **walk** up a wooded burn and valley side. You can return in a loop along the lower reaches of Chapel Fell to Daddry Shield which offers superb views of the facing hills. The unclassified road to Langdon Beck climbs over Harthope Moor (2,057 feet), giving outstanding views of the moors of Weardale and Teesdale.

Ireshopeburn

As you come into Ireshopeburn from the east, you pass the wonderful two-storey **High House Chapel**, which could be mistaken for a Georgian manor house. John Wesley preached here 13 times, first by a thorn tree before the chapel was built in 1760. It's the oldest Methodist place of worship in continuous weekly use in the world (services on Sundays at 10.45) and it's also the most striking of any of the early Methodist chapels, particularly its interior which has a Victorian wooden organ and pews that curve around the corners of the room. Next door, the volunteer-run **Weardale Museum** (*01388 517433; www.weardalemuseum.co.uk; open Wed–Sun 14.00–17.00 Easter and May–Oct; and every afternoon in Aug*) is a great little folk museum with a recreated 19th-century living room, mineral and archaeological collections and an exhibition dedicated to John Wesley about Methodism in Weardale.

Methodist chapels

With increasing industrialisation and population expansion came new forms of Christianity, but the one that had the most profound impact in the North Pennines was Methodism. John Wesley, the founder of the Methodist movement, preached in the valleys many times during the 18th century and established some of the earliest Methodist chapels here. Today, though many are now private homes, you'll still see Primitive and Wesleyan chapels in every town and village and scattered on even the most remote fells such as at Pry Hill and at West Garret's Hill near Sinderhope (between Allendale and Allenheads).

Turning off the main road onto a lane signed for New House, go over the stone bridge and take the footpath along the wooded riverside for a walk on the Weardale Way, or continue uphill. Facing you is the grand façade of **Newhouse**, the headquarters of the mine agent in the 19th century. At the back of the complex, which includes a blacksmiths and workshops, is the old **Candle House** where miners would purchase candles for their lanterns.

Burnhope Reservoir, Cowshill and up onto the moors

Continuing westwards along the river from Ireshopeburn, you soon come to Wearhead, close to the thickly wooded and remote **Burnhope Reservoir**. To get here, turn off the main A689 just before the bridge when you enter the village from the east and continue uphill to the reservoir car park. Outstanding views of the valley and hills await, but once you set foot on the lakeside trail, dark conifers gather around.

The scenery becomes more remote the further west you go, particularly on rising out of **Cowshill** – a quiet hamlet with an old church cowering under bossy hills. The lane striking uphill from the bridge (opposite side to the hotel) leads up onto the moors where you can turn to the east and follow an old packhorse bridleway across Middlehope Moor to Rookhope, six miles away. Purple fluorspar – one of the Pennines' many minerals – appears in places on the track. Returning to Cowshill via the Weardale Way makes a varied route of 15 miles.

From Cowshill to Killhope, the road rises steeply where only the odd farmstead, conifer plantation, chapel and cluster of cottages interrupts the expansive view of heavy moors pressing into each other and of the silver chain Wear below. But, that's just a taste of what's to come. From Killhope to Nenthead, the **A689** climbs to over 2,000 feet making this the highest classified road in England.

⑬ Killhope Lead Mining Centre

Near Cowshill DL13 1AR ☏ 01388 537505 ⓦ www.killhope.org.uk; open daily 1 Apr-beginning of Nov; café and shop.

Surrounded by moors bearing centuries-old scars from mining and quarrying operations, Britain's best-preserved lead mine is now one of the leading attractions in the North Pennines. It's very much an outdoor museum (except for the mine itself which can be entered on tours) with wagon lines, a mineshop (where the workers lodged during the week), machinery, a reservoir (reached on a walk via wildlife hides in the adjacent forest where you may see red squirrels) and the largest waterwheel in the north of England. All the operational areas are laid out as they were, evoking the processes of extraction, transportation and separation.

The **'washing floor'** occupies the central area of the mine where 'washer boys' working outside separated the lead ore – or 'galena' – from waste material using water from the burn and a contraption that's essentially a large sieve. Children today seem to enjoy having a go of these 'hotching tubs' and using the mallets to break real stone.

Mining became increasingly mechanised in the 19th century with the assistance of the **Killhope Wheel** – a precious relic and one of only three waterwheels designed by the Victorian industrialist and hydroelectric engineer, Lord Armstrong, still in existence. Water from a purpose-built reservoir on the hill-top turned the wheel that powered machines in the adjacent 'jigger house' that crushed and washed the galena.

You'll need wellies, a hard hat and torch to go into the **mine tunnel**, all of which are supplied by the museum as part of your entry fee. It's not one for the claustrophobic but most will find wading

through the dark tunnel quite exciting, and you'll see where lead ore veins were hacked into and a huge underground waterwheel.

The **indoor museum** and **Magnificent Minerals** display give a glimpse of the astonishing geology of the North Pennines – the first UNESCO-designated European Geopark in Britain. One of the most fascinating collections is the **Victorian spar boxes** – a folk art that developed in mining communities that involved fashioning the purple, green and amber fluorite crystals, quartz and other rocks into miniature worlds: street scenes and grottos with little people. They were displayed in wooden cabinets and taken to exhibitions and country fairs.

⑭ Nenthead

There are no signs of poverty, but abundant signs of work; men and boys washing, sorting, and crushing ore, amid the splashing of water, the thumping of machinery, and clattering as of falling stones when the wagons from the mines drop their burden. From the heaps of ore at one end of the premises, to the slime-pits on the other, resolute industry prevails.
W White *Northumberland, and the Border*, 1859

Veins and hushes

Evidence of lead mining in the North Pennines appears from medieval times, though it's very likely the Romans also mined here (land this rich in minerals so close to major Roman forts would surely not have gone unnoticed). Boom time came in the mid 18th century and lasted for over 100 years but the industry crashed quite suddenly in the 1870s when cheaper markets for lead opened on the continent. At its peak in the 1860s, the North Pennines produced a quarter of Britain's lead.

Lead ore or 'galena' forms **'veins'** – long ribbons, sometimes miles long, between the limestone that could be just a few inches wide or several feet thick. Finding these veins was key and much time and expertise was devoted to mapping the landscape and plotting its mineral veins.

A technique called **'hushing'** was used to get at the lead ore. It involved building a dam at the top of a hill above a vein and when sufficient water had collected, it was breached allowing the force of the water surging down the hill to strip away debris and loosen the rock. Successive flushing of debris from the hillside in this way created gullies, which today look like natural fissures in the hillside but they are very much manmade features. Good examples are **Coldberry Gutter** in the Hudeshope Valley, near Middleton-in-Teesdale, and **Hazely Hush** at Killhope Museum.

A complete lead-mining village (still with its mine) built by the Quaker owned London Lead Company in the 18th century, Nenthead is a somewhat utilitarian village hunkered beneath frowning hills with all the components that make it so distinctively a North Pennine lead-mining community and not a coal-mining settlement in Durham or Northumberland. You see a few miners' terraces and, in the centre, a reading room ('Lead Company's Workmen's Reading Room'), a chapel, fountain and school. The lead mine itself is no longer open to visitors as a museum but you can still walk through the site.

The London Lead Company had a good deal of authority over the inhabitants and fostered an orderly community where houses were well kept and children obedient and educated. The afore-quoted author described this scene on his visit in 1859: 'What a clattering of clogs there was when the school broke up, and the children swarmed out upon the street! They are not remarkable for beauty, but they are remarkable for cleanliness, and appear to be robust alike in heath and limb.'

Teesdale

Invigorated from its run through Cauldron Snout, the River Tees flows eagerly under Cronkley Scar and enters a sweeping sun-filled pastoral landscape at

Langdon Beck. The lasting memory is of lambs in fields of buttercups, cyclists whizzing downhill, vigorous waterfalls and the inconsolable curlew who cries all through spring, this is a landscape evocative of Cumbria and the Yorkshire Dales with the white stone cottages of the former and the drystone walls and luxuriant meadows of the latter.

West of Cow Green Reservoir and Middleton-in-Teesdale, the moors rise to form an expansive heather plateau. You'll find some of the North Pennines' most remote and desolate scenery around Moor House National Nature Reserve.

Downriver between Middleton-in-Teesdale and the town of Barnard Castle, the hills mellow and you encounter an appealing string of old stone villages, culminating in the largest market town in the region. Barnard Castle lures arts and antiques lovers and a scattering of historic buildings (including a colossal medieval castle) nearby make for memorable day excursions.

This section starts on the eastern edge of Teesdale and takes a leisurely route westwards into the hills of Upper Teesdale in search of outdoor adventures, wildlife and step-back-in-time villages.

⑮ Barnard Castle

Affectionately known to locals as 'Barney', this large market town on the eastern edge of the North Pennines gets its name from the 12th-century founder of the fortress, Bernard de Balliol. Despite its crumbling walls and secluded location behind houses on the main thoroughfare, from the riverside the **Castle** (*01833 638212; www.english-heritage.org.uk; open daily 1 Apr–30 Sep*) appears thoroughly in control at the top of a steep bank. It's reached at the end of Galgate. Inside the curtain walls, the fortress is split into three main wards and has a keep which can be climbed (good views from the top).

Galgate, Horse Market and Market Place form one continuous broad road of 18th- and 19th-century houses through the centre of Barnard Castle, culminating in the **Market Cross**. The name is misleading but that's what the stone 1747 octagon building at the bottom of the street is known as when not being referred to as the Butter Market. But, forget about what it's called and take a closer look at its venerable stonework and the bullet holes in the weather vane. An unofficial shooting contest between two men in 1804 was staged using the vane as a target.

On **Horse Market**, you'll find plenty of tea rooms and the odd gallery (eg: **Mouncey Fine Art** ceramics and paintings). Market Day is Wednesday and there's a farmers' market on the first Saturday of the month where you can pick up local foods including Cotherstone Cheese (see box on page 296).

Charles Dickens's trail

If you should go near Barnard Castle, there is a good ale at the King's Head. Say you know me, and I am sure they will not charge you for it.
Newman Noggs in Charles Dickens's *Nicholas Nickleby* 1838

Dickens visited Barnard Castle while researching the notorious Yorkshire boarding school for *Nicholas Nickleby*, and stayed at the **King's Head** on Market Place (no longer a pub but the building is unchanged). He visited the **William Shaw Academy** in nearby Bowes which provided inspiration for Dotheboys Hall in the novel and its cruel headmaster, Wackford Squeers. Conditions at the real life school (which still stands but is no longer a school) were by all accounts pretty horrific and Shaw was prosecuted when students went blind because of the unsanitary conditions. A Dickens heritage trail leaflet in the **tourist information centre** on Flatt's Road (*01833 696356*) lists the locations of all the places the author visited on his trip.

Opposite the Market Cross is **St Mary's Church** which has surviving Norman and Transitional masonry despite its largely Victorian exterior.

Turning downhill onto **The Bank**, passing the **Teesdale Gallery** (paintings, photography and crafts) on the corner, you enter Barnard Castle's well-known road of **antiques shops**. Plenty of vintage finds await browsers here, as well as two traditional toy and gift shops with delightfully unchanged frontages. A few other antiques places dot the town, including the **Hayloft** next to the butchers on Horse Market. Halfway down The Bank, **Blagraves House** is a Tudor building with steps up to its door and it lays claim to being the town's oldest house (and foremost restaurant); a quartet of stone musicians plays above its windows.

Bowes Museum
Barnard Castle DL12 8NP ① 01833 690606 Ⓦ www.thebowesmuseum.org.uk; open daily year round; café.

Built in the style of a French château in the 19th century and described by architectural writer Nikolaus Pevsner as 'gloriously inappropriate', Bowes Museum stands above formal gardens and fountains and externally is astonishingly grand and ostentatious – fitting only for the treasures inside, not for the Durham countryside. Just why such riches came to Teesdale is explained by the marriage in 1852 of its founders, John Bowes (a Durham man and illegitimate son of the 10th Earl of Strathmore who inherited his estate, but not his title) and a French actress. Their love of the arts (and tremendous wealth) is much in evidence, but sadly, neither lived to see the museum's completion.

The purpose-built museum houses a staggering array of European paintings, porcelain and silverware from the 14th to the 20th century and is reached in ten minutes on foot from Barnard Castle's Market Cross by following Newgate. In all, there are some 15,000 objects including a large number of 18th-century French landscape paintings and Sèvres porcelain and the odd Gainsborough, Turner and Canaletto; but the star attraction is a 230-year-old life-size silver automaton swan that 'performs' every day at 14.00 catching a fish to the delight of all those gathered around to see the eccentric spectacle. Also don't miss the dress collection which includes sumptuous Victorian gowns and early 20th-century haute couture.

Along the river: Egglestone Abbey and Rokeby Park

A leafy riverside footpath (the Teesdale Way) leads to **Egglestone Abbey** (*0870 333 1181; www.english-heritage.org.uk; open daily*), which appears quite wonderfully above the river about a mile from the town centre. Founded by Premonstratensian 'white canons' in the late 12th century, enough of the church remains standing to clearly appreciate its nave and most of its walls. The abbey's cloisters became an Elizabethan house at one time, but even that is now in ruins.

If you continue downriver for another mile and a half, still following the Teesdale Way, you come to **Rokeby Park** (*01609 748612; www.rokebypark.com; open 14.00–17.00, Mon and Tue from Jun–Sep*), an 18th-century Palladian villa in parkland that's been in the same family for almost 250 years. Its stately rooms are adorned with oils, statues and ornate original plasterwork and on the stairwell hang intricate 18th-century needlework 'paintings'.

Food and drink

In Barnard Castle town centre, there are plenty of cafés and the odd pub on Horse Market and Market Place. **NeST art gallery** on Newgate is also a contemporary café serving light lunches. Also consider the tea rooms at **Bowes Museum** up the same street.

Blagraves House Restaurant 30–2 The Bank ① 01833 637668
Ⓦ www.blagraves.com. Oliver Cromwell is said to have dined here on 'burnt wine and oat cakes'. You can expect something rather more refined today in this upmarket timber-beamed house dating to the 16th century. Its snug interior with open fires and an antique touch form a fine setting for British/French dishes such as rabbit and onion pie, beef braised in Allendale ale and poached coley with a leek and mussel sauce.

⑯ Raby Castle

Staindrop DL2 3AH ① 01833 660202 ⓦ www.rabycastle.com; castle open Sun–Wed
13.00–16.30 (parkland open all day) on Easter weekend and May, Jun and Sep, Jul–Aug
open Sun–Fri; compulsory free guided tours on weekdays, no booking required; café.

As you descend over the hills from the north, Raby Castle appears in the vale
below looking majestic with turrets, walls and embattlements rising through
the trees. It's on a similar scale to Alnwick Castle – in other words what children
might call 'a proper castle', and what architectural historians rate as one of the
finest medieval fortresses in England.

Originally the Nevilles lived here from the 14th century until 1569 when
700 knights gathered at Raby Castle under the part command of Charles
Neville to stage a rebellion against Elizabeth I in support of Mary, Queen of
Scots. The Rising of the North failed and Neville fled to the Netherlands never
to be seen again – except on canvas in the medieval passage where he welcomes
visitors at the start of castle tours. The Crown initially took possession of the
castle before selling it to the Vanes, later the Lords Barnards. Currently the
11th Lord Barnard resides at Raby who happens to be a direct descendent of
the Nevilles, so the ownership has come full circle.

Structurally, Raby is essentially 14th century though small amounts of
masonry from the Norman period survive as well as one or two recent additions.
Deer have roamed the 250-acre parkland since Norman times. Within the
wider grounds is a formal **walled garden** with rose bushes and tremendously
high yew trees that have merged into one another to create an organic-shaped
wall (it takes two gardeners one month to cut it). Behind the gardens is the
impressive **Coach House** and a **tea room** occupies the old stables.

Inside Raby Castle

Entry into the rooms once you're within the curtain walls is via the formidable
Nevill Gateway. Notice how the courtyard (with the largest cobbles you may
ever see) is not quite wide enough to turn a carriage, hence why they travelled
straight into the Entrance Hall and exited out the far door.

Inside, the rooms are impressive from the start – stately with huge chandeliers,
drapes and paintings, but none comes closer in opulence and grandeur than
the **Octagon Drawing Room**, intact from the 1840s when it was adorned
with the most jaw-dropping crimson and gold furnishings imaginable. Also
impressive is the **Barons' Hall** where the above-mentioned knights grouped.

At the other end of the scale of lavishness is the **Servant's Bedroom** furnished
around 1900, and the **Old Kitchen** – a fine example of a surviving medieval
kitchen, built in 1360 and little changed since then, except perhaps for the
1950s-era sky blue gloss paintwork; the decorators even gave the grandfather
clock a coating. Cooks will be in awe of the range, and the dazzling array of
copper teapots, saucepans and jelly moulds. A passageway near the top of the
ceiling runs around the kitchen and was used by servants entering the Barons'
Hall and by soldiers on watch duty.

Raby Castle is stuffed with **curios**, including: the musical cabinet and ornamental Chinese pagodas in the library; a cocker spaniel rug (an interesting variation on the more usual tiger or leopard skin) and a Flemish painting within a painting in the Ante-library; a trinket tray of lockets, rings and miniatures in the Octagon Drawing Room; five outstanding Meissen porcelain animals in the Barons' Hall; wooden pew ends in the chapel; a stuffed fox curled up by the fire in the Entrance Hall; and the 19th-century horse-drawn fire engine in the Coach House.

Middleton-in-Teesdale and its outlying villages

Leaving Barnard Castle for Middleton-in-Teesdale, road-users dip in and out of a handful of very well-kept villages with much in the way of heritage and natural scenery to entice – and a couple of good places to eat thrown in.

⑰ *Cotherstone*

A peaceful village stretched out for three-quarters of a mile along the main winding thoroughfare, Cotherstone is topped and tailed with two village greens and has some conspicuously grand houses as well as a post office, small shop and a few pubs.

Picnickers will find plenty of spots to take lunch by the **River Tees**, reached by taking a footpath signed just before the bridge at the northern end of Cotherstone. You can pick up the **Teesdale Way** riverside trail here and follow it through woods all the way to Romaldkirk (two miles north) looking out for goosanders, dippers and wagtails as you go. After a visit to the Rose and Crown pub, return via the **Tees Railway Walk** – a flat route with expansive views of the hills and rolling pastures and a viaduct.

⑱ *Romaldkirk*

Romaldkirk stands amid hay meadows watching the centuries go by and is instantly appealing with its neat 18th-century stone houses around a wide village centre, excellent pub (see opposite), old church and centre filled with the chatter of sparrows and jackdaws.

A sweet square of cottages conceals a side entrance into the church ground. Some masonry in **St Romald's Church** goes back to Anglo-Saxon times and a good deal remaining dates to the Norman period, particularly the nave arcade

Cotherstone Cheese

Cotherstone's well-known crumbly cheese has been produced in Teesdale for hundreds of years; now just one farm continues the tradition. You'll find the cheese stocked in most delis, butchers and local shops in Teesdale (including the Orchard Deli and butchers in Barnard Castle) as well as in Cotherstone post office shop.

and isles. An effigy of a medieval nobleman (in chain mail) who died in battle against the Scots in 1305 lies in the north transept. A couple of pews near the door bear a mouse carved into the wood identifying Yorkshireman Robert 'Mouseman' Thompson as the craftsman.

Food and drink

Rose & Crown Romaldkirk, Barnard Castle, Co. Durham DL12 9EB ℗ 01833 650213 ⓦ www.rose-and-crown.co.uk. This top-end restaurant in a traditional Georgian inn gets booked up quickly so if you are not staying in the plush hotel, make sure you make a reservation in advance. The adjoining brasserie is more informal and there's a snug bar with a coal fire and an outside beer garden/terrace. For a four-course evening dinner for two with wine in the restaurant, expect to pay close to £100. Nothing too adventurous on the menu (steak and chips, goats cheese salad, lamb and veg) but the quality of dishes and produce (locally sourced from top farms and fisheries), fine-dining surroundings and service are high. Fish cakes, sausage and mash and sandwiches (not cheap) for lunch in the brasserie.

⑲ *Egglestone*

You'll need to cross the River Tees over a bridge that dates to the 15th century (rebuilt in the 17th century) to reach Egglestone, an oddly shaped village trailing down a steep hillside. **Egglestone Gardens** (*01833 650230; open daily*) is nestled among trees not far from the bridge. Set in the grounds of Egglestone Hall (not open to the public), which was built in the early 19th century off the back of lead-mining money, the gardens, nursery, beehives and restored greenhouses are enclosed by Victorian walls. A **ruined church** dating to the 17th century is reached at the end of a very short garden trail. It must have been dilapidated for some years for such a thick-waisted tree to sprout through its centre and rare snake's-head fritillaries to establish inside the ruin.

Food and drink

Egglestone Gardens Coach House Café DL12 0AG ℗ 01833 650553. Modern café/restaurant in the restored coach house with views out of the arched entranceways (now windows) and a sunny patio area. Soups and sandwiches as well as restaurant-standard dishes such as grilled haddock, sausages and mash, and risotto.

⑳ *Middleton-in-Teesdale*

Middleton used to be a fairly ordinary workaday town – at least that's how I remembered it – until I revisited in 2012 and found it more convivial and definitely somewhere you'd think of stopping for lunch or a wander. A main thoroughfare runs through its centre flanked by a wide, linear green on one side

White and blue cottages

What makes Upper Teesdale distinctive from Weardale, apart from natural landscape features, are its white cottages and farmsteads. They look wonderfully picturesque and provide a visual reminder of the extent of the huge land-owning Raby Estates which owns them all – as well as pretty much all the grouse moors from here to the Cumbrian border.

A well-known local story goes that while out hunting one day, Lord Barnard of Raby Castle sought shelter during inclement weather at one of the cottages he believed to be his, but he picked one of the few residences that didn't belong to his estate and was thus turned away. Thereafter he had all his cottages painted white so he could identify his property in future.

and smart stone houses on the other and mixed with some tempting shops and cafés. Locals were enjoying lattes in the sun, chatting outside shops, waving at acquaintances passing in cars, and the streets were busy with ramblers picking up supplies before heading into the hills, cyclists saddling up after lunch and so on. An antiques shop selling glass chandeliers and vintage bird cages had opened since I was last here.

On Chapel Row (the cobbled lane with a Co-op) a lovely little shop sells traditional hand-knitted children's cardigans and blankets and further up is a run of good market town shops with old frontages and awnings. In the Market Place is a **tourist information centre** (*01833 641001; open daily 10.00–13.00*).

Food and drink

Café 1618 Market Place. On the sunny side of the street with outside tables and a garden out the back, this all-singing, all-dancing bistro, bar and restaurant (but mainly the former) is a friendly place for lunch or coffee. Inexpensive sandwiches and soup as well as more substantial dinners (swordfish was on the menu and priced similarly to an upmarket restaurant).

Hudeshope Valley and its industrial heritage

At the western end of Middleton, a road signed for Stanhope leads steeply uphill into one of the most prosperous lead mining areas of the 19th century. Keep heading north on a lonely track (or burnside walking trail) and you emerge from the trees to enter open countryside pitted with shafts and mine entrances and cut by hushes. The stone buildings at **Coldberry Mine** (*grid reference NY941289*) still stand in their remote spot above **Coldberry Gutter** – a deep manmade chasm and the largest hush (see page 291) in the region. Closer to Middleton is **Skears Limekilns** (*grid reference NY948271*), four well-preserved stone kilns, one of which dates to the 18th century.

Into the hills

Outstanding valley and moorland scenery awaits between Middleton-in-Teesdale and Cow Green Reservoir. Whitewashed cottages and farmsteads dot the hillsides – overlooking livestock in meadows – and the black metal barns so characteristic of Teesdale are seen here and there along with the occasional stone barn built into the drystone walls, as is more commonplace in the Yorkshire Dales. There's less in the way of large villages and places to eat, but more natural delights with at least two nationally renowned waterfalls and superb wildlife-watching and hiking opportunities. Birders in spring and early summer will be glued to their binoculars, but who needs binoculars when a flock of 30 lapwings tumbles through the valley?

Upper Teesdale National Nature Reserve encompasses a broad sweep of this landscape renowned for its bird and plant life and variety of rare upland habitats including the largest juniper woodland in England, extensive blanket bog, high altitude hay meadows and limestone grasslands. There are alpine plants up here that have hung on since the last Ice Age and they are of national significance, particularly the eye-catching blue spring gentian. The area around Cow Green Reservoir should be top of the list of places to visit by birders and botanists. The Pennine Way and an old packhorse route, the Green Trod, over Cronkley Fell will lead you to some of the best spots.

㉑ The North Pennines' Lake District

A steep climb up Romaldkirk Moor through farmland leads to a nest of five reservoirs on the moorland fringes. They're all within close reach of each other – though separated into two groups by a ridge of pastureland: **Selset** and **Grassholme**, and **Balderhead**, **Blackton** and **Hury**. The view is one of rushy grasslands, old stone farmsteads and meadows dotted with sheep sloping down to the water's edge, and drystone walls trailing up the hillsides (very Yorkshire Dales-like) to heather-topped moors. You may see farmers rounding up sheep, cyclists, horseriders, anglers and dingy sailors. **Grassholme** offers the most in terms of facilities (bird hide, café, toilets and a small visitor centre).

The Pennine Way connects the two groups of lakes, and there are a few other lakeside trails, but really this watery upland landscape is best explored on two wheels and you'll find many miles of quiet paved tracks line all the reservoirs, providing outstanding views of the Upper Teesdale countryside.

Hannah's Meadow Nature Reserve

Grid reference NY937186; signed off the unclassified road west of Romaldkirk and between Blackton and Baldershead reservoirs; Durham Wildlife Trust.

Where the Pennine Way drops down to Blackton Reservoir, it crosses a pasture and two glorious hay meadows that have been trapped in a kind of ecological time warp, providing a glimpse of the flower-rich grasslands that used to cover much of the hillsides of the North Pennines.

Hay time

A North Pennine hay meadow in summer is a sight to behold: swathes of yellow rattle, pignut, meadowsweet, great burnet, clovers, lady's mantle, buttercups and wood crane's-bill. You won't see all these plants in flower at the same time of course, and the grasslands change colour throughout the season: rusty reds and purples when great burnet and melancholy thistle flowers in July; and the yellows of late spring are particularly striking.

High-altitude meadows like those found on the southern edge of Hury Reservoir in Upper Teesdale, behind Ireshopburn in Weardale and around Wooley, south of Allendale are exceedingly rare in Britain and of the estimated 2,500 acres of traditional upland hay meadow left in the UK, 40% is in the North Pennines.

Since the early noughties, the Hay Time project run by the North Pennines AONB has been restoring meadows by transplanting seeds from donor sites onto less botanically rich grasslands and supporting hill farmers to manage them in the traditional, low-intensive way including mowing late in the season when the plants have seeded.

Beyond the first rough pasture (a haven for curlews, snipe and lapwings in spring) are two meadows filled with yellow rattle, globe flower, ragged robin and wood crane's-bill flower and an abundance of grasses such as sweet vernal-grass (smell its head) and meadow fox-tail. The best time to visit is in June and early July before the meadows are cut.

Mechanised farming methods, chemical sprays and a shift towards silage production instead of traditional hay-making quickly reduced the species diversity found in upland meadows after World War II – but not here. Before the Durham Wildlife Trust took over the running of the site, these grasslands were managed by an extraordinary farmer, Hannah Hauxwell, who lived alone in a stone hut (now an information point) without electricity or running water and managed the land for over 50 years in the time-honoured way: cutting the meadow late in the year after the flowers have seeded and without adding anything to the land.

Hannah, who is now in her eighties and living in Cotherstone, became well known in the 1970s after an article ran in the local paper titled, 'How to be happy on £170 a year'. Her autobiography *Seasons of my Life* became a best-seller in the 1990s, and she went on to make television programmes while continuing to live a simple, frugal life at Low Birk Hatt Farm with a couple of cows for company.

㉒ Newbiggin-in-Teesdale

We rode through rain and wind to Newbiggin-in-Teesdale. Being but a poor horseman, and having a rough horse, I had just strength for my journey and none to spare; but, after

resting awhile I preached without any weariness.
John Wesley, founder of Methodism, writing in his journal dated 16 June, 1784

This unassuming old hamlet with its fetching rows of white cottages and flower-filled meadows deserves a stop just for a wander or a picnic by the burn (there are a few benches around if the grass is wet). A glance at an Ordnance Survey map will reveal a good number of short uphill trails direct from the hamlet that can be made into a loop of a mile or so. Expect expansive valley views and plenty of birds (look out in particular for yellow wagtails).

The **Methodist Chapel** is the oldest in continuous use in the world (though services are infrequent), as the blue plaque states. John Wesley's journal shows he visited Newbiggin several times and preached from the pulpit inside. You can borrow keys from the Bowlees Visitor Centre, Middleton-in-Teesdale tourist information centre or Alston Road Garage.

Gibson's Cave forms an amphitheatre around a secluded waterfall and is reached on a short walk through woods behind the quaint hamlet of **Bowlees** just up the road. Ask for directions in Bowlees chapel (now a visitor centre) as the signage was really poor at the time of writing.

㉓ High Force and Low Force

The waterfalls are between Middleton-in-Teesdale and Langdon Beck about 1½ miles apart; a minibus service (Upper Teesdale Bus Link) from the public toilets in Middleton currently operates three times a day on Wednesday and stops at Bowlees, the High Force Hotel and Langdon Beck (call 01833 640213 for times).

Geological events 295 million years ago created **High Force**, one of the highest and mightiest waterfalls in England. Upriver, the Tees ripples along quite merrily after recovering from its tumultuous journey through Cauldron Snout, only to reach an igneous precipice near Forest-in-Teesdale where the entire river plunges 71 feet into a foaming pool. Molten rock forced upwards through the earth solidified forming a hard layer of dolerite between the softer limestone and sandstones. Glacial meltwater and rivers eroded the softer rock over time leaving the harder 'Whin Sill' which now stands as high as a four-storey building.

Two main vantage points provide equally stupendous views: one is not quite as busy as the other, involves a walk, has no closing time and is free (see walk on page 303); the other is best for those less mobile (along a wide gravel slope suitable for wheelchairs) and is close to a car park but for these conveniences you must pay a few pounds to Lord Barnard of Raby Castle (*use honesty box in the low*

Birding in Upper Teesdale

Exceptional numbers of breeding wading birds inhabit the **meadows** and **pastures** rising out of the valley basin – probably in greater densities than you will see anywhere else in England. Curlews and lapwings are particularly conspicuous, but redshanks, snipe, oystercatchers and woodcock are not infrequently seen (or heard). Also look out for yellow wagtails in the meadows.

On the **moorland** plateau where there's heather, golden plover and merlin should be on your tick list. Red grouse and meadow pipits are everywhere of course. Lucky walkers may come across a ring ouzel singing in a wooded gully. There's plenty of heather habitat for breeding hen harriers in the North Pennines, but nests are extremely rare and only really occur on the RSPB's Geltsdale reserve over the border in Cumbria, and away from the shooting estates. The birds come into conflict with landowners and gamekeepers because they occasionally take red grouse chicks. At dawn you can watch the spring courtship display of the rare black grouse at Langdon Beck (see page 305).

Dippers merrily bob up and down on stones in pretty much every **burn** and **river** in the valley. Common sandpiper, grey wagtails and goosanders are the other obvious river-dwelling birds about. Broadleaved **woodland** along the riverbanks support all the usual tits, finches, thrushes and woodpeckers.

A couple of superb areas for spring and early summer birdwatching are **Widdybank Fell** (bordering Cow Green Reservoir) and **Harwood Beck**, which flows into the Tees from the northwest. A really memorable spot is along the Pennine Way where it follows the River Tees under **Cronkley Scar**. Not only is the valley scenery exceptionally beautiful – and geologically fascinating with Whin Sill strewn cliffsides – there's always the chance of seeing ravens, peregrine falcons and ring ouzels.

The above-mentioned bird sightings apply mostly to spring and summer; come autumn, the waders feast at the coast, but from over the North Sea come migrant geese and ducks which choose the windswept barren landscape around the **reservoirs** to sit out the following few months (it's mild here in comparison to Scandinavia). With them comes an influx of thrushes to the valleys: redwings and fieldfares gorge on thorn bush berries and, memorably, in the **juniper woods** north of High Force. This is also a pretty good time of the year to go raptor-watching with good sightings of short-eared owls (day flying large creamy-brown coloured owl) and hen harrier possible on the moors.

Wildlife watching

For organised wildlife watching trips in the North Pennines, try **Northern Experience Wildlife Tours** (*01670 827465; www.northernexperiencewildlifetours. co.uk*) and **Wild North Discovery** at the Durham Dales Centre (*01388 529154; www.natureholiday.co.uk*) who also specialise in bush craft and walking trips.

season; manned ticket hut Easter–Oct until 16.00 daily). The car park is signed off the B6277 next to the High Force Hotel (and pub).

If it weren't for High Force, **Low Force**, a short walk from the hamlet of Bowlees, would still draw the crowds as it is quite some waterfall in its own right albeit smaller and more of a cascade.

Waterfalls walk

Low Force and High Force are easily reached on foot from Bowlees Visitor Centre – a walk of two miles described in brief here.

From Bowlees, turn right onto the B6277 and cross the road. After a few yards, follow a (signed) path through a meadow and woods all the way to the riverside. Cross Wynch Bridge, turn right and follow the well-trodden Pennine Way upriver passing a sculpture of two sheep which children like to sit on, and Low Force.

High Force is a mile and a bit ahead – just stick on the Pennine Way. The riverside path is flat as far as Holwick Head Bridge and really scenic with globeflowers, mountain pansies, bird's-eye primrose and water avens and a deep dark pool where the river flows either side of a large island.

Don't cross the Holwick Head Bridge but climb uphill on the Pennine Way through dense juniper 'woods' until you reach an obvious viewing area from which to take in the sight of High Force.

To vary the return route (this bit requires an Ordnance Survey map) continue ahead for another mile or so beyond High Force, passing Bleakbeck Force and climbing up through more juniper. Opposite ragged Dine Holme Scar, the Pennine Way noticeably swings right and off to the north. Here, you turn left onto a path that connects a little way ahead with an old packhorse trail. Turn left onto this prominent grassy track which crosses Holwick Fell and eventually becomes a paved lane leading under Holwick Scar and straight to the Strathmore Arms. After a pint, it's just a short descent back to the river and Bowlees.

Food and drink

Strathmore Arms Holwick DL12 0NJ ☎ 01833 640362. Towards the end of a dead end lane on the west bank of the Tees, is this wonderful real ale inn (serves typical pub food) under the gaze of the Holwick Scars crags and surrounded by luxuriant hay meadows. It's less than a mile's walk to Low Force and the Pennine Way that leads to High Force.

㉔ Cow Green Reservoir and Cauldron Snout

Cow Green Reservoir is a bleak place: a metallic sheet of water surrounded by green slopes but with one of the best upland birdwatching sites in the UK on its doorstep in the form of **Widdybank Fell**. Cow Green's leading attraction for most visitors is **Cauldron Snout** – where the Tees tumbles down a powerful

Alpine flora

Upper Teesdale supports rare plants that are thought to have survived since the last glaciation including a couple of species found here and almost nowhere else in Britain, like the spring gentian (bright blue and unlikely to be confused with any other plant) and Teesdale violet. Also look out for alpine cinquefoil, hoary rockrose, spring sandwort, bird's-eye primrose, alpine bistort and hoary whitlowgrass.

The most productive spots are where you see exposed **'sugar limestone'** – a crumbly marble with sugar-like texture which was formed by the heat from the molten Whin Sill rock 'baking' the carboniferous limestone millions of years ago. You'll find it most conspicuously on the top of **Cronkley Fell**. Swathes of this rare habitat were destroyed when Cow Green was flooded in the 1970s to make the reservoir.

cascade through a rocky chasm of dolerite Whin Sill below the reservoir, before continuing its journey under the rock strewn Whin Sill cliffs, known as Falcon Clints – and later Cronkley Scar. The waterfall is reached by following a paved path (suitable for wheelchairs) from the Cow Green Reservoir car park along the water's edge. Only the nimble-footed will be able to descend down the steep trail to the bottom of Caudron Snout to look back and view the raging fall in its entirety. As you drive along the lane to the reservoir, watch out for lapwing chicks on the road in spring.

Walking along the Pennine Way in the other direction (westwards) with the Maize Beck as your companion, you'll reach the startlingly dramatic **High Cup Nick** where the deepest and most perfect glacial valley opens up before you. Poet W H Auden described it as 'one of the holy places of the earth'.

Fells and moors

It goes without saying that the rambler who savours stillness and who wishes to walk all day without meeting another, will find the North Pennine moorlands particularly alluring, especially at places like **Moor House National Nature Reserve**, **Dufton Fell** and **Alston Moor**. It's really stark up here: just the odd flush of vegetation with plants such as mountain saxifrage, bog asphodel and cotton-grass; derelict shepherds' huts; patches of bilberry and cloudberry; gullies and scree slopes; red grouse springing from cover; a golden plover, perhaps even a dunlin on the highest peaks or a merlin striking out low and fast over the vegetation; but otherwise just miles of heather, blanket bog, grasses and silvery burns.

Pennine Way walkers see some of the best tracts of upland landscape on offer in the North Pennines – as well as a gruelling run of three peaks. **Cross Fell**, **Little Dun Fell** and **Great Dun Fell** create a striking panorama on the western edge of the North Pennines with views out towards the Lake District

5am at the black grouse lek

lek = a small gathering of birds performing a courtship ritual; from the Swedish leka, meaning 'to play'

A grey-yellow light is seeping through the blackness of a March night sky on Langdon Common, revealing the rough sides of the facing fells and picking out its bumps and scars. The ghostly throbbing of snipe and the plaintive cry of curlews provide an eerie background soundtrack to the bleak scene as I scan the rushy grasslands for black grouse – a rare upland bird emblematic of the North Pennines with a scarlet cap and white bustle-like tail feathers. They appear through the dim light, already sizing each other up and in exactly the same grassy arena as on previous visits. A quick count shows they're doing well with 21 individuals – up from 12 and 18 in earlier years.

Hiding in the tussocks, the hens have taken up their ring-side seats to watch potential mates exert their strength, fitness and ranking. Facing each other in pairs about a yard apart and with a look of intent, the males charge forward, jousting their opponent until full battle commences and they lock together, jump and tussle. When the fight is over, one bird turns and sees another possible challenger through the grasses: he advances and repeats the ritual. All the while, the strangest low burbling sound comes in waves across the grasslands.

Black grouse perform their mating ritual in March and April and can be viewed on the unclassified road branching off the B6277 about a quarter of a mile west of the Langdon Beck Hotel. Go over two cattlegrids and 500 yards later you'll see a pull-in gravel area on your right by fence line. Look for a flattish area of grass about 400 yards to the southeast. Arrive before dawn and stay in your car with the engine turned off. Do not get out of your car or walk across the fields as this will certainly disturb these rare birds.

mountains and below into the Eden Valley. Even if you don't climb them, the chain is visible from miles away with the white 'golf-ball' radar station identifying Little Dun Fell, and Cross Fell nudging the clouds ever so slightly more than the others at nearly 3,000 feet.

Index

Main entries in **bold**.